# WHO WAS WILLIAM SHAKESPEARE?

# WHO WAS WILLIAM SHAKESPEARE?

## *An Introduction to the Life and Works*

## DYMPNA CALLAGHAN

A John Wiley & Sons, Ltd., Publication

This edition first published 2013
© 2013 John Wiley & Sons Ltd

Wiley-Blackwell is an imprint of John Wiley & Sons, formed by the merger of Wiley's global
Scientific, Technical and Medical business with Blackwell Publishing.

*Registered Office*
John Wiley & Sons Ltd, The Atrium, Southern Gate, Chichester, West Sussex, PO19 8SQ, UK

*Editorial Offices*
350 Main Street, Malden, MA 02148-5020, USA
9600 Garsington Road, Oxford, OX4 2DQ, UK
The Atrium, Southern Gate, Chichester, West Sussex, PO19 8SQ, UK

For details of our global editorial offices, for customer services, and for information about how
to apply for permission to reuse the copyright material in this book please see our website at
www.wiley.com/wiley-blackwell.

The right of Dympna Callaghan to be identified as the author of this work has been asserted in
accordance with the UK Copyright, Designs and Patents Act 1988.

Wiley also publishes its books in a variety of electronic formats. Some content that appears in
print may not be available in electronic books.

Designations used by companies to distinguish their products are often claimed as trademarks.
All brand names and product names used in this book are trade names, service marks, trademarks
or registered trademarks of their respective owners. The publisher is not associated with any
product or vendor mentioned in this book. This publication is designed to provide accurate and
authoritative information in regard to the subject matter covered. It is sold on the understanding
that the publisher is not engaged in rendering professional services. If professional advice or
other expert assistance is required, the services of a competent professional should be sought.

*Library of Congress Cataloging-in-Publication Data*

Callaghan, Dympna.
  Who was William Shakespeare? : an introduction to the life and works / Dympna Callaghan.
       p. cm.
  Includes index.
  ISBN 978-0-470-65846-8 (cloth) – ISBN 978-0-470-65847-5 (pbk.)   1. Shakespeare,
William, 1564-1616. I. Title.
  PR2894.C27 2013
  822.3'3–dc23

                              2012022347

A catalogue record for this book is available from the British Library.

Cover image: A death mask thought to be that of English dramatist William Shakespeare.
Photo (c) Hulton Archive/Getty Images
Cover design by www.simonlevyassociates.co.uk

Set in 10/13 pt Galliard by Toppan Best-set Premedia Limited
Printed in Malaysia by Ho Printing (M) Sdn Bhd

1   2013

*For Chris*

# CONTENTS

# Note on the Text

I have adopted the via media in relation to the issue of modernized versus original spelling in using quotations from texts and documents from the period. I have left original spellings except where I felt it would make the language unduly difficult to understand for a non-specialist audience or when a quotation is taken from an already modernized edition. My objective here is to introduce readers to the singular eloquence of sixteenth- and seventeenth-century English with its sometimes alien locutions and resonances and to do so without making early modern spelling an impediment to reading excerpts from the period's texts and documents. Although I have tried throughout to keep notes to a minimum, there are rather more of them in sections that make extensive reference to primary documents and historical materials.

References to the *Oxford Dictionary of National Biography* (*ODNB*) can all be found in its online edition at http://www.oxforddnb.com/.

# ACKNOWLEDGMENTS

First and foremost I want to thank the very best of editors, Emma Bennett at Blackwell, for her faith in me and in this project. She made a world of difference. Ben Thatcher also has my heartfelt thanks for seeing it through the press. I am very grateful for the indefatigable labors of my copy editor Felicity Marsh who has been a joy to work with. I have incurred many debts of gratitude along the way, especially to Gail Kern Paster, Georgianna Ziegler and the staff of the reading room at the Folger Shakespeare Library. Denise Walen kindly lent her expertise to the chapter on theatre, and David Kathman was a wonderfully generous resource for matters pertaining to the geography and organization of theatre in early modern London. I am especially grateful to Paul Hunneyball who provided invaluable information on naming practices in early modern England. Jason Peacey also liberally added to my store of duplicate names to put with those of Shakespeare's sisters. To David Cressy I am almost as grateful for his most recent research on literacy and many other matters early modern as I am for the gift of his friendship. The late Irvin Matus was a generous interlocutor over many a Folger tea, and I am so very sad he is not here to see the finished product.

This book – like everything else I have ever accomplished in academic life – has benefited immeasurably from the guidance and unstinting intellectual generosity of Jean Howard. I am also immensely grateful for the incisive comments and constructive suggestions of an anonymous manuscript reviewer for the press.

Many friends and colleagues listened to my dilemmas about how to frame and organize my materials. Among the most long-suffering are Denise Albanese, Heidi Brayman Hackel, and Deanne Williams. Rory Loughnane proved himself a fabulous and stimulating colleague throughout; Laurie Maguire never tired of talking Shakespeare with me, and I owe a huge debt, as always, to her impeccable scholarship. Despite being a historian of medieval France, Samantha Kahn Herrick provided illuminating insights on our drives to Cazenovia. Frances Dolan always makes me believe that all things are possible, and without her support, intellectual energy, and friendship this book would have been not only much the poorer, but also much less fun to write. Amy Burnette and Rinku Chatterjee provided invaluable research assistance and did so with untiring efficiency and good cheer. I also owe a great debt of gratitude to my students at Syracuse University, past and present, whose encounters with Shakespeare so enhance my own appreciation and understanding of his work. I fervently hope to incur even heavier debts to them in the future.

Last, but by no means least, I must thank my family: my sister, Margaret Newcombe, offered wise counsel upon listening with superhuman patience to weekly installments of where I was with this book. My husband, Chris Kyle, read the script from first to last with unfailingly generous perspicacity and with his extraordinary knowledge of early modern England. I dedicate this book to him.

# PART I

# THE LIFE

# 1

# WHO WAS WILLIAM SHAKESPEARE?

In 1841 a canon of Cologne Cathedral, Count Francis von Kesselstadt, died. His passing promised to answer definitively the question that is the subject of this book: Who was William Shakespeare? This was because among the count's dispersed possessions was a death mask bearing the label "Traditionen nach Shakespeare,"[1] and marked on the reverse "Ao Dm. 1616," the year of Shakespeare's death (see Figure 1.1). Believed to have been purchased in England by one of the count's ancestors, who had been attached to an embassy at the court of James I, the curiosity was recovered in 1849 from a secondhand shop in Darmstadt and brought from Germany to the British Museum by a man named Dr Ludwig Becker as the death mask of none other than England's national poet.[2] Unfortunately, the unpainted death mask is *not* an image of Shakespeare, but the belief that it was such epitomizes the persistent desire to capture Shakespeare's identity.

The death mask is perhaps what Shakespeare *ought* to look like, unlike the figure mounted on the north wall of the chancel in Holy Trinity Church at Stratford-Upon-Avon in 1622, pen and paper in hand (see Figure 1.2). Apart from the engraving executed by Martin Droeshout on the First Folio (the collection of Shakespeare's plays compiled in 1623), this unprepossessing figure is the only reliably authentic image of Shakespeare left to posterity. It is singularly unfortunate, then, that the figure on the funeral monument in Holy Trinity, as the critic Dover Wilson once remarked, looks "like a self-satisfied pork butcher."[3] Dissatisfaction with the bust grew almost directly in proportion to Shakespeare's posthumous reputation, which gathered increasing momentum through the seventeenth and eighteenth centuries. By the nineteenth century, fascination with the Kesselstadt death mask was excited by what was felt to be

*Who Was William Shakespeare?: An Introduction to the Life and Works*, First Edition.
Dympna Callaghan.
© 2013 John Wiley & Sons, Ltd. Published 2013 by John Wiley & Sons, Ltd.

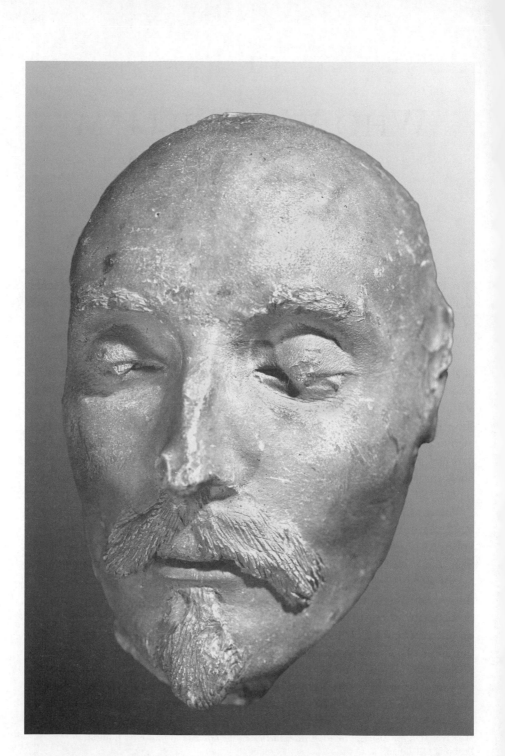

**Figure 1.1** The Kesselstadt Death Mask. Image reproduced by kind permission of Universitäts- und Landesbibliothek Darmstadt.

**Figure 1.2** The Shakespeare memorial bust from Holy Trinity Church, Stratford-Upon-Avon. © John Cheal "Inspired Images 2010."

the inadequacy of the Holy Trinity monument. When A.H. Wall, who had spent many years as a professional portrait artist, addressed the Melbourne Shakespeare Society in 1890 in a paper called "Shakespeare's Face: A Monologue on the Various Portraits of Shakespeare in Comparison with the Death Mask . . ." he described the monument as "a failure," "clumsy," "crude, inartistic, and unnatural."[4]

Whatever the alleged deficiencies, the Stratford monument (and it is, admittedly, no great work of art) must have offered at least a minimally adequate likeness of Shakespeare because his wife, Anne, and daughters, Judith and Susanna, his sister, Joan, as well as other relatives, friends, and denizens of Stratford who knew the poet well would have seen it every time they went to church. The dissatisfaction Wall articulates, however, extends beyond artistic merit to the ideological reconstruction of Shakespeare's face by the Romantics as a serene and high-browed poetic countenance that probably bears little or no similarity to Shakespeare's actual face – which the monument no doubt creditably, if not very artfully, resembles. In contrast, the marble statue at University College Oxford by Edward Onslow Ford of the handsome young poet Percy Bysshe Shelley, who drowned in 1822, looks exactly as a dead poet should (see Figure 1.3). Little wonder, then, that by the time the Kesselstadt death mask was discovered, many prominent artists and experts were eager to proclaim the likeness to be truly Shakespeare's. After the "discovery" of the death mask, Ronald Gower, opined, "Sentimentally speaking, I am convinced that this is indeed no other but Shakespeare's face; that none but the great immortal looked thus in death, and bore so grandly stamped on his high brow and serene features the promise of an immortality not of this earth alone."[5] Although, periodically, claims for its authenticity resurface (the most recent advocate being Dr Hildegard Hammerschmidt-Hummel of the University of Mainz in 2006), the death mask's authenticity has now been wholly discredited, and it does not any longer form part of the British Museum collection, having been consigned to the provincial obscurity of the Grand Ducal Museum in Darmstadt, Germany. David Piper of the National Portrait Gallery in London has queried whether the artifact even genuinely dates from the period. He claims that if it had been an authentic Jacobean artifact, "it must be the only death mask of a subject other than royalty known to have been made let alone survived at this period."[6] What the death mask unequivocally demonstrates, however, is the degree to which ideas about authorship inherited from the nineteenth century still shape ideas and understandings of Shakespeare's life and work. It is, after all, the disparity between the Shakespeare to be found in the historical record and exalted ideas about dead poets that have led Oxfordians and others to dismiss the real, historical Shakespeare as the mere "man from Stratford."

**Figure 1.3**   Memorial Sculpture of Percy Bysshe Shelley by Edward Onslow Ford. Photograph by Dr Robin Darwall-Smith, FSA, FRHistS. Used by the permission of the Master and Fellows of University College Oxford.

We might expect that Shakespeare would have at the very least merited the services of one of the greatest artists of his time, some English Michelangelo: perhaps Nicholas Stone, who sculpted the magnificent full-length statue of John Donne in his shroud for St. Paul's cathedral in 1631. Stone was already receiving important commissions by 1614 when he was only fifteen years old, and two years later, in the year of Shakespeare's death, he was appointed to royal service. Or perhaps Maximilian Colt, who completed the marble sculpture of Elizabeth I for Westminster Abbey, and who in 1608 was appointed master carver to the king, would have been a worthy recipient of the commission. Despite the disparagement heaped on the artistic inadequacies of Shakespeare's funeral monument, its artist, Gheerart Janssen (sometimes anglicized as Gerard Johnson), the son of a Dutch sculptor of the same name who had settled in London around 1567 and established a notable family business near the Globe theatre in Southwark, was, in fact, a perfectly respectable choice to execute the likeness of the poet. The Janssens had sculpted the handsome monument for

Edward Manners, the third Earl of Rutland, who died in 1587. This work is on a vastly larger and grander scale than Shakespeare's effigy. It includes evidence of the scope of Rutland's political power in the kneeling alabaster figure of Rutland's granddaughter, Elizabeth, whose marriage he had arranged to none other than the grandson of Elizabeth's chief minister, William Cecil, Lord Burghley. A second tomb (which also interned his wife Elizabeth) was made for Edward's brother, John, the fourth Earl of Rutland, who died only a year later. For this aristocratic charge – two tombs and four paintings erected at St Mary the Virgin in Bottesford, Leicestershire – Janssen the elder was paid two hundred pounds in 1590. When Roger, the fifth earl died, the Janssens were employed again for a recumbent alabaster effigy of the earl and his wife. Shakespeare probably knew about these tombs because the sixth Earl of Rutland, Francis Manners, was a friend of Shakespeare's patron, the Earl of Southampton. Indeed, Rutland and Southampton had been brought up together as wards of Lord Burghley. Further, Rutland hired Shakespeare along with Richard Burbage for forty-four shillings apiece to design an *impresa* – a chivalric device of an emblem with a motto – which would be displayed on the combatant's shield, for the Accession Day Tilt, an annual jousting tournament, of 1613.

A comparison between the full-sized, elaborate, recumbent effigies of the earls of Rutland replete with ancillary figures and Shakespeare's modest edifice is instructive. Shakespeare was a poet, a playwright, and a player, not an aristocrat, and his funeral monument, commemorating a life begun in Stratford, where he was baptized in 1564 and buried in 1616, is an instance in which art accurately mirrors life, or at least social status. This is exactly how early moderns thought things should be. For, as John Weever observed in *Ancient Funerall Monuments* (1631), "Sepulchers should be made according to the qualitie and degree of the person deceased, that by the Tombe one might bee discerned of what ranke he was living."[7] The image in Holy Trinity Church, reflects rather accurately, then, the status of a poet and playmaker in early modern England, even one of Shakespeare's unparalleled talent. By these standards, the bust is appropriate, and thus successfully fulfills the purpose for which it was intended. Indeed, Nicholas Rowe records in his 1709 volume of Shakespeare's works that in 1634 an early visitor, a Lieutenant Hammond, described it as a "neat Monument."[8] The image in fact tells us a great deal about what it meant to be an author at a time when no one then living could ever have envisaged that the gifted Warwickshire native would vie with Elizabeth I as the most important figure of late sixteenth-century England.

Shakespeare's immediate family almost certainly commissioned the monument, and they probably employed Gheerart Janssen because he had executed the full-length, recumbent alabaster effigy of fellow-Stratfordian, John Combe, which also lies in Holy Trinity Church. Combe was the friend who left "Mr.

William Shackspere five pounds" in his will, and when the poet himself died, he bequeathed his sword to another member of the Combe family, Thomas, John's nephew. Shakespeare's image is just the torso and is made of the cheaper, local Cotswold limestone and would have been considerably less expensive than Combe's more elaborate monument that cost sixty pounds in 1588. However, what most distinguishes the monuments of these friends is that Combe is depicted lying down in peaceful repose whereas Shakespeare is alert, upright, and at work. This posture is not unique to Shakespeare but simply accords with representational convention. The chronicler of London, John Stow, for example, is also thus depicted. Yet, that Shakespeare, almost completely bald, whiskered, and wearing a red doublet and a black sleeveless gown, holds the tools of his trade in his hands – a quill and paper – conveys the sense that even Shakespeare's afterlife would be in some way about writing rather than resting in peace.

The bizarre phenomenon of the Kesselstadt death mask, however, promised something more than a face better fitted to Shakespeare's plays than Janssen's rendering. Had it indeed proved genuine, the mask would constitute the material vestige of Shakespeare's actual visual identity in a way that a mere sculpted depiction does not. What is more, the Janssen bust is one of only two verifiably authentic portraits of Shakespeare – the other being Martin Droeshout's engraving on the First Folio.[9] The yearning, represented by the death mask, for an image that would take us closer to Shakespeare is understandable in so far as his lineal descendants had died out before the end of the seventeenth century and there are no truly personal traces, such as diaries, letters, or possessions, not even the much-vilified second-best bed that Shakespeare bequeathed to his wife. Probably the closest we get to Shakespeare-the-man is his will, which is simply an inventory of his possessions and their disposal. Little wonder, then, that, even in the late twentieth century, Susan Sontag wished for an impossibly vivid connection with Shakespeare: "Having a photograph of Shakespeare would be like having a nail from the True Cross . . . , something directly stenciled off the real, like a footprint or a death mask."[10] The German mask had, in fact, promised precisely such a hallowed and evidentiary trace: red facial hair was still attached to the plaster on the inside.[11]

Thus, the fascination with Shakespeare's image has persisted despite Ben Jonson's famous verse directing readers to the works rather than the engraving on the First Folio: "Reader look / Not on his picture, but his book." Written seven years after Shakespeare's death and printed under an engraving of the Holy Trinity bust, Leonard Digges's verse panegyric issues a similar reminder:

> when that stone is rent,
> And time dissolves thy Stratford monument,
> Here we alive shall view thee still. [in] This book[12]

The monument did indeed begin to fall apart rather early on: the fingers had broken off and the paint peeled away by 1748. But then, in 1793, the Shakespearean editor Edmond Malone persuaded James Davenport, then vicar of Stratford, to whitewash the bust in the mistaken belief that this restrained, classical style must have been its original color. For his pains, Malone – whose editorial labors, though lauded by many contemporaries, also had their vocal detractors – was rewarded with an epigram inserted in the Stratford Visitors' Book:

> Stranger, to whom this monument is shewn,
> Invoke the Poet's curse upon Malone;
> Whose meddling zeal his barbarous taste betrays,
> And daubs his tombstone, as he mars his plays![13]

In 1861, the "daubed" image was repainted, this time in the belief that Shakespeare was represented to borrow his own words in "his very habit as he lived."[14]

I begin this volume with the end in mind, the end, that is, both of Shakespeare's life in his funeral monument and the posthumous reputation that so far outshines it – he was voted Man of the Millennium, for instance, in 2000. Shakespeare's life does not and cannot explain his works, but it can, I trust, help us to more fully understand them. The central theme of this book is how Shakespeare's personal circumstances together with historical events and conditions, as well as political, social, and institutional frameworks, helped constitute his identity as a writer. This book takes a counterintuitive approach to Shakespeare's life, not examining how it was different from the lives of other Elizabethans, but rather the ways in which it occupied common ground with theirs. What made Shakespeare exceptional was not, after all, his life (his extra-literary pursuits) but his identity as a writer, his literary and theatrical career. Above all, this book endeavors to understand what it meant to be a writer in a world long before the rise of the novel. This entails an examination of the intellectual, social, and political forces – educational institutions, systems of patronage, and new institutions such as the printing house and the public theatre – that molded a writer and created the category of the author, the creative literary artist as we have come to know it. Endeavoring to understand Shakespeare's life and writing also necessitates understanding the complex political and religious forces that upheld and opposed his art. For Shakespeare was part of the Elizabethan Renaissance, that remarkable flowering in English letters that occurred towards the end of the sixteenth century, a period which produced, at an exponential rate, some of the greatest authors in the language: Philip Sidney, Edmund Spenser, John Donne, Ben Jonson, and Christopher Marlowe – along with a host of other writers whose very considerable successes are often dwarfed by the titanic proportions of their contemporaries. However, the post-Reformation Protestant regime in which Shakespeare lived also saw some of the most voluble objections to literature as a discourse that promulgated untruth and ungodliness, and to the theatre as a place that fostered idolatry and immorality.

That the established "facts" of Shakespeare's life for which there is irrefutable documentary evidence are relatively few is a circumstance neither unusual nor one that tarnishes the veracity of the facts themselves. It is a "fact" that, according to historians of the period, the survival rate for early modern documents is low and that Shakespeare lived in a world prior to the systematic, all-inclusive collection of data that provides the foundation of modern bureaucracy. Shakespeare's life left two kinds of texts in its wake. The first takes the form of various church and legal documents of which he was not the author but which sometimes refer to him or, in the case of his will, for instance, bear his signature. The parish register duly notes his baptism, marriage, and death, while legal records, especially relating to property transactions and bequests, provide the far from scant evidence for his life. This volume does not aim to detail every legal document, every property transaction, or every record that can be connected with Shakespeare, because this would merely be to traverse rather dry ground that is already amply covered elsewhere. We are fortunate that Shakespeare's art is left to us in a much more abundant supply than these secondary documents, even though neither the plays nor the poems, any more than the legal records, offer the kind of material that allows anything other than speculation about Shakespeare's inner world, his emotions, relationships, or political opinions. Even if information about other matters pertaining to a writer's life, such as his opinions and emotions, his political and religious adherences, and so forth, is sparse, what is remarkable about Shakespeare's life is that the interstices of all that counts as "evidence" and "fact" are crammed with literary production.

In brief, the substantive details of Shakespeare's life, chronologically arranged (but excluding the often very problematic dates of performance and publication of his plays) are as follows: He was born the eldest son of John Shakespeare and his wife Mary, née Arden. His father, a glove maker, was a prominent tradesman in Stratford-Upon-Avon and became a bailiff in 1568. An older sister, Joan, had been born in September 1558 and seems to have died in infancy, a fate that also befell John and Mary's next daughter, Margaret, born in 1562 and buried the following year. Shakespeare, christened on April 26, 1564, was luckier and survived an outbreak of plague in the area during his infancy. His brother Gilbert was born to them in 1566, another child, also named Joan, in 1569, and their daughter Anne, in 1571. Anne, however, died at only eight years of age, and indeed, of Shakespeare's four sisters only Joan, reached adulthood, dying in 1646. Two more brothers, Richard, born in

1574 and Edmund, born in 1580, completed the family. Of his male siblings, only the much younger Edmund followed Shakespeare's path to London and became an actor. None of his brothers survived him, though they all lived to adulthood.

Since there was a thriving grammar school in Stratford, that is undoubtedly where Shakespeare received his education. We do not know why in 1582 Shakespeare was issued a marriage license by the bishop of Worcester to marry Anne Whateley of Temple Grafton, but it is most likely simply the result of a clerical error since when he was eighteen, in November 1582, he married Anne Hathaway from Shottery, nearby to Stratford. Shakespeare's first child, Susanna, although born in wedlock was conceived some months outside it. She was baptized on May 26, 1583, and two years later, on February 2, 1585, William and Anne's twins, Hamnet and Judith, were christened. By 1587, Shakespeare's father's fortunes, which had been on the decline for at least ten years, had fallen so low that he was expelled from the corporation of Stratford. By 1592, when Shakespeare was twenty-eight, he was clearly a force to be reckoned with in the London theatre because he was attacked as an "upstart crow" in *Greene's Groats-worth of Wit*, a book purportedly written by Robert Greene. Shakespeare had secured the patronage of the Earl of Southampton by 1593, and the earl was the dedicatee of the narrative poem of that year, *Venus and Adonis* and, in the following year, of *The Rape of Lucrece*. By 1595, Shakespeare was a member of the Lord Chamberlain's Men, who were engaged for royal performance. In 1596, tragedy struck, and his son, Hamnet, was buried on August 11. On his father's behalf, in the following year, Shakespeare applied to the College of Arms for a patent of gentility, and in 1597 he purchased New Place, the finest house in Stratford. Also in 1597 he was mentioned by Francis Meres in *Palladis Tamia* as, at that point in time, the author of twelve plays and a number of unpublished "sugar'd sonnets," which were in restricted manuscript circulation. In Warwickshire in 1599 he was reported by the borough survey as hoarding eighty bushels of malt during a period of dearth. Meanwhile in London that year, the Globe theatre was built in Southwark on the south bank of the Thames. On September 8, 1601 his father was buried. In 1603 Shakespeare was still working as an actor, playing a leading role in Ben Jonson's *Sejanus*. In 1602 and 1608 he pursued two of his debtors in Stratford, for a total of less than £10. He purchased tithes in the Stratford area in 1605 for £440, and records of 1614 show his involvement in William Combe's attempts to enclose common land in the parish of Welcombe near Stratford. In 1607, his daughter Susanna married the physician John Hall, while the following year saw the death of his mother. In 1609, his *Sonnets* were published, long after the English sonnet craze of the 1590s had passed. He gave evidence in a lawsuit at the Court of Requests in 1612 in relation to a marriage contract which he had facilitated while lodging at the home of Christopher Mountjoy and his family in Silver Street. In 1613, the same year that the Globe was razed to the ground by a fire ignited during a performance of *Henry VIII*, he purchased the gatehouse at Blackfriars, although he never lived in the property. The Globe reopened the following year. Two months before his death, Shakespeare's youngest daughter, Judith, married Thomas Quiney, who had already fathered a child upon another woman, Margaret Wheeler, and was sentenced by the consistory court for his offence. Wheeler was buried with her infant on March 15, 1616. A month later, Shakespeare was buried himself, on April 25, 1616. Anne Shakespeare, his wife, survived him and died in 1623. Although he remembered both of his children in his will, the bulk of his property went to his eldest daughter, Susanna.

In a life begun and ended in Stratford, Shakespeare had chosen not to shake the dust from his native place but rather to consolidate his status there. As he put it in the narrative poem *The Rape of Lucrece* (1594), "The aim of all is but to nurse the life / With honour, wealth and ease in waning age" (*ll.*141–2). These lines strike a decidedly Elizabethan note with their articulation of the relatively modest aspirations to social respectability and comfort in a poem set just before the dawn of the Roman republic where imperial and dynastic ambitions rather exceeded the desire to amass sufficient wealth to stave off destitution in old age. That said, wealth and ease were hardly negligible considerations in Shakespeare's world.

The popular fascination with Shakespeare's life has, if anything, increased in recent years, despite the ostensible paucity of documentary evidence. Similarly, interest in the so-called authorship controversy remains unabated. If it strains the credibility of those skeptical about Shakespeare's authorship that a man who never went to university and who did not have an illustrious aristocratic background authored his plays, we might do well to consider the case of Shakespeare's friend and fellow-dramatist, Ben Jonson, about whom there is no authorship controversy. We do not know the Christian names of either of Jonson's biological parents, and his stepfather's name, Robert Brett, was only uncovered in the latter part of the twentieth century. The absence of such material is neither unusual nor mysterious given the survival rate for early modern documents. Nor was Shakespeare's social standing or education unusual for a writer in his day. Christopher Marlowe, Shakespeare's great contemporary and rival in the late sixteenth century, was the son of a Canterbury cobbler. Unlike Shakespeare, Marlowe had attended Corpus Christi College in Cambridge, but the immensely learned Jonson, who notoriously charged that Shakespeare had "small Latine and lesse Greeke," did not attend university at all. After receiving his elementary education at the school of St Martin-in-the-Fields in London, Jonson attended Westminster School under the great antiquary William Camden. The stepson of a bricklayer, he followed his adoptive father into the trade, and indeed maintained his right to work as a paid-up member of the Tylers and Bricklayers Company even at the height of his literary career, when his identity as a playwright and poet was thoroughly established. Understandably wishing to avoid arguments that purport to unseat the "man from Stratford" as the author of Shakespeare's works, instructors are sometimes reluctant to engage with the issue of Shakespeare's life at all. Unfortunately, this works to cut off one of the main reasons that readers are initially interested in Shakespeare and one of the primary reasons that students sign up for Shakespeare classes. What underlies this fascination with the authorship issue is the perfectly legitimate interest in the contours of Shakespeare's life. Readers are right to want to know how it came to be that Shakespeare wrote so many of the world's literary masterpieces and to ask precisely what kind of life he was living while he was writing them.

I begin with three of the most significant issues that shaped Shakespeare's identity: these are education, religion, and social status. Indeed, the last two of these were inescapably conditions of every Elizabethan life, and, of these, social status, the fundamental hierarchy of Shakespeare's world, based on wealth, property, and lineage, was by far the most important force in determining the trajectory of all lives in early modern England. For Shakespeare personally, of course, education, the very real and substantial source of his literary achievements, was the most important factor in allowing him as a gifted individual to become a writer. Access to that education, however, was also a direct index of status. A boy in Elizabethan England did not need to be from an exalted or aristocratic background to receive a grammar school education, but he still needed at least modest means, which, small though it might be, was nonetheless far beyond the mass of the laboring population. The remaining category, religion, was, of course, a vexed, highly fraught dimension of life in the post-Reformation era of Shakespeare's time, as English Christianity, splintered by schism, took new and unprecedented forms. That church attendance, far from being a voluntary expression of devotion, was mandatory, while heresy and atheism were subject to severe legal censure, meant that prescribed belief was compelled by the state, which often ensured compliance by violent means. In these ways, religion infused almost every aspect of early modern life. Far from being, then, the backdrop for Shakespeare's writing, religion formed the crucible in which his secular drama was generated.

The subject of Chapter 2 is, literally, writing and the humanist institution that most fundamentally shaped Shakespeare's art, namely the Elizabethan educational system. Shakespeare, Marlowe, Jonson, and many others were all beneficiaries of the Protestant revolution in education and, in particular, of the Elizabethan grammar school system in a way that was unique to their generation. There is no evidence whatsoever that the parents of arguably the greatest writer who ever lived could write. John Shakespeare, though prosperous, was uneducated and never signed his name but always used the conventional, and in his case, the neatly crafted, substitution for it, his "mark." That even this fact has been a source of contention amongst commentators arises only from the refusal to credit the reality of Elizabethan provincial life where well-to-do people often remained unable to write.

An unreliable anecdotal account of Shakespeare's early years from the eighteenth century reports that he initially followed his father's trade, though the story has him slaughtering animals (which was not, in fact, a dimension of John Shakespeare's employment) and making tragic speeches upon dispatching a calf. Despite paucity of all other evidence, however, one thing we know definitively about Shakespeare is that his move to London represented a definitive decision *not* to follow his father any further (if indeed he had ever followed him at all) into the trade of whittawer, or whitener of leather (one who "taws," that is dresses skins with alum and salt), and glover. When Gonzalo in *The Tempest* ponders a utopia where "letters" (literacy) are unknown (2.1.150), his speech, though indebted to Michel de Montaigne's account of the indigenous inhabitants of Brazil, would also have reminded those in his audience who were the first generation of literate people in their families, of a world to which they could now never fully return. Stratford produced not only Shakespeare but also the printer Richard Field, who was only three years his senior and the son of a tanner, a trade very much related to that of Shakespeare's father. Field also went to London to become a stationer's apprentice. In the immensely successful pursuit of his vocation he published some of the most important works of his era, including Shakespeare's *Venus and Adonis* (1593), George Puttenham's *Arte of English Poesie* (1589), and Sir John Harington's translation of Ariosto's *Orlando Furioso* (1591). Field, too, was an important part of the burgeoning literary enterprises of the era. Thus, although literacy rates for the overall population were low, even boys of humble background who attended the grammar school, might make something of themselves far beyond the crafts and trades that their forefathers had practiced in the provinces. The chasm opened up by education between the lettered and unlettered that comes up in so many of the plays (*Romeo and Juliet* and *The Tempest*, for example) allows us to ask what it means to be a professional writer in this period and precisely where that occupation stood along the spectrum from basic literacy to literary authorship.

Chapter 3, "Religion," addresses the fundamental conundrum of dealing with the years in which Shakespeare lived in anonymity before the establishment of his London career. Theories about Shakespeare's religious identity have shaped the lacunae of information pertaining to this period in his life. While critics have argued variously that Shakespeare was a staunch Protestant, a devout crypto-Catholic, a furtive nonbeliever, or the holder of any one of a range of positions in between, this chapter stresses instead the ways in which the impact of the Reformation, religious persecution, and anxiety about religious identity invariably informed Shakespeare's theatrical practice as well as his identity as a writer.

Chapter 4, "Status," treats Shakespeare's application, on his father's behalf, for a coat of arms, which would allow him the status of a gentleman: Wm. Shakespeare, Gent. But what exactly did that shift in status mean in early modern England? What procedures were involved in attaining official ratification of the fact that Shakespeare had crossed the vast social chasm that separated commoners from the gentry? In addressing these questions, we will see that Shakespeare's reach for upward mobility did not go uncontested and that the obstacles he encountered at the College of Arms reflect some of the most tumultuous changes in his society, changes which he in turn addresses in his plays. Although the structure and function of the College of Arms remain opaque or obliquely referenced in most extant biographies, it was one of the most important institutions in early modern England. Further, the College provides one of the most illuminating sources of information on the lived experience of class identity in the period. This chapter is especially concerned to explain its operations with utmost clarity.

The final chapter in this section addresses the social and professional conditions that molded Shakespeare's theatrical career in London. Astonishingly, the first printed account of Shakespeare is very negative indeed, but this may be accounted for by the fact that it was written by one of his rivals (though not necessarily the one whose name is on the title page) in a pamphlet entitled *Greene's Groats-worth of wit* (1592). Shakespeare's success had clearly ruffled some feathers because the pamphlet's author disparages him as an "upstart crow" and a "*johannes factotum*" (jack-of-all-trades) who believes he is the only "shakes-scene" in the country. These comments indicate something of the competitive environment of early modern theatre, which, paradoxically, also required collaboration in order to meet the tremendous demand for new plays. This chapter goes on to address the nature of theatre as a new urban institution with a fixed location as well as the pressures of censorship on both performance and print, and, finally, the rather anomalous situation of actors and their companies in comparison with other situations of employment in the capital.

The chapters that comprise Part II treat individual plays from every genre in Shakespeare's oeuvre. The analyses of the plays also include reference to Shakespeare's sources and the status of early texts of each play as well as evidence, where available, for first performances. Included here are also reminders (relatively unobtrusive, I hope) of the plot, which will be a little more comprehensive in chapters covering plays that are less often staged and therefore likely to be less familiar to the majority of readers. Reasons of space preclude the treatment of every play and poem, and I extend my apologies in advance to readers who find their favorite work omitted. If it is any comfort, several works very close to my own heart could not be included in the final selection. Nonetheless, while no single volume can do justice to Shakespeare's achievement, what remains offers a representative sample of the variety of his writing as a poet for both page and stage.

There is little in the way of irrefutable evidence to support the view that *The Comedy of Errors* was Shakespeare's first play, but simply because this has been a traditional assumption about the order in which the plays were written, Part II begins there. The genre categories under which the plays are considered are comedies, histories, and tragedies, as well as a category not to be found in the First Folio, namely, romances. Four of Shakespeare plays share the magical and improbable plotlines and the redemptive happy endings that characterize romance, namely *Cymbeline, Pericles, The Winter's Tale*, and *The Tempest*. The latter two, being far more often staged and read, are addressed in this book. Even though *The Tempest* was placed first in the list of Shakespeare's comedies in the Folio, these plays have come to be understood to merit a discrete category because they represent the trajectory of Shakespeare's writing within the genre of comedy towards the end of his career. This development is significant to any biographical account of Shakespeare's work, or what the title page of *Pericles* calls "the true relation and whole Historie, adventures, and fortunes" of our poet.

Chapter 6, "Comedies: Shakespeare's Social Life," addresses the great range of experience in Shakespeare's comedies, some of which press the genre to the very edges of its boundaries. What all the plays addressed here have in common is that they demonstrate the way that comedy is an intrinsically *social* genre about how men and women go about the business of interacting with one another so as to achieve a certain connectedness, either as conjugal pairs or as a cohesive community. Using information about Shakespeare's day-to-day life in Stratford and London, each reading in this chapter examines the extraordinary power and complexity of the comic perspective. The discussion of *The Comedy of Errors*, for example, revolves around the fact that Shakespeare had two sisters who were named Joan and uses extensive archival evidence to show how the early modern practice of duplicate naming operated and how it illuminates the treatment of social identity in the play. *The Taming of the Shrew* section examines the way this play pays homage to Shakespeare's rural Warwickshire roots. Indeed, the play proves insistently domestic in being a comedy of marriage rather than a comedy of courtship. The analysis of *Love's Labour's Lost* takes Shakespeare's connections with the translator John Florio, who lived for a time at the French Embassy in London, as a way of beginning to understand what the representation of brilliant and glittering French court culture might mean in England. The section devoted to *A Midsummer Night's Dream* considers Shakespeare's creative and conceptual engagement both with his female sovereign and with the sovereignty of art that he sets so skillfully against the flora and fauna of his native place. In contrast, that on *The Merchant of Venice* considers all that Shakespeare encountered that was not marked by familiarity and domesticity, particularly those Jews and Italians who were, like himself, entertainers for the court. The next section considers the title of *Much Ado About Nothing* and specifically its bawdy double entendres, which were regularly recorded in language from the streets of Shakespeare's London in court depositions relating to women indicted for prostitution. The slander of an aristocratic woman, like the vilification of lower-class women arraigned by authorities, raises the question of who gets to adjudicate a woman's chastity. The Forest of Arden returns us to Shakespeare's native county in the next section on *As You Like It* as Arden has a direct topological connection with Warwickshire as well as being his mother Mary's maiden name. In this play, the forest is a refuge where Shakespeare uses the license of comedy, exile, and displacement to explore some of the most profound political questions of his day – and indeed of ours – about the nature and extent of political liberty. The proximity of the Paris Garden bearbaiting ring to the Globe is the spur to this analysis of *Twelfth Night*. Here, Shakespeare examines both cruelty and festivity as the motivations for laughter. Shakespeare turned to the landscape of the city in *Measure for Measure*, so this section uses the French-speaking population of London, with which Shakespeare was intimately involved, as a means of juxtaposing the threatened decapitation of Claudio with an actual instance of decapitation for sexual misconduct in Calvin's Geneva.

The plays analyzed in Chapter 7, "English and Roman Histories: Shakespeare's Politics," focus on political concepts, structures of law, and government more than on individuals and localities. The objective here is not to discern Shakespeare's own political opinions, to which we do not have access, but to assess to what degree "Peace, freedom, and liberty!" (*Julius Caesar* 3.1.110) motivated the popularity of this genre in its own time. The readings here show how Shakespeare navigated the treacherous waters of some of the most volatile political and newsworthy issues and events of his day, from plots against Elizabeth to the circulation of seditious, contraband European writings against tyranny. In particular, *Richard II* was arguably Shakespeare's closest encounter with the ire of the Elizabethan state, while *Richard III* (written before *Richard II*) exposed, via the compelling histrionics of its eponymous protagonist, the sometimes astonishing contiguities between theatre and power. *The First Part of King Henry the Fourth* examines the play as unique among Shakespeare's histories with its dramaturgically remarkable counterpoints between high and low culture, history, and comedy, and its widespread disposition of social groups.

The play shifts between registers, from the blank verse sphere of high politics to Welsh lyricism to the prose world of those who haunt taverns and commit highway robbery. This chapter ends with two Roman histories, *Julius Caesar* and *Coriolanus*, even though the editors of the First Folio, John Heminges and Henry Condell, placed these plays under the heading of tragedy because these are profoundly and explicitly political tragedies. The section on *Julius Caesar* begins with the emperor's historical connection with England, arising from the fact that he had invaded the country in 54 BC, and examines the degree to which autocracy in ancient Rome might be understood as analogous to absolute monarchy in England. The section on *Coriolanus* examines the play's action-hero, warrior protagonist as, in an important sense, the antithesis of Shakespeare, construed, for the purposes of this analysis, as a reader – that is, as someone intimately engaged with books. Indeed, this play provides telling evidence of how Shakespeare read history with a view to transposing what he read onto the medium of theatre.

Chapter 8, "Tragedies: Shakespeare in Love and Loss," addresses *Romeo and Juliet*, *Hamlet*, *Othello*, *King Lear*, *Macbeth*, and *Antony and Cleopatra*. I explore the irreducibly literary dimension of tragedy as well as its intersection with commonplace social incidents of grief and loss, some of them in Shakespeare's own family. Shakespeare's sorrows are ordinary: the loss of a child, the loss of a father. What is extraordinary, however, is the way that he turns these nearly ubiquitous forms of loss, these everyday heartbreaks, into the great tragedies of this period.

The section on *Hamlet* explores the extraordinary onomastic coincidence between the play's title and his dead son, Hamnet, as well the "muddy death" of a young woman from a village close to Stratford, Katherine Hamlett. In fact, names in Shakespeare often hold biographical clues, and the discussion of *King Lear* begins by asking why Shakespeare gave one of his greatest villains the same name as his brother. The great paradox considered in the section on *Othello* is that although the play is in so many ways decidedly un-English, so indebted to the idea of Africa and to its Italian source, it is nonetheless a domestic tragedy. *Othello* addresses matters very close to home, especially the slander of the virtuous wife, to which any woman, including Shakespeare's own daughter Susanna might fall victim. The two love tragedies considered here, *Romeo and Juliet* and *Antony and Cleopatra* are addressed in the light of less immediately personal issues. The former bespeaks Shakespeare's intense engagement with Petrarchan poetry, and the latter evidences his interest in the essentially theatrical problem of how to present goddess-like power and femininity.

The final chapter, "Romances: Shakespeare and Theatrical Magic," addresses *The Winter's Tale* and *The Tempest*, written towards the close of his career, in which families are ultimately reunited by means of extraordinary theatrical magic. The analysis of *The Winter's Tale* begins with its court performance in 1611 before the royal couple who were bitterly familiar with the loss of children and whose marital strife about fostering their eldest son and heir in the 1590s had been made public by means of newsletters. News and current events also play a significant part in *The Tempest*. While these plays are traditionally viewed as Shakespeare's retrospective on his career in theatre, it is also important that he was, even in his later work, still attuned to matters of immediate interest both to himself and to his audience. *The Tempest* (now understood to have been followed by collaborative work with John Fletcher), is the focus of the final section, which considers the rather astonishing fact that Shakespeare himself, despite transporting his audience to strange and exotic climes in this play, probably never left England.

What follows, then, is an account of Shakespeare's writing aimed at readers who have a healthy appetite for information about Shakespeare's life. This exposition is intended to provide a clear guide to Shakespeare and his works and to deepen readers' knowledge about Shakespeare's literary achievement and his historical moment. My aim throughout this book is to make Shakespeare's personal, social, and literary identity more vividly present. In so doing, I hope also to demonstrate how Shakespeare incorporated the life around him into his plays and how his works show that process as one which in turn might alter, transform, or astonish the reality that had first shaped it.

# Notes

1 Samuel Schoenbaum, *Shakespeare's Lives* (Oxford: Clarendon Press, 1991), p. 338.

2 Schoenbaum, *Shakespeare's Lives*, p. 338; James Walter, *Shakespeare's True Life* (London, 1889); David Piper, *"O Sweet Mr Shakespeare: I'll Have His Picture"* (London: National Portrait Gallery, 1964), p. 36.

3 Quoted in Samuel Schoenbaum, *William Shakespeare: A Documentary Life* (New York: Oxford University Press, 1975), p. 254.

4 A.H. Wall, *Shakespeare's Face: A Monologue On the Various Portraits of Shakespeare in Comparison with the Death Mask Now Preserved as Shakespeare's in the Grand Ducal Museum at Darmstadt* (As read before the Melbourne Shakespeare Society, in Australia) (Herald Printing Office: Stratford-Upon-Avon, 1890), p. 4.

5 Quoted in Schoenbaum, *Shakespeare's Lives*, p. 338.

6 Piper, *"O Sweet Mr Shakespeare"* p. 36; Nigel Llewellyn, *Art of Death: Visual Culture in the English Death Ritual, c.1500–c.1800* (London: Reaktion), p. 54.

7 Quoted in Roy C. Strong, *English Icon: Elizabethan and Jacobean Portraiture* (New Haven: Yale University Press, 1970), p. 29.

8 Schoenbaum, *Documentary Life*, p. 185.

9 See Susan Sontag, *On Photography* (New York: Picador 1977, 1st edn 1973), p. 154.

10 Sontag, p. 154.

11 See Jonathan Gil Harris, "Shakespeare's Hair: Staging the Object of Material Culture," *Shakespeare Quarterly* 52 (2001): 479–91.

12 Walter, *Shakespeare's True Life*, p. 266.

13 Schoenbaum, *Documentary Life*, p. 256.

14 Schoenbaum, *Documentary Life*, p. 255.

# 2

# WRITING

In a humorous soliloquy in the first act of *Romeo and Juliet*, Capulet's unnamed and illiterate servant is given a list of people he must invite to the Capulet ball: "I am sent to find those persons whose names are here writ, and can never find what names *the writing person* hath here writ" (1.2.40–2).[1] Perplexed, the servant finds himself in the comic predicament of being the intermediary between two entities, both of whom are, in different senses, illegible to him: the author of the list, that shadowy figure, "the writing person," and the "persons whose names are here writ." Conscious of his deficiency, the serving-man jokes about his unsuitability for the job at hand with a comic analogy: "It is written that the shoemaker should meddle with his yard and the tailor with his last, the fisher with his pencil [paintbrush], and the painter with his nets" (1.2.38–40). Jokingly, he assigns the tools of the crafts mentioned to the wrong tradesmen: it is a shoemaker who uses a last, not a tailor; a tailor, not a shoemaker, uses a yard; while fishermen, as we know, use nets and painters, brushes. Interestingly, the manual laborers in his itinerary were not always illiterate, and tailors in particular could often read and write. It is also significant that the serving-man's dirty joke about tradesmen who play ("meddle") with their own – as well as possibly other men's – (sexual) equipment ("yard" and "pencil" were slang terms for the male organ) begins with the mildly blasphemous use of the term that typically prefaced readings and quotations from scripture: "It is written." The authority of scripture was paramount in this society and had been lent greater power by the advent of the printed word, but this was also the period in which authorial identity in a specifically literary sense

*Who Was William Shakespeare?: An Introduction to the Life and Works*, First Edition.
Dympna Callaghan.
© 2013 John Wiley & Sons, Ltd. Published 2013 by John Wiley & Sons, Ltd.

emerges to greater prominence. At last, the serving-man alights on the only possible solution to his quandary: "I must to the *learned*" (1.2.40–2; my emphasis). While the gulf between "the learned" and the unlearned, "the writing person" and the illiterate, is bridged here by comedy, it remained one of the starkest divisions in Shakespeare's society. For Shakespeare, like many others, that division scored through his family as well as his world. This chapter explores what it meant in such a context for Shakespeare to be a "writing person."

Shakespeare must have covered sheaf upon sheaf of paper with ink during his working life. Of all that labor, not one manuscript of any of the plays printed in the First Folio survives in Shakespeare's hand. There are only six indisputable autographs, all on legal documents: six relatively inconsiderable traces of Shakespeare's signature. Notwithstanding Oliver Wendell Holmes's contention that to spell any word the same way twice is evidence of a lack of imagination, that none of these signatures are spelled the same way would not, from our twenty-first-century point of view, seem to indicate that Shakespeare was a highly literate person. The spelling of inexperienced writers in the period sometimes bespeaks a more phonetic expression than that to be found among those with more highly developed literacies, but such generalizations are difficult to sustain because early modern spelling is notoriously erratic. Standardized spelling was not introduced until the eighteenth century, and spellings such as "aboute," "younge yeares," "sonne," and "paste" (for "past"), are not *wrong* in our modern sense. Nor are they necessarily the product of a person of mean estate, of someone low on the totem pole of early modern social hierarchies. In fact, these examples are taken from a letter found in the Folger Library's Bagot collection that was written by the aristocrat Lady Markham to her brother in 1610.[2]

Shakespeare's wayward spelling, then, while it may not distinguish him from the minimally or partially literate, does not necessarily make him one of them. That Shakespeare writes in the distinctive cursive script known as secretary hand, on the contrary, indicates a person who writes regularly and with some rapidity. Importantly, in Shakespeare's day, those who were most fully engaged in the material practices of writing were not authors themselves, who were referred to as "poets," but scribes who made "fair copies" of both legal and literary documents either for manuscript distribution or for print. Indeed, this kind of writing was sometimes disparaged as mere penmanship, or as Martin Billingsley put it in *The Pen's Excellencie* (1618), as "onely a hand-labour,"[3] that is, as manual work that did not require the use of the intellectual faculties. That writing was time consuming and physically demanding labor is noted by the scrivener in *Richard III*, who reports that he has been ordered to copy a legal document: "Eleven hours I have spent to write it over" (3.6.5).[4]

Only three manuscript pages by "Hand D" from the coauthored play *Sir Thomas More* exist as presumed autographic evidence of Shakespeare's creative expression. It is instructive, too, that Shakespeare's signature does not survive on his poetic scribbles but on the documents early moderns considered most important, namely those pertaining to legal proceedings and the transfer of property: the deed for the gatehouse property at Blackfriars and the mortgage for the Blackfriars' property; a court deposition in the dowry dispute known as the Belott-Mountjoy case (in which he was called as a witness); and his will. Indeed, three of Shakespeare's extant signatures were affixed to his will, and all but the final one – the most important one on a legal document – probably represent contractions of his full name rather than misspellings of it as such. The oddity of Shakespeare's signatures aside, what is not in doubt (except perhaps among Oxfordians and Baconians), though it seems trite to say it, is Shakespeare's own literacy. Not only was Shakespeare literate, but also, we might say, he was hyper-literate because his facility in reading and writing was above and beyond all norms. Although within the context of early modern education, which prized facility in classical languages, Shakespeare's literacy had its limitations. Ben Jonson famously derided his literacy skills because, or so Jonson charged, Shakespeare possessed "small Latine and lesse Greeke."[5] These are limitations that even a literate character like Romeo admits to in his exchange with Capulet's servant:

SERVINGMAN:   God gi' good e'en. I pray, sir, can you read?

ROMEO:   Ay, mine own fortune in my misery.

SERVINGMAN:   Perhaps you have learned it without book. But, I pray, can you read anything you see?

ROMEO:   Ay, if I know the letters and the language.

SERVINGMAN:   Ye say honestly. Rest you merry!

ROMEO:   Stay, fellow, I can read. (1.2.56–62)

It is clear that the servant takes Romeo's joke about not being able to read foreign alphabets and languages as an admission of complete illiteracy because "Rest you merry" is a conventional expression of farewell. Similarly, in Christopher Marlowe's poem *Hero and Leander* the "illit'rate hinds" (*l.* 218)[6] probably refers to people who cannot read Latin rather than to people who simply cannot read English. Distinctions among degrees of literacy – in the vernacular or in Latin, in European languages or in Greek – were important. Shakespeare himself would have fallen into the category described in ecclesiastical usage as "litteratus," that is, someone who knew Latin but lacked a university degree.[7] The questions, "I pray sir, Can you read?" or "Are you not lettered?" (*Love's Labour's Lost*, 5.1.43)[8] were freighted with cultural significance and much more momentous in a world where, despite these impressive humanist advances in education, the majority of the population remained unable to read and write: "the illiterate, that know not how / To cipher what is writ in learned books" (*The Rape of Lucrece*, *ll.* 810–11).[9] Approximately one man in five in Elizabethan England could sign his own name, but the figures were much lower for women: one in twenty.[10] There is, however, considerable debate about the statistics for literacy in the period, and especially about whether women, in particular, but also the lower orders in general, might be able to read but not write – and thus be categorized as literate. Also, since reading and writing were taught independently, the inability to write does not *necessarily* betoken the inability to read. To complicate matters further, Wyn Ford has demonstrated that "good handwriting was not always linked to competence in other aspects of literacy."[11] The "sir" in the serving-man's question to Romeo indicates also that literacy did not invariably correlate with class status. Although Shakespeare's mother, Mary Arden, came from a well-to-do family, and though his father achieved positions of civic distinction, neither signed their name. Neither civic nor social prominence was incompatible with minimal literacy skills, and most people acquired knowledge by extra-textual means, often aided by very well-developed arts of memory: "You have learned it without book" (*Romeo and Juliet*, 1.2.58).

Shakespeare's father, John, who became Stratford's bailiff in 1568, signed only with his mark on all surviving documents. He witnessed legal documents with a cross, perhaps indicating that he made his mark before God and understood the "signature" to have the significance of an oath, and on other documents he sometimes drew a pair of compasses, "the instrument used for measuring and making ornamental cuttings on the back of gloves. Once he appended a different sign, which has been interpreted as a glover's stitching clamp, or 'donkey.'"[12] According to Ford, elaborate marks of this type "lend weight to the hypothesis that rudimentary penmanship was learnt by some without pretensions to literacy."[13] Unletteredness was common among members of John Shakespeare's trade, and few glovers, especially in the provinces, could sign their names. Like her husband, Shakespeare's mother, Mary, used a mark to witness the sale of their Snitterfield property in 1579. There has been considerable resistance to these facts on the part of those Shakespeare biographers who imagine that literacy patterns in early modern England must have been like those of the present. Historians, too, have debated whether a mark represents the inability to write or simply a creative choice. For instance, when John Shakespeare's neighbor, Adrian Quiney, whose developed literacy is established by other documents, signed the Stratford Council register with an inverted form of his initial "Q," was he just choosing on that occasion to sign with a mark? In fact, he was not. The distinction between initialing a document and making a creative mark is that Quiney is able, as his illiterate neighbors were not, to deploy the letter of the alphabet that corresponds with his name. As David Cressy has pointed out, whether a person signed with a mark or with a signature was "a question of capacity, not of choice."[14]

Although the inability to read was a socially acknowledged deficiency, the skills Shakespeare's parents probably required more urgently in their everyday conduct of business were basic numeracy and arithmetical ability. Fortunately, there were readier aids for arithmetic (objects and instruments that were part of the fabric of everyday life) in Shakespeare's time. In *The Winter's Tale*, when faced with a calculation, the clown confesses, "I cannot do't without counters" (4.3.36),[15] while in the *Sonnets* ("Nor need I tallies thy dear love to score," 122.10) and *2 Henry VI* ("Our forefathers had no other books but the score and the tally," 4.7.32–3), Shakespeare refers to "the score and tally" system of marking sticks with notches in order to keep a record of monetary transactions.[16]

In order to understand the context in which Shakespeare's acquisition of literacy followed early modern educational and social norms, we need to grasp the puzzling coexistence of hyper-literacy and unletteredness. Illiteracy was a fate that could very easily have been visited on Shakespeare had his father, perhaps, never been appointed an alderman (a post which entitled his son to attend the grammar school), or had his father's financial misfortunes occurred earlier in the poet's childhood. If we look at the next generation, we do not know whether Shakespeare's son, Hamnet, (who died at age eleven in 1596) went to school, though it is likely that he did so. Certainly, the twin sister who survived him, Judith, signed with a mark as a full-grown woman of twenty-six in 1611. She made a mark twice as witness to a deed for the sale of a house belonging to Elizabeth and Adrian Quiney. While the illiteracy or partial literacy of Shakespeare's parents (they might have been able to read but not write) is perhaps surprising, it remains one of the most astonishing facts surrounding Shakespeare's biography that his own daughter, Judith, could not sign her own name. It seems almost incomprehensible that the daughter of England's greatest ever writer could not write herself. Yet the Judith Shakespeare who has been most often the object of critical consideration is not a real person at all, but the playwright's hypothetical sister invented by Virginia Woolf in *A Room of One's Own* (1929). Woolf demonstrates that a woman, though endowed with literary talents equal to Shakespeare, would not have been able to attain his achievements:

> She was not sent to school. She had no chance of learning grammar and logic, let alone of reading Horace and Virgil. She picked up a book now and then, one of her brother's perhaps, and read a few pages. But then her parents came in and told her to mend the stockings or mind the stew and not moon about with books and papers.[17]

For all that Woolf's intriguing fantasy draws attention to the impediments women with literary aspirations would have encountered, it also deflects attention from the real Judith Shakespeare.

John Hart's *A Methode or Comfortable Beginning for All Unlearned, Whereby They May Bee Taught to Read English in a Very Short Time* (1570) casts an interesting light upon the acquisition of literacy, noting that some precocious children (of whom Shakespeare himself was no doubt one) make remarkable and rapid progress. Did Judith Shakespeare, in contrast, lack aptitude or "towardness," as it was known in Elizabethan English, or did Shakespeare's pursuit of his own career mean that he was not there to teach her, or did he not think writing a valuable skill for a woman? Whichever was the case, the evidence for the literacy of Shakespeare's youngest daughter offers a stark contrast with the learned women of his plays and poems. For example, in *Titus Andronicus*, Lavinia's knowledge of the Roman poet Ovid allows her to reveal the identities of the men who have raped and mutilated her, while the ravished Lucrece is shown in the throes of epistolary composition:

> Her maid is gone, and she prepares to write,
> First hovering o'er the paper with her quill.
> Conceit and grief an eager combat fight;
> What wit sets down is blotted straight with will.
> This is too curious-good, this blunt and ill:
>     Much like a press of people at a door,
>     Throng her inventions, which shall go before.
>                                    *The Rape of Lucrece* (*ll.* 1296–302)

This is not the halting hand of a woman whose deficient and underdeveloped writing skills cause her to be unable to express emotion within the constraints of perceived epistolary convention. The violated Lucrece struggles not only to find the balance between writing something too contrived ("conceit," "curious-good") and something too poorly articulated ("blunt and ill"), but also to express her crowded thoughts ("like a press of people at a door") in a logical, orderly fashion. Shakespeare sets the scene here with the material implements of writing – paper and quill – as the interface between intellectual invention and written expression. The writing process is a three-staged one of thinking, writing, and correcting – setting down and immediately blotting out. "Wit" and "will" are particularly interesting words here because their early modern meanings are somewhat different from our own. "Wit" denoted the faculty of thought and reason, as well as a capacity for apt expression, and was not then associated so firmly as it is today with sophisticated humor or a talent for the *bon mot*. "Will" was a complex word that carried both literary and theological associations. Here it means the emotion that overwhelms Lucrece's intellectual powers in the act of writing. Sir Philip Sidney had used the term "erected will" in his *Apology for Poetry* and had, furthermore, used it in conjunction with "wit" to describe how human weakness overwhelms rational virtue: "Our erected wit maketh us know what perfection is, and yet our infected will keepeth us from reaching unto it."[18] "Will" was also, of course, Shakespeare's name, something he puns on repeatedly in the *Sonnets*. (He uses the word twelve times in Sonnet 135: "Will in overplus" (*l.*2). Given the literary context for these words, it is impossible not to feel that Shakespeare was, in *Lucrece*, describing something of his own process of composition. The association – as well as the distinction – between the writing Lucrece and Shakespeare himself is even more compelling when we consider also the way Lucrece *blots* her lines in conjunction with a remark Ben Jonson made about Shakespeare's preternatural fluency in composition: "I remember the players have often mentioned it as an honor to Shakespeare that in his writing, whatsoever he penned, he never blotted out line. My answer hath been, would he had blotted a thousand."[19]

Secretary and italic were the two forms of handwriting Shakespeare would have learnt in school. Secretary hand was used in many legal and ecclesiastical records, and was also the script used for play texts. Unfortunately, as we have noted, of Shakespeare's "foul papers," that is, the plays written in his own handwriting, only the script known as "Hand D" in the collaboratively written play *Sir Thomas More* survives.[20] There, he was clearly writing quickly and fluently, and the speed with which Shakespeare could transcribe his thoughts was no doubt impressive enough to make Jonson jealous. Shakespeare is certainly engaged by the mental aspect of composition because he refers to it again in the *Sonnets* when he asks, "What's in the brain that ink may character . . . ?" (108.1). "Character" refers here quite specifically to the inky letters themselves as well as the more general sense of "character" as description. There is another telling reference to a letter or character in *Love's Labour's Lost*: "Fair as a text B in a copy-book" (5.2.42), and on this occasion it is from a writing manual, the standard handwriting textbook of Shakespeare's day, Jean de Beau Chesne and John Baildon's *A Booke Containing Divers Sortes of Hands As Well the English as French Secretarie with the Italian, Roman, Chancelry and Court Hands* (1571), which contained an ornate character, a heavily inked capital B. Thus, like Quiney's inverted "Q," the "character" is a letter freighted with significance in a way that a mere mark was not, and the writing process it bespeaks is of a much higher order of complexity.

In 1647, Susanna, Shakespeare's oldest daughter, had been widowed for more than a decade when, at sixty-four, she signed her name on the deed to New Place. She had been married to the well-educated physician John Hall, who died in 1635. Susanna could write her name, but she could not recognize her own husband's handwriting. As Samuel Schoenbaum remarks, this is odd. Does it mean, he inquires, that she possessed "learning sufficient only to enable her to sign her name?" As Schoenbaum observes,

> Susanna Hall could sign her name to legal documents, but, although lauded as witty beyond her sex, she could not identify her husband's distinctive handwriting in his Latin medical diaries. So we learn from the visit, around 1642, of the Warwick surgeon James Cooke to New Place, where he came to examine the books that the celebrated physician, lately deceased, had left behind. "I, being acquainted with Mr. Hall's hand," Cooke recalls, "told her that one or two of them were her husband's, and showed them her – she denied; I affirmed, till I perceived she begun to be offended."[21]

Her epitaph specifically lauds her as a woman possessed of singular intellectual gifts:

> Witty above her sex, but that's not all,
> Wise to Salvation was good Mistress Hall.
> Something of Shakespeare was in that, but this
> Wholly of him with whom she's now in bliss.

If Susanna's "wit," her native intelligence (which the epitaph attributes to genetic inheritance from her father) made her cleverer than most women, it did not necessarily mean that she was also better educated. Yet commentators invariably equate the wit here ascribed to Susanna as equivalent to or inclusive of full literacy, which it most probably was not.[22]

Susanna, in fact, may not have been literate as a child or as a young woman since early moderns often acquired literacy skills not as a matter of course but as the need arose. Thus, she may have learned to write only after the death of her husband, and even then, the extent of her literacy may have been confined to the capacity to sign her name, especially given what Elizabeth Rivlin calls the "multiplicity and variety of early modern literacies."[23] Whatever the limitations of Susanna's education, Schoenbaum's assessment is that she was simply more intelligent than her sister: "Judith Shakespeare presumably had less wit than her sister, for she never learned to sign her name."[24] For Katherine Duncan-Jones in *Ungentle Shakespeare: Scenes from his Life*, Judith is the slighted daughter, not necessarily the least intelligent one:

> Judith, it seems, was not a favourite daughter. She may have suffered, in her father's eyes, from having had the insensitivity to stay alive so many years after the death of her much loved twin brother Hamnet at the age of eleven. Though Susanna, "Witty above her sex", commanded some degree of literacy, Judith seems to have

had none. She signed documents only with the crudest of marks. She may well
have been intelligent, but no time or money had been devoted to her early education, nor was she to enjoy the later advantage that Susanna did of marriage to a
highly educated husband.[25]

It is far from clear that Susanna's capacity to write (in the event that she indeed
possessed it at twenty-four, the age of her marriage to Dr John Hall in 1607)
was the motivating factor in the making of that alliance, although Susanna
certainly gained advantages in marrying an educated man. For Duncan-Jones
there consists in the difference between a mark and a signature a vast distinction
between the two sisters that might even have helped Susanna to her advanta-
geous match.

From the historical point of view, then, the problem of the illiteracy and
especially the unletteredness of women that was the context for Shakespeare's
own achievements is a fractious one. Most recently, Germaine Greer has cham-
pioned a highly literate Anne Hathaway in *Shakespeare's Wife* as an alternative
to the potentially illiterate woman who might never have read anything Shakespeare wrote. (Greer's Anne even reads to Shakespeare on his deathbed.) Greer
is fully aware of the evidentiary problems presented in determining who was
and who was not literate in Shakespeare's family, and she remarks, tongue-in-
cheek, "Certainly it is possible, even entirely possible, that Ann [*sic*] could not
read. It is also possible, given the absolute absence of evidence to the contrary,
that she was blind."[26] Blindness, however, was an unusual circumstance that
would have been noted, and indeed there was a convention for recoding inability to sign because of physical incapacity: "*non subscripsit quia cecus.*" Greer
bizarrely proposes yet another scenario for Anne: "She may have been illiterate
when Shakespeare met her, and he may have spent the long hours with her as
she watched her cows grazing on the common, teaching her to read."[27] Greer,
however, swiftly dismisses this possibility in favor of the idea that the "staunchly
Protestant" Hathaways would not have tolerated a daughter who could not
read her Bible.[28] This may or may not have been true, since in pious households
wives were required to defer to their husband's spiritual authority.[29] In addition,
it is likely that, as Kirsi Stjerna maintains, "the educational provisions of the
Protestant Reformation, while nurturing the traditional female values of modesty
and submissiveness, etc., limited girls' education to rudimentary reading and
writing skills and, generally speaking, provided a poorer standard of basic education than they had received in the convents."[30] Greer's revisionist perspective
regards critics who propose the possibility that Shakespeare married an illiterate
woman as disparaging of women in general. Stephen Greenblatt is singled out
for attack because, he argues, "it is entirely possible that Shakespeare's wife
never read a word that he wrote, that anything he sent her from London had

to be read by a neighbor . . ."[31] The demographics, however, are with Greenblatt on this one because literacy rates were much lower in the provinces than
in London, and even in the capital, it was not until the end of the seventeenth
century that female literacy showed a significant increase.

In contrast to the members of his immediate family, then, Shakespeare was
afforded the privilege of a very good education denied to most of those around
him. We know that Shakespeare read Montaigne's *Essays* and that his profound
and life-long debt to the *Metamorphoses* began at the grammar school where
he first encountered the classical Roman poet Ovid. What is fascinating, however,
is that on the opposite end of the continuum with such immensely influential
books is the very first book he ever read, a text known as the hornbook. This
book places him closer to the ordinary, everyday world of Stratford than his
subsequent reading. The hornbook was not, in fact, a book with leaves and a
cover, but a square wooden paddle bearing the alphabet in capital and lower
case black letters, and it was one of the objects most familiar to everyone who
learned to read in sixteenth-century England. Its name derives from the sheet
of horn processed in a sequence of soaking, heating, and pressing to produce
a transparent protective covering for the pasted parchment. There was sometimes a hole in the handle, and the hornbook was small enough to be worn
around a child's neck or on a belt. It was with this object that all literacy began,
and thus, it is with the hornbook that Shakespeare inevitably started his literary
career.

William Kempe, in *The Education of Children in Learning* (1588), summarized the work of the hornbook as, "The scholler shall learne perfectly, namely,
to knowe the letters by their figures, to sound them aright by their proper
names, and to joyne them together, the vowels with vowels in diphthongs, and
the consonants with vowels in other syllables."[32] In *Ludus Literarius* (1612),
John Brinsley urged that once children became "cunning in their letters, if you
make them to understand the matter which they learne, by questions, for a little
at the first, they will goe on in reading, as fast as you will desire."[33]

Shakespeare's intimate acquaintance with the hornbook, then, is important
in a sense, not because this experience is peculiar to him, but precisely because
it is not. In this, as in every aspect of his subsequent literary training, there
is nothing to distinguish Shakespeare's schooling from that of his fellows.
Instead, the significance of the obvious fact that the author of *Hamlet*, the
*Sonnets*, and the rest began by learning his ABCs lies in the social and institutional conditions specific to sixteenth-century culture that shaped the means by
which the most rudimentary aspects of literary language were acquired.

The very first symbol on the hornbook, on the left-hand side, where reading
was to begin, was not a letter but a figure: the Greek cross, and it is mentioned
as the "crossrow" in *Richard III* (1.1.55). This was followed by the alphabet,

and then by a syllabary with combinations of vowels and consonants that pupils were required to recite aloud. Among the essentials of early modern literacy contained in the hornbook are the *In-nomine* ("In the name of the Father and of the Son and of the Holy Ghost, Amen") and the *Pater Noster* (the "Our Father"). The inclusion of such prayers, still known by their Latin names even when recited in English, is indicative of the fact that literacy and religious instruction were well-nigh inseparable. Humanism, the resurgence of interest in the classical past and its languages, had gained momentum from the Reformation's break with the Roman Catholic Church initiated in England by Henry VIII, and England followed the European reformers' commitment to reading the Bible in the vernacular. Shakespeare's *Henry VIII* reflects this commitment when Katherine Parr (Henry's sixth wife), who was herself a translator of one of the most popular devotional books of the age, asks to pray in English as opposed to Latin, the pan-European language of prayer among Catholics. Humanist educator Roger Ascham demonstrates the ideological weight of this difference in 1570 when he remarks that "In our forefathers tyme . . . fewe bookes were read in our tongue," because "Papistry, as a standing poole, covered and overflowed all England."[34] Church Latin for Ascham, then, not only stood for all that was stagnant and foul, but also for what actively stifled vernacular expression.

The English language itself thus took on new significance in the wake of the Reformation. Protestantism, as a religion of the "Word," emphasized direct access to the Bible – newly available in English – and therefore required literacy as one of its preconditions. The reformed Church of England also sought to have everyone learn the catechism and thus avoid all manner of theological error and heresy. To this end, basic literacy became the ready means of instilling religious conformity. However, the state also sought conformity in other aspects of education, including non-religious books. William Lily's *An Introduction of The Eyght Partes of Speche* (popularly known as "Lily's Grammar") "and none other" was authorized by a proclamation of Henry VIII in 1542, which was also printed in the front matter of the text: "Fayle not to apply your scholars in learninge and godly education," the proclamation urged as it attempted to stem the tide of "the diversitie of grammers and teachinges,"[35] which were believed to be a hindrance to effective education. This cannot have been entirely successful since in 1545 a further proclamation attempted to outlaw "the diversity of primer books that are now abroad."[36] Other authorized books included Alexander Nowell's *A Catechisme or First Instruction and Learning of Christian Religion* (1571). In 1543 the Act for the Advancement of True Religion stated that such authorization was intended "for the Abolishment of the Contrary" and, in a surprisingly early argument for universal literacy, encouraged "the multitude of the people," including "women, artificers, 'prentices . . . and laborers" to read.[37] Henry VIII claimed that he had put aside "the manifold business and most weighty affairs pertaining to our regal authority" in order to attend to the education of "tender babes and youth of our realm," a concern which further attests to powerful fresh impetuses to literacy.[38]

In the wake of the new interest in education and as part of the rise of print, schoolmasters and tutors began to commit their thoughts on teaching to the new medium, and these theories of pedagogy were influential in the transformation of education which began in the sixteenth century and continued through the reign of James I. For example, the aforementioned John Brinsley's *Ludus Literarius* (1612), dedicated to Henry Prince of Wales, also included advice on the instruction of the very young: "The pleasantest way to teach the little ones, to pronounce their letter, and to spell before they know a letter; and how to doe it."[39] Indeed, there was no want of innovative pedagogical strategies aimed at young children. Another writer reported that a father of his acquaintance made a little carousel of the alphabet so that only one letter would be revealed at a time – much to the delight of his young son, who eagerly pronounced his letter when it was presented to him in this entertaining fashion.[40]

Given his parents' deficit in literacy, Shakespeare is unlikely to have acquired the fundamental skills of reading and writing at home. The "petty school," as it was known, was the place where children too young (under seven) to attend the grammar school were taught their letters. In Stratford, the small chapel of the Guild Hall served as a schoolroom for this purpose. Two petty school-teachers were licensed in Stratford when Shakespeare was a boy: the curate, William Gilbard (who also drew up wills for the illiterate and kept the town clocks),[41] and Thomas Parker, whose license was renewed in 1604. The bailiff and burgesses of Stratford noted in their petition to the chancellor of Worcester that Parker "hath for a reasonable time of continuance employed himself to the teaching of little children (chiefly such as his wife one time of the day doth practice in needlework), whereby our young youth is well furthered in reading and the Free School greatly eased of that tedious trouble."[42] This is interesting from a gender point of view since only male pupils were admitted to the grammar school and these same children appear to be learning needlework. The Corporation praises Parker because the boys were fully literate when they reached the grammar school as a result of his labors with them. This is especially important because the Ordinances of Stratford made literacy a specific prerequisite for entry to the grammar school: "at the least ways entered or reddy to enter into their . . . principalles of grammer."[43] The renewal document intimates that Parker's wife was also involved in education, at least in teaching sewing. In Shakespeare's own rendition of early childhood instruction in *Love's Labour's Lost*, however, the schoolmaster, Holofernes, seems to teach both sexes: "If their sons be ingenious, they shall want no instruction; if their daughters be capable, I will put it to them" (4.2.78–80). Yet when the saucy page, Moth, makes of fun him, Holofernes is referred to as only teaching boys: "he teaches boys the horn-book" (5.1.44). Certainly the rigid division of the sexes was less rigorously enforced with small children, who began at the petty school at about four years old, and while girls were not admitted to grammar school, women teachers were involved in elementary literacy education. As Brinsley urged,

> Thus may any poore man or woman enter the little ones in a towne together; and make an honest poore living of it, or get from that towards helping the same. Also the Parents who have any learning, may enter their little ones laying with them, at dinners and suppers, or as they sit by the fire; and finde it very plesant delight.[44]

However, whether such teachers were competent instructors was questionable. Francis Clement, in *The Petie Schole* (1587), was less optimistic about this scenario, complaining that coarse, unsuitable individuals, "men and women altogether rude," were teaching children in private.[45]

Clement's text begins with a verse listing the various principal livelihoods of those who might teach as a sideline. As in the Stratford of Shakespeare's youth, the parish clerk "is made a Teacher meete," that is, he is perfectly suitable, made for the occupation. Literacy was, of course, for him a fundamental job requirement, as was his suitability to teach children their catechism. More surprisingly, Clement shows, the weaver's craft as well as that of the tailor and the seamstress can also be combined with teaching "petties":

> Come, little childe, let toyes alone,
>     and trifles in the streete:
> Come, get thee to the parish Clarke,
>     H[e]'is made a Teacher meete [suitable].
> Frequent ye now the Taylers shop,
>     and eeke the Weavers lombe:
> Ther's neither these [both of these], but can with skill
>     Them teach that thither come.
> The Semstresse she (a Mistresse now)
>     hath lore as much to reade,
> As erst [ever] she had in many yeares
>     compast by silke and threede.
> I can not all by name rehearse,
>     For many moe you see:
> Come make your choyce, let toies alone,
>     and trifles: Learne A, B.[46]

The poem suggests also that the combination of pedagogical and other labors refutes our notion of the radical separation of manual and intellectual labor, and argues instead for their coexistence. John Hart's 1570 reading manual makes a similar point: "Some one such in a house as now can read our present manner may be able to teach it to all the rest of the house, even whilst their hands may be otherwise well occupied in working for their living, or otherwise being idle or sitting by the fire, without any further let [hindrance] or cost."[47] Notably, textile crafts, not just the skills of clerkship, are thought to be the right kinds of occupations to combine with teaching. Tailors, weavers, and seamstresses are understood to do indoor work that allows them to listen to children pronouncing their letters and syllables from the hornbook. All literate individuals were eligible to obtain teaching licenses from the bishop, provided that they accepted the Thirty Nine Articles of the Church of England, the fundamental tenants of Protestantism which were introduced in 1563, the year before Shakespeare was born. The seamstress is singled out in Clement's poem as someone who now covers more narrative ground by reading ("hath lore as much to reade") than she ever achieved, "compast," or encompassed, by embroidery and ordinary stitching ("silke and threede"). Some needlewomen in early modern England told remarkably complex and beautiful stories in their embroidery. Indeed, John Taylor's book of embroidery patterns, *The Needle's Excellency* (1631), assumes that embroidery is a more difficult art than reading, but he promises that his book will allow its readers to create ornate figures "as plaine and easie as are A B C."[48]

It is not impossible that Shakespeare's first teacher was a seamstress, since there are surviving accounts by men of their first tutelage at the hands of women. James Fretwell, born in the late 1590s in Yorkshire, was sent to a female neighbor to learn to read, while Oliver Sansom, a Berkshire yeoman born in 1636, recalls that, "When I was about six years of age, I was put to school to a woman, who finding me not unapt to learn, forwarded me so well that in about four months time, I could read a chapter in the Bible pretty readily."[49] Certainly, in *Othello*, Shakespeare's imagination plays with the idea of a needle-woman whose creative powers can imbue an object with magical properties when his protagonist describes the creative *agon* that generated the handker-chief with the strawberry motif:

> 'Tis true: there's magic in the web of it.
> A sybil that had numbered in the world
> The sun to course two hundred compasses,
> In her prophetic fury sewed the work (3.4.71–4)[50]

From whomever Shakespeare learnt to read, however, he would also have begun to acquire the rudiments not only of the writer's skill but also an introduction to some of those skills required by an actor. The way that reading was taught all the way from the petty school to the grammar school was by reading and reciting aloud and by rote, so that even young children were drilled in their Christ-cross row. Charles Hoole describes the conventional pedagogical method as follows: "The usual way to begin with a child, when he is first brought to Schoole, is to teach him to know his letters in the horn-book, where he is made to run over all the letters in the Alphabet or Christ-cross-row both forwards & backwards, until he can tell any one of them, which is pointed at, and that in the *English* character."[51] Shakespeare makes specific reference to this practice when, in *Love's Labour's Lost*, Moth impudently inquires, "What is a, b, spelt backward with the horn on his head?" and answers his own joke with "Ba! most silly sheep with a horn" (5.1.44–7). The first letters of the hornbook are also the summation of learning with the Bachelor of Arts degree, "BA," and Moth's suggestion is that the graduate has simply reversed himself rather than progressed.

Importantly, young children learnt their letters and syllables without writing any of them down, and indeed, as we have noted, reading was taught quite separately from writing and always preceded it. This may have been in part dictated by the relative expense and scarcity of writing materials. So, for example, the scholar is instructed that if he comes upon a difficult passage in the Psalms, he should "marke it with a pin, or the dint of his nayle" (fingernail).[52] The process of learning to read emphasized memorization and pronunciation. Francis Clement, in *The Petie Schole* (1587), instructs, "Let the childe learne the vowels perfectly without the booke, so that he can readily rehearse them in this manner. The vowels be, a, e, i, o, u, y."[53] These were also, of course, key ingredients of the actor's art. *An English Grammar* (1641), explains:

> Teachers ought to have a speciall care, so to frame and fashion the tender and stammering tongues of children, that they do not with a continuall volubility of the tongue, either to hastily utter their speech, as that they never cease untill their breath fail; or contrariwise, at every word make a long pause, foolishly breaking off the tenour of their talk, by belching, laughter, hicket [hiccups], spitting, cough, or such like.[54]

Children must also, this author argued, be prevented from acquiring "those vices, which do seem almost proper to our common people," that is, pronouncing words with a regional accent, with "too full and an undecent sound."[55] Northerners are particularly guilty on this score, but Shakespeare may also have had to overcome a Midlands' accent when he learned to read.[56] The insistence on pronouncing letters aloud undoubtedly gave the process of learning to read a declamatory emphasis. *An Introduction on the Eyght Partes of Speche* (1542), the textbook that was known in early modern England as "Lily's Grammar,"[57] further insisted on the spoken aspects of language; for example, it defined an interjection as "a parte of speche, whiche betokeneth a pasion of the mynde, under an unperfect voyce" that is caused by either mirth, sorrow, or silence.[58]

Beginning readers then moved on from the hornbook to the primer, the A.B.C. book or the "Absey-book," as it is referred to in *King John* (1.1.196).[59] The next step was the grammar school, but there was some debate about how to discern when a scholar was ready to progress from the petty school to the next stage of his education. Chapter 42 of Richard Mulcaster's *Positions* (1581) advocated allowing the pupil's development to unfold naturally over time, especially in gauging the optimum moment for transition between petty school and grammar school and grammar school and university: "The incurable infirmities which posting hast[e] worketh in the whole course of studie. How necessarie a thing sufficient time is for a scholer."[60] His defense of measured and unhurried educational development remarkably resembles some of Shakespeare's own language about adolescent development. For Mulcaster, "ripeness is all" (*King Lear*, 5.2.11)[61]:

H[a]stie preasing onward is the greatest enenmie, which any thing can have whose best is to ripe at leasure. For if ripenes be the vertue, before it is greene, after it is rotten: and at the least be cast away, without any more losse, . . . The defect to plucke before ripenes, breedes ill in the partie which tasteth therof . . . I have appointed in my elementarie traine *reading, writing, drawing, singing, playing:* now if either all these be unperfectly gotten, where all be attempted, or some, where some: when the childe is removed to the grammer schoole, what an error is committed? The thinges being not perfect, to serve the consequence, either die quite if they be not sevearly called on: or come forward with paine, where the furtherance is in feare.[62]

While Jaques's "Seven Ages of Man" speech from *As You Like It* offers the paradigm of the full span of life with uninterrupted progress from mewling infancy to feeble old age (2.7.140–67),[63] more often than not Shakespeare presents us with the specter of undeveloped or blighted potential: "That yon green boy shall have no sun to ripe / The bloom that promiseth a mighty fruit" (*King John*, 2.1.472–3). These are poignant and recurrent images. In *Venus and Adonis* (1593), Shakespeare treats the arguments for "ripening" tragicomically when Adonis, whose life will be violently cut short by the end of the poem, argues that he is too young to entertain the aggressive attempts at seduction on the part of the goddess of love: "Who plucks the bud before one leaf put forth?" (*l.* 416); "The mellow plum doth fall, the green sticks fast, / Or being early plucked is sour to taste" (*ll.* 527–8).

Interestingly, too, acting, or "playing," along with drawing and singing, is one of the arts in which Mulcaster believed the student should be trained. Indeed, performance of plays in Latin was a key component of education not only at the grammar school but also at the university. Boys (and boys alone) began grammar school when they were seven. Having already learnt to read and write English, their grammar school career consisted of learning to read, write, and speak Latin, and indeed, the name "grammar school" derives from its fundamental purpose, namely the inculcation of Latin grammar. The records for the grammar school in Stratford do not survive, but as the son of an alderman, Shakespeare would have been entitled to a free place there. He probably remained at the school until he was about fifteen, although he may have left earlier on account of his father's serious financial losses, or what Shakespeare's first biographer, Nicholas Rowe, writing in the eighteenth century, referred to as "narrowness of . . . circumstances."[64] The school he himself attended had been founded in the second half of the fifteenth century in connection with the Guild of the Holy Cross. Although the guild had sub-sequently been proscribed, after the Reformation the school was given a new charter by Edward VI in 1553 under the title, the "King's New School."[65] It was at the grammar school that writing, as opposed to just reading, was specifi-cally taught, and where boys were trained in the arts of Latin composition. Orthography was defined as the art of "writing rightly: by which wee are taught with what letters every word is to be formed."[66] Once the mechanics of literacy had been mastered, skills in reading, rhetoric, and composition were developed at much higher levels.

Grammar school education in Shakespeare's day was truly extraordinary, and far more demanding than even the most rigorous curriculum in our own time. The first part of Lily's *Grammar* was written entirely in Latin and the second in English. The boys essentially memorized the various Latin word endings (declensions) and verb inflections (conjugations). In *The Merry Wives of Windsor*, the Welsh schoolmaster Hugh Evans, possibly – especially given the relative proximity of Stratford to Wales – a parody of one of Shakespeare's own school-masters, drills young William on his Latin and is observed proudly by the boy's mother who is clearly sympathetic to Latin education even though her husband is not: "My husband says my son profits nothing in the world at his book" (4.1.14).[67] The boy not only shares Shakespeare's Christian name but also belongs to the same social stratum. Evans tries to instruct his pupil: "I pray you have your remembrance, child: *accusativo hing, hang, hog*" (4.1.42–3), only to have Mistress Quickly, who is also observing, superimpose her own ideas: "'Hang-hog' is Latin for bacon, I warrant you" (4.1.44). By the time William arrives at "Genitive *horum, harum, horum*" (4.1.55), a horrified Mistress Quickly exclaims, "Vengeance of Ginny's case [vagina]; fie on her! Never name her, child, if she be a whore" (4.1.56–7), and she accuses his master of doing "ill to teach the child such words" (4.1.59).

Although education, and especially education beyond the level of minimal literacy, was directed toward males, England's star pupil was a woman, the queen herself. Her tutor, Roger Ascham, lauded her achievements: "It is your shame, (I speake to you all, you young Gentlemen of England) that one mayd should go beyond you all, in excellencie of learnyng, and knowledge of divers tonges." Elizabeth had achieved fluency and had obtained "perfect readines, in Latin, Italian, French, & Spanish . . . [and] Greek." Not only could she read, understand, and speak these languages, but she could also produce original compositions in them. The phrase that Ascham uses to describe this skill is a telling one, namely that Elizabeth composes "both wittely with head, and faire with hand," and does it so well that, rather like Shakespeare in the realm of dramatic composition, she outmatches the university wits, writing as well "as scarce one or two rare wittes in both the Universities have in many yeares reached unto."[68] As can be discerned from Jonson's jibe at Shakespeare's educational deficiencies in ancient languages, a profound distinction among the literate population was the capacity to read and write in Latin, Greek, and European languages. To be able to read Greek, with its non-Roman alphabet, was a further step towards humanist mastery of language. While Ben Jonson's charge that Shakespeare had "small Latine" may be an exaggeration, there are more grounds for believing that he did indeed possess "lesse Greeke."

While Latin grammar was indeed the key to an early modern grammar school education, boys also read fiction and poetry. Children in the lower forms read Aesop's fables while more advanced scholars read the gamut of classical literature, especially the poetry of Virgil, Horace, and Ovid and the comedies of Plautus and Terence that so profoundly informed Shakespeare's writing. Indeed, the Elizabethan curriculum placed great emphasis on versification. In *Ludus Literarius*, John Brinsley's lists of things an Elizabethan grammar schoolboy should know included *writing poetry* "with delight" and crucially, "without any bodging at all"; he should also be able to quote Ovid, Virgil, and other classical authors.[69] Fluency in pronunciation and reading aloud was also required. At Winchester College, for example, at mealtimes the scholars were required to read the Bible "distinctly and apertly."[70]

We might well wonder how such rigorous training in Latin could have produced Shakespeare as the greatest of *English* writers: "THE writing person," so to speak. Indeed, while the value of Latinity was a cultural given, the dialog about education in Brinsley's book nonetheless reflects what was also probably a genuine concern of the time, namely, "That there is no care had in respect, to traine up schollars so, as they may be able to expresse their minds purely and readily in our owne tongue."[71] Hoole reports the rather different concerns of those who felt that Latin would be unnecessary in the practice of a skilled trade or of husbandry.[72] His own argument was that even a "little smattering" would help in reading English and especially in discerning the puzzling Latinate constructions that those who liked to "slant it in Latin" delighted in.[73] On the one hand, then, humanist education emphasized Latin, but on the other, the Reformation had promoted vernacular religious expression. Thus, in 1545, Henry VIII issued a proclamation in the hopes that "our people and subjects . . . may pray in their vulgar tongue, which is to them best known, that by the means thereof they should be the more provoked to true devotion"[74] As a result, Latin and the culture of the ancient Roman world became available by default as a secular and indeed pagan language and culture now, ostensibly at least, entirely distinct from the Latin of the Mass and from Roman Catholicism. This is important in relation to Shakespeare's career because the theatrical culture of metropolitan London in which it flourished was decidedly secular.

While we have no direct knowledge of how Shakespeare felt about school, certainly his dramatic representations of it are not entirely positive. In *As You Like It*, Jaques describes,

> . . . the whining schoolboy, with his satchel
> And shining morning face, creeping like snail
> Unwillingly to school. (2.7.146–8)

That wonderful image of childhood, the "shining morning face," summons up the idea of a well-scrubbed boy, and the shining face creates a link with the instrument used commonly to tell the time, the sundial. Thus, it is both early in the day and early in the boy's life. The "whining" (no doubt familiar to parents throughout the ages) was perhaps justified in Elizabethan England where, apart from Thursdays and Saturdays, which were half days, the school day ran from six or seven in the morning for twelve hours a day, and where the focus of the curriculum was on Latin. Several extant images of early modern schoolrooms, both in England and the rest of Europe, show the use of the birch, and indeed, one of the foremost features of schools in Shakespeare's day was the exercise of corporal punishment, despite the arguments against it by some of the most notable humanist pedagogues of the day. The 1557 edition of William Lily's *A Short Introduction of Grammar* bears a woodcut on the frontispiece of a child and a devil accompanied by a quotation from Psalm 119: "Whereby shall a Childe clense and amende his waie? / By ruling himselfe, according to thy worde, O Lorde."[75] This is symptomatic of early modern, and especially Protestant, education, premised on the idea of the fallen nature of humankind, of young boys in particular, and as such that children needed the devil beaten out of them.

Elizabeth I's own tutor, Roger Ascham, felt that brutality in the classroom was abhorrent, ineffective, and unnecessary, and wrote *The Scholemaster* (1579) in part as an antidote to it. His text is framed in terms of a dinner conversation at Windsor Castle that took place in 1563 where the latest news was that "diverse Scholers of Eaton, be runne awaie from the Schole, for feare of beating."[76] However, not all children felt terrorized by their masters. Ben Jonson loved and revered his schoolmaster, William Camden, at Westminster School, whom he described as his friend. Robert Willis, born only a year before Shakespeare, attended the grammar school in Gloucester, where his gentle teacher was a graduate of Pembroke Hall in Cambridge and future secretary to Lord Chancellor Ellesmere. His affection for his master, whose lodgings were directly above the school, reached such an intimacy that the two became "bedfellows," "which made me also love my book, love being the most prevalent affection in nature to further our studies and endeavours in any profession."[77] While in our own day the authorities would have no doubt that such a confession meant that the relationship between Willis and his master was inappropriate and sexual, no one in early modern England seemed to put that construction on it. Willis himself went on to an illustrious career as secretary to Lord Brooke, Chancellor of the Exchequer, then to the Earl of Middlesex, Lord High Treasurer of England, and finally to Lord Coventry, Lord Keeper of the Great Seal. Like Shakespeare, Willis never attended the university and so attributed all his successes to his extraordinary schoolmaster: "Though I were no graduate of the University, yet (by Gods blessing) I had so much learning as fitted me for the places whereunto the Lord advanced mee, and (which I thinke to bee very rare) had one that was after a Lord Chancellors Secretary to be Schoolemaster."[78]

That Stratford's grammar school excelled in the education it provided was a tribute to several factors – such as a well remunerated headmaster who received twenty pounds per annum, and to the well-established practice of hiring outstanding teachers in a period of intensified consciousness around education. As Brinsley's book on the grammar school put it, "[we are] born and live in the most glorious light, and knowledge; in which, if the experiments of sundry of the learnedest, & most happily experienced Schoolemasters and others, were gathered into one short sum, all good learning (which is the chiefest glory of a nation) would daily flourish more & more."[79] Bishop Hall's preface to Brinsley's volume worries about how far the Jesuits had monopolized education as a powerful implement of faith. Protestants, it seems, need to close the gap: "The Jesuits have won much of their reputation, and stolen many hearts with their diligence in this kind. How happie shall it be for the Church and us, if we excite our selves at least to imitate this their forwardness? We may out-strip them, if we want not to our selves."[80] These "servants of [the] Antichrist," as

Brinsley terms them, "bend all their wittes . . . onely to the advancement of Babylon."[81] In fact, Shakespeare's grammar school education may also have been influenced by Catholic intellectualism.

In 1564–5 also, a year after Shakespeare was born, Stratford hired for its master of the grammar school John Brownsword, a Latin poet in his own right who had been a student of John Bretchgirdle of the renowned school at Witton, where he had established an ambitious curriculum.[82] The tradition of able masters continued, and Simon Hunt was the master during part of the period throughout which Shakespeare is likely to have been in attendance, c.1571–5. Thomas Jenkins then served from 1575–9 and was succeeded by John Cottom. Although the Queen's injunctions of 1559 decreed "that all teachers of children, shall stir and move them to the love and due reverence of God's true religion, now truly set forth by public authority,"[83] Shakespeare's masters had decidedly Catholic connections: Thomas Jenkins attended St John's College in Oxford, where he was an associate of Edmund Campion, the man regarded at the time as England's most notorious Jesuit. If the identification is correct, John Cottom's younger brother, Thomas, has an even stronger Campion connection – he was the Catholic priest who was executed with Edmund Campion in 1582. However, Shakespeare is unlikely to have been taught by Cottom, though no doubt everyone in Stratford and everyone with ties to the town would have known the fate of his brother as a Catholic martyr alongside Campion. While none of this proves that Shakespeare was trained in Catholicism at the grammar school, it does demonstrate that the ideological ends of Protestant education might have been thwarted there.

What remains most important about Shakespeare's grammar school experience, however, is not religion but that this was where he learned the essentials of his craft as a poet and playwright. Boys read the plays and poems of the ancients and learned how to versify themselves as well as how to declaim and perform: "a readines to speake, a facilitie to write, a true judgement, both of his owne, and other mens doinges, what tonge so ever he doth use."[84] In other words, they learned to read without "bodging" [botching] and to write without "blotting," to translate verse, and to do so with facility and *sprezzatura* rather than labored eloquence. This sense of fluency and effortless grace – *sprezzatura* – was important training for Shakespeare, who rattled out some of the greatest works of English literature with staggering ease and alacrity.

# Notes

1    All references to *Romeo and Juliet* are from Callaghan, ed., *Romeo and Juliet:* *Texts and Contexts* (Boston: Bedford/St. Martin's, 2003).

2  See Callaghan, *Romeo and Juliet*, p. 331.

3  Martin Billingsley, *The Pens Excellencie, or The Secretaries Delighte* (London, 1618) STC / 30625, sig. C3v.

4  William Shakespeare, *King Richard III: The Arden Shakespeare*, ed. James R. Siemon (London: Methuen Drama, 2009).

5  *Ben Jonson*, ed. C.H. Herford, Percy Simpson, and Evelyn Simpson, 11 vols (Oxford: Clarendon Press, 1925–51), Vol. 1, p. 35.

6  Christopher Marlowe, *The Complete Poems and Translations*, ed. Stephen Orgel (New York: Penguin, 2007).

7  David Cressy, *Shakespeare Encyclopedia*, ed. Patricia Parker (Westport, CT: Greenwood Press, forthcoming).

8  William Shakespeare, *Love's Labour's Lost: The Arden Shakespeare*, ed. H.R. Woudhuysen (Walton-on-Thames: Thomas Nelson and Sons, 1998).

9  References to Shakespeare's poems are from William Shakespeare, *Shakespeare's Poems: Venus and Adonis, The Rape of Lucrece and the Shorter Poems*, ed. Katherine Duncan-Jones and H.R. Woudhuysen (London: Arden Shakespeare, 2007).

10  Nigel Wheale, *Writing and Society: Literacy, Print and Politics in Britain 1590–1660* (New York: Routledge, 1999), p. 41.

11  Wyn Ford, "The Problem of Literacy in Early Modern England," *History* 78 (1993): 36.

12  Samuel Schoenbaum, *William Shakespeare: A Compact Documentary Life* (New York: Oxford University Press, 1987), p. 37.

13  Ford, "The Problem of Literacy," p. 31.

14  David Cressy, *Literacy and the Social Order: Reading and Writing in Tudor and Stuart England* (Cambridge: Cambridge University Press, 1980), p. 58. See also Eric Sams, *The Real Shakespeare: Retriev-*

*ing the Early Years 1564–1594* (New Haven: Yale University Press, 1995), p. 5.

15  William Shakespeare, *The Winter's Tale: The Arden Shakespeare*, ed. John Pitcher (London: Arden Shakespeare, 2010).

16  William Shakespeare, *Shakespeare's Sonnets: The Arden Shakespeare*, ed. Katherine Duncan-Jones (London: Methuen Drama, 2010); William Shakespeare, *King Henry VI. Part 2: The Arden Shakespeare*, ed. Ronald Knowles (Walton-on-Thames: Thomas Nelson, 1999).

17  Quoted in Juliet Dusinberre, *Virginia Woolf's Renaissance: Woman Reader or Common Reader* (Iowa City: University of Iowa Press, 1997), p. 11.

18  Sir Philip Sidney, *A Defence of Poetry* in *Miscellaneous Prose of Sir Philip Sidney*, ed. Katherine Duncan-Jones and Jan van Dorsten (Oxford: Clarendon Press, 1973) p. 79.

19  *Ben Jonson*, ed. Herford, Simpson, and Simpson, Vol. 8, pp. 583–4.

20  John Jowett writes of the case for Hand D as Shakespeare's, "Much of the evidence is strong, and some of it is decisive" in *Sir Thomas More: The Arden Shakespeare* (London: Methuen Drama, 2011), p. 439.

21  Samuel Schoenbaum, *Shakespeare's Lives* (New York: Oxford University Press, 1970), pp. 27–8.

22  For an account of partial literacy in the period, see Heidi Brayman Hackel, *Reading Material in Early Modern England: Print, Gender, and Literacy* (Cambridge: Cambridge University Press, 2005), pp. 55–60; and for the scholarly controversy over literacy, see Ford, "The Problem of Literacy," p. 35; Frances E. Dolan, "Reading, Writing, and Other Crimes," in Valerie Traub, M. Lindsay Kaplan, and Dympna Callaghan, eds, *Feminist Readings of Early Modern Culture: Emerging Subjects* (Cambridge: Cambridge University Press, 1996), pp. 142–67; Margaret Spufford, *Small Books and*

*Pleasant Histories: Popular Fiction and Its Readership in Seventeenth Century England* (Cambridge: Cambridge University Press, 1981).

23 Elizabeth Rivlin, "Theatrical Literacy in *The Comedy of Errors* and the *Gesta Grayorum*," *Critical Survey* 14 (2002): 64.

24 Schoenbaum, *Shakespeare's Lives*, p. 28.

25 Katherine Duncan-Jones, *Ungentle Shakespeare: Scenes from His Life* (London: Thomson Learning, 2001), pp. 268–9.

26 Germaine Greer, *Shakespeare's Wife* (New York: HarperCollins, 2007), p. 52.

27 Greer, *Shakespeare's Wife*, p. 52.

28 Greer, *Shakespeare's Wife*, p. 52.

29 Cressy, *Literacy and the Social Order*, p. 128.

30 Kirsi Stjerna, *Women and the Reformation* (Oxford: Wiley-Blackwell, 2009), p. 44.

31 Quoted in Greer, *Shakespeare's Wife*, p. 52.

32 William Kempe, *The Education of Children in Learning* (London, 1588) STC / 14926, sig. F2r.

33 John Brinsley, *Ludus Literarius* (London, 1612) STC / 3768, p. 20.

34 Roger Ascham, *The Scholemaster or Plaine and Perfite Way of Teaching Children, to Vnderstand, Write, and Speake, the Latin Tong* (London, 1570) STC / 832, p. 27.

35 William Lily, *An Introduction of the Eyght Partes of Speche* (London, 1542) STC / 15610.6, verso of title page.

36 Paul L. Hughes and James F. Larkin, eds, *Tudor Royal Proclamations*, 3 vols (New Haven: Yale University Press, 1964) Proclamation 248, 1545, 37 Henry VIII, Vol. 1, pp. 349–50.

37 Henry VIII, "Act for the Advancement of True Religion," in *The Statutes of the Realm*, 11 vols (London: Dawson of Pall Mall, 1963), Vol. 3, p. 896.

38 Hughes and Larkin, Proclamation 216, Vol. 1, p. 317.

39 Brinsley, *Ludus Literarius*, p. 315.

40 See Charles Hoole, *A New Discovery of the old Art of Teaching Schoole* (London, 1661) Wing / H2688, pp. 8–9.

41 See Duncan-Jones, *Ungentle Shakespeare*, p. 150; and Cressy, *Literacy and the Social Order*, p. 39.

42 T.W. Baldwin, *William Shakespeare's Petty School* (Urbana: University of Illinois Press, 1943), p. 137; Richard Savage and Edgar Innes Fripp, eds, *Minutes and Accounts of the Corporation of Stratford-upon-Avon*, 4 vols (London: The Dugdale Society, 1921–9), Vol. 3, p. xi, n.1.

43 Baldwin, *Petty School*, p. 138; Savage and Fripp, Vol. 1, p. 34.

44 Brinsley, *Ludus Literarius*, p. 20.

45 Francis Clement, *The Petie Schole with an English Orthographie* (London, 1587) STC / 5400, p. 4.

46 Clement, *The Petie Schole*, p. 9.

47 John Hart, *A Method or Comfortable Beginning for All Unlearned, Whereby They May Bee Taught to Read English in a Very Short Time* (London, 1570) STC / 12889, Epistle Dedicatory. Quoted in Cressy, *Literacy and the Social Order*, p. 38.

48 John Taylor, *The Needles Excellency* (London, 1631) STC / 237755, sig. A4v. See Dympna Callaghan, "Looking Well to Linens: Women and Cultural Production in *Othello* and Shakespeare's England," in Jean Howard and Scott Shershow, eds, *Marxist Shakespeares* (New York: Routledge, 2000), p. 78.

49 Margaret Spufford, "Women Teaching Reading to Poor Children in the Sixteenth and Seventeenth Centuries," in Mary Hilton, Morag Styles, and Victor Watson, eds, *Opening the Nursery Door: Reading, Writing and Childhood, 1600–1900* (London: Routledge, 1997), pp. 53–4.

50 William Shakespeare, *Othello: The Arden Shakespeare*, ed. E.A.J. Honigmann (Walton-on-Thames: Thomas Nelson & Sons, 1997).

51 Hoole, *A New Discovery*, p. 4.

52 Hoole, *A New Discovery*, p. 22.

53 Clement, *The Petie Schole*, pp. 12–13.

54 R.R., *An English Grammar or, A Plain Exposition of Lilie's Grammar In English, with Easie and Profitable Rules for Parsing and Making Latine* (London, 1641) Wing / L2262, p. 3. This was one of the varying titles of Lily's textbook, updated and revised by "R.R."

55 R.R., *An English Grammar*, p. 3.

56 Lily, *Eyght Partes of Speche*, p. 3.

57 H. S. Bennett, *English Books and Readers 1475 to 1557: Being a Study in the History of the Book Trade from Caxton to the Incorporation of the Stationers' Company*, 3 vols, 2nd edn (Cambridge: Cambridge University Press, 1990) Vol. 1, p. 89.

58 Lily, *Eyght Partes of Speche*, pp. 35–6.

59 William Shakespeare, *King John: The Arden Shakespeare*, ed. E.A.J. Honigmann (London: Methuen and Co., 1954). See Hoole, *A New Discovery*, pp. 4, 20; although published in 1661, Hoole's text was written in 1637, according to Herbert C. Schulz, "The Teaching of Hand-writing in Tudor and Stuart Times," *Huntington Library Quarterly* 6 (1943): 329.

60 Richard Mulcaster, *Positions Wherin Those Primitive Circvmstances Be Examined, Which Are Necessarie For The Training Vp of Children, Either for Skill in their Booke, or Health in their Bodie* (London, 1581) STC / 18253, p. 259.

61 William Shakespeare, *King Lear: The Arden Shakespeare* (Walton-on-Thames: Thomas Nelson and Sons, 1997).

62 Mulcaster, *Positions*, p. 259.

63 William Shakespeare, *As You Like It: The Arden Shakespeare*, ed. Juliet Dusinberre (London: Arden Shakespeare, 2006).

64 Nicholas Rowe, ed., *The Works of Mr William Shakespeare*, 6 vols (London: Printed for Jacob Tonson, 1709), Vol. 1, p. ii.

65 Thomas Spencer Baynes, *Shakespeare Studies and Essay on English Dictionaries*, ed. Lewis Campbell (London: Longmans, Green, and Co., 1894), p. 177.

66 R.R., *An English Grammar*, p. 1.

67 William Shakespeare, *The Merry Wives of Windsor: The Arden Shakespeare*, ed. H.J. Oliver (London: Methuen, 1971).

68 Ascham *The Scholemaster*, p. 21.

69 Brinsley, *Ludus Literarius*, sig A1v.

70 George A. Plimpton, *The Education of Shakespeare: Illustrated from the School-Books in Use in His Time* (London: Oxford University Press, 1933), p.57.

71 Brinsley, *Ludus Literarius*, p. 22.

72 Hoole, *A New Discovery*, p. 23.

73 Hoole, *A New Discovery*, p. 20.

74 Hughes and Larkin, Proclamation 348, 1545, 37, Henry VIII, pp. 349–50.

75 William Lily, *A Short Introduction of Grammar* (Geneva, 1557) STC / 15611.7, frontispiece.

76 Ascham, *The Scholemaster*, sig. B2v.

77 R. Willis, *Mount Tabor. Or Private Exercises of a Penitent Sinner* (London, 1639) STC / 25752, pp. 97–8.

78 Willis, *Mount Tabor*, pp. 98–9.

79 Brinsley, *Ludus Literarius*, p. 3.

80 Hall, Preface to Brinsley, *Ludus Literarius*, §2.

81 Brinsley, Dedicatory Epistle, *Ludus Literarius*, 4v.

82 Schoenbaum, *Compact Documentary*, p. 65.

83 See Schoenbaum, *Compact Documentary*, p. 62.

84 Ascham, *The Scholemaster*, 2v.

# 3

# RELIGION

The insuperable obstacle to be confronted throughout this volume is that Shakespeare is much more significant a figure dead than he was alive. During his lifetime, even after his London career, neither his carefully amassed wealth nor the magnitude of his reputation can begin to compare with the significance posterity would rightly accord him. This situation is naturally exacerbated in the years prior to the beginning of his London theatrical career, when he possessed neither the status nor the wealth that would have placed him in any conspicuous position in the historical record. As a young married man, we know almost nothing about him, what he did, how he felt, how he supported his family, or how he came to settle on a theatrical career. Biographers have scratched their heads over the decade 1582–92, for which no documentary trace of his whereabouts remains. This chapter will show that religion has been the most important element in shaping this decade-long lacuna of evidence in the poet's life at the point where the paper trail peters out in Stratford, diminishing to a few mentions of his name in the legal transactions of his family.

Religion speaks powerfully to what *we do not know* of Shakespeare's life, and Catholicism in particular has been used to speculate about *where* Shakespeare might have been after his marriage. More broadly, religion constitutes one of the most contentious, pervasive, and politically significant aspects of Shakespeare's culture. It is also one of the vital pressure points in the knotty conjunction between art and life that this volume aims to explore. For religion is everywhere in Shakespeare, as pervasive as it was in his culture, and yet, perhaps

*Who Was William Shakespeare?: An Introduction to the Life and Works*, First Edition. Dympna Callaghan.
© 2013 John Wiley & Sons, Ltd. Published 2013 by John Wiley & Sons, Ltd.

because this is art and not life, its presence never announces its partisanship, except perhaps in its depiction of those vocal enemies of the stage, the Puritan factions of radical Protestantism, such as the "precise" Malvolio in *Twelfth Night* and the hypocritical Angelo in *Measure For Measure*.

The paucity of information for the period between Shakespeare's firmly documented residence in Stratford at the time of his marriage and his London career, known as "the lost years," has opened the door for a range of unverifiable hypotheses. The earliest is by the seventeenth-century antiquary, John Aubrey, whose *Brief Lives* reports anecdotal evidence that he was a school teacher: "Though as Benjamin Jonson says of him, that he had but little Latin and less Greek, he understood Latin pretty well: for he had been in his younger years a schoolmaster in the country."[1] Other biographers have suggested that the intimate knowledge of the law that permeates Shakespeare's work indicates that he must have been a law clerk. More recently, E.A.J. Honigmann and others have revived the claim that Shakespeare resided, initially as a tutor, with the Catholic family the Hoghtons at Hoghton Hall in Lancashire, that he there became a member of an acting troupe, and that this sojourn in Lancashire accounts for his whereabouts during the "lost years." The difficulty with this hypothesis is that the historical record does not show that William Shakespeare resided with the Hoghtons. One of Hoghton's servants (though perhaps not a player) named William Shakeshafte clearly did live with them because in his will of 1581, Alexander Hoghton requests that Sir Thomas Hesketh "be friendly unto Fulk Gyollme and William Shakeshafte now dwelling with me and either take them unto his service or else to help them to some good master, as my trust is he will."[2] Since it turns out that there were a great many Shakeshaftes in sixteenth-century Lancashire, we cannot justify the conjecture that Shakespeare was Shakeshafte by another name.[3] While this line of research has not uncovered new evidence about Shakespeare's beliefs, it has succeeded in establishing two very valuable general points in terms of the historical contexts of Shakespeare's life: first, the extent to which theatrical culture was available and accessible in the provinces in the houses of noblemen. Secondly, this work has established the pervasively Catholic religious practice that still persisted in many areas of England after the Reformation.

It is important first to understand what the pan-European phenomenon of the Reformation was all about in order to grasp the ways in which its influence on Shakespeare was inescapable. Corruption in the medieval church, especially in dissolute monastic life and the selling of indulgences (that is, the system of "guaranteeing" a reduced sentence in purgatory before achieving heavenly bliss) had provoked criticism of the church by the likes of the Dutch humanist scholar, Desiderius Erasmus. But eventually dissatisfaction with the Church culminated in Martin Luther's articulation of a fully-fledged alternate theology. The most prominent feature of this reformed Christianity was the proposition that salvation was the result of faith alone, *sola fidei* (rather than being achieved by good works, as Catholics maintained), combined with a new understanding of what exactly occurred when the words *Hoc est corpus meum*, or "This is my body," were uttered by the priest over the communion wafer in the eucharistic ritual. Traditional Catholic theology held that at the very moment of the priest's pronouncement, the bread and wine became the body and blood of Jesus Christ. This was because Catholics understood the ritual of the Mass as a reenactment of Christ's sacrifice on the cross. For them, his body, blood, soul, and divinity were made present by the priest's actions and words according to the doctrine of transubstantiation. For Luther, in contrast, that Christ was made present in ordinary foodstuffs remained a mystery of faith but for him, the words of the priest did not have the power to effect the miraculous transformation: that was "hocus-pocus," (a parody of *hoc est corpus meum*) magic, not religion. He espoused instead the doctrine of consubstantiation, and the analogy he used to explain eucharistic transformation was that of red-hot iron in the fire – the fire was in the iron, but the iron remained. Other Protestant writers went further in refusing such a viscerally material interpretation of a sacramental act. No sixteenth-century English Protestant, however, ever denied that the Eucharist was central to Christian life or argued that Christ was not present in some form in this ritual – it was the *nature* of Christ's presence that was at issue. Over such distinctions, wars were fought and martyrs made. Importantly too, from the perspective of literature and art, these disputes inflamed those Protestants who sought to close the allegedly immoral and ungodly theatres and who condemned all fiction as lies and art as idolatry.

In part because they had been a source of corruption in the medieval church, the veneration of saints, the preservation and veneration of relics, the practice of saying the rosary, and especially, devotion to the Virgin Mary, were also vilified by Protestants as idolatrous practices and popish superstition. As a result, authorities attempted to excise all visual evidence of popery, although with mixed success. In areas where adherence to the old faith remained strong, parishes did their best to keep their church interiors intact, whereas, in areas of zealous Protestantism, even tombs were desecrated. In 1560, a proclamation was issued prohibiting the further destruction of funeral monuments, arguing that these were "only to show a memory to . . . posterity . . . and not to nourish any kind of superstition."[4] Nonetheless, authorities ordered that church interiors be denuded of sacred ornament, forbidding the "decking of churches" as John Jewel called it in a homily of 1563. Statues, paintings, rood lofts, elaborate copes and other vestments, and an array of ritual objects were ordered defaced or destroyed. The degree to which such orders were enforced or ignored depended in large measure on the local bishop and the theological leanings of the churchwardens and local ministers. The wall paintings in Shakespeare's parish were, like so many others, whitewashed over, and the altar was removed from the Guild Chapel. Throughout the land this radical interior renovation created the spare – and not inelegant – aesthetic of plain walls and simple communion tables that have come to be associated with Protestantism.[5]

In English churches, the service of Holy Communion from The Book of Common Prayer replaced the Catholic Mass. Edward VI first instituted The Prayer Book in 1549, and it is, as Lori Anne Ferrell has noted, "what made the Church of England *English*."[6] The Prayer Book served to wean the English people from the Catholic liturgy and became a more defining document of religion in England than even the Bible. There was even a penalty of life imprisonment for clergy who used any other liturgical form. The years of the Catholic Mary Tudor's reign, 1553–8, afforded what can have only been a doctrinally confusing hiatus in the development of English Protestantism. At Holy Trinity Church, the first casualty of the return to Protestantism with the accession of Elizabeth I was the Catholic Roger Dyos, who had a year earlier baptized Joan, Shakespeare's older sister, and was in 1559 removed from office.

In the past several years, critical debate has focused on the question of Shakespeare's own religious identity – Catholic or Protestant? Indeed, the question of religious identity has now overshadowed the old chestnut about the poet's equally unknowable sexual preferences. The problem is that if Shakespeare was indeed a Catholic, or if he cherished a certain sympathy with Rome, he would have been compelled to hide it or face persecution. Even if new evidence were to come to light, the reality is that we can never know what, in his heart of hearts, were Shakespeare's religious sympathies and allegiances.

What we do know is that he was baptized in the Protestant Church of England, as everyone was after the accession of Elizabeth in 1558, that he was married in it and buried in it, as were they. In 1608, Shakespeare found himself once again at the baptismal font when he became the godfather of William Walker, whom he remembered in his will with twenty shillings. Contrary to earlier claims that godfathers had to be sound Anglicans,[7] this may, in fact, simply have meant that they observed the mandatory attendance at the weekly communion service. Further, apocryphal evidence has Shakespeare as godfather to a child of Ben Jonson, and since Jonson, who had converted to Catholicism in prison, was hardly a sound Protestant himself, he was unlikely to have required fervent orthodoxy in the persons he invited to become his children's godparents. It is true that Shakespeare was never indicted for recusancy, that is, the failure to attend the Protestant service on Sunday, but since church attendance was mandatory rather than optional, this can hardly be adduced as evidence of his sincere, heart-felt Protestantism.

From this point of view, the heated debate about Shakespeare's religious identity is somewhat spurious. What is truly significant, indeed momentous, is that a more attentive reading of religion and religious identities in early modern England has shown that Catholicism persisted long after the Reformation in myriad practices, among many people and in manifold structures of thought. The debate has also further emphasized the fact that everyone, Catholic and Protestant, and every shade of religious opinion those designations might conceivably encompass, was compelled simply as an effect of historical circumstance to live cheek by jowl with neighbors, kin, masters, and servants, whose religious views (whether deeply held or superficially observed) were ones to which they might well feel themselves bitterly opposed. Crucially, in respect to Shakespeare's own religious proclivities, while the evidence marshaled on the Catholic side has been unable to establish his sympathies incontrovertibly, the debate has upturned the secure and long-held identity of Shakespeare as the great *Protestant* national poet. Symptomatic of this long-held view is A.L. Rowse's confident pronouncement that "he was an orthodox, conforming member of the Church into which he had been baptised, was brought up and married, in which his children were reared and in whose arms he at length was buried."[8] We may not know decisively if Shakespeare was a Catholic; but crucially, neither do we know that he was a stalwart Protestant.

We know two things for certain about religion in Shakespeare's England. First, everyone without exception had had Catholic grandparents, and second, no one living in early modern England could fail to be defined by the Elizabethan Protestant Church of Shakespeare's time. The queen's subjects were either within its fold or defined by their decision to remain apart from it, like Catholics and sectaries of the overheated Protestant variety. Shakespeare himself had been born too late to experience the volte-face around religious affiliation that took place when Elizabeth's older half-sister, Mary Tudor, had ascended the throne and turned the decidedly Protestant realm of their half-brother, Edward VI, into a place where Protestantism, instead of Catholicism, was now a heresy and those unfortunate to be punished for it were burned at the stake. What exactly was signified by the troubled transformation of England from a completely Catholic country at the beginning of Henry VIII's reign to the decidedly Protestant regime of Elizabeth and her successor, James I, is still a matter of heated scholarly debate. Henry was not, by personal inclination, at least, a Protestant. In fact, he received the title "Defender of the Faith" from Pope Leo X in 1521 for his defense of the church against Luther's ninety-five theses nailed to the door of the parish church in the German town of Wittenberg on October 31, 1517. It was famously a private sexual matter and, debatably, a matter of conscience that led Henry to initiate this great religious transformation when he consistently failed to gain papal approval for the annulment of his twenty-year marriage to Catherine of Aragon, widow of his older brother and mother of his own eldest daughter Mary. His personal desire was to marry Anne Boleyn, future mother of Elizabeth I, and he professed belief that his marriage to Catherine was contrary to scripture as evidenced by the union's failure to produce male heirs to secure the dynasty. Thus, this cataclysmic rupture in English society was instigated, at least initially, somewhat inadvertently. However, once unleashed from Rome, Henry discovered further, specifically financial, incentives to pursue autonomy. Prior to the Henrician Reformation monasteries and convents had been key institutions of medieval England, and Henry's dissolution of them had a huge economic impact as well as a specifically religious one on their local environments. Henry was essentially swept along with the tide of religious reform that had taken Europe by storm since Martin Luther made his new theology public, and, in the end, fiscal rather than theological reasons made him disinclined to extricate himself from it.

Shakespeare writes in the *Sonnets* of "art made tongue-tied by authority" (Sonnet 66.9)[9]. Sensitive matters of religion – among many other topics that might have the whiff of sedition about them, as we shall see in Chapter 5 – were unlikely to get past the authorities who licensed printed works (the Stationers' Register) and public performances (the Master of the Revels). Catholicism was officially proscribed, while Protestantism itself contained many and mottled shades of religious difference at the end of the sixteenth century. For all that, the Thirty-Nine Articles of the Church of England (1563) constituted the required rather than voluntary codification of religion in this era. Recusants (people who did not attend church) were subject to fines, set at twenty pounds a month in the anti-Catholic legislation of 1585, and should they be found to be still practicing Catholicism, they would potentially be subject to drastic further punishment. Those who could not pay had all their goods and a third of their land confiscated. For those in possession of little in the way of property, this spelled utter devastation. John Whitgift, bishop of Shakespeare's diocese of Worcester since 1577, conveyed the list of names of those who were "noted to bee greate myslikers of the religion now professed and do absent themselves from the churche."[10] Shakespeare's father was on the list: his recorded failure to attend the mandatory Protestant service after the Privy Council had sent commissioners to flush out recusants, priests, and suspected Catholic sympathizers still survives. Given the potential outcome of such investigations, the effect on those who remained Catholic was undoubtedly chilling. The Privy Council's purge on residual papistry was in response to the arrival in England in 1580 of a mission by members of the Society of Jesus, founded by the Spaniard Ignatius Loyola, and recognized by the pope in 1540, to bring England back to what they regarded as the one true faith. It is the second report of the Commission that names John Shakespeare as a recusant, although his first citation before the Queen's Bench in Westminster was in 1580, when he was fined twenty pounds for non-appearance there. This first charge may have been for a lapse in religious conformity because when he is explicitly named as a recusant in the 1591 list, his name appears as one "heretofore presented," in other words, a repeat offender. Thus, it is in the course of a sporadic purge that John Shakespeare's name appears for posterity. However, the record states that he did not attend church "for fear of process for debtte." There is no reason to question this evidence, and despite the fact that the law forbade arrests taking place in a church, John Shakespeare would have been vulnerable on his way to and from services.

Although the play is set in Catholic Italy and the service with which she is faced is that of marriage, when in *Romeo and Juliet* the irate Capulet threatens to have his daughter dragged to church "on a hurdle" (3.5.155) if she refuses to marry Paris, Shakespeare summons up both the idea that going to church can be brutally compelled as well as the spectacle of those Catholics who were dragged through the streets to ignominious execution. However, for Protestants in the audience, it may have summoned up the specter of their coreligionists executed in both Henry VIII's and Mary's reigns, especially since Juliet is to be dragged to St Peter's church, the name of which had indelible associations with the first pope. These deaths were vividly imaged in the woodcuts of one of the most popular books in early modern England, John Foxe's *Acts and Monuments*, popularly known as the *Book of Martyrs* (1563), a volume that was chained, along with the Bible, in every parish church in the land.

In Elizabeth's reign, although the persecution of Catholics was neither always consistent nor effective, it remained nonetheless a terror to those who still heard the now proscribed Mass. Search for suspected Catholics might be instigated directly by the Privy Council, by the House of Commons, by an official commission, or by the notoriously sadistic torturer and rabid Protestant, Richard Topcliffe. The queen, who although "not liking to make windows into men's hearts," as Sir Francis Bacon put it,[11] did require uniformity of religion, and was fully apprised of Topcliffe's activities, and indeed, actively encouraged them. During one royal progress, she made a point of informing him of "sundry lewde Popishe beasts" in Buxton who required his attentions.[12] The Jesuit poet Robert Southwell fell into his hands in 1592, by which time and Topcliffe's reputation as "the cruellest tyrant of all England"[13] had raised questions about the legality of his interrogation methods. While torture had long served as a government instrument, its use escalated sharply toward the end of the century. However, although Topcliffe benefitted throughout his career from the support of the queen, he was briefly imprisoned in the Marshalsea in 1595 for maligning members of the Privy Council who now sought to rein him in. He wrote to Elizabeth, "By this disgrace . . . the freshe deade bones of Father Southwell at Tyburne and Father Wallpoole at Yorke, executed bothe since Shrovetyde, will dance for joye."[14]

To harbor or "receive" a Jesuit or a seminary priest, that is, to hide one or to allow him to say Mass in your home or even to be found in his company, was a felony, thus rendering the practice of Catholicism a serious crime. Usually trained and ordained at one of the English Catholic colleges in Europe, Douai or Rheims, or at the English College in Rome, these priests were the very well-educated emissaries of the pope in England, and the state feared their success in the reconversion of the English populace. Of all the Catholic martyrs of this era, Edmund Campion, who was executed in 1581, was probably the most famous. In the 1586 edition of *Holinshed's Chronicles* (those texts which provide sources for Shakespeare's history plays as well as *Macbeth* and *King Lear*), his former student, Richard Stanihurst, extolled Campion as "so rare a clerk, so upright in conscience, so deep in judgment, so ripe in eloquence."[15] Even at the scaffold, Campion protested his allegiance to the queen. However, Pius V's papal bull of 1570 pronouncing Elizabeth's excommunication had made the lives of English Catholics much harder, essentially making it impossible to profess loyalty to the queen if they maintained an allegiance to Rome. Indeed, it is important to understand that Elizabeth's excommunication essentially absolved subjects from political loyalty and could thus be used as a pretext for assassination, a very serious matter in a country where Protestantization was proceeding slowly. Allegiance to the pope was not, however, necessarily a benign matter of personal religious commitment, but was indeed sometimes actively seditious. While Campion may personally have posed no threat to the queen's life, the same could not be said for his fellow missionary, Robert Parsons, who was deeply implicated in a plot to kill her. Catholic pressure to depose Elizabeth was unremitting, and in the face of it, her words to Topcliffe about "Popishe beasts" may appear as an expression of well-founded fear. In 1569, for instance, the rebellion of the northern earls received papal backing and sought to reinstate Catholicism. Again, in 1586, the Babington Plot was an attempt to put Elizabeth's Catholic cousin, Mary Queen of Scots, on the throne in her place. In James I's reign, too, the Gunpowder Plot of 1605 (to which Shakespeare refers in both *King Lear* and *Macbeth*) was a foiled attempt to blow up the Houses of Parliament while the king was there. Guy Fawkes was discovered with the explosives in the cellars at Westminster. His co-conspirators were in Shakespeare's native Warwickshire, one of the counties of the English Midlands, an area to which all were connected, close by to Coombe

Abbey, near Coventry, from where they planned to seize James's daughter, the young Princess Elizabeth.

How does such political unrest and doctrinal turbulence intersect with the specifics of Shakespeare's biography? Most importantly, the systems of surveillance, interrogation, and persecution that were in place to root out Catholicism were also applied to other forms of perceived sedition, especially those that took writers as their target. This cultural climate, then, is the context for all of Shakespeare's work. He clearly knew how easy it would be to fall afoul of the implicit restrictions on creative expression. Further, the limitations imposed blurred the boundary between specifically religious issues and other ideas and topics authorities might find objectionable. Topcliffe, a man who clearly relished his work, was the instigator of one of the most famous cases of early modern censorship, namely the suppression of a no longer extant play by Ben Jonson and Thomas Nashe called *The Isle of Dogs* (1597). The playwrights were imprisoned in the Fleet, and Topcliffe interrogated Jonson and two actors. Ben Jonson's fate in the hands of Topcliffe was especially parlous since he had converted to Catholicism (probably at the instigation of another detainee, the Jesuit Thomas Wright in 1598) while in prison for the slaying of a fellow actor, Gabriel Spencer. Jonson and his wife, Anne, were charged repeatedly with recusancy in 1606. In addition, Jonson was accused of "seducing of youth . . . to the popishe religion."[16] However, he rejoined the fold of the Church of England after the assassination by a Catholic, François Ravaillac, of King Henry IV of France in May 1610 when James I, anxious for his own safety from Catholic radicals, compelled a stronger oath of allegiance.

Catholic connections were to be found everywhere in the literary world. Jonson's friend and apostate John Donne was born into a Catholic family tied to the Catholic statesman and martyr, Sir Thomas More. Donne's brother, Henry, was discovered in the company of a Catholic priest, William Harrington. Harrington was hanged, drawn, and quartered, a fate that Henry escaped only by dying in prison. Donne, whose secular career had been blighted by an imprudent marriage, went on to occupy one of the most prominent clerical positions in Protestant England as Dean of St Paul's Cathedral. Although a convert to the English Church, Donne remained supremely conscious of the fate that might befall Catholics. In *Pseudo-Martyr* (1610), he wrote, "As I am a Christian, I have been ever kept awake in a meditation of Martyrdom, by being derived from such a stock and race." In the face of such fears and indeed, in face of state coercion, how freely Protestants in early modern England embraced the beliefs dictated to them by their government must remain open to question.

Perhaps unsurprisingly in the midst of such internecine struggle, a certain skepticism arose about Christianity altogether. The Scottish poet William

Drummond, who recorded his conversations with Ben Jonson, observed disapprovingly in 1619 that Jonson had proclaimed that he was "for any religion as being versed in both."[17] But there were those who denied adherence to religion of any stripe, a position that had been made available by the humanist rediscovery of the texts of the ancient world of Greece and Rome. In its way, the study of these pagan cultures was every bit as disruptive to early modern systems of belief as the Protestant Reformation. As the result, especially of an exposure to the Roman world and its pagan deities, there arose a kind of Latinate secularism. Disengaged as it was in Elizabethan England from "popish Latin," the language of the Church of Rome, and especially of the theologically discredited sacrifice of the Mass, Latin was now more firmly situated in a definitively secular sphere. Thus, the relative autonomy of classical humanism from religion created a space not just for religious skepticism through its alternative culture of what were regarded as morally suspect deities, but also for the potential disavowal of Christianity. Christopher Marlowe, Shakespeare's greatest rival in his early career, was accused of atheism and blasphemy and eventually met his death under dubious circumstances when he was murdered aged only twenty-nine, ostensibly over the bill, the "reckoning," at an establishment in Deptford whose proprietor was a woman named Eleanor Bull. Indeed, his plays, especially *Doctor Faustus*, whose eponymous hero strikes a deal with the devil, as well as his translation of the Roman poet Ovid's elegy on the death of Tibullus, with its admission of "secret thoughts" denying the existence of God (*Elegies* 3.8.35–6), lend some weight to these suspicions. Marlowe was alleged to have said that religion was only invented to ensure docile subjection to those in power, to "keep men in awe." He was also reported to have said that Moses was a juggler and Christ a bastard who had a sodomitical relationship with St John the Evangelist.[18]

While no such controversy attaches itself to Shakespeare, what he has most crucially in common with Marlowe is his love of Ovid. Shakespeare refers to Ovid more often than to any other author. All grammar school boys had some experience of this pagan and profane Ovidian world, though rarely would they have had Marlowe's capacity to enter into it as fully as his extraordinary facility in Latin allowed. Contemporaries were immensely conscious of the fundamentally religious and doctrinal problem presented by classical literature, and there were attempts to ban its teaching throughout the period.[19] Even those who embraced non-Ovidian, classical paganism were extremely cautious about doing so. Clergyman Stephen Batman's 1577 book *The Golden Booke of the Leaden Goddes. Wherein is Described the Vayne Imaginations of Heathe[n] Pagans, and Counterfaict Christians* is a case in point.[20] For Batman, "counterfeit Christians" were those who, like Shakespeare and most of his literary contemporaries, were indebted to the stories of the Greek and Roman world, and who, in

Batman's view, conformed outwardly to Christianity but were in fact idolaters invested in the veneration and manufacture of profane images in poetry and plays. Shakespeare's glorious and immensely popular narrative poem, the epyllion *Venus and Adonis* (1593), which entirely eschews Christian sexual morality, falls decisively into this category, with its depiction of the amorous pursuit of a reluctant paramour by the goddess of love. Such were the "erroneous trumperies" with which, Batman maintained, "Antiquitie hath bene nozzled" [bamboozled].[21] Indeed, Batman dedicated books to Henry Carey, first Baron Hunsdon, who became Lord Chamberlain in 1585 and was the patron of Shakespeare's acting company, the Chamberlain's Men. He is likely to have been Hunsdon's chaplain because Shakespeare's patron also owned the Paris Garden, close to Newington Rectory, where Batman served as minister from 1570–84. In a culture riven by this very contradiction, it seems to escape Batman that he is promulgating the pagan culture he so vigorously condemns. Caught in the cultural crosshairs Batman nonetheless urged readers "not to disregard the spiritual value of 'papisticall' texts, whose contents he tried to accommodate to his beliefs . . ."[22] The religious unity that was in medieval England the incontrovertible horizon of society and culture was now subject to "chopping and changing" that "produced a level of de facto religious pluralism unprecedented in English history."[23] It is important to remember, however, as we have seen, that religious heterogeneity far beyond the confines of Christianity had become available with the advent of humanism. This is especially significant because the Renaissance was founded as much on a return to Rome (in the cultural sense) as the Reformation was founded on a departure from it (in the religious sense). Shakespeare's Roman plays offer testimony to the popular interest in the political struggles of the most powerful civilization the world had known, albeit one which was only belatedly (with the conversion of the Emperor Constantine) – as early moderns put it – penetrated by the light of the gospels. Shakespeare also reminded his audience in *King Lear*, set in ancient Britain, that their ancestors, too, were pagans, and not even pagans of the culturally sophisticated classical kind.

One important distinction, however, between Christianity of all stripes and classical paganism, was that the former was available as a religious rite and practice, and paganism was not – it was, rather, a conceptual horizon that permitted a view beyond the limits of orthodoxy. One might go to the Anglican church with impunity, or to hear Mass, albeit fearing discovery, but one could not participate in rites at the temple of Isis or of Venus – at least not literally. However, the new awareness of "paganism" also intensified consciousness of another, still very much extant, "heathen," "infidel" religion, namely that of Islam, which was the religion of the Ottoman Empire. However, Islam was not thought to be any worse than Catholicism. In *Othello*, Shakespeare takes as his protagonist a converted African Muslim to lead the fight of Christian Venice against the Turks, and throughout his plays he demonstrates his interest in racial and religious "others."

The form of religious alterity most available in Shakespeare's England was that of the Jews, whose Old Testament practices offered a culturally legitimate window on cultural difference. Although Judaism was a recognized antecedent to Christianity, substantial communities of Jews in York, London, and other cities, had been viciously persecuted in England during the Middle Ages, and Jews had been expelled altogether in 1290. Although not officially readmitted until the mid-seventeenth century, Jews were to be found in England, and Judaism itself had taken on a new importance. Among the reasons for this development was the momentous advent of the vernacular Bible (people could now read about the ancient civilization of the Jews in English), references to which saturate Shakespeare's work. Shakespeare's most prominent debts are to the Geneva Bible of 1560 and the Bishops' Bible of 1568. The King James Bible, which achieved status as the authorized version of the scriptures, was published in 1611 after years of immense scholarly labor by a team of translators. With translation (from Latin, Greek, Aramaic, and Hebrew) came new attention to the language of the Hebrew bible, and this, together with the Protestant emphasis on the belief that the conversion of the Jews was a vital element in Christian eschatology, led to a new cultural interest in the first "Chosen People" as precursors to English Protestants. The latter were now believed to be God's chosen race to turn the world from the perceived evils of papistry. Once again, Henry VIII had ignited the focus on Judaism (both philo-semitic and anti-semitic) by bringing Hebrew scholars to England to help provide scriptural authority for his case that his first marriage to Catherine of Aragon was null and void because she was the widow of his older brother, Arthur. Indeed, a renewed interest in Jews and Judaism no doubt informed Shakespeare's decision to write *The Merchant of Venice*.

What are we to make, then, of this complex religious context? Catholic invocations, "Jesu Maria" and the like, pepper Shakespeare's plays, but they also still imbued the language he heard spoken every day. In the play he wrote with John Fletcher (*Henry VIII*), however, the Reformation is the most conspicuous omission, and indeed it includes no representation of religious schism, which the topic would seem to require. Instead, the play is most famous for the fact that during its performance at the Globe, a canon was discharged, setting the thatch on fire, which razed the theatre to the ground.

In relation to Shakespeare's own family, the context of Catholic persecution that constitutes a vital document in the paper trail leads only to Shakespeare's father, although whether this constitutes evidence of his Catholicism remains moot. It could be that John Shakespeare was caught up in the Earl of Leicester's attempted persecution of the Catholic Ardens, which led to his withdrawal from civic government and even from the life of his parish.[24] In 1757, in the course of the re-roofing of a house belonging to a descendent of Shakespeare's sister in Stratford, a document was discovered (though it is now lost again) which it was claimed was "John Shakespeare's Spiritual Testament." The document was based on a form established during a period of plague by the Italian Cardinal Carlo Borromeo, Archbishop of Milan. Until recently, critics believed the document to have been brought into England by Edmund Campion and Robert Parsons. However, careful detective work by Robert Bearman has demonstrated conclusively that this is not possible. Bearman further claims that it was an eighteenth-century forgery.[25]

More compelling evidence in relation to matters religious is John Speed's attack on Shakespeare during his lifetime, linking him with the Jesuit priest Robert Parsons: "This Papist and his Poet, of like conscience for lies, the one ever faining, the other ever falsifying the truth."[26] Speed's grievance with Shakespeare centers around his objection to Shakespeare's portrayal of Sir John Oldcastle, in life a Puritan and therefore close to Speed's heart, but transformed by the playwright into the laughable fat man of *1 Henry IV*. This is an interesting accusation, to say the least, and that a contemporary wrote it carries some weight. On the other hand, "papist" is by definition decidedly pejorative, and because it represents everything that Speed loathes, detests, and reviles, it is also the worst thing he can call anyone.

Further evidence for Shakespeare's Catholicism has been adduced from an assertion of the alcoholic chaplain Richard Davies,[27] of Corpus Christi College in Oxford, who, in his notes on Shakespeare made half a century after the poet's death, writes, "He dyed a Papist." Whether he did or not is anyone's guess.

## Notes

1 Samuel Schoenbaum, *William Shakespeare: A Compact Documentary Life* (New York: Oxford University Press, 1987), p. 110; John Aubrey, *Brief Lives, Chiefly of Contemporaries, Set Down by John Aubrey, Between the Years 1669 and 1696*, ed. A. Clark, 2 vols (1898).

2 E.A.J. Honigmann, *Shakespeare: The Lost Years* (Manchester: Manchester University Press, 1998, 1st edn 1985), p. 3.

3 Robert Bearman, "'Was William Shakespeare William Shakeshafte?' Revisited," *Shakespeare Quarterly* 53 (2002): 83–94. "The preponderance of Shakeshafte families in the Preston area thus coincides neatly with the epicenter of the Hoghton family's sphere of influence, and, had the Shakeshafte of Hoghton's will been christened Thomas, it is difficult to imagine anyone disagreeing with the proposition that he must have been a local man,

drawn into the Hoghton household in a perfectly natural way" (p. 89).

4 Quoted in Dympna Callaghan, ed., *Romeo and Juliet: Texts and Contexts* (Boston: Bedford/St. Martin's, 2003), p. 437. All references to *Romeo and Juliet* are taken from this edition.

5 Russell Fraser, *Young Shakespeare* (New York: Columbia University Press, 1988), 48.

6 Lori-Anne Ferrell, *The Bible and the People* (New Haven: Yale University Press, 2008), p. 79.

7 T.W. Baldwin, *William Shakespeare's Petty School* (Urbana: University of Illinois Press, 1943).

8 A.L. Rowse, *William Shakespeare: A Biography* (London: Macmillan, 1963), p. 43.

9 William Shakespeare, *Shakespeare's Sonnets: The Arden Shakespeare*, ed. Katherine Duncan-Jones (London: Methuen Drama, 2010).

10 Peter Alexander, *Shakespeare's Life and Art* (New York: New York University Press, 1939), p. 21.

11 James Spedding, *The Letters and Life of Francis Bacon* (London, 1872), Vol. 1, p. 98.

12 Charles Nicholls, *The Lodger Shakespeare: His Life on Silver Street* (New York: Penguin, 2007), p. 217; William Richardson, "Topcliffe, Richard (1531–1604)," *ODNB*.

13 Richardson, "Topcliffe."

14 British Library, Harleian MS 9889.

15 Michael A.R. Graves, "Campion, Edmund [St Edmund Campion] (1540–1581)," *ODNB*.

16 *Ben Jonson*, ed. C.H. Herford, Percy Simpson, and Evelyn Simpson, 11 vols (Oxford: Clarendon Press, 1925–51), Vol. 1, p. 138.

17 *Ben Jonson*, ed. Herford, Simpson, and Simpson, Vol. 1, p. 690; Ian Donaldson, "Jonson, Benjamin (1572–1637)," *ODNB*.

18 Park Honan, *Shakespeare: A Life* (New York: Oxford University Press, 1999), p. 124; David Riggs, *The World of Christopher Marlowe* (New York: Henry Holt, 2004), p. 328.

19 See Dympna Callaghan, "The Book of Changes in a Time of Change: Ovid's *Metamorphoses* in Post-Reformation England and *Venus and Adonis*," in Richard Dutton and Jean Howard, eds, *A Companion to Shakespeare's Works: Vol. IV: The Poems, Problem Comedies and Late Plays* (Malden, MA: Blackwell, 2003), pp. 27–45; Dympna Callaghan, "Comedy and Epyllion in Post-Reformation England," *Shakespeare Survey: Shakespeare and Comedy* 56 (2003): 27–38.

20 Stephen Batman, *The Golden Booke of the Leaden Goddes. Wherein is Described the Vayne Imaginations of Heathe[n] Pagans, and Counterfaict Christians* (London, 1577) STC / 1583.

21 Batman, *The Golden Booke*, Dedicatory Epistle 3v.

22 Wallace T. MacCaffrey, "Henry, First Baron Hunsdon (1526–1596)," *ODNB*.

23 Peter Lake, "Religious Identities in Shakespeare's England," in David Scott Kastan, eds, *A Companion to Shakespeare* (Malden, MA: Blackwell, 1999), pp. 57–8.

24 Peter Thompson, *Shakespeare's Professional Career* (Cambridge: Cambridge University Press, 1994, 1st edn 1992), p. 13.

25 Robert Bearman, "John Shakespeare's 'Spiritual Testament': A Reappraisal," *Shakespeare Survey*, 56 (2003): 184–202, with specific reference to p. 190.

26 John Munro, ed., *The Shakespeare Allusion Book*, 2 vols (London, 1909), Vol.1, p. 224. See also Richard Wilson, *Secret Shakespeare Studies in Theatre, Religion and Resistance* (Manchester, 2004), p. 12.

27 See Schoenbaum, *Compact Documentary*, p. 98.

# 4

# STATUS

Prior to Shakespeare, the individual who had achieved most prominence in Stratford-Upon-Avon was Hugh Clopton (c.1440–96). Though not aristocratic, his family had lived the village of Clopton, near Stratford, since the thirteenth century. Hugh made the family name and reputation by his ventures in trade. He was apprenticed to a mercer (a cloth trader) in London when he was fifteen or sixteen years old and eventually became a member of that company, and rose to become Lord Mayor of London. He made his career in the metropolis but maintained his connections with Stratford, building Clopton Bridge and New Place, a "praty howse of brike and tymbar." Clopton features in Shakespeare's biography because in 1597, a year after being granted his coat of arms, Shakespeare bought this "pretty house of brick and timber," and upon his retirement from the theatre, New Place became his home. However, Clopton's further significance is that he represents, even a hundred years before Shakespeare, a pattern of provincial achievement: make good in London and return to enjoy wealth and status in one's native place. Like Shakespeare, Clopton forged his own success in the world, and contrary to critics, who typically refer to Clopton as "Sir Hugh," in fact, he was never knighted. For all that, his will (which records bequests of the enormous sum of almost two thousand pounds, nine properties in Stratford, and two manors elsewhere) attests to his status as "citizen, mercer and alderman."[1] Although he died a bachelor in Stratford, by Shakespeare's time the wealth that Hugh Clopton had dispersed was evident in the fortunes of his wider kin. In 1580, Joyce Clopton, the daughter of his great-nephew, married George Carew (1555–1629), Earl

*Who Was William Shakespeare?: An Introduction to the Life and Works*, First Edition.
Dympna Callaghan.
© 2013 John Wiley & Sons, Ltd. Published 2013 by John Wiley & Sons, Ltd.

of Totnes and Baron Carew of Clopton. This was an exceptional trajectory of wealth and status, but if Shakespeare also aspired to it, he would have been disappointed since none of his descendants survived so long after him, and none ever ascended to the ranks of the nobility.

This chapter will explore the ways in which class hierarchy shaped Shakespeare's career and experience, especially at the point where he sought to climb the social ladder and achieve the status of a gentleman. While the great noble families and even the minor aristocracy were far above most country gentry, the biggest gulf in class status, and the one hardest to traverse, was that fundamental divide between the common, those who were described as being "without name," and the "gentle sort," whose names revealed their established and propertied positions in society.

What follows is an attempt to understand the social order of Shakespeare's world, not from our own received ideas about a class society, but rather by looking in detail at the specific hierarchies encountered by Shakespeare and his fellow Elizabethans. It should be remembered also that while Shakespeare's audience at the Globe was a heterogeneous group ranging from peers to fish-wives, and while his characters range from the indigent to the princely, the characters in whom his plays are most invested, his tragic heroes, and his comic principles are all "persons of quality" because their stories, their joys and mis-adventures, were considered – and not just by Shakespeare – worth the telling.

The ladder of Elizabethan social hierarchy was very long indeed and very hard to climb. Composed of a great many rungs, everyone knew exactly where they – and everyone else – stood on it. However, the static certainties of status as the expression of social function were shaken by the development of trade, the vast expansion of the metropolis of London, and the accretion of those factors that made up the new economic formation described as nascent capital-ism. So, for example, Hugh Clopton's career path, rare though it was in the late medieval era, was a less unusual phenomenon in early modern England. While it would be dangerously inaccurate to exaggerate the degree of social mobility achievable in sixteenth-century England, it was certainly the case that there was far more room for maneuver than hitherto. Both Shakespeares, father and son, then, were part of the transformation of social identities in early modern England. They were part of the social upheaval attendant on that transformation where wealth was generated by what is recognized with hindsight as birth of capitalism, a hitherto unknown form of economic organization.

However, greater social mobility did not mean the absence of social hierarchy. Everyone, except the sovereign, had a master, and the most parlous condition of all was to be "masterless" because it meant falling out of the hier-archy, almost outside society altogether, and thus being unable to secure the basic material necessities for the maintenance of life. The lack of a master gravely imperiled the prospects of survival of vagabonds, beggars, and the similarly impoverished. Those who thrived and who felt assured of being able to maintain their comfortable state, in contrast, might then seek status. The Shakespeares were unquestionably a thriving family in the playwright's early years. Shakespeare's mother, Mary, came from the well-to-do Ardens, and John Shakespeare's speculations in wool seem to have strengthened the family's financial position. His election to alderman and then bailiff, further bolstered his modest wealth with provincial status. While holding office was indeed one path to gentle status for those who were not born to it, the connection between the two was far from automatic or inevitable. The titles of alderman (attained in July 1565) and bailiff (1567) confirmed on Shakespeare's father the right to be addressed as "Master Shakespeare," but they still did not permit him the dignity of gentle status. For that, he would need a coat of arms from the College of Heralds. A coat of arms would confirm, consolidate, and enhance his status in his community.

But what precisely did this status mean? William Harrison explained in his *Description of England* (1577):

> We in England, divide our people commonly into four sorts, as gentlemen, citizens or burgesses, yeomen, and artificers or labourers. Of gentlemen the first and chief (next the king) be the prince, dukes, marquesses, earls, viscounts, and barons; and these are called gentlemen of the greater sort, or (as our common usage of speech is) lords and noblemen: and next unto them be knights, esquires, and, last of all, they that are simply called gentlemen.[2]

At the very bottom of the hierarchy are those who have "neither voice nor authoritie in the common wealthe, but are to be ruled and not to rule." Crucially, the least significant among the gentry are the "bare gentlemen," that is those without further title or entitlements, as Harrison puts it "they that are simply called gentlemen." That first step in climbing the social hierarchy was probably also the most difficult. To those in the higher echelons of the social order, a "bare gentleman" was hardly a mark of distinction. For all that, a vast chasm opened up between the commoner and the bare gentleman. To move from being someone with "neither voice nor authoritie," as William Harrison defined the undistinguished majority, into even this unadorned, "bare" gentry status was nonetheless to traverse the biggest social division in England, one whose significance cannot be overemphasized.

There is in Shakespeare a keen sense of the importance of being a person "of name," which means in this period someone of rank, the implication being that those without name, that fundamental marker of identity, are devoid of social and even human significance. News from the wars at the start of *Much Ado About Nothing*, tells us that the casualties have been light, that "few of any sort" are dead, and "none of name" (1.1.6).[3] Two words here refer to status, "sort" and "name." Contrary to our modern sense, which would be something like, "We have lost none of any kind," "sort," in early modern parlance, means "rank," while "name" refers not just to the nobility, but to the kinds of social distinction associated with the possession of a coat of arms, the visual representation of one's name and the "ocular proof" (*Othello* 3.3.363)[4] of social identity. Those who are "none of name," the overwhelming majority, are the "food for powder" (4.2.65–6),[5] the cannon fodder of *1 Henry IV*. Their lives are expendable and their corpses are literally disposable, "good enough to toss" (4.2.65) into the mass graves that were a standard feature of the early modern battlefield. In *Henry V*, "None else of name"[6] is also used at the end of the Battle of Agincourt when "the number of our English dead" is being accounted, and the king is given a paper detailing the fatalities:

> Edward the Duke of York, the Earl of Suffolk,
> Sir Richard Keighley, Davy Gam Esquire;
> None else of name, and of all other men
> But five-and-twenty. (4.8.104–7)

Unlike the messenger in *Much Ado*, Henry at least sees fit to enumerate the dead among those whose defining characteristic is the lack of "name" and whose losses are negligible, not so much because they are few but because these lives are insignificant from vantage point of the top of the Elizabethan social hierarchy. The death toll is called in order of status because in this period military rank was determined entirely by social standing. Deaths in battle among the nobility were always reported; not so those of common soldiers. Shakespeare places these no-names in stark juxtaposition to those on whom there has been "bestowed much honour" (*Much Ado* 1.1.10). In Shakespeare, this kind of recognition is invariably a mixed thing, as it is in *Macbeth* when becoming Thane of Cawdor sows the seeds of regicide. Similarly, in *Much Ado*, Claudio no sooner receives martial honors than he almost kills his fiancée by making unfounded allegations against her. Again, in *The Rape of Lucrece*, the violation of the noble Roman matron is presented as a direct consequence of "the heraldry in Lucrece's face" (*l.* 64).[7] This is because it inspires in her rapist the ambition to achieve, even by the most violent means, the honors symbolically represented there.

Heraldry, the coat of arms emblazoned on a heraldic shield harks back to a medieval understanding of social status or "degree." The coat of arms was a residue of the feudal class formation that obtained in the Middle Ages when knights went into battle literally bearing arms and carrying shields decorated with their armorial bearings. This world of chivalry no longer existed, even if the class distinctions it had created survived fully intact. The College of Arms was presided over by the Earl Marshal, who at the time of Shakespeare's application was Robert Devereux, second Earl of Essex. The college hierarchy in many ways mimicked the delineations of status, the numerous distinctions among the gentle class it policed and produced. Directly under the Earl Marshal was the Garter King of Arms, then William Dethick, who dealt with Shakespeare's application and oversaw all operations at the college. In addition, there were (and still are) heralds who presided over specific geographical regions, such as Norroy and Clarenceux, a York Herald, a Chester Herald, and a range of other officers, including a class of "Pursuivants" with old French titles worthy of a video game: Portcullis, Rouge Croix, Rouge Dragon, Bluemantle, and Rose Rouge.

So, having attained the highest office in Stratford and having served as a Justice of the Peace, in about 1568 John Shakespeare took the momentous step of making his application to the College of Arms for a coat of arms. If awarded it, John Shakespeare who had made good would become "John Shakespeare, Gent.," and thus would have crossed the Rubicon of social status that divided England cleanly in two with the gentry and nobility on one side and the vast majority, the common people, on the other. Such status was far from abstract. For example, in the event of a tied contest, the candidate who had the most votes from "gentlemen" would be given the election.[8] Arguably less significant were the entitlements to wear silk and the color purple, which were part of the system of "sumptuary laws," an elaborate dress code whereby class status was visible and could be determined at a glance. While such rules were honored as much the breach as in the observance in the capital (especially among affluent theatre-goers who dressed to impress), it remained the case that social distinctions were meant to be kept visible and in plain sight.

John Shakespeare's initial application to the College of Arms clearly made some progress before being abandoned because, during one of the periods of "Heraldic Visitation" (as the tours of inspection during which heralds verified the credentials of applicants were called) he was issued with a "pattern," that is to say a preliminary drawing, of his coat of arms.[9] However, several further stages incurring much more expense would have to be gone through before a grant of arms could be issued. For reasons that are not clear, though probably ones related to impecuniosity, the process of application was suspended. At sometime around 1576 John Shakespeare's fortunes, and thus his family's prospects, went into precipitous decline. He had stopped attending council meetings by that date, and ten years later he was replaced as alderman. By 1591, as we have noted in the previous chapter, he had ceased attending church services "for fear of process," wary of prosecution by his creditors.[10]

It is very likely that his business ventures had failed. This was a period in which all business was a perilous undertaking. Anyone seeking to profit from it, as Shakespeare put it in *The Merchant of Venice*, "must give and hazard all he hath" (2.7.16).[11] This risk was not only the result of natural calamities like plague, dearth, or shipwreck, but also the consequence of vast and unanticipated fluctuations in supply and demand. In addition, at this stage of economic development, transactions were based largely on "trust," which led to byzantine complexity in chains of debt and credit that could imperil the fortunes of a very large number of people.[12]

John Shakespeare's social aspirations languished until his son revived them with a new application in London. Shakespeare applied in his father's name, not only because John Shakespeare was the eldest male of the family but also because, as Samuel Schoenbaum points out, "former bailiffs rated higher than playwrights."[13] For although he could not sign his name, John Shakespeare had held public offices of "dignity and worship"[14] as his son never did, and the career of the father has left a paper trail at all only because of the status he achieved, however precarious that might have been. John Shakespeare thus received the patent in 1596, and Shakespeare himself would simply have inherited it 1601 when his father died. Thus, Shakespeare, though he could never be "a gentleman born," was set to become a second-generation gentleman, though hardly someone with established lineage and inherited honor. Toward the end of his career, in *The Winter's Tale*, Shakespeare makes sport of the newly elevated shepherd who proudly tells his son, the clown, "thy sons and / daughters will be all gentlemen born" (5.2.124–5).[15] Of course, daughters will *not* become gentleman under any circumstances, and even social elevation will not change the irremovable fact of lowly birth.

Shakespeare achieved this grant of arms only four years after he was first recorded as being a playwright in London in 1592. He was a parvenu who had made money and made it fast. Accompanying the heraldic patent was the coat of arms itself. This was a heraldic pun on the Shakespeare name – a golden spear – topped by a silver falcon and bearing the motto, *Non sans droict*, "not without right." That it was written in old French also intimated ancient, Norman lineage. *Non sans droict*, has overtones of the defensive claim of the social aspirant, the nouveau riche.

Not surprisingly, Shakespeare's works demonstrate an intimate familiarity with the tropes of heraldry, the systematic arrangement of devices on a shield – the armorial assignments, escutcheons, and the old French words used to designate colors on a shield: "gules" (red); azure (blue); "sable" (black), and so on. In *Hamlet*, Shakespeare describes Pyrrhus in burning Troy as emblazoning his sable arms with blood:

*With heraldry more dismal, head to foot*
*Now is he total gules, horridly tricked*
*With blood of fathers, mothers, daughters, sons.*
*Baked and impasted with the parching streets, . . . (2.2.394–7)[16]*

"Tricked" was a technical word used to indicate the initial sketch for a coat of arms where the colors are represented by symbols. Status is solidified here, but only as the congealed baked-on blood of enmity.[17] This is a price even higher than any Shakespeare paid for his arms, although we do not know how much it cost him in 1596. Solgadio in Jonson's *Every Man Out of His Humour* pays thirty pounds for his arms, and Katherine Duncan-Jones speculates that Shakespeare may have paid as much as one hundred pounds.[18] Essentially, Shakespeare had purchased his father's honor and his own. Yet, in the world of bribes and kickbacks that regularly lubricated early modern bureaucracies, this was not unusual. Thomas, fourth Duke of Norfolk (1538–72), had tried to regularize the proceedings at the College of Arms in order that pedigrees "bear true evidence" of entitlement, but since in the volatile world of Elizabethan politics, he was executed for treason, his reforms were never realized.[19]

As money rather than lineage began to exert much more of an influence in Shakespeare's world, there emerged profound contradictions and ambiguities about what made someone a gentleman. In *The Merchant of Venice*, Shakespeare puns insistently upon the relation between being "gentle" (virtuous, merciful, and Christian) and being a "gentile," and shows that the relation between mercy and Christian behavior is strained to the breaking point in the mercantile world, where money rather than blood (also, incidentally, two of the play's key themes – Shylock's thirst for Antonio's blood and the fiduciary values that define them both) is the governing value system. Ostensibly, gentle status was a matter of pedigree *conferred* by blood. The College of Arms purported to keep a perpetual record of the genealogies of all families in order to establish and ratify gentle status on these grounds. In order to be eligible for a heraldic award, the applicant had to prove his pedigree – that is, prove that he fulfilled the requirements of the much sought after state of gentility. John Shakespeare based his claim to armigerous status on these grounds (his ancestor had been of service in battle to Henry VII), as well as on his marriage to Mary Arden. Historically, the Ardens were an illustrious and landed Warwickshire family. This justification via pedigree barely disguised the fact that in 1596 Shakespeare's main qualification for gentry status was money.

There were, moreover, increasing numbers of people who had the cash to become gentlemen. That is, they could, as William Harrison put it, bear the "port and charge" of a gentleman, even though they possessed none of the other qualifications. This development did not go uncontested. Sir Thomas Wilson's was but one of many voices raised in objection to such practices.[20] One of the most fundamental notions about status was that the "countenance of a gentleman" required living, as William Harrison noted, "without manual labour."[21] Yet, even this foundational notion that the condition of gentility absolutely proscribed manual labor was now in question.[22] Clearly, John Shakespeare had not abandoned manual labor as a glover in Stratford, either at the time of his first application or at the second. Nor had John Dudley, Elizabeth I's pastry chef, or "sergeant of pastry" as he was known, or the two other royal cooks who were awarded patents for arms along with him. This was a society in which the time-honored distinction between those who labored with their hands and those who did not was fast coming undone. Lawyers, doctors, and a new generation of educated persons whose wealth did not lie in land created even further pressure on already strained social categories that had not been created to accommodate them.

The College of Arms, where Shakespeare made his application, has stood on the same site in London since the reign of Mary Tudor, and it became increasingly important in this period as a vital and active instrument of class formation. The heralds, that is the officers of the College of Arms, were charged with giving official recognition – as if it were a pre-existing state – to those who were in essence *already* gentlemen (primarily because of blood and sometimes because of office), but were simply unrecognized as such. Despite all rhetorical fast-footwork to the contrary, this so-called recognition of gentry status was in reality synonymous with its manufacture.[23] "Recognition" took the form of a grant of arms. The grantee and his heirs, having attained the much sought after armigerous status, would then be permitted to style themselves as gentlemen, thus, "William Shakespeare, gent.," or, as he is styled on the title page of the First Folio, "Mr. William Shakespeare," and to display his crest and coat of arms, his heraldic devices in stained glass, in civic memorials, in embroidery, in portraits, banners, and the like. Wives and daughters would simultaneously become ladies – not, of course, gentlemen, as envisaged by the shepherd in *The Winter's Tale*. The bastard says in *King John* 1.1.184: "Well, now can I make my Joan a lady."[24] Joan was a name synonymous with women of the lower orders, and Shakespeare himself had, as we have seen, two sisters of that name, the first of whom died in infancy. Gentry status augmented wealth and property, and these were the magnetic points of the compass of a person's life in Shakespeare's world.

The Crown sought to keep a check on the number of gentry and to that end periodically sent out officials – heralds and Kings of Arms from the College of Arms – on official visitations to every county in England. What was unusual in Shakespeare's time was the unprecedented number of arms being issued, which led to complaints by contemporaries about the failure of the heralds – including and especially William Dethick who issued Shakespeare's arms – to police the bounds of the fundamental hierarchy, namely that between the common and the gentle, on which social organization depended. Although it was unofficial knowledge, everybody knew that "One of the chief purposes of granting arms was to establish the gentility of persons whose status was doubtful."[25] On their visitations, the heralds sought to "remove false arms and arms devised without authority" and "to take note of descendants."[26] In 1580, William Dawkyns was put in the pillory and had his ears cut off for impersonating a herald and concocting spurious pedigrees.[27] Mutilation did not deter him, however, and in 1597, a warrant for his arrest described him as "a notable dealer in arms and maker of false pedigrees."[28] Dawkyns had forged these for almost a hundred families in Essex, Hertfordshire, and Cambridgeshire.[29] However, in a world where money and status were no longer so closely coincident as they had been in feudal England, pedigrees might be fabricated and honors bought and sold, not only by the likes of Dawkyns, but also by the college itself. In *De Republica Anglorum*, Thomas Smith claimed that gentlemen "be made good cheape in England . . . a King of Heralds shall also give him for money arms newly made and invented, the title whereof shall pretende to have beene found by the said Herald in perusing olde registers, where his auncestors in times past had been recorded to beare the same."[30] The College of Arms needed to make sure that it – and not imposters like Dawkyns – authorized, and thus profited from, the trade.

Conferring gentle status was an immensely lucrative business, and business in the sixteenth century was booming with more grants of arms being awarded than ever before as more people could pay the fees required by the college, augmented, of course, by bribes and sweeteners. The rule, more often violated than observed, was that "persons bearing Arms by descent from the old families should be able to deduce an unbroken Lineage from some ancestor whose claim has been allowed by the Heralds, and recorded in these documents and such only have a right to use them."[31] Both William Dethick (Garter 1586–1606) and Robert Cooke (Clarenceux 1566–93) were accused of taking bribes to grant arms. Furthermore, Cooke's own credentials were said to be highly questionable since, at least according to his enemies, he was the son of a tanner.[32] Cooke was never formally censured, even though Sir William Segar (Dethick's successor) charged that he "confirmed & gave Armes and Creastes without number to base and unworthy persons for his private gaine onely without the knowledge of the Earl Marshall."[33] Accusations flew back and forth, and when Ralph Brooke tricked Sir William Segar into granting the arms of Aragon and Brabant to Gregory Brandon, the hangman of the City of London (whose son Richard is believed to have executed Charles I), King James I was outraged and imprisoned them both.[34] As for Dethick, in 1597 only a year after Shakespeare's grant of arms, he was found by Lord Burghley to have propounded a false pedigree for George Rotheram, entitling him to the arms of Lord Grey of Ruthin.[35] He was accused of even more egregious falsifications such as forging "a most false pedigree" for John Roberts of Cardiff, "which Robert's father was a peddler and bastard."[36] Finally, in 1602, Dethick was dismissed from office, but he simply refused to go and was able to persist in this resolution by virtue of having taken the precaution of copying his own Great Seal patent, which authorized his office, and done it so well that only the color of the wax betrayed the fact that it was not original.[37] Dethick's disgrace was, at any rate, temporary, and was followed by a knighthood the next year. This was James I's expression of gratitude for Dethick's good offices in 1587 when he helped organize the funeral of the king's executed mother, the disgraced Mary Queen of Scots.

What we see here is a hierarchy creaking at every point. Bloodlines were almost impossible to verify, and new forms of social status were beginning to compete with them. The principal purpose and primary duty of the College of Arms was to separate the base and the unworthy from the rest, and since, officially, the duty of heralds was to watch over and preserve the genealogies of families, the heralds were clearly falling down on the job. Yet, the crisis in the College of Arms in large measure simply mirrored the social crisis about status and class that was being generated by new and unprecedented economic and social conditions. This was no longer a world where land was the only source of wealth, and thus new money might easily trump ancient bloodlines, at least in terms of cash value, if not in terms of that ineffable quality, "honor." As Falstaff points out in *Henry V*, honor is an intangible, and, in a society that increasingly valued substantive, material gain, there were numerous points in the social system where the line between the gentleman and commoner had worn very thin indeed.

The heralds fought bitterly among themselves over the rich spoils of their office and about matters of jurisdiction and protocol. Shakespeare's own award of arms was imperiled by internecine dispute when one of the heralds, Ralph Brooke, charged that "mean" [lowly, common] persons had been granted arms. He accused Dethick in particular of professional impropriety and urged that arms inappropriately granted should be revoked. It was not only to Shakespeare's grant that Brooke took exception: he also claimed that a common plasterer had been given arms very similar to the royal coat. Next to a sketch of Shakespeare's arms that had been awarded by Dethick, Garter King of Arms, he wrote with telling derision: "Shakespear ye Player, by Garter." Clearly, a plasterer and a player were regarded as social equivalents. The essence of the problem was outlined by Sir Henry Peacham, in *The Compleat Gentleman* in a chapter rather pretentiously entitled "Of Armorie, or Blazon of Armes, with the Antiquity and Dignitie of Heralds." For Peacham, it was important to "discerne and know an intruding upstart, shot up with the last night's Mush-rome, from an ancient descended and deserving Gentleman."[38] Peacham demands "the redress of this unsufferable abuse." Shakespeare, the "upstart crow," was exactly the sort of parvenu, "shot up with the last night's Mush-rome" that Peacham had in mind. His name appears on Brooke's list of improper awards because he, a mere player, has been granted arms that resemble too closely those of a peer of the realm, Lord Mauley, even though that line had long dwindled into extinction because of the lack of male heirs, and the last Lord Mauley had died in 1415.[39]

Such was the minefield of social distinction that was bartered, negotiated, and muddled through by the College of Arms. Its head, the Earl Marshal, also presided over the High Court of Chivalry, where contested cases were heard. Despite Brooke's objections, Shakespeare's case never reached it, probably because Dethick, head of all the heralds, and beneath only the Earl Marshal's Lieutenant and the Earl Marshal himself, was too far up the chain of command to suffer serious challenge.

Much about the operations of the College of Arms can be gleaned from William Dethick, the key official in Shakespeare's case. Dethick's own genealogy rested more on a deftly wrought fiction than on heredity and blood. His grand-father was a German immigrant, and his father had risen to prominence in the College of Arms by claiming descent from the noble family of the same name in Derbyshire. Dethick married Thomasine Young, the daughter of a London fishmonger. He was also in gross violation of the idea that gentle status implied a set of virtuous behaviors, or as Shakespeare satirically puts it in relation to the newly elevated country clowns in *The Winter's Tale*: "We must be gentle now we are gentlemen" (5.2.149–50). Notoriously violent, Dethick had attacked the wife of a fellow herald as well as a priest and his own father. This first assault was so vicious that he was branded with a hot iron by way of pun-ishment. Branding offered a permanent visual representation of misfeasance, just as much as arms were the visual and emblematic representation of honor. When approached by Dethick during his failed coup in 1601, the chivalric Earl of Essex, who was none other than the Earl Marshal of the College of Arms, is reported to have rebuffed him thus: "I see no herald here but that branded fellow, whom I took not for a herald."[40]

The fracas over Shakespeare's own grant of arms may be reflected in the *Sonnets* in his own meditations on branding: "Thence comes it that my name receives a brand" (Sonnet 111.5).[41] That it is his name that is mutilated and not his person is because the poet contemplates here not the branding with a hot iron but rather, the heraldic version of the felon's brand. This consisted of a black strike or bar through the coat of arms that denoted an illegitimate scion of an armigerous family. "Thence comes it that my name receives a brand" essentially means he must suffer the most egregious calumny As Shakespeare knew from his representations of Don John the bastard in *Much Ado*, Edmund in *King Lear*, and the bastard in *King John*, illegitimacy was a profound social stigma that was not erased by the mere fact of biological descent from a noble family. When Shakespeare's nephew, his brother Edmund's illegitimate son, was buried in St Saviour's churchyard, he was recorded in the parish register as "base born." "Base" was not only "out of wedlock," it was also the opposite of "gentle." Thus "the bastard shame" the poet suffers from in the *Sonnets* is a slur on the poet's reputation of the most serious kind.

Indeed, in Elizabethan and Jacobean England, if you were a gentleman the brand of a felon might be less of a social obstacle than the loss of name and reputation. Shakespeare's illustrious contemporary Ben Jonson was branded on the thumb when he was convicted of murdering fellow actor Gabriel Spencer. Jonson escaped hanging because he was able to recite the "neck verse," the fifty-first psalm and thus claim "benefit of clergy." This misadventure had no discernible impact whatsoever upon his literary career. Jonson had a Scottish coat of arms from his biological father. If that was not enough, his honorary MA from Oxford – (like Shakespeare, he never attended university) also met another of the qualifications for gentle status, which Shakespeare also lacked. Born with this kind of privilege Jonson had no need to seek it at the College of Arms. In fact, in *Every Man Out of His Humor*, performed in 1599, he made sport of Shakespeare's social aspirations in the figure of a rustic simpleton, Sogliardo, who has sold land to buy fancy clothes and a coat of arms. More-over, Sogliardo's motto, "Not without mustard," is clearly a satire on Shake-speare's own, "*Non sans droict*," not without right. Mustard, that vivid yellow relish for ordinary fare or "common victual," is heraldic gold to a commoner. Indeed, one of the key distinctions between persons in early modern England is what they ate, and crucially, what they could afford to eat. William Harrison describes "the hard and pinching diet"[42] which consisted of bread, cheese, small beer, and garden greens, and the scarcity of food for a substantial propor-tion of the population. For Jonson, mustard is a more appropriate garnish for a player's reputation than armorial gilding. In *Poetaster*, Jonson sneers at common players who, despite the law which classified them as indigents, none-theless aspire to heraldic distinctions: "They forget they are i'th statue, the rascals, they are blazoned there, there they are tricked [sketched], they and their pedigrees: they need no other heralds, iwis."[43]

Yet Jonson also provides some sense of the complexities of status in early modern England because, while he was a gentleman born, if also a branded one, he was also for most of his career as a playwright and poet and a dues-paying member of his stepfather's livery company, the Bricklayers. Further, all of the London companies, through which manufacture and trade in the city were organized, also had coats of arms, and these, like family arms, were granted by the self-same College of Arms that awarded Shakespeare his much sought after pedigree. Perhaps because of the art and design aspects of their occupations, many officers of the college were themselves members of the Painters and Stainers' Company. Thus, the line between gentry and trade was far less clear than is usually imagined. Increasingly, too, there are claims in the period for the dignity of honest labor that are expressed in terms of gentility. In *Eastward Ho!* "honest pains" are seen to be the source of true honor:

> What ere some vainer youth may term disgrace,
> The gain of honest pains is never base;
> From trades, from arts, from valour, honour springs,
> These three are founts of gentry, yea of kings. (1.1.172–5)[44]

Similarly, shoemaking was known as the "gentle craft," an idea explored in Thomas Middleton's comedy *The Shoemaker's Holiday*. Francis Beaumont's *The Knight of the Burning Pestle* parodies the chivalric pretentions of apprentices, the pestle being the sign of the Apothecaries and the "burning pestle," or penis, being a joke about the discomforts of venereal disease. Shakespeare himself explores a related fantasy about status, and indeed, one rather more apposite not only to his own situation but also to the many younger sons of gentry who, because of the system of primogeniture, by which the eldest son inherited everything, were obliged to take up apprenticeships in trades. Orlando in *As You Like It* is a younger son deprived (in this case by his elder brother) of his right to gentlehood and set to menial labor: "The spirit of my father grows strong in me, and I will no longer endure it: therefore allow me such exercise as may become a gentleman" (1.1.66–7).[45]

Shakespeare, however, was as cognizant as Jonson of the folly of the late sixteenth-century heraldry craze. He jokes about magisterial office as a qualification for and enhancement of gentlemanly status in *The Merry Wives of Windsor*, where "Robert Shallow, Esquire" is also Justice of the Peace, Custos Rotulorum, "and a gentleman born" with a "dozen white luces" to contribute to the armorial bearings of his heirs. Shallow is, to quote *Hamlet*, "Well ratified by law and heraldry" (1.1.86) to the point of comic excess. Shakespeare may even be laughing at himself and at genealogical claims to status when in *The Taming of the Shrew* he has Christopher Sly, a native of Burton Heath (Barton-on-the-Heath), a village near Stratford, claim his descent from the erroneously named Norman king, "Richard [i.e. William] the Conqueror." More seriously, Shakespeare also interrogates the conceptual basis of status itself. In *King Lear*, elemental humanity, "the bare forked [two-legged] animal" (3.4.106) that is man, dresses himself in robes of wealth and office in a futile attempt to deny the inherent vulnerability of the mortal condition, to which everyone, regardless of rank, is subject. In *King Lear*, to deny this commonality is the source of depravity. A "bare gentleman" is just more socially palatable than a "bare forked animal." The gravedigger in *Hamlet* makes a similarly radical observation when he claims that Adam was the "first gentleman": "There is no ancient gentlemen but gardeners, ditchers, and grave-makers" (*Hamlet* 5.1.29–30).[46]

It was also the case that heraldic colors were a highly decorative form of conspicuous consumption.[47] Individuals who were either unable or, on account of the trouble and expense, unwilling, to justify a claim before the College of Arms, might just go ahead anyway and garnish their homes and possessions without authorization. Henry Peacham made loud complaint about this practice, especially when he found a coat of arms copied from the French nobility proudly displayed above tradesman's door: "Neither can their owne Inventions consent them, but into what land or place soever they travaile, if they espy a fairer Coate then their owne (for they esteeme Coates faire or good, as our Naturals, according to the varietie of colours) after their return they set it up in Glasse for them and their heirs."[48] Displaying arms without title to them, or borrowing foreign heraldic colors because they were prettier – like "Naturals" or congenital idiots is the added jibe here – was a clear contravention of the law, yet it seems to have been too pervasive a practice for the College of Arms to completely stamp out.

No matter what the objections to Shakespeare's arms, at least he had gone about obtaining them through official channels. Nor was 1596 the only year that the Shakespeares had dealings with the College of Arms. John Shakespeare applied again in 1599, only a year before *Hamlet* was written, to have his arms "quartered" or "impaled" (that is, combined with) the Arden arms, Shakespeare's maternal line. The quartered arms would display the alleged aristocratic connection with the family of the earls of Warwick by dividing the shield vertically, with the Shakespeare arms on the dexter (right) half, and Arden ones on the left, or sinister, as it was termed in heraldic parlance. In *A Midsummer Night's Dream*, Helena describes her closeness to Hermia as "an union in partition . . . like coats in heraldry, / Due but to one, and crowned with one crest" (3.2.210–14).[49] As far as Henry Peacham was concerned, this practice was but another form of abuse: "Such a medley (I had almost said Motley) of Coates, such intrusion by adding or diminishing into ancient families and houses."[50] In this subsequent petition to the college, the Shakespeares had probably overreached themselves since the original design was scrapped in favor of those of a lesser family of Ardens, and, in the end, they did not adopt the new coat at all.[51] Curiously, too, John Shakespeare was still described as a yeoman – not a gentleman – in January 1597 when he sold a strip of land to George Badger.

John Shakespeare might well have been one of those allegedly ignominious persons whose social ambitions far overstretched their means. William Harrison commented that these people were not too big for their boots, but rather too small for them, "who peradvenure," "will go in wider buskins [boots] than [their] legs will bear."[52]

Perhaps because of the turbulence created in the social hierarchy consequent upon the influx of new wealth and the development of London, there was a new market for books on heraldry. Peacham's was prominent among them, as well as a volume by Augustine Vincent, who, of course, blazed his own status on the title page: "Baron Upton, Gerrard Leigh, Master Ferne, Master Guillim (late Portculleis pursivant)." Indeed, William Jaggard, the printer of Shakespeare's First Folio, also published many books on heraldry, and the Folio itself went through the press at approximately the same time as Vincent's treatise.[53]

To sum up: the herald Brooke's derisive annotation of Shakespeare, as "ye [the] player" despite his already enormous theatrical success in London is an important clue about how to read the operations of status and hierarchy in this society. *We* value Shakespeare much more than Lord Mauley; *they* did not. No one living in Elizabethan England would ever have suspected that when the dust of history had settled, it would be William Shakespeare, "ye player," who would stand far above all his peers as the most eminent of the Queen's subjects.

# Notes

1  M.R. Macdonald, "Clopton, Hugh (c.1440–1496)," *ODNB*.

2  Harrison's *Description of England in Shakespeare's Youth. Being the Second and Third Books of His Description of Britaine and England.* Edited from the first two editions of Holinshed's Chronicle, A.D. 1577, 1587, by Frederick J. Furnivall, pt 1 (London: The Shakespeare Society, 1877) pp. 128–9 (spelling modernized).

3  All references to *Much Ado About Nothing* are from William Shakespeare, *Much Ado About Nothing: The Arden Shakespeare*, ed. A.R. Humphreys (London: Methuen Drama, 1981).

4  William Shakespeare, *Othello*, ed. E.A.J. Honigmann (Walton-on-Thames: Thomas Nelson and Sons, 1997).

5  William Shakespeare, *King Henry IV. Part I: The Arden Shakespeare*, ed. A.R. Humphreys (London: Methuen Drama, 1960).

6  William Shakespeare, *Henry V*, ed. T.W. Craik (New York: Routledge, 1995).

7  References to Shakespeare's poems are from William Shakespeare, *Shakespeare's Poems: Venus and Adonis, The Rape of Lucrece and the Shorter Poems*, ed. Katherine Duncan-Jones and H.R. Woudhuysen (London: Arden Shakespeare, 2007).

8  Sir John Ferne, *The Blazon of Gentrie (1586)*, STC / 10824; Sir John Ferne, *The Blazon of Gentrie (1586)*, STC / 10824; Katherine Duncan-Jones, *Shakespeare's Life and World*, London: The Folio

Society, 2004), p. 117. See also Raymond Carter Sutherland, "The Grants of Arms to Shakespeare's Father," *Shakespeare Quarterly* 14 (1963): 379–85 at 383.

9 See Sutherland, "Grants of Arms," p. 383.

10 For the documents bearing out these facts, see David Thomas, ed., *Shakespeare in the Public Records* (London: Her Majesty's Stationery Office, 1985), p. 5.

11 William Shakespeare, *The Merchant of Venice: The Arden Shakespeare*, ed. John Russell Brown (Walton-on-Thames: Thomas Nelson, 1998).

12 Keith Wrightson, *Earthly Necessities: Economic Lives in Early Modern Britain* (New Haven: Yale University Press, 2000), p. 191.

13 Samuel Schoenbaum, *William Shakespeare: A Documentary Life* (New York: Oxford University Press, 1975), p. 227; Sutherland, "*Grants of Arms*," pp. 379–85.

14 Sir John Ferne, *The Blazon of Gentry (1586)*; quoted in Samuel Schoenbaum, *William Shakespeare: A Compact Documentary Life* (New York: Oxford University Press, 1987) at p. 38. For a list of the offices in the College of Arms see G.E. Aylmer, *The King's Servants: The Civil Service of Charles I, 1625–1642* (London: Routledge and Kegan Paul, 1961), p. 482.

15 William Shakespeare, *The Winter's Tale: The Arden Shakespeare*, ed. John Pitcher (London: Arden Shakespeare, 2010).

16 William Shakespeare, *Hamlet: The Texts of 1603 and 1623*, ed. Ann Thompson and Neil Taylor (London: Arden Shakespeare, 2006).

17 See Margreta de Grazia, *Hamlet without Hamlet* (Cambridge: Cambridge University Press, 2007), p. 94.

18 Katherine Duncan-Jones, *Ungentle Shakespeare: Scenes from His Life* (London: Arden, 2001), p. 85.

19 See Anthony Wagner, *Heralds of England* (London: HMSO, 1967), p. 215, and, on Shakespeare, p. 203.

20 Wrightson, *Earthly Necessities*, p. 22.

21 Harrison, *Description of England*, p. 128.

22 See Thomas Woodcock and John Martin Robinson, *The Oxford Guide to Heraldry* (Oxford: Oxford University Press, 1990), pp. 35–8.

23 Sutherland, "*Grants of Arms*," p. 382.

24 William Shakespeare, *King John: The Arden Shakespeare*, ed. E.A.J. Honigmann (London: Methuen and Co., 1954).

25 Wagner, *Heralds of England*, p. 204.

26 Woodcock and Martin, *Oxford Guide to Heraldry*, p.145; see also Aylmer, *King's Servants*, p. 43.

27 A.L. Rowse, *The England of Elizabeth: The Structure of Society* (New York: Macmillan, 1951), p. 247; Wagner, *Heralds of England*, p. 237.

28 Wagner, *Heralds of England*, p. 237.

29 Wagner, *Heralds of England*, p. 238.

30 Quoted in Felicity Heal and Clive Holmes, *The Gentry in England and Wales, 1500–1700* (Stanford: Stanford University Press, 1994), pp. 29, 390.

31 Frederick Wilson Kittermaster, *Warwickshire arms and Lineages: Compiled from the Heralds' Visitations and Ancient MSS* (London: 1866), p. viii.

32 Mark Noble, *A History of the College of Arms* (London: J. Debrett, 1804), p. 169.

33 Wagner, *Heralds of England*, p. 207.

34 See Wyman H. Herendeen, "Brooke, Ralph (c.1553–1625)," *ODNB* and Basil Morgan, "Brandon, Richard (*d.* 1649)," *ODNB*.

35 Wagner, *Heralds of England*, p. 215.

36 Wagner, *Heralds of England*, p. 205.

37 I am grateful to Nigel Ramsey for this information.

38 Henry Peacham, *The Compleat Gentleman* (London: 1622), p. 138.

39 For complaints about the College of Arms, see William Smith, Rouge Dragon, "A Brief Discourse of the Causes of Discord Amongst the Offices of Armes," MS. Folger V.a.157; MS V.a.199. The

scribal copy is dedicated to Elizabeth's chief minister, Lord Burghley.

40 Katherine Duncan-Jones, *Ungentle Shakespeare*, p. 102; Noble, *History of the College of Arms*, p. 199.

41 William Shakespeare, *Shakespeare's Sonnets: The Arden Shakespeare*, ed. Katherine Duncan-Jones (London: Methuen Drama, 2010).

42 Quoted in Wrightson, *Earthly Necessities*, p. 33.

43 Schoenbaum, *Compact Documentary*, pp. 229–30.

44 George Chapman, Ben Jonson, and John Marston, *Eastward Ho!* ed. R.W. Van Fossen (Manchester: Manchester University Press, 1999).

45 William Shakespeare, *As You Like It: The Arden Shakespeare*, ed. Juliet Dusinberre (London: Arden Shakespeare, 2006).

46 Noble, *History of the College of Arms*, p. 33.

47 Peacham, *Compleat Gentleman*, pp. 142, 145.

48 Peacham, *Compleat Gentleman*, p. 150.

49 Schoenbaum, *Compact Documentary Life*, p. 230; William Shakespeare, *A Midsummer Night's Dream: Texts and Contexts*, ed. Gail Kern Paster and Skiles Howard (Boston: Bedford/St. Martin's, 1999).

50 Peacham, *Compleat Gentleman*, p. 39.

51 Schoenbaum, *Compact Documentary Life*, p. 230.

52 Quoted Wagner, *Heralds of England*, p. 187; Harrison, *Description of England*, pp. 128–9 (spelling modernized).

53 Edwin Eliott Willoughby, *A Printer of Shakespeare: The Books and Times of William Jaggard* (P. Allan, London: 1934), pp. 267–75.

# 5

# THEATRE

The first account of Shakespeare's theatrical career was not encouraging. It appeared in a pamphlet called *Greene's Groats-worth of Wit* (1592) that describes Shakespeare as concealing "a Tyger's heart" beneath a benign player's exterior:

> There is an upstart Crow, beautified with our feathers, that with his Tyger's hart wrapt in a Players hyde, supposes he is as well able to bombast out a blanke verse as the best of you: and beeing an absolute Johannes fac totum, is in his own conceit the onely Shake-scene in a countrey.[1]

The bitter disparagement of Shakespeare as "Shake-scene" whose own words are turned against him in a parodic allusion to the wicked Queen Margaret in the theatrically successful though as yet unpublished play *3 Henry VI*: "O tiger's heart wrapp'd in a woman's hide!" (1.4.137).[2] His detractor's paraphrase of this line from Shakespeare's *3 Henry VI* may also be a glance at the animal skins of his father's trade. But if ever Shakespeare had followed his father's footsteps he was no longer doing so by 1592, and clearly had been pursuing for some years a form of employment that barely existed in John Shakespeare's youth, when the life of an itinerant player would have been the only theatrical vocation imaginable.

William Shakespeare became an actor, playwright, and sharer (one of the cooperative of investors who owned and ran the company) in a theatrical enterprise with a fixed London location and thus participated in a venture that was

*Who Was William Shakespeare?: An Introduction to the Life and Works*, First Edition.
Dympna Callaghan.
© 2013 John Wiley & Sons, Ltd. Published 2013 by John Wiley & Sons, Ltd.

historically unprecedented. However, the new economic and social conditions that sustained the theatre lasted for a relatively brief period in the late sixteenth and early seventeenth centuries. There were mounting cultural energies that sought to suppress drama altogether. Stephen Gosson's *The Schoole of Abuse* (1579) and John Northbrooke's *A Treatise Wherein Dicing, Dauncing, Vaine Playes or Enterludes are Reproved* (1577) were among the many attacks on the stage for its cross-dressed performers, its alleged "vice," "wantonnesse," "impuritie" (as Northbrooke put it), and more fundamentally, its fictions, as the propagation of untruth. Within twenty-five years of Shakespeare's death, political turmoil erupted as the result of the power struggle between Crown and Parliament. In 1640 Puritans wrested the political initiative away from the Crown and closed the theatres in 1642.[3] The traditional account of the closing of the theatres with its straightforward equation of Puritanism with rabid antitheatricality, however, has been significantly revised and complicated by the work of Margo Heinemann and David Kastan. The professed intention to quell "spectacles of pleasure, too commonly expressing lascivious Mirth and Levity," for example, was not, Kastan argues, the primary impetus behind the order to close the theatres. Instead, the order was "motivated by practical concerns for security more than by religious zeal."[4] This is significant in relation to understanding the theatre of Shakespeare's time because it speaks to the way that authorities of all stripes (the Crown, the City of London, town councils, and the like), both before and after the outbreak of the Civil War in 1642, sought to control the *conditions* of theatrical representation itself (which were secular and involved public assembly) as much as its *contents* – such as mirth and levity. While the Common Council of London passed an ordinance in 1574 aimed at content (what Elizabethans called the "matter" of the entertainment the "words" and "doings" especially those that tended towards "unchastity, sedition," and "such like")[5], it nonetheless remains the case that the issues plays addressed might have been less controversial than the vehicle for their expression, the medium of theatre itself. Crucially, restrictions imposed on representation by the Crown and also by civic government – both the control of theatre as an institution and the system of censorship applied to its scripts – did not simply suppress and stifle artistic expression. Thinking historically rather than anachronistically about such legal impediments, they can be seen to have constituted the cultural shape of artistic production in Elizabethan and Jacobean England, which, paradoxically, saw the greatest ever achievements of English theatre. When the theatre reopened with the Restoration of the monarchy in 1660, the public theatre as Shakespeare knew it was gone for good.

This chapter will offer a detailed historical and literary context for the first reference to Shakespeare in London, exploring both the limitations and possibilities presented by a theatrical career in Elizabethan London.

In Shakespeare's childhood, his exposure to drama would have come through the companies of travelling players who had been licensed to perform – the Queen's Servants, Worcester's Servants, Leicester's Servants, Warwick's Servants, Derby's Servants, and Lord Berkeley's Servants. Indeed, in 1569, during his tenure as bailiff, John Shakespeare himself twice authorized performances in Stratford. We do not know if Shakespeare also witnessed the lavish entertainments put on by the Earl of Leicester at nearby Kenilworth for Queen Elizabeth in 1575, or the Coventry cycle of mystery plays, which were preformed up until their suppression in 1578.

There was a vigorous native tradition of drama in England, predominantly religious drama. Even popular festivities were tied to the ecclesiastical calendar – for example, Shrove Tuesday, or Mardi Gras, the day prior to the Lenten observances that commence with Ash Wednesday; Whitsuntide (celebrating the descent of the Holy Spirit upon Christ's apostles); and the June feast day that celebrated the institution of the Eucharist, Corpus Christi. The most well-developed aspects of the pre-Shakespearean dramatic tradition were the mystery cycles, or miracle plays – the religious dramas staged by the medieval guilds which addressed the central moments in Christian eschatology from the Creation to the Last Judgment. Rural areas as well as towns saw all manner of revels and entertainments, including short secular interludes, often derived from the folklore of Robin Hood. Maypoles and May festivities, however, harked back to the pagan fertility rites of ancient Britain, along with folk dances, such as the Morris dance and other long-practiced pastimes. Shakespeare's plays have their roots in popular festivities, which were often the occasion for revel, riot, and rebellion, not to mention a resurgence of Catholic ritual that authorities endeavored to contain. The Corporation of Stratford, for example, tried to suppress the annual Ascension Day Pageant of St George in 1547.

Such festivities were celebrated all over England, and there was simply no sense that the culture of performance and entertainment was focused on the capital until the mid-sixteenth century. The mystery cycles were performed in important provincial towns; Wakefield, Coventry, Chester, and York were the sites of the most prominent cycles that have come down to us. The performers of these plays were townspeople and members of medieval guilds rather than professional actors. This was similarly true of another type of drama that preceded Shakespeare, the morality plays, such as *Everyman*. Characterized by heavily didactic emphases and allegorical form, performances of these plays occurred on carts, outside churches, and sometimes in the halls of grand houses. In contrast to the world of Shakespeare's forebears, devoid of professional actors and purpose-built theatres, huge changes in economic organization – the complex shift from a feudal society to a mercantile capitalist one attendant upon the immense growth of trade and the exponential growth the metropolis – had made way for the professional player, the professional playwright, the theatre as a building, indeed for the new institution of English theatre itself.

In this novel environment *Greene's Groats-worth of Wit* was published under the name of the recently deceased, university-educated playwright Robert Greene. Greene was a notorious celebrity who, as the scholar and writer Gabriel Harvey opined, was known for "dissolute, and licentious living . . . ruffianly haire, unseemly apparrell, and more unseemly Company."[6] Greene's life of dissipation was well-documented, but whatever his other transgressions, he most probably did not write this pamphlet. Most likely, his death simply offered the opportunity to attribute its acerbic content to him. Scholars suggest two possible contenders for its authorship, either Henry Chettle, who ostensibly prepared the manuscript for the press, or another of the "university wits" on the London theatrical scene, Greene's friend Thomas Nashe. Chettle denied having written *Groats-worth*, and in the second edition of his prose work *Pierce Pennilesse*, in 1595, Nashe also vigorously denied having done so.[7] He expostulates, "God never have care of my soule, but utterly renounce me if the least word or syllable in it proceeded from my pen."[8] Katherine Duncan-Jones's recent and persuasive case for Nashe's authorship, however, has tipped the balance in favor of him.[9] As an up and coming rival, clearly Shakespeare had excited envious derision. The pamphlet vilifies Shakespeare as an upstart and a plagiarizer ("beautified with our feathers") who is over-confident about his ability to compose dramatic poetry. The verb "to bombast" means to stuff or expand, to fill out. In this case it is a line of blank verse that is being filled out, that is, a line of unrhymed iambic pentameter with its five stresses, which Shakespeare, a mere actor, a player, believes himself as well able to do as the best-educated of his peers. In his preface to Greene's *Menaphon* (1589), Nashe had earlier complained about those who used bombast verse "to vent their manhood . . . to the spacious volubility of a drumming decasillabon [decasyllabic verse or iambic pentameter]." While such throbbing rhythms were immensely popular, for Nashe they are crude and unsubtle, "loud," and do violence to the language. Nashe attacks – and parodies with clanging alliteration – those "who thinke to out-brave better pennes with the swelling bumbast [bombast] of bragging blank verse."[10] Later in his career, Shakespeare has the malevolent Iago, jealous of his rival's promotion, echo the precisely the terms of disparagement used about "Shaks-scene" in *Greene's Groats-worth*: "But he, as loving his own pride and purposes evades them with a bombast circumstance horribly stuff'd with epithets of war" (*Othello*, 1.1.11–13). In fact, the principal job requirement of a playwright was to "bombast [fill] out blank verse," to put matter into the metrical frame of the iambic line. Moreover, in Elizabethan theatrical culture, where rivalry and collaboration coexisted as its predominant if contradictory energies, "bombast" was simply the epithet of choice.

The "tyger's heart" slur, however, appends a kind of brutal aggression to the other charges that sits uneasily with the "gentle Shakespeare" of Jonson's commendatory poem in the First Folio. Yet, Shakespeare's run-ins with the law were invariably in relation to fiscal matters rather than to physical violence. Even in 1596, when William Wayte sought surety of the peace against him (a sort of early modern restraining order), the petition also names Francis Langley, who built the Swan playhouse, and two others, and the litigant's objective seems to have been to bring financial ruin upon Langley.[11] In this, Shakespeare is unlike some of his most notable contemporaries. Ben Jonson murdered a fellow actor, Gabriel Spencer, and he boasted about his violent exploits in battle in the Low Countries. Similarly, Christopher Marlowe and Thomas Watson were indicted in the street-fight murder of an innkeeper's son, William Bradley; and Marlowe was himself murdered in Deptford. Some of Shakespeare's most distinguished contemporaries, then, were enmeshed in the violent, turbulent world of early modern London in a way that he was not. Given this, "tyger's heart" perhaps suggests ferocious ambition and professional ruthlessness rather than personal malice. In the cutthroat context of the London theatre, probably his adversaries could see Shakespeare's potential to kill the competition.

Perhaps more serious is the allegation of plagiarism, of borrowed feathers. Accusations of theft were probably inevitable in Shakespeare's theatrical milieu where almost half the plays written were coauthored in order to speed production and meet the voracious appetite of audiences for new shows. The extent of writers' collaborative contributions varied considerably, even in cases where the work clearly belonged to at least one other playwright who was its primary author. Thomas Heywood, for example, claimed to have "a hand" or "at least a main finger" in approximately 220 works written over a forty-year period. Sometimes, though not always, shared authorship was recorded in the entry in the Stationers' Register. The lost play *Cardenio*, for example, was entered as having been written by Shakespeare and John Fletcher, as was *Two Noble Kinsmen*, a play omitted from the First Folio and first published in 1634. Late in Shakespeare's career, he allegedly wrote *Pericles* with George Wilkins (which similarly fails to appear in the First Folio), and yet its title page lists only Shakespeare as the author:

The Late, and Much admired Play, Caled Pericles, Prince of Tyre. With the true relation and whole Historie, adventures, and fortunes of the said Prince: As also, The no lesse strange, and worthy accidents, in the Birth and Life, of his Daughter Mariana. As hath been divers and sundry times acted by his Majesties Servants, at the Globe on the Banck-side. By William Shakespeare. Imprinted at London for Henry Gosson, and are to be sold at the signe of the Sunne In Pater-noster row, &c 1609.

Wilkins, an unsavory character whom Shakespeare had met while lodging in Silver Street,[12] probably wrote the better part of the first two acts, while Shakespeare wrote the remainder of the play. There is evidence for the presence of "other hands" in a number of Shakespeare's plays including, for example, *Titus Andronicus*, which he may well have written with George Peele, and *Macbeth*, which includes scenes by Thomas Middleton. Writing was not always evenly divided between collaborators, who typically worked independently of one another on those scenes or dimensions of the plot for which they had assumed responsibility.

However, the accusation in *Groats-worth* is not that a fellow writer has claimed credit for something he did not pen, but rather that a *player* has done so. The exact nature of the charge is obscure, but essentially the claim is that a Johnny-come-lately and Jack-of-all-trades-master-of-none, a mere actor who has been adorned with lines composed by the university wits, Robert Greene, George Peele, Christopher Marlowe, and Nashe himself, now thinks he can be a poet along with the best of them. Whatever else he may be, it is clear that Shakespeare is known as a "player," and he is thus referred to twice in the scant personal records we have of him from the early 1590s – by the herald Ralph Brooke (as we have seen in the previous chapter) and by the author of *Groats-worth*. In both instances, the use of the term is pejorative. The word "player," originally associated with revelry and making merry, was commonly used to refer to actors but was a category broad enough to encompass entertainers ranging from great tragedians to a motley assortment of clowns, tumblers, and jig-makers.

Despite his posthumous reputation, then, Shakespeare had not entered an illustrious profession. This particular slight in *Groats-worth*, "the player's hyde," discloses not only something about the status of actors during this period, but also about Shakespeare's theatrical career. Shakespeare does indeed seem to have been unique among his contemporary dramatists in being an actor as well as a writer. He performed in at least two plays by Ben Jonson. His name heads the cast list of the Folio text of 1616 of *Every Man in his Humour* (1598), an indication that he played a major role, and he acted in *Sejanus* (1603). In contrast, Jonson himself abandoned acting as soon as he had made a reputation as a playwright because he "was never a good Actor, but an excellent Instructor."[13] Good acting was valued, however – even by Nashe, whose chameleon-like persona, could change as required by the expanding market for print culture in the new metropolis. Nashe praised the power of drama and singled out Shakespeare's *Henry VI* in particular:

> How would it have joyed brave *Talbot* (the terror of the French) to thinke that after he had lyne two hundred yeares in his Tombe, hee should triumphe againe

on the Stage, and have his bones newe embalmed with the teares of ten thousand spectators at least (at severall times), who in the Tragedian that represents his person, imagine they behold him fresh and bleeding.[14]

Here, the actor, "the Tragedian that represents his person" receives his due, and indeed, Shakespeare's own company boasted the great tragic actor, Richard Burbage, but it is his counterpart in the rival Admiral's men, Edward Alleyn, who received Nashe's highest praise. No actor even in classical times, Nashe writes, "could ever performe more in action than Ned Allen." Comic actors too, the clowns, Will Kempe and Richard Tarlton, also achieved celebrity status in their day. Fynes Moryson noted in *Unpublished Chapters of the Itinerary*, "as there be, in my opinion, more Playes in London then in all the partes of the worlde I have seen, so doe these players or Comedians excell all other in the worlde."[15] Shakespeare and his fellow actors may have been consummately skilled in the exercise of their art, but in a period prior to the establishment of professional identities, they held a parlous and marginal status in Elizabethan society.

Actors were routinely the primary targets of the period's anti-theatrical prejudice, as attempts to regulate them as a group attest. Actors, minstrels, and other entertainers were lumped together with recalcitrant idlers who could not even claim the excuse of infirmity for their destitute condition. Such "sturdy beggars" were targeted by the Elizabethan Poor Laws, which sought to restrict the peripatetic lives of the idle and insolvent and to provide minimal relief for the indigent poor who were enfeebled by age, disability, or sickness. The 1572 statute, "An Acte for the Punishment of Vagabonds and for the Relief of the Poore & Impotent" stated that "Common Plaiers in Enterludes . . . shall bee adjudged and deemed Rogues Vagabonds and Sturdy Beggars."[16] In the epilogue to *As You Like It*, when the actor playing Rosaline steps out of his role to address the audience, Shakespeare resists this conflation between beggars and actors and, from the vantage point of theatre as a fixed location, arguably claims new status for actors: "I am not furnished like a beggar, therefore to beg will not become me. My way is to conjure you . . ." (Epilogue 9–11).[17] There were attempts during this period to differentiate the "common" player from the professional actor. John Stephens, in *Essayes and Characters* (1615) observed, "Therefore did I prefix an Epithite of *common*, to distinguish the base and artlesse appendants of our citty companies, which often times start away into rusticall wanderers and then like Proteus start backe again into the Citty number." Here again, the worry is not acting per se but vagrancy. Authorities feared the menacing underclass known as "masterless men" or "rogues, vagabonds, and mighty valiant beggars" as the 1572 statute calls them. This was the army of the itinerant poor who wandered from parish to parish because communities were reluctant to have additional burdens thrust on already hard-pressed resources. Now that actors had a fixed address they had grounds for differentiating themselves from this group and some defense against arguments like Stephen Gosson's volcanic diatribe in *Playes Confuted in Five Actions* (1582), which defined players as "the Sonnes of idlenesse."

One of the most important innovations of the later part of the sixteenth century was the development of fixed locations for theatrical performance – that is, the advent of theatres themselves. From at least the mid-1550s, a number of inns had served as venues for theatrical performance:[18] the Bell Savage on Ludgate Hill, the Bull in Bishopsgate Street, and the Bell and the Cross Keys in Gracechurch Street.[19] The Bell and the Cross Keys were well within the walls of the City of London.[20] Unlike taverns and alehouses, inns were self-regulated and therefore of less concern to City authorities. In these *ad hoc* performance spaces, plays were staged amid the not uncongenial everyday activities of the "common Inne or victualinge howse whereunto dyvers persons resorte for lodging and victuallys."[21] Theatre historians do not know precisely when playing at these inns ceased, but by about the mid-1590s, regular playing at these locations seems to have terminated.

Despite the misleading name – it sounds more like an inn – the first purpose-built theatre was the Red Lion in Stepney, built in 1567 by a grocer, John Brayne.[22] Brayne undertook a second theatrical venture together with his brother-in-law, James Burbage, who was involved with the Earl of Leicester's company and built the aptly named Theatre, the first ever round, outdoor theatre, in 1576, in Holywell or Halliwell Street in Shoreditch, north of the City. Brayne, together with his wife, Margaret, quarreled violently with Burbage and suffered financial ruin, while – whatever the rights and wrongs of the case, and from historical distance it is difficult to tell – Burbage thrived. James Burbage's family included his sons Cuthbert and Richard. Cuthbert vaunted his father's playhouse as England's first, while Richard was the great tragedian of Shakespeare's company. When, in 1597, James Burbage's lease was up on the land on which the Theatre was built, he had it dismantled and shipped across the Thames to build the Globe, the theatre that has become synonymous with Shakespeare's name, and which was erected in 1599.

Not only did actors have a newly fixed address, they were offered some protection under the law. A clause in the 1572 legislation urged that actors were to be treated as beggars and whipped to the next parish boundary *unless* they belonged to "any Baron of this Realme or to[wardes] any other honorable Personage of greater Degree." Thus, the objective in this instance was to enable rather than to suppress theatrical performance. Indeed, this document urges authorities throughout the kingdom to permit performances without "lettes, hynderaunce, or molestation." Players who were under the retainer of a social superior were thus regarded as being legitimately employed because, in effect, they had a master and were thus a recognizable part of the social hierarchy rather than the detritus governed by no employer or social superior.

Aristocratic patronage was therefore the surest form of protection from prosecution for theatrical companies. The Earl of Leicester, Robert Dudley, was the most important patron at the start of Elizabeth's reign, and his playing company, The Earl of Leicester's Servants, received a royal patent in 1574 authorizing its theatrical activities.[23] Upon Leicester's death, patronage of this company devolved upon Ferdinando Stanley, Lord Strange. ("Lord Strange" was historically the title given to the Earl of Derby's heir until such time as he inherited the earldom). This was the company with which Shakespeare began and continued his entire theatrical career under the auspices of various patrons. Thus, when, in October 1593, Lord Strange inherited his father's title, the company became the Earl of Derby's, and after he died in turn a year later, it became the Lord Chamberlain's, under the aegis of Henry Carey, the first Lord Hunsdon. The name, the "Lord Chamberlain" referred to a powerful office in the royal household. The household above stairs (that is, not including the kitchens, cellars, etc.) was known as the Chamber and employed over six hundred people with the Lord Chamberlain as its head.

By the time of Shakespeare's ascendency in the theatre, two playing companies dominated the London scene: actors under the patronage of the Lord Howard of Effingham, the Lord Admiral, a company first mentioned in 1586 and renamed as Prince Henry's in the reign of James I, and those under the patronage of the Lord Chamberlain. But these aristocratic patrons were largely figureheads. Shareholders, like Shakespeare, bore collective financial and managerial responsibility for the company.[24] More important than aristocratic patrons in terms of financial success were the business and managerial figures who led these playing companies: James Burbage was the financial mind behind the Lord Chamberlain's Servants while Philip Henslowe provided the entrepreneurial energy for the Lord Admiral's Servants. Indeed, Henslowe's accounts, popularly known as *Henslowe's Diary*, offer one of the most valuable sources of information about early modern theatre. The Admiral's Men, whose chief actor was Edward Alleyn, took Marlowe's plays as an established part of their repertory, while the Chamberlain's Servants, whose chief actor was Richard Burbage, took Shakespeare's plays. Other important companies were the Queen's, founded under royal warrant in 1583; Lord Worcester's, which became Queen Anne's during the reign of her husband, James I; and Lord Pembroke's, first mentioned in 1593. There were also two companies of boy actors, the Children of Paul's and the Children of Queen Elizabeth's Chapel, the "eyrie of children, little eyases" of *Hamlet* (Folio 2.2.337–8). On James's accession all recognized companies passed under royal patronage, and the Chamberlain's Servants became the King's Servants. While this new status afforded actors continued social protection it did not endow them with social preeminence.[25] Nor was aristocratic protection *carte blanche* for actors.

For all their associations with aristocracy, acting was still a tainted profession. John Davies of Hereford's praise of Shakespeare in *Microcosmos* (1603) makes its excuses: "Though the stage doth stain pure gentle blood, / Yet generous ye are in mind and mood."[26] In fact, "common" is an adjective redolent of class hierarchy that frequently attached to theatre, though it sometimes means "public" as in the "common stages" and "common players" mentioned in *Hamlet* (2.2.340, 346).[27] Arguably, Shakespeare may himself have shared some of these scruples about theatre if his *Sonnets* are indeed autobiographical. In Sonnet 111, the poet regrets that the goddess Fortune did not provide for him other than "public means" to make his living – "public means which public manners breeds" (*l.* 4).[28] The trade the poet identifies with here is that of the dyer: "my nature is subdued / To what it works in, like the dyer's hand" (Sonnet 111.6–7). Since the dyer's art entailed staining hides as much as dyeing cloth, Shakespeare here forges a connection, albeit by antithesis, with his father's craft as a glove maker and whitener, of leather. There is an important literary allusion here also to Shakespeare's favorite poet, Ovid, especially in the English translation of the *Metamorphoses* by Arthur Golding. In Book 6, the gifted young weaver Arachne, confident in her artistic supremacy, enters into competition with the goddess Athena, who is disguised as an old woman. The vindictive goddess cruelly punishes Arachne's presumption and her extraordinary skill by transforming her into a spider. As with Shakespeare, devoid of an elite heritage, Arachne's art is her only means of livelihood: "This Damsell was not famous . . . for her stocke, but for her Arte" (*Metamorphoses* 6.10–11). Like Shakespeare's father too, Arachne's father, "a *pelting* Purple Dier" treats animal skins or pelts; only her father dyes the skins with the color purple. In Shakespeare's sonnet, the poet applies vinegar ("potions of eisell," Sonnet 111.10) as a stain remover – a solvent that might restore his stained reputation that is the consequence of an inherently degraded public profession.

Importantly too, dyeing had other tangible connections with Shakespeare's career. The theatre manager and entrepreneur, Philip Henslowe, whose Rose theatre staged Shakespeare's *Titus Andronicus* and *Henry VI* plays, began his business life as apprentice to a dyer called Woodward. He then married the dyer's widow and subsequently apprenticed his young actors in the Dyers Company.

Trades in London were organized around the City's livery companies, whose members took on young apprentices. The apprentices were "bound" (contracted) to their masters, usually for a period of seven years, at which time their training was complete, and they were eligible to become "freemen" of their company, recognized as citizens of London. Shakespeare's fellow-actor and the coeditor of the First Folio, John Heminges, was apprenticed to the grocer James Collins and made a freeman of London through the Grocers Company in 1587. Heminges then took on two apprentices himself, Thomas Belte and Alexander Cooke, whom he trained as actors in the mid-1590s. (Eight more apprentices later followed these in the early part of the seventeenth century.) Cooke went on to become a freeman of the Grocers and took on apprentices of his own, even though, like him, they had received actors' training and were only nominally grocers despite their allegiance to that livery company. Acting apprenticeships typically began when boys were thirteen or fourteen, and their first parts were often women's roles: Cooke was apprenticed at thirteen and Belte at sixteen. Since Cleopatra, Lady Macbeth, and Hamlet's mother, Gertrude, not to mention comic roles like Rosaline in *As You Like It*, demand extraordinary skill, they demonstrate Shakespeare's confidence even in his youngest actors. We know that one of Heminges's grocer apprentices, Richard Sharpe, was a very gifted actor and female impersonator because he played the title role in John Webster's powerful tragedy *The Duchess of Malfi*. This evidence suggests the caliber of at least some of the actor apprentices, even though their "official" trades offer no connection whatsoever with the theatre.

Significantly, the "rude" or unsophisticated "mechanicals" of *A Midsummer Night's Dream*, no matter their work-a-day trades (weaver, joiner, tailor, carpenter, bellows mender, tinker), are also a company of (albeit amateur) actors who perform for their ruler. Early modern England was a place where the social status we associate with the word "profession" had not yet been established. There is a telling rendition of social encounter between the ruling class and the laboring class in the opening lines of *Julius Caesar*. In a scene that no doubt reflected daily life in Shakespeare's London more than that in ancient Rome, a cobbler is peremptorily accosted by his social superior: "(Being mechanical), you ought not walk / Upon a labouring day, without the sign / Of your Profession? Speak, what trade art thou?" (1.1.3–5).[29] "Mechanical," "profession," "trade," and "laboring" are of a piece here.

Theatre was very much a part of the politics and the fabric of London, a city whose ancient walls could no longer contain it. City authorities, composed of the Lord Mayor, the Aldermen, and the Common Council, had jurisdiction over the area approximately within the boundaries of the medieval city wall. Theatres were located primarily on land that was either physically beyond the reach of the City fathers, in the suburbs (the Globe and the Rose were south of the Thames in Southwark), or within the City boundary in an area that, because it had been monastic land prior to the Reformation (like Blackfriars, Shakespeare's indoor theatre) was exempt from City governance.[30] Players and playwrights could take a certain degree of license in the "licentious Liberties" and in the suburbs, but this did not mean that they were given free rein.[31] Traditionally, theatre historians have associated the City with Puritan anti-theatricalism and the Crown with watchful encouragement of the drama, but the real picture, as we have noted in relation to the closing of the theatres, is probably more complicated than that. Certainly, the neat division between Crown and City does not square with the sheer scale and extent of flourishing civic entertainment recently uncovered by Ann Lancashire and Tracey Hill.[32]

Drama, as we have seen, had been primarily religious up until the mid-sixteenth century, and it was especially religious content that authorities, both civic and sovereign, sought to suppress. On May 16, 1559, the queen issued the proclamation, written in her own hand, which pronounced that she "doth straightly forbyd" all theatricals that had not been awarded official permission.[33] Elizabeth was clearly concerned about something more than simply crowds congregating at entertainments because she also includes private theatricals, and adds that her officers must not allow plays "wherein either matters of religion or of the governaunce of the estate of the common weale shall be handled or treated, beyng no meet matters to be wrytten or treated upon, but by men of authoritie . . ."[34] Elizabeth here articulates the key objectives of both theatrical and print censorship, namely those of curbing heresy and stifling sedition.[35]

The contours of Shakespeare's plays and poems were thus defined not just by what they said, but crucially, by what they could not say, what, as we noted in Chapter 2, in the *Sonnets* the poet calls "arte made tung-tied by authority" (66.9). To be tongue-tied is not to be completely muzzled or mute, but rather to be capable only of partial and imperfect articulation. It is a free imagination denied its fullest expression. One of the most important historical facts Shakespeare's modern readers must grasp is that his was a society that was devoid of both freedom of religion and freedom of speech. This does not, however, mean that Elizabethan England was a world in which art was merely a set of cleverly coded messages to be deciphered. Anagrams, puzzles, and emblems were indeed popular in England in Shakespeare's time, but neither in performance nor in print did drama take that form. Censorship was simply part of the day-to-day reality in which Shakespeare worked and achieved a level of artistic expression unmatched by eras ostensibly characterized by absolute freedom of expression.

The basic legal framework of censorship was as follows: In 1414 Parliament passed an act giving ecclesiastical authorities the right to take action against heretical books and their authors, and this legislation intensified with the onset of the Reformation. In 1529 and 1530 proclamations were issued against heretical books and a licensing system was instituted in 1538 that put the Privy Council in control of the dissemination of printed matter, whether produced in England or on the Continent. Furthermore, the first Protestant king, Edward

VI, issued a proclamation in 1551 which insisted that pamphlets, plays, and ballads should be devoid of anything that might be "unseemly for Christian ears."[36] These regulations were further elaborated in Shakespeare's lifetime by both statute and proclamation. Physical mutilation was one of the possible punishments for violating these restrictions. When in 1579, in a pamphlet called *Discovery of a Gaping Gulf*, John Stubbes speculated about the queen's marriage, both he and his publisher lost their right hands.[37]

Thus, in Shakespeare's lifetime, neither the performance nor the printing of plays could be undertaken without a license. If a text was not approved as it stood, an author might make changes, motivated by the powerful incentive to retain all his body parts. Censorship enforced by draconian penalties was, to a large extent, simply accepted as a normal part of the social fabric, and was not something that aroused particular protest or objection. Such a view is certainly indicated by Thomas Nashe's letter to the printer of the second edition of *Pierce Pennilesse* (1595). Nashe, who had gone up to the country to escape an outbreak of plague, writes that "if the sicknesse cease before the third impression, I will come and alter whatsoever may be offensive . . ."[38] Yet, playwrights and poets, risking parlous consequences, did sometimes cause offense and risked punishment. This was the case with Ben Jonson's *Sejanus* (1603), a play in which, as we have noted, Shakespeare played one of the leading parts. At the instigation of Henry Howard, first Earl of Northampton, Jonson was summoned before the Privy Council to answer charges of "popery and treason."[39] Scholars do not know the precise nature of the matter that caused offense because, of course, Jonson was obliged to change it before the play was printed. Even as it stands, Jonson's play text reflects upon this very issue of state surveillance, albeit from the distance of ancient Rome, and upon an environment in which every other dinner guest "Is a fee'd spy, t'observe who goes, who comes, / What conference you have, with whom, where, when" (*Sejanus*, 2.445–6). Other writers, too, fell foul of the authorities. In 1599, Marlowe's translation, *All of Ovid's Elegies*, was burnt on episcopal order along with the satires of John Davies. Thomas Kyd, author of *The Spanish Tragedy*, one of the most important plays of the period and a crucial precursor of *Hamlet*, had been put on the rack earlier in the decade to answer questions about his notorious associate Christopher Marlowe.

Shakespeare seems to have been more successful in evading the ire of the authorities. Yet, even he did not escape entirely. When *Richard II* was first printed in 1597, and in the two reprints of 1598, part of Act 4, Scene 1 was excised. The potentially controversial matter here was both the representation of Parliament itself, the proceedings of which, theoretically at least, were secret (*arcana imperii*), as well as the deposition of Richard II. This episode was no doubt believed to offer an historical precedent for deposing an anointed monarch. As a female ruler, Elizabeth was especially vulnerable on this point. After all, her cousin Mary had been deposed in Scotland, but at least Mary had an heir. In England, the succession question could lead to a potential civil war if Elizabeth were somehow deposed or killed. Colored by and intensified by religious conflict, these were the dangers posed by *Richard II*. However, the play was duly licensed with the deletion of the offending episode. But that was not the end of the matter. In February 1601, Shakespeare's company was hired to perform the play the night before the Essex Rebellion, the ill-fated attempt by the Earl of Essex to force the queen to bend to his will. Once the uprising was quelled, the actor Augustine Phillips, Shakespeare's fellow sharer in the Lord Chamberlain's company, was called to explain the matter to the Privy Council. Phillips reported that he and his fellow actors were asked "to have the play of the deposing and killing of King Richard the Second to be played the Saturday next" for eleven shillings more than their ordinary fee. He testified that the actors "were determined to have played some other play, holding that play of King Richard to be so old and long out of use that they should have small or no company at it."[40] However, the queen herself was in no doubt about its relevance to current events and famously pronounced: "I am Richard II. Know ye not that?"

Nor were authorities wrong to fear outbreaks of public disorder in the playhouses. In 1597, *The Isle of Dogs* allegedly instigated a riot among spectators. The Privy Council responded not only by imprisoning its authors, including Ben Jonson, but also by ordering the demolition of the playhouses. In the end, however, only the Swan theatre, which had staged the offending play, was deprived of its license.[41] The Privy Council issued another order on June 22, 1600 permitting only the Globe and the Fortune to exhibit plays, and further stating that there were to be only two performances per week. Fortunately, these directives were completely ignored.

There were a number of different concerns that might lead to restrictions on theatrical performance, and invariably, some were religious. Playhouses closed every year during the six weeks of Lent, which was observed as a period of fasting and penitence; nor were plays to be performed during the times of Sunday worship, for the obvious reason that it would conflict with mandatory church attendance.[42] The Tudor horror of crowds, of mobs, of the power of the "many-headed multitude" (*Coriolanus*, 2.3.16–17) was yet another dimension of the restrictions on theatre, as Nicholas Ling put it in *Politeuphuia: Wit's Commonwealth*: (1598): "The seeds of rashness & lust, are nourished in a disordinate [*sic*] multitude." Crowds drew criminal interest – prostitutes and pickpockets – and might even constitute a direct threat to the Crown.

There were restrictions on performance during plague outbreaks, since large assemblies would indeed have promoted the spread of disease. England had been bedeviled with plague since the fourteenth century, and sporadic outbreaks, high death rates, quarantined households, as well as people fleeing to the countryside, continued to disrupt cultural and civic life, especially in London where the density of population produced rampant spread of infection.[43] The Lord Mayor of London, Sir Nicholas Woodrofe (or Wooderooffe), writing to Lord Burghley on June 17, 1580, argued that playhouses and other "houses of resort," such as bawdy houses and alehouses, exacerbated the problem by bringing God's wrath upon the city in the form of further visitations of the pestilence: "Some things have double the ill both naturally in spreading the infection, and otherwise in drawing God's wrathe and plague upon us, as the erecting and frequenting of houses very famous for incontinent rule out of our liberties and jurisdiction."[44]

While most of our own theatre-going experiences take place in the evening, and even if we attend a matinee, the performance invariably takes place in a darkened auditorium, a public theatre in early modern England was essentially an amphitheatre along the lines of a modern sports pavilion, although of vastly diminished proportions – the famous "wooden O" (Prologue.13)[45] referred to in *Henry V*. For all that, the polygonal structure of the Globe is thought to have held approximately three thousand spectators – a very considerable number given the population of early modern London. Plays were performed in the middle of the day on a stage that, although partially sheltered from the elements by a canopy, protruded out into the pit, right into the midst of the mass of spectators who had paid a penny for standing room around the stage. More affluent play-goers paid an extra penny for a seat in the upper gallery or threepence for a seat in the middle. Those who were as anxious to be seen as to see might sit on the stage itself. Shakespeare's other more up-scale theatrical venue, a private theatre, Blackfriars, was indoors, a hall-style space whose illumination depended on artificial lighting.

Early modern theatres like the Globe, and even the indoor Blackfriars, were very different theatrical spaces from the model that is still in most of our minds synonymous with what we think of as the stage. Our dominant idea of theatre is not only of an indoor space but includes the curtain and proscenium arch, or the elaborate stage sets that were *de rigueur* for most of the nineteenth and twentieth centuries. Shakespeare's stage was probably not quite "the Empty Space" of director Peter Brook's ideal.[46] In fact, the theatrical companies possessed a surprisingly large number of theatre properties. For all that, plays moved much more rapidly from scene to scene than in most modern productions of Shakespeare. The "two-hours traffic of our stage" (Prologue.12)[47] as the Chorus in *Romeo and Juliet* specifies for the duration of performance, bespeaks a very much smarter pace than most modern productions can muster. When we consider that many of Shakespeare's spectators were standing in the pit at the Globe, up-close to the theatrical action, and not averse to loudly expressing their displeasure, it seems unlikely that they would be taxed with unduly protracted dramatic action.[48] It is likely that plays performed indoors were longer because companies made use of act breaks while musicians played.[49]

Public theatre in the capital was booming. Phillip Henslowe, Burbage's counterpart and rival, built the Fortune, also south of the Thames, in 1600. There were numerous other theatres, including the Curtain (1577); the Rose (1587), which saw the staging of Shakespeare's *Henry VI* plays; the Red Bull (c.1604); the Swan (1595); the Boar's Head Inn (an inn converted to a theatre); the Hope; the Fortune (1600); the Cockpit, in which Shakespeare acted in Ben Jonson's *Sejanus* in 1603; and further afield in Newington Butts, a theatre was built in 1576. More than twenty-five thousand people attended plays each week when the season was at full flourish.[50] In addition, the private theatres, Whitefriars, Blackfriars, and the child actors of St Paul's, also fed the city's appetite for theatrical entertainment.

In Shakespeare's time, as the Lord Mayor pointed out in a letter to Sir Christopher Hatton in 1580, the City was a densely built urban environment: "This City being so overpressed with the multitudes, that the meaner sort are not able to live by one another,"[51] and playwrights depended on the exponential growth of London – its density of population and its new wealth – for their audiences. As Muriel Bradbrook once remarked, "Drama is the poetry of the City."[52]

# Notes

1   Robert Greene, *Greene's Groats-worth of Wit* (1592), sig. A3v.

2   William Shakespeare, *King Henry VI. Part 3: The Arden Shakespeare*, ed. Andrew S. Cairncross (London: Methuen, 1964).

3   For a helpful summary of the critical and historical arguments relating to the closing of the theatre, see N.W. Bawcutt, "Puritanism and the Closing of the Theatres in 1642," *Medieval and Renaissance Drama in England* 22 (2009): 179–200.

4   David Kastan, *Shakespeare after Theory* (London: Routledge, 1999), p. 204; Margot Heinemann, *Puritanism and Theatre: Thomas Middleton and Opposition Drama under the Early Stuarts* (Cambridge: Cambridge University Press, 1980), pp. 20, 34.

5   Quoted Richard Dutton, *Mastering the Revels* (Iowa City: University of Iowa Press, 1991), p. 29.

6   Gabriel Harvey, *Four Letters* (London, 1592), sig. B2.

7   For a full discussion of Nashe's possible authorship of *Greene's Groats-worth of Wit*, see Katherine Duncan-Jones, *Ungentle Shakespeare: Scenes from His Life* (London: Thomson Learning, 2001), pp. 43–53.

8   Thomas Nashe, *Pierce Pennilesse: his Supplication to the Divell* (1595) STC/18375, sig. A2v.

9 Duncan-Jones, *Ungentle Shakespeare*, pp. 43–53.

10 Thomas Nashe's preface to Robert Greene, *Greenes Arcadia or Menaphon* (1610) STC/122274 (first published in 1589 as *Menaphon*), sig. A2.

11 David Thomas, *Shakespeare in the Public Records* (London: Her Majesty's Stationary Office, 1985), p. 6. See also Samuel Schoenbaum, *William Shakespeare: A Compact Documentary Life* (New York: Oxford University Press, 1987), p. 199.

12 Charles Nicholl, *The Lodger Shakespeare: His Life on Silver Street* (New York: Penguin, 2007), p. 207.

13 John Aubrey quoted in *Ben Jonson*, ed. C.H. Herford, Percy Simpson, and Evelyn Simpson, 11 vols (Oxford: Clarendon Press, 1925–51), Vol. 1, p. 182.

14 Thomas Nashe, *Works*, ed. R.B. McKerrow (Oxford, 1958); *Pierce Pennilesse*, *Works*, Vol. 1, p. 212.

15 Quoted in Walter A. Raleigh, Sidney Lee, and C.T. Onions, eds, *Shakespeare's England*, 2 vols (Oxford: Clarendon Press, 1916), Vol. 1, p. 28.

16 E.K. Chambers, *The Elizabethan Stage*, 4 vols (Oxford, 1923), Vol. 4, p. 270; Dutton, *Mastering the Revels*, p. 26.

17 William Shakespeare, *As You Like It: The Arden Shakespeare*, ed. Juliet Dusinberre (London: Arden Shakespeare, 2006).

18 David Kathman, "Innyard Playhouses," in Richard Dutton, ed., *The Oxford Handbook of Early Modern Theatre* (Oxford: Oxford University Press) pp. 153–67 with special reference to p. 155.

19 David Kathman, "Alice Layston and the Cross Keys," *Medieval and Renaissance Drama in England* 22 (2009): 144–78 with special reference to p. 144.

20 David Kathman, "Innyard Playhouses," p. 153.

21 Kathman, "Alice Layston" pp. 167, 155.

22 Peter Thompson, *Shakespeare's Professional Career* (Cambridge: Cambridge University Press, 1992), pp. 58–60.

23 Dutton, *Mastering the Revels*, pp. 26, 28.

24 Andrew Gurr argues that Shakespeare's company had "conceived a management system that made its actors their own managers and financiers, creating the only effective democracy of its time in totalitarian England." Andrew Gurr, *The Shakespeare Company, 1594–1642* (Cambridge: Cambridge University Press, 2004), p. xiii.

25 J. Leeds Barroll observes: "The new patent that created Shakespeare and his fellows Servants of the King was largely irrelevant to their basic situation as common players . . ." *Politics, Plague, and Shakespeare's Theatre: The Stuart Years* (Ithaca: Cornell University Press, 1991), p. 14.

26 Samuel Schoenbaum, *Shakespeare's Lives* (Oxford: Clarendon Press, 1970), p. 55.

27 William Shakespeare, *Hamlet: The Texts of 1603 and 1623*, ed. Ann Thompson and Neil Taylor (London: Arden Shakespeare, 2006).

28 William Shakespeare, *Shakespeare's Sonnets: The Arden Shakespeare*, ed. Katherine Duncan-Jones (London: Methuen Drama, 2010).

29 William Shakespeare, *Julius Caesar: The Arden Shakespeare*, ed. David Daniell (London: Thomson Learning, 2004).

30 *John Stow's Survey of London (1598)* ed. C.L. Kingsford (Oxford: Clarendon Press, 1909), 2 vols.

31 Stephen Mullaney, *The Place of the Stage* (Ann Arbor: University of Michigan Press, 1995), p. 44.

32 Anne Begor Lancashire, *London Civic Theatre: City Drama and Pageantry from Roman Times to 1558* (Cambridge: Cambridge University Press, 2002); Tracey Hill, *Pageantry and Power: A Cultural History of the Early Modern Lord Mayor's*

*Show: 1585–1639* (Manchester: Manchester University Press, 2010).

33   Dutton, *Mastering the Revels*, p. 22.

34   Quoted in Dutton, *Mastering the Revels*, p. 22.

35   For a comprehensive account of print censorship in the period, see Cyndia Susan Clegg, *Press Censorship in Elizabethan England* (Cambridge: Cambridge University Press 1997) and Cyndia Susan Clegg, *Press Censorship in Jacobean England* (Cambridge: Cambridge University Press 2001).

36   Debora Shuger, *Censorship and Cultural Sensibility: The Regulation of Language in Tudor–Stuart England* (Philadelphia: University of Pennsylvania Press, 2006), p. 64.

37   See Richard Dutton, "Jurisdiction of Theater and Censorship," in Arthur Kinney, ed., *A Companion to Renaissance Drama* (Oxford: Blackwell, 2002), p. 232.

38   Thomas Nashe, *Pierce Pennilesse: his Supplication to the Divell (1595) STC.* 18375, sig. A2v. On the critical debates about censorship see Richard Dutton's Preface to *Licensing, Censorship and Authorship in Early Modern England: Buggeswords* (New York: Palgrave 2000), pp. ix–xx.

39   See Donaldson, "Jonson, Benjamin," *ODNB*.

40   Chambers, *Elizabethan Stage*, Vol. 2, p. 205.

41   See Janet Clare, *Art Made Tongue-Tied* (Manchester: University of Manchester Press, 1990), p. 30

42   Chambers, *Elizabethan Stage*, Vol. 2, pp. 87–8; Dutton, *Mastering the Revels*, p. 28.

43   For a comprehensive account of the plague, especially in relation to Shakespeare's Jacobean period, see Barroll, *Politics*.

44   Quoted in Mullaney, *Place of the Stage*, p. 49.

45   William Shakespeare, *Henry V*, ed. T.W. Craik (New York: Routledge, 1995).

46   Peter Brook, *The Empty Space* (Harmondsworth: Penguin, 1968), pp. 105–7.

47   William Shakespeare, *Romeo and Juliet: Texts and Contexts*, ed. Dympna Callaghan (Boston: Bedford/St. Martin's, 2003).

48   Andrew Gurr argues that plays lasted between two and three hours in *The Shakespearian Playing Companies* (Oxford: Clarendon Press, 1996), pp. 8–12.

49   Gurr, *Shakespearian Playing Companies*, p. 81.

50   Figures quoted are from James Shapiro, *A Year in the Life of William Shakespeare: 1599* (New York: Columbia University Press 2005), p. 9.

51   Sir Nicholas Harris Nicolas, *Memoirs of the Life and Times of Sir Christopher Hatton, K.G.* (London: 1847), p. 145.

52   M.C. Bradbrook, *English Dramatic Form: A History of its Development* (London: Chatto and Windus, 1965), p. 41.

# PART II

# THE PLAYS

# 6

# COMEDIES
## Shakespeare's Social Life

### *The Comedy of Errors*

Shakespeare had two sisters named Joan. The first was the eldest child of John and Mary Shakespeare and was christened on September 15, 1558: "Jone Shakspere daughter to John Shakspere."[1] A second Joan was baptized eleven years later on April 15, 1569. This oddity is typically dismissed by means of the explanation that the first girl must have died before the second was born, although since her burial record does not survive, we do not know this for a fact.[2] Since the first Joan never again appears in the historical record, however, we must assume that she did indeed die. The practice of giving a child the same name as a dead sibling probably strikes most modern sensibilities as profoundly macabre. Yet, this was not how Elizabethans would have regarded the matter

*Who Was William Shakespeare?: An Introduction to the Life and Works*, First Edition.
Dympna Callaghan.
© 2013 John Wiley & Sons, Ltd. Published 2013 by John Wiley & Sons, Ltd.

since they both recycled names of deceased siblings and duplicated names of living children within the same family without our deference to names as markers of implacably individual identity. However, while Shakespeare's two Joans pass without much comment on the grounds of historical difference, the same cannot be said about the duplicate names in *The Comedy of Errors*. Unlike Shakespeare's other great twin play, *Twelfth Night*, with its more decorously comic fantasy of identical fraternal twinship whose distinct identities are nonetheless finally guaranteed not only by a difference in gender but also, and perhaps even more importantly, by different names (Viola and Sebastian), the duplicate names in *Errors* seem like comic overkill that was long held to be symptomatic of the play's weaknesses.

Why, then, did Shakespeare introduce the apparently outrageous implausibility of having two sets of same-sex twins in *The Comedy of Errors* who share the same names, one pair named Antipholus and the other named Dromio? Traditionally, the most common explanation has been that the play is believed to be one of Shakespeare's earliest plays, possibly written in 1589 or even earlier. With that, until the later twentieth century (when, as we shall see, both the play's date and its achievement were revisited) *Errors* was dismissed as "derivative, slapstick, [and] slight."[3]

Aristotle's telling remark in the *Poetics* that while the origins of tragedy as a genre were well established, those of comedy remained obscure "because it was not at first treated seriously"[4] might well be applied to *The Comedy of Errors*. Taking its cue from Aristotle, this section will explore the grounds for taking this hilarious comedy seriously and for reading it historically, and will examine in particular the cultural ramifications of the common early modern practice of duplicate naming.

The insistently implausible plot of *Errors* begins twenty-three years before the action of the play when Egeon and his wife, Emilia, became the parents of identical twin boys. The same night they were born, in the self-same inn, another set of identical twins was born to an impoverished family, and these children were bought by Egeon to become servants to his own sons. Alas, while the family was on voyage at sea, when the children were still infants, they were separated when a rock split the ship cleanly in two. In this thoroughly symmetrical sundering, the mother, with one of her twin sons and one of the twin servants, was swept away on one half of the vessel, the father on the other with the other two children:

> For ere the ships could meet by twice five leagues,
> We were encounter'd by a mighty rock,
> Which being violently borne upon,

> Our helpful ship was splitted in the midst;
> So that in this unjust divorce of us,
> Fortune had left to both of us alike
> What to delight in, what to sorrow for. (1.1.100–6).[5]

The initial multiplications – two sets of twins, two people named Antipholus and two named Dromio – is comic, in the ancient tradition in which fecundity and increase, along with accumulation, abundance, bounty, and excess, are cause for joy and laughter, because they are associated with survival. However, the subsequent division, isolation, and separation effected by the shipwreck are associated with death and are traditionally the matter of tragedy. Events are described in terms of an arithmetical language. Thus, the ships are not ten leagues away from one another but "twice five" (1.1.100). Indeed, division, addition, and multiplication as concepts applied to human life are precisely what the play is about. These are the mathematical deviations, the "errors," or in the Latin meaning of *error*, a "wandering away," from unity and back to it again. These mathematical notions are closely related to the specifically artistic idea of mimetic depiction as a form of duplication, as in Hamlet's instructions to the players to "hold as 'twere the mirror up to Nature" (3.2.21–2).[6] However, just as a mirror reverses reality, the artistic image – whether painterly or poetic – also deviates from the original either because it is a fictionalized rendition of nature or because the artist lacks the technical skill to achieve mimetic exacti-tude. What gives *Errors*, even in its darker moments, an insistently comic cast is that there is an emphasis on duplication and multiplication even in the midst of catastrophe, when we might more properly expect loss, subtraction, division, and decrease.

Egeon of Syracuse narrates the story of the shipwreck at the opening of the play because he must explain to the Duke of Ephesus why he is there, in viola-tion of a decree that all Syracusians found in Ephesus must pay an exorbitant fine (which Egeon does not have the means to pay) or be subject to execution. The division and duplication on which the play is premised is especially evident in Egeon's opening narrative. He recounts the parted family's rescue by two different boats, with the result that they have been separated ever since. Egeon has lived in Syracuse with his son and his son's servant, but when the Syracusian Antipholus turned eighteen, his curiosity led him to go, with his servant, in search of his brother. Fearful that he had lost his only remaining son, Egeon then set out in search of him, and as the opening of the play informs us, has been seeking for him throughout the past five years "in farthest Greece" and "clean through the bounds of Asia" (1.1.132–3). Egeon is taken off to prison, resigned to his fate, not knowing the whereabouts of either of his sons. The Syracusian Antipholus and Dromio are alive and well and have just arrived in Ephesus, though they are unaware of the existence of their Ephesian counterparts.

Crucially, in Ephesus things divide and multiply at a prodigious, almost supernatural, rate within the structure of the classical unities of time and place (all the events of the play occur in the course of one day in one place) that Shakespeare typically does not observe. Antipholus of Ephesus is thriving with a well-established life in which his unwitting brother becomes enmeshed. The former is married to Adriana, who is much troubled by his infidelity, and Dromio of Ephesus is betrothed to a decidedly uncomely kitchen wench. When the bachelors from Syracuse find themselves addressed by name by strangers, they believe some sort of magic is at work. Adriana invites the wrong Antipholus to supper (only to have him court Luciana, her sister) and inadvertently locks her real husband out of the house, so that he dines with the courtesan instead. When the Dromio twins get paired up with the wrong masters and when merchants demand payment for a gold chain provided to Antipholus of Syracuse instead of Antipholus of Ephesus, the problem of personal identity takes on a further social dimension. The play proceeds at a helter-skelter pace through such scenes of misrecognition and mistaken identity – the "errors" named in the play's title. These are resolved by having both sets of twins together on stage at last – although we do not know how Shakespeare's twins were played in his lifetime, whether with two actors throughout, or with one actor briefly duplicated in the final scene. Whatever the case, as if to maximize, as well as to exaggerate and inflate the comic satisfaction of the end of the play, Antipholus of Syracuse is paired with Adriana's sister, and the abbess of the priory at Ephesus reveals herself to be none other than the mother of the Antipholi. Now united with his long-lost wife and family, Egeon is then spared his punishment, and the family and the servant Dromios are all together at last.

The frame of the play concerning Egeon and Emilia is from the Greek romance *Apollonius of Tyre*, a source Shakespeare used again in *Twelfth Night* and in the late play *Pericles*. The episode in which Adriana locks her husband out of the house is from Plautus's *Amphitruo*. However, Shakespeare borrowed the main outline of the plot from another Plautus play, *Menaechmi*. Plautus, in turn derived his plot from an earlier Greek source, a play called *Twins or As Like as Two Peas*. Instead of diminishing the play's implausibilities as he found them in Plautus, where one of the twins becomes lost in a crowd, what is interesting about Shakespeare's version is that he chose to compound them, adding, for instance, the second set of twins. Among Shakespeare's other sources is *The Pattern of Painful Adventures* (1576) by the uncannily named Laurence Twine, a book whose title anticipates Sigmund Freud's work on recurrence. Freud was concerned with the tendency to repeat and replay distressing events or circumstances that have previously been the cause of emotional and psychological anguish. Repetition and onomastic coincidence intimate the degree to which veracity and facticity are rarely life-like. Interestingly, this is exactly what Dionysius Lambinus, the early modern editor of Shakespeare's Plautine source, observed: "*quo id credit, quod non est: non credit quod est*" / "one believes that which is not true and does not believe that which is."[7] Further, the imitation of life or nature for artistic and literary purposes is overshadowed by the notion that it is in some way a deception of the senses. When presented with the two Antipholi at the end of the play, Adriana, the wife of Antipholus of Ephesus, declares, "I see two husbands, or mine eyes deceive me" (5.1.331).

In *The Comedy of Errors*, most of the characters, as is appropriate to the genre in which they are written, are comically two-dimensional, although they remind us of the paradox tragically discovered by Narcissus when he drowned in his own watery reflection, namely that surfaces are not ultimately superficial. Shakespeare's twins in *Errors* are like mirror images, characters that trick us into perceiving depth when we are in fact looking only at a two-dimensional surface. The play's comic complication arises from the fact that each set of twins shares both a physiological identity with his brother and a name. The duke's confusion, "I know not which is which" (5.1.364), gestures toward the perceptual error incumbent upon the way art imitates reality – which came first, which is real or original, and which is the copy?

At the play's opening, Egeon confusingly suggests the difference between his sons is birth order – in other words that temporal progression distinguishes identities. However, Antipholus of Ephesus is described as "the latter-born" (1.1.78), but later in the same scene Egeon claims his Syracusian brother as "my youngest boy" (1.1.124). However *any* distinction (older/younger, married/single, etc.) is annulled by their single onomastic identity, the bizarre fact that the Syracusians have retained the names of their Ephesian counterparts and vice versa. This represents an important deviation from Shakespeare's Plautine source where the father had traveled abroad with only one child, whom he then lost at a festival, only then giving the boy who remained in Syracuse his brother's name.

For all that, the fact that two sets of twins have the same name is intended to be comic, and duplicate naming appears to be the place where Shakespeare most definitively parts company with social reality. However, no matter how bizarre it seems to us, committed as we are to the concepts of development of a fully individuated identity as fundamental to psychological well-being, it is nonetheless the case that in early modern England, people gave the same name to different children in the same family. Very often the name of a child who had died and who had been christened after its parent, grandparent, or godparent was used again for a later infant. Thus it was that, for example,

Ben Jonson had two sons named Ben. However, there are numerous instances where this was done even when one child had not died, almost in anticipation of such a tragedy, or as insurance against it, thus giving two siblings the same name. Interestingly, the practice of duplicate naming applied mainly to boys.[8] It was a practice that reflected a desire to remember and also to honor parents, in-laws, and other relatives, but there is also what we might call a psycho-cultural sense in which replicating names was stimulated by a fear of impending loss.

There were cases where a surviving parent returned to the same name for a child with a new spouse. Thus, Sir Edmund Ludlow (d.1624) named the first sons by each of his two wives "Henry," making them half-brothers with the same name. The eldest apparently became a member of Parliament in 1601 and 1604, and died in 1639, while the younger became Sir Henry Ludlow, MP in 1640 (d.1643). We also find brothers with the same name who have the same father *and* mother. In the Sparke family of Plymouth, both John Sparke's father and his paternal uncle (i.e. his father's brother) were named John. Each man, father and uncle, reached the age of at least thirty, dying in 1603 and 1597 respectively, and they were undoubtedly contemporaries.[9] Similarly, John Barton and his brother both became prominent lawyers and both sat in Parliament. (Presumably in the family, the elder would have been referred to as John, while his brother might have been called by a diminutive, such as "Jenkin").[10] Another case is that of the Speaker of the House of Commons, John Wood, whose heir was his brother John, who also sat in Parliament. Serjeant at law, John Hoskins had a younger brother, a Church of England clergyman also called John. John Stow of the famous Chronicles of London had a younger brother named John Stow. In yet another example, Sir Richard White MP, had an older brother also named Richard, and both Richards had the same parents and both men reached adulthood.[11] Incidentally, the younger Richard was a servant of Shakespeare's patron, the Earl of Southampton, a fact whose relevance to Shakespeare's play may be quite direct since Southampton was also a member of Gray's Inn, where *The Comedy of Errors* was performed for the Christmas festivities in 1594.[12] At any rate, these examples demonstrate the contention that "the duplicability of names, the fact that they can have multiple referents, prevents them being a reliable marker of identity."[13]

Chief among the play's few but telling exceptions to the principle of two-dimensionality is Adriana, the aggrieved wife of Antipholus of Ephesus, who seems like a "real" individual. Adriana is a figure much amplified from Shakespeare's source. She makes a moving plea, in eloquent verse, for the return of her erring husband's love in lines that endow her with an emotional and psychological complexity that far exceed the typical characterizations of farce:[14]

> Ah, do not tear away thyself from me;
> For know, my love, as easy mayst thou fall
> A drop of water in the breaking gulf,
> And take unmingled thence that drop again
> Without addition or diminishing,
> As take from me thyself, and not me too (2.2.124–9).

She speaks from a specifically Christian understanding of sexual relations derived from St Paul, and every churchgoer in England knew the Letter to the Ephesians (and, perforce, everyone *was* a churchgoer). Paul famously used a somatic analogy to describe the husband as the head to whom the wife should submit even while urging the reciprocal duties of husbands. Adriana tells her husband that he can no more separate himself from her than a drop of water poured into the ocean can be retrieved again. In a sense, her argument for marital unity reminds him that his former, discrete identity as a bachelor is forever lost.

In her plea for the integrity of marriage: "easy mayst thou fall . . . / And take unmingled thence that drop again," Adriana refers the audience back to the watery history of the characters outlined earlier in the play, of which the audience is aware, but of which Adriana herself knows nothing. When the travelling Antipholus arrived in Ephesus in Act 1 in search of his lost brother, he announced, "I to the world am like a drop of water / That in the ocean seeks another drop" (1.2.35–6). Montaigne's essay "Of the Resemblance Between Children and Fathers" (John Florio's translation was published in 1603) pondered the complexities of genetic inheritance encapsulated in a drop of seminal fluid. He used imagery strikingly similar to that of *The Comedy of Errors*:

> Wee need not go to cull out myracles, and choose strange difficulties: me seemeth, that amongst those things we ordinarily see, there [in Nature] are such incomprehensible rarities, as they exceed all difficultie of miracles. What monster is it that this *tear or drop of seede*, whereof we are ingendred brings with it; and in it the impressions, not only of the corporall forme, but even of the very thoughts and inclinations of our fathers? Where doth this *droppe of water* containe or lodge this infinite number of forms? And how bear they these resemblances, of so rash, and unruly a progress, that the child's chile shall be answerable to [look like] his grandfather, and the nephew to his uncle? (my emphasis)[15]

Note again the similarity to Adriana's line: "easy mayst thou fall . . . / And take unmingled thence that drop again / Without addition or diminishing." Further, "Addition" refers us to the complex algebra of multiple births and "diminishing" to the tragic subtractions of the shipwreck, as well as to the body of water in which Egeon and Emilia proved far from inseparable from one another. Shakespeare forged a further thematic link relating to marriage and identity by describing the parents of Antipholi as being "*divorced*" by the shipwreck:

> Our helpful ship was splitted in the midst;
> So that in this unjust *divorce* of us
> Fortune had left to *both of us alike,*
> What to delight in, what to sorrow for. (1.1.103–6, my emphasis)

Egeon and Emilia have here become like the twins "both . . . alike" – "Fortune had left to *both of us alike*" – even as they are severed from one another. In other words, their separation, their sorrow, has compounded their affinity. In this clever analogy, a married couple become like twins – almost literalizing the old adage that people who live together start to look alike by dint of long and intimate association.

In *The Comedy of Errors*, the search for one's other self bespeaks the fear we will never be known even in our most intimate relationships and simultaneously dread that we will be discovered in all our hideous inadequacy. The fantasy is that this could be resolved if only we could meet someone "just like us." One of the questions the play raises is, if we met our "other half," would that other half be our mirror image or our antithesis, or would it be our twin sibling or our spouse? All of these possibilities are explored by the play. When the Dromios meet, Dromio of Syracuse is relieved that the fat kitchen wench "now shall be my sister, not my wife" (5.1.416), while Dromio of Ephesus remarks, "Methinks you are my glass, and not my brother" (5.1.417). At the ending of *Errors*, in some productions, while the servant Dromio characters pair up happily, the Antipholi are, as they are in the text, somewhat wary and distrustful of one another. People who look alike are not necessarily alike in other ways, as Montaigne points out, "never were there two opinions in the world alike, no more than two haires or two grains."[16]

In the theatre, the challenge and opportunity presented by this play lies in the way the flat surface of farce is used to extrapolate the most profound dimensions of human identity as twinning represents issues of both multiplied and divided identity – do the twins represent a divided whole, that is, halves of one complete identity, one divided by two? Or do they represent addition, one plus one equals two? Comparisons may be invidious but we make them all the time. Antipholus the married man is different from Antipholus the bachelor, even as he is just like him. Shakespeare probes this way we have of constantly processing the world, considering how like or unlike one thing is to another, or more importantly, one person is to another. When the twins are brought together at the end of *The Comedy of Errors*, assuming that only one of the pair is real while the other is some sort of apparition, the alarmed duke inquires, "And so of these, which is the natural man, / And which the spirit? Who deciphers them?" (5.1.333–4).

The duke's confusion at the end of the play arises from his assumption that one identity has been divided rather than doubled. Shakespeare extends this conundrum inherent in the sibling relationship of the twins by juxtaposing it with the idea of conjugal identity where, to reiterate the biblical sense so pervasive in the Renaissance, the two become one flesh (Ephesians 5.31), a new, metaphysically indivisible identity.[17] This is precisely Adriana's argument about how Antipholus can never really regain his former identity as a single individual. This idea has its roots in the *Symposium* of Plato (428 – 327 BC), where he tells Aristophanes' story that all human beings were once quadrupeds, male and female conjoined in one creature, who were split in half when they incurred the wrath of the gods. From that time on, humans were destined to search and long for the lost part of themselves. In light of Plato's ontology, the conjugal relationship becomes an attempted recovery of a perceived loss, and is, in some sense, a reenactment of the original, founding moment of identity. However, in this story, the process of splitting off itself both generates identity and propagates art – as a separated, reflective dimension of reality.

Shakespeare addresses the big philosophical questions in *The Comedy of Errors*: How do we know who we are? Who do we think we are? and What is the source of our longing to be recognized? However, he also poses as a fundamental theatrical problem familiar to all (honest) spectators, namely the difficulty of telling characters apart. After all, who has never (except possibly my husband) leaned over to ask a companion at the cinema, "Is he the bald one who killed the blond woman, or is that the other bald one?" Shakespeare's play, then, addresses absolutely practical and fundamentally theatrical issues about character identification, as well as the more troubling issues of what constitutes individual onomastic identity.

The play offers a utopian comic resolution to these issues via the Dromio twins, who are the very last to leave the stage. They exit after a discussion about how they should determine seniority and thus who should go first, the Syracuse Dromio cheerfully deferring to his brother. Then, however, the pair hit upon a happy resolution to their ostensibly irreconcilable similarities:

> We came into the world like brother and brother,
> And now let's go hand in hand, not one before another. (5.1.425–6).

The play must have been popular because, if it was indeed an early composition, it was still being performed at court in 1604. (It was not printed until the

First Folio of 1623.) The play has continued to enjoy considerable success in recent performance. James Cellan-Jones's 1983 production, set in the *comedia del arte* tradition and starring Roger Daltrey of The Who as Dromio times two, demonstrated that the play could be hilarious rather than silly, while Tim Supple's acclaimed 1996 Royal Shakespeare Company production at Stratford's Other Place and at the Old Vic emphasized the play's tragic dimensions as much as its hurly-burly farce. Such productions show that a different kind of complexity can emerge from the interactions of the depthless comic characters who populate this play than from those characters whom Shakespeare so adeptly endows with an apparently real inner life and fully developed thoughts and feelings. These impressive productions reignited a critical interest in the play that is consistent with the predominant aesthetic attributes of postmodernity, namely image, surface, and the accelerated temporality of the modern world. These qualities constitute the antithesis of the slow-depth and profundity that were conventionally assumed to be the predominant constituents not only of great works of art, but also of individuals themselves. This shift has allowed reassessment of the merits of a play that interrogates at break-neck pace precisely such understandings of identity.

A final aspect of the case for *Errors* as a play that merits more sustained critical attention is the claim that the play is not an early work but was in fact written for the play's first recorded performance during the Christmas season of 1594, when the new theatrical company of the Lord Chamberlain's Men performed it at Gray's Inn.[18] If this dating is correct, it would mean that Shakespeare wrote this rambunctious, knock-about comedy around the time that he was working on what he called the "graver labor" of the narrative poem, *The Rape of Lucrece*, and only a year after *Romeo and Juliet* and *A Midsummer Night's Dream*.[19] This compositional context, then, challenges the conventional narrative of Shakespeare's development as a writer for whom *Errors* was nothing more than an apprentice piece.

## *The Taming of the Shrew*

Because it marks the beginning of his professional career, and because Shakespeare's life can be examined with the advantage of a few hundred years of hindsight, his arrival in London appears to be the most momentous and consequential transition of his life. The greatest step of a lifetime as most Elizabethans understood it, however, was not a professional one. It was, on the contrary, the moment when individuals entered into what the Book of Common Prayer referred to as "the holy estate of matrimony." In our own day, financial and social status, and even sex itself can be quite unrelated to marriage, but in early modern England conjugality more often wrought powerful and conspicuous economic, social, and personal transformation. Significantly, Shakespeare did not make this momentous transition from bachelor to married man in London, but instead made a provincial match (perhaps, given Anne's pregnancy, of necessity rather than choice) in the county he grew up in. It is, then, arguably not a coincidence that in a play about precisely the transition from the single state, "the life that late I led," $(4.1.120)^1$ to the married one, Shakespeare begins in his home county of Warwickshire with a beggar, Christopher Sly from Burton Heath near Stratford. Indeed, in *Shrew*, Shakespeare juxtaposes, in a single play, the homely, provincial world that served as the background to his own nuptials, with the more literary and generally foreign settings that are the locations of his other plays.

The ur-text of transition and sudden transformation was Shakespeare's favorite, Ovid's *Metamorphoses*, translated by Arthur Golding in 1567. Shakespeare's references to it, especially in the Induction scenes that frame the main action, this chapter will argue, offer important clues about how we are to interpret this perplexing play. Even more important, however, is the way Ovidian transformation informs every aspect of the text. Like Ovid, in *Shrew* Shakespeare invites us to consider the mystery of metamorphosis, but unlike Ovid, he does so within an insistently social context of subjugation. This was a pressing and perennial early modern problem: how could unruly subordinates – whether political rebels or domestic ones (wives, servants, animals) – be compelled to obey? The most common answer to that question in Shakespeare's world was that violence or threat of it was the only means of ensuring obedience. However, *Shrew* poses further questions as to whether transformation from unruliness to compliance – wrought by taming, training, or teaching (all modes of transformation present in the play) can ever really be effected from the outside; about whether one person's will can truly subdue another's, or whether, in the case of human beings at least, genuine transformation only ever occurs from within.

In concert with the provincial setting of the Induction scenes, the very title of *The Taming of the Shrew* alludes to the decidedly unglamorous household problem of rodent infestation. A shrew is a small gnawing mammal known for its long pointed snout and sharp, high-pitched squeal. These "nosy," noisy pests fit perfectly the period's misogynous image of the unruly woman, known then – and now – as a shrew. Although possessed of a vicious bite, shrews could be put in their place and stomped underfoot. In this sense, the threat or danger they presented was not very serious. While hawks or dogs or horses might be tamed, pesky vermin would undoubtedly be exterminated rather than accommodated into domestic life in the manner of more tractable beasts. This makes the play's title something of an oxymoron; further, *taming* indicates that this is *not* a comedy of courtship. Typically in comedy, the plot achieves wedlock as a final outcome, but instead this play is a somewhat anomalous *comedy of marriage* that focuses on a specific aspect of marital union, namely the *transition* from the single state to the married one. In grand settings such as palaces and great country estates where marital discord was unlikely to trouble neighbors, the story is over once conjugal and dynastic alliance has been cemented. In contrast, the social cohesiveness of everyday life among ordinary mortals required marital harmony so that even though the main body of *Shrew* takes place in the rather exotic environs of Padua, it nonetheless retains a domestic flavor.

In *Shrew* the process of entering into the married state is precisely a process of submission to authority, a struggle for power and the achievement of male dominance. The shrew of the title role, Katherine, or "Kate," the elder daughter of Baptista Minola, a wealthy merchant of Padua, is a termagant who takes out her rage upon anyone who comes within her orbit, but especially on her younger sister, the beautiful and eminently marriageable Bianca, with whom the young Lucentio has fallen in love. However, the girls' father has stipulated that Bianca will not be permitted to marry until Katherine has a husband. This provides the incentive for Bianca's suitors to find someone who will marry her truculent sister. Fortunately, one of them, Hortensio, has a friend, the belligerent, eccentric Petruchio, "a mad-brain rudesby" (3.2.10), who is newly arrived from Verona and whose only motivation in marriage is wealth. Despite refusing and resisting Petruchio's suit, when he seemingly fails to arrive at the church for their wedding (he does eventually turn up, late and in tatters) Kate experiences the anguish of public humiliation. Indeed, this incident is but one element of a carefully planned strategy to "tame" Kate. After undergoing a series of fairly brutal ordeals designed to break her spirit, Kate capitulates. Her transformation occurs in Act 4, at the point when the wedding is over and the marriage has begun. In Act 4, Scene1 Petruchio starves Kate and deprives her of sleep, and in Act 4, Scene 3 a tailor makes her fine clothes, but Petruchio rips them to rags claiming that they are ill-made and inadequate. Petruchio does all of this under cover of being a solicitous husband: "This is a way to kill a wife with kindness" (4.1.188), he confesses to the audience in a Machiavellian soliloquy at the end of the scene that draws attention to political sovereignty and household government: "Thus have I politicly begun my reign" (4.1.168). By the last scene of Act 4, Petruchio has won the war of attrition, having successfully executed his plan to domesticate his wife. Hitherto, she had insisted on her independent identity, a sense of autonomy that was encapsulated onomastically: "They call me Katherine that do talk of me" (2.1.182). By the end of Act 4, however, Petruchio seems to have achieved his earlier stated purpose of bringing her "from a wild Kate to a Kate / Conformable as other household Kates" (2.1.269–70). In a dramatic turning point, Kate surrenders to her husband's right to name the world (reminiscent of Adam's God-given power in Genesis) and swears the sun is the moon and an old man is a maid because "What you will have it named, even that it is, / And so shall it be so for Katherine" (4.5.22–3). This victory, however, is arguably qualified by the fact that she still announces her identity as "Katherine" rather than as "Kate."

At the end of the play, when the husbands make a wager on whose wife is most docile, Kate is able to perform abject compliance to her husband's will in a way that neither her sister (who eloped with Lucentio and married him without the knowledge or consent of her father), nor the widow who has married Hortensio can match. What is clear is that Kate and Petruchio's marriage is a legitimate union, fully sanctioned by Baptista and that it has produced an obedient wife (be that obedience real or feigned) whereas Bianca's elopement with Lucentio is, even at the wedding feast, already producing marital discord. This is all the more surprising because at the beginning of the play, Bianca's virtues seemed to conform perfectly to the Renaissance ideal of docile femininity.

The play offers no real clue about whether Katherine's submission is pretended or genuine, or about whether she is merely overpowered by her husband's will, or whether her acquiescence is voluntary. Thus, we do not know if this initially hostile alliance has grown into a love match. This is not a play that provides deep insights into the thoughts and feelings of its characters, but rather carefully keeps them at a distance, revealing only the caricatures of humanity that are appropriate to the kind of rambunctious comedy that conforms to the specifications of farce. This distancing is much facilitated by the Induction scenes that serve as a link between the English work-a-day world, the familiar, the petty, the everyday culture that produced the folkloric shrew-taming stories, and the Italianate comedy of the rest of the play.

In the Induction, the drunken beggar Christopher Sly is quarreling with the hostess of a tavern to whom he offers physical violence: "I'll pheeze you" (Induction 1.1). This is a prelude to the battle of the sexes that is the subject of the body of the play. Sly is found sleeping it off by a lord and his companions. They contrive to play a trick on him so that when he wakes they will make him believe he is himself a lord who has been gravely ill and lost his memory. Key to their contrivance is the role of Sly's supposedly aristocratic wife, who is to be played by the page, Bartholomew. A prelude to the main plot, where an unruly woman is trained in how to become a wife, Bartholomew will take instruction from one of the company of traveling players on how to behave like a proper lady: "Such duty to the drunkard let him do / With soft low tongue, and lowly courtesy" (Induction 1.109–10). These instructions remind the audience both that this is a transvestite stage, which requires as a structural principle the feigned transformation of sexual identity, and that being a wife is a role created by social expectations. The Induction plays out the way that social convention requires of women not only appropriate conduct but also the enactment of a fundamentally masculine, patriarchal ideal of womanhood. Being soft-spoken and submissive are the two behaviors marked as key to the effective performance of aristocratic womanhood. While the visual aspect of playing the woman's part was relatively easy to achieve, the female voice presented a formidable obstacle to convincing female impersonation on the early modern stage. Further, although conduct literature continually urged women to be "chaste, silent, and obedient," qualities that were also construed as synonymous, the female tongue was an ever-present reminder of women's own power and agency. The lord's remark on the elocution lesson to be given to Bartholomew is also reminiscent of Lear's lament for Cordelia, the daughter who had "Nothing" to say in response to his command to say how much she loved him: "her voice was ever soft / Gentle and low an excellent thing in a woman" (*King Lear* 5.3.270–1).[2] When the lord instructs that Bartholomew's impersonation should also include explicitly sexual behavior "kind embracements, tempting kisses" (Induction 1.114), he draws attention to the very "lewd" practices for which some of Shakespeare's contemporaries condemned the stage for its defiance of the biblical proscription against men donning "women's raiment" (Deuteronomy 22.5). The lord's directions also amplify the idea of the kind of behavior men expect from women, and potentially imply that his power over his subordinate has gone too far. There are indeed a range of performance and interpretive possibilities inherent in this scene, from the benign to the sinister. Is the lord offering theatrical direction: "I know the boy will well usurp the grace / Voice, gait, and action of a gentlewoman"? (Induction 1.127–28). Or is he a master abusing his authority over his young servant?

The Induction ends when the players perform a play – which is, of course, *The Taming of the Shrew*, and Sly soon sits to "mark" the play (1.1.247). The presence of observers onstage thus serves to further remind the audience that what they see is the product of artifice, verisimilitude, that is, the appearance of reality rather than reality itself. From an Ovidian point of view, the lord's control over Sly's reality and Bartholomew's behavior is reminiscent of the abuse of power, which is Jove's absolute prerogative in the *Metamorphoses*. As Shakespeare puts it in the late romance play *Pericles*: "And if Jove stray, who dare say Jove doth ill?" (1.1.105).[3] Jove's dominion is often enacted as rape, that is, as the imposition of his sexual desires without regard to the will of those he violates. Similarly, Sly is offered sexual entitlements when he awakens to transformed external circumstances:

> Or wilt thou sleep? We'll have thee to a couch
> Softer and sweeter than the lustful bed
> On purpose trimmed up for Semiramis. (Induction 2.35–7)

The very name of the Assyrian queen, Semiramis, was synonymous with sexual indulgence and erotic adventure, but also, interestingly, with specifically female sexual power and prowess. Sly is certainly eager to accept this aristocratic privilege. When his "wife," the cross-dressed Bartholomew inquires, "What is thy will?" Sly's first command in his new role is: "Madam, undress you and come now to bed" (Induction 2.113). Indeed, the aesthetic and the erotic are frequently aligned in the Induction, especially around painted versions of stories from the *Metamorphoses*:

> Dost thou love pictures? We will fetch thee straight
> Adonis painted by a running brook,
> And Cytherea all in sedges hid,
> Which seem to move and wanton with her breath
> Even as the waving sedges play with wind. (Induction 2.47–51)

Ovid's stories were popular subjects for European painting, and here include the ideal in both masculine (Adonis) and feminine form (Cytherea or Venus). The latter is naked and hidden only by reeds whose appearance of movement is itself erotic. Subsequent topics for art offered to Sly are freighted with more disturbing connotations than that of mere voyeurism offered in the first description of painting:

> We'll show thee Io as she was a maid,
> And how she was beguilèd and surprised,
> As lively painted as the deed was done. (Induction 2.52–4)

"Beguilèd" and "surprised" are the sugar-coated euphemisms for deception and rape. That a vivid depiction of sexual violation is the matter for art prepares the audience for the spectacle of sexual control they are about to see in the main plot. For all that, the metamorphoses entailed in the story of Io involve not only another instance of how cunningly rapine Jove effects a sexually violent intrusion into the mortal realm where he preys upon his hapless female victims (in this case by means of a change in the weather, a dense fog) but also the transformation of Io from "maid" to ravished woman:

> . . . Jove intending now in vaine no longer tyme to lose,
> Upon the country all about did bring a foggie mist,
> And caught the maiden, whom poore foole, he used as he list.
>
> (*Metamorphoses*, 1.742–4)[4]

When Jove's jealous wife finds out, Io is changed again, this time from woman to cow, who bereft of the definitively human power of speech, can only complain by lowing like a beast. Io is especially interesting because while most subjects of transformation never recover their former fully human identity, Io does become human again:

> . . . Io took her native shape in which she first was borne,
> And eke became the selfsame thing the which she was beforne.
> For by and by she cast away her rough and hairy hide,
> Instead whereof a soft smooth skinne with tender flesh did bide . . .
> In fine, no likeness of a Cow save whiteness did remain.
>
> (*Metamorphoses*, 1.924–7, 932)

This later stage in Io's transformation is undeniably an improvement on her bestial condition, and arguably it is, perhaps, this part of Ovid's story that correlates with the main plot where the "rough" Kate learns how to be mild. However, while Io is fully restored, even in her recovered form, she remains afraid to speak:

> And though she gladly would have spoke: yet durst she not so do,
> Without goode heed, for fear she should have lowed like a Cow.
> And therefore softly with her selfe she gan to practice how
> Distinctly to pronounce her words that intermit[tent] were.
>
> (*Metamorphoses*, 1.935–8)

The reference to Io looks forward to the subjugation of Kate in the main plot as well as backwards to the "voices" of animals described when the lord and his hunting party first encounter Sly, particularly an unnamed bitch (the other dogs have names) who bays deeply: "the deep-mouthed brach" (Induction 1.14).

The final painting described to Sly is Apollo's attempted rape of Daphne, who is, so to speak, the one who got away in classical mythology:

> . . . Daphne roaming through a thorny wood,
> Scratching her legs that one shall swear she bleeds,
> And at that sight shall sad Apollo weep,
> So workmanly the blood and tears are drawn. (Induction 2.55–8)

The depiction of a bleeding Daphne, scratched by thorns as she tries to flee from her pursuer, suggests her victimization. In Ovid, Apollo tells Daphne that neither her own desires nor even her father's approval are relevant: "Thy will and his consent are nothing in this case" (*Metamorphoses*, 1.592). Like other

Ovidian allusions, here the story of Daphne prepares the audience for the main plot where Petruchio overrides the will of a very willful Kate, but additionally suggests that his success in doing so may not be as complete as it seems. In flight from her rapacious pursuer, Daphne prays that she will not be forced to cede her chastity. Her prayer is granted, but at a price: she escapes Apollo but instead of liberation, she achieves only another form of containment by being turned into a tree.

All of these episodes from Book 1 of the *Metamorphoses* suggest distinct but related ways of understanding – and problematizing – the main body of the play and the kinds of transformation that occur there. Act 1, Scene 1 further picks up on these references to the *Metamorphoses* when Lucentio first sets eyes on Bianca:

> O yes, I saw sweet beauty in her face,
> Such as the daughter of Agenor had,
> That made great Jove to humble him to her hand
> When with his knees he kissed the Cretan strand. (1.1.161–4)

The reference here is to the story of Europa, daughter of Agenor, who was abducted by Jove, who deceived her by taking on the guise of a bull:

> The fairest beast to looke upon that ever man beheld.
> For why? His colour was as white as any winter's snow
> Before that either trampling feet or southern winde it thow [thaw] . . .
> His hornes were small, but yet so fine as that ye would have thought
> They had bene made by cunning hand or out of wax bene wrought.
>
> (*Metamorphoses*, 2.1064–6, 1069–70)

Ovid presents the preposterous spectacle of a woman seduced by an extraordinarily good-looking bull and simultaneously emphasizes and annuls the connotations of bestiality by stressing the bull's attractiveness. He has no "grisly look" like other bulls "But so demure as friendship seemed to crave" (*Metamorphoses*, 2.1073–4). As a consequence of Jove's disguise and deception, Europa's defenses are down when her encourages her to pet and fondle, "stroke and coy," him while he licks her hands (*Metamorphoses*, 2.1084). This seduction by deception bears on the main plot of *Shrew* in that in one sense it is the antithesis of the more straightforward imposition of will that Petruchio employs on Kate. In another, however, this bovine deception is analogous to the plan "to kill a wife with kindness" (4.1.188).

This apparently casual reference to the Europa story offers a mythological gloss on assuming a false identity as a strategy of control that is key to the subplot itself, which is indebted to George Gascoigne's aptly titled *Supposes*

(1566). Lucentio and his servant Tranio switch roles so that the former can gain access to Bianca by purporting to be her Latin tutor in a fashion that recapitulates the metamorphosis of class identity that is the primary transformation of the Induction scenes. What particularly draws attention to this specifically as a class issue is that when Lucentio's father, Vincentio, arrives in Padua and discovers the fraud, he articulates fears shared by many early moderns about the potentially lethal consequences of subordinates seizing power: "He hath murdered his master!" (5.1.73). Of course, his fears are soon allayed. However, that they have been voiced at all reveals, albeit for a moment, the substructure of the social hierarchy that is not only vulnerable to violent overthrow but that is also alarmingly maintained by force, just as the glance at Europa reveals the potential violence of sexual hierarchy. Shakespeare, however, adds a twist to the Ovidian story when, at the end of the play, Bianca as a wife is no longer the docile, compliant girl she appeared to be when she was still a maiden. Thus it may be Bianca who really deceived Lucentio, while he revealed his true identity and his purpose in assuming the role of her tutor from the very beginning of their relationship. That Shakespeare inserts this Ovidian moment in the midst of Lucentio's otherwise orthodox and conventional expression of Petrarchan desire: "I burn, I pine," (1.1.149) also suggests the inherent perversity of desire and even its potential for deviance. By increments, Europa comes to trust the bull: "fear by little driven away," (*Metamorphoses*, 2.1083), but there is a critical moment when she decides to mount the bull (who at first merely paddles in the water at the sea shore) and too late realizes that escape is impossible: "where was no meanes to scape with life away" (*Metamorphoses*, 2.1092). In other words, bovine Jove trains his prey and deceives her into compliance with his will until she has no choice but to go along with his desires.

Shakespeare has thus embedded yet another Ovidian taming story that reflects on power relations between the sexes. This is "rape" in the now obsolete sense of abduction, although the distinction is far from absolute since, as in this case, abduction presumably precedes violation. In Golding's translation, Europa is now described as Jove's "pretty trull" (a prostitute) implying that she had lost her status as virgin and maiden at the moment the god had "Tane [taken] landing in the Ile of Crete" (3.3). Like Agenor, who is left to wonder about the fate of his daughter, Baptista is also the victim of deception, even if it is a deception in which, to quote John Donne's defense of his elopement with Anne Moore, both Lucentio and his daughter have "adventured equally."[5]

In early modern England, for a man, to "wive it wealthily" (1.2.73) meant to acquire the economic advantage of marrying a woman with a hefty dowry, which might be the biggest engine of transformation wrought by marriage. For a woman, in theory at least, intrinsic to this changed state from maid to wife was the loss of her virginity. However, one signally absent aspect of that transition in *Shrew* is any indication of consummation itself. We simply do not know if this is deferred until the end of Act 5. The text does not reveal whether Kate is tamed before the marriage is consummated, or whether specifically sexual subjugation is itself one of the methods of achieving spousal obedience. Petruchio's determination to prevail over Kate makes it clear that her consent is irrelevant: "Will you, nill you, I will marry you" (2.1.263). The process of humiliation after the nuptials, then, is potentially suggestive of something that could extend to – or be intrinsic to – this defining aspect of conjugality.

Certainly, in the play's induction, Sly has been made to believe not only that he is a lord but also that he has a young and attractive wife. He wants to be "off to bed" immediately. His "wife," however – the transvestized page, Bartholomew – fobs him off, and the two watch the play together instead. This strategy also renders the entire action of the main plot a form of belated consummation.

In an important sense, the issues raised by the play are not amenable to resolution because they are constituent parts of an on-going cultural debate about the status of women, the *querelle des femmes*, literally the argument about women, a vigorous debate in books and pamphlets about the nature, role, and status of women in early modern society. Material pertaining to this debate was published across Europe and translated into English. But England had its own homegrown varieties of the genre, such as Joseph Swetnam's *The Arraignment of Lewd, idle, froward, and unconstant women or the vanity of them* . . . First published in 1615, the pamphlet was reprinted again in 1615, 1619, 1628, 1634, 1645, and 1690. As was often the case in the *querelle*, Swetnam's publication provoked a reply, Rachel Speght's *A Mouzell for Melastomus; Jane Anger, her Protection for Women To defend them against the Scandalous Reports of a Late Surfeiting Lover* . . . (1589). What is fascinating about this debate, to which the accessibility of print lends energy, is that writers (who may have been real women or just men impersonating the offended sex) responded, defending women against charges that they were as Swetnam's title put it, "lewd, idle, froward [forward] and unconstant." Since the entire sex was deemed to possess such degenerate characteristics, it followed that women required absolute subjugation. The biblical origins of the power imbalance between the sexes rested first and foremost on the Book of Genesis. Eve had not set a good precedent for women in the Garden of Eden and was blamed by many early modern writers for the predicament of fallen humanity when they claimed that the Bible offered evidence of divinely ordained subjugation even before the Fall (Eve was taken from Adam's rib in the second of Genesis's accounts of human creation), and exacerbated thereafter when God condemns the pair to perpetual strife, and Eve to subjection ("under his [her husband's] heel"). St Paul's injunction in the New Testament that "wives must be subject to your husbands" was taken as further scriptural authority for innate conjugal inequity, although this position was moderated somewhat by the Protestant emphasis on marriage as a state of harmony in which partners might be helpmeets to one another.

The precise tone of these debates is often difficult to gauge, and the same difficulty is to be found in Shakespeare's play. *Shrew* contains material that can be staged to achieve the full range of tonal effects from high-spirited, flirtatious badinage to uproarious comedy and to outright brutality, and any of these may be activated to become the dominant coloring of a given production. One of the play's wittiest and specifically erotic exchanges, for example, at their first meeting, ends with Kate striking Petruchio:

PETRUCHIO:   Who knows not where a wasp does wear his sting? In his tail.
KATE:   In his tongue?
PETRUCHIO:   Whose tongue?
KATE:   Yours, if you talk of tales, and so farewell.
PETRUCHIO:   What, with my tongue in your tail? Nay, come again,
   Good Kate, I am a gentleman.
KATE:   That I'll try. *She strikes him.* (2.1.211–5)

Certainly, the debate in the pamphlet literature *was* a game of sorts, with its outrageous claims and hyperbolic rhetoric. Sometimes there is clearly a sense of harmless banter, but there were also more biting exchanges, and both sides made frequent recourse to the Bible to support their arguments. A case in point, where the debate is on the lighter side and where no truly scurrilous charges are made against women, is the delightful manuscript exchange between the queen's godson, Sir John Harington, and Lady Mary Cheke. This is a playful, witty game where both parties demonstrate their linguistic dexterity and their facility with verse. Harington's poem initiates the exchange, with the deliberately preposterous claim that it could be deduced from the Latin biblical text *erat quidam homo*, "there was a certain man" (a phrase often repeated in the bible, especially at the beginning of narratives) that there were no women in the Bible. Lady Mary's refutation urges that "though wee by men be overswayed [overruled]" women, such as Christ's mother, are vitally important to the Christian documents of salvation. Any preacher who believes such nonsense as that there are no women in the Bible, she insists, should be ashamed, "And blush his Sermon was no Better suited / Than by a Woman thus to bee confuted."[6] Yet, even this genteel badinage takes the opportunity to poke fun at incompetent biblical exegesis – both writers do this – and in addition, Lady Mary's riposte bespeaks a seriousness of purpose, defending both the virtue of her sex and women's significance in Christian history and eschatology. That these poems constitute an actual exchange – poems written back and forth – demonstrates both dialog and creative collaboration even in opposition. This case is an interesting one in relation to *The Taming of the Shrew* because it too is a literary game, and one where the stakes are similarly high despite initial appearances to the contrary.

The play itself may be a deliberate theatrical intervention into an on-going debate, since an earlier play, *A Pleasant Conceited History of The Taming of A Shrew* (1594), was popular enough to be reprinted in 1596 and 1607, and was in wide circulation by the time Shakespeare wrote his play at some time before its first performance 1591 or 1592 (although it was only first printed in the Folio in 1623). While there is no single source for Katherine–Petruchio plot of *The Taming of the Shrew*, it everywhere reflects folk culture in which unruly women were subjugated, often with extraordinary brutality. For example, in the anonymous ballad *A Merry Jest of a Shrewd and Curst Wife Lapped in Morel's Skin* a wife is beaten and then wrapped in the salted hide of a horse without anything in the way of explanation or insight as to individual actions and feelings. Evidence that this kind of punishment was more than fiction survives in contraptions such as the scold's bridle (a metal device modeled on a horse's bridle used to prevent women from speaking),[7] and the ducking stool (a kind of chair, which served as an instrument for semi-drowning unruly women into meek subjection). The debate continued after Shakespeare's treatment of the *Shrew* when John Fletcher intervened with *A Woman's Prize or The Tamer Tamed* (written 1609–10). In Fletcher's riposte, Petruchio is now a widower, and it is *he* who must now be tamed by his second wife.

## Love's Labour's Lost

The half-Italian linguist and translator John Florio (1553–1625) inspired the anticipation of romantic disappointment in Shakespeare's title *Love's Labour's Lost*. In his language manual, *Florio his First Fruits* (1578) Florio writes, "It were a labour lost to speake of Love."[1] Florio's connections in literary London were many. He had married the sister of the poet Samuel Daniel in 1580 and was a good friend of Ben Jonson. More importantly, echoes of Florio's greatest literary achievement, his translation of the *Essays of Montaigne* (1603), are also to be found in *The Tempest* and *King Lear*. This was, of course, well after Shakespeare had written *Love's Labour's Lost*, composed sometime between 1593 and 1595. Taken together, these textual and personal interconnections that persisted through the entire course of Shakespeare's literary career would seem to indicate that in the small world of writers in early modern

London Shakespeare and Florio knew one another well. There was, however, yet another connection: Florio tutored Shakespeare's patron, the Earl of Southampton, in Italian. There is a direct quotation from Florio in the play – "*Venetia, Venetia, chi non ti vede non ti pretia*" (only those who have not seen Venice will fail to praise her; 4.2.92–3)[2] – from *Florio's Second Fruits* (1591) that, in addition to Shakespeare's Italian borrowings in *The Taming of the Shrew*, would seem to indicate Shakespeare's extensive familiarity with Florio's language books. These were devoted to genteel pastimes and behaviors and aimed at helping the English finesse their way through the sophistications of continental culture at a time when behaviors of court culture were being appropriated by a non-aristocratic readership. Arguably, this is also the motive of Shakespeare's play: to make available the brilliant, glittering world of aristocratic refinement and sparkling wit for those who did not see themselves, as Shakespeare's courtly audience might have done, as already reflected there.

Like Shakespeare, then, Florio was positioned at the literary intersection of aristocratic and urban culture, and *Love's Labour's Lost* demonstrates Shakespeare's literary and intellectual connections both with Florio and with the Continent. In many ways – more than simply in terms of its setting – the play's plot is French rather than English, a fact perhaps not coincidentally related to the fact that Florio lived at the French Embassy in London between 1583 and 1585 when he was tutor to the French ambassador's daughter. However, this circumstance is also related to the reputation of aristocratic French culture as being the most sophisticated as well as the most extravagant and luxurious in Europe. Something of the glamour of this world as well as the clear division between lords and ladies who line up like opposing teams is evident in the *Memoirs* of Marguerite de Navarre:

> Our residence, for the most part of the time . . . was at Nérac, where our court was so brilliant that we had no cause to regret our absence from the Court of France. We had with us the Princess of Navarre, my husband's sister, since married to the Duke of Bar; there were besides a number of ladies belonging to myself. The King my husband was attended by a numerous body of lords and gentlemen, all as gallant persons as I have seen in any Court.

What Robert Codrington said in 1654 about the French court at this period could well be applied to *Love's Labour's Lost*: "Mars and Venus were for a long time the two culminating planets."[3] Shakespeare follows the same pattern of a gender-segregated gathering of beautiful people via the preposterous comic premise of the play, namely the exclusion of women from the Court of Navarre. In an attempt to create a pristine, humanist academy devoid of sexual distraction, King Ferdinand of Navarre has decreed, "no woman shall come within a mile of my court" (1.1.119–20). His injunction might have reminded the audience that there were no actual women on the stage and that the elaborate mating dance they were about to witness was the public theatre's version of the fantasy and artifice associated with court entertainment. The king and his courtiers (Berowne, Dumain, and Longaville – named after actual, historical figures) take a solemn oath to abjure the company of women and to devote themselves to the study of philosophy for a period of three years. However, their resolve is tested when the Princess of France arrives as an emissary from the French king on a diplomatic mission concerning the status of the province of Anjou. Ladies-in-waiting – the dark beauty, Rosaline with whom Berowne falls in love, Katherine, and Maria – accompany the princess. Sexual separatism is shown to be distinctly impracticable when the king decides to house the ladies in the fields and when philosophy does not save the young men from falling in love. The men try to save face as, one after another, they break every vow they have taken. Their stoic resolutions cannot withstand the force of desire, and yet, they do not succeed in winning the hearts and minds of the women they woo. Indeed, Shakespeare ends the play making his audience endure the same uncertainty as the wooers. The princess and her entourage now impose conditions that parallel the men's oaths at the beginning of the play, namely, the suspension of courtship for the period of a year and a day. The difference in this new commitment is that while Navarre's oath was frivolous and taken on a whim, the princess's terms are motivated by genuinely weighty concerns and comport with the requisite period of mourning for her father, the king of France, news of whose death arrives toward the end of the play. This is not the satisfying finale expected of comedy, but rather is at best a deferral and at worst a failure of comic resolution: "Our wooing doth not end like an old play; / Jack hath not Jill" (5.2.867–8).

As a play focused on courtly and linguistic artifice, on the stately dance of aristocratic marital alliance, on courtly pastimes such as sonnet writing, wooing, masques, and other entertainments, Shakespeare emphasizes the performance of civility and the superficiality of aristocratic refinement. Yet, the disquieting rupture of the finale serves to cast an ominous shadow over all that has gone before, even though that shadow, while so carefully and unobtrusively drawn, has been there from the start in the form of the play's topical allusion to the real historical figure Henri of Navarre and to the wars of religion in France, waged from 1562 to 1598. Interestingly, Shakespeare's great theatrical rival Christopher Marlowe had also dealt with part of this dark episode in French history in the tragedy *Massacre At Paris*, performed in 1593. Marlowe's play took as its subject the St Bartholomew's Day Massacre of August 1572 when as many as three thousand Protestants living in Paris were brutally murdered at the instigation of the Duke of Guise. In what has been called the "demi-monde" of French and Francophile London, Shakespeare may have known literary allusions to and renditions of these events in French, including a drama of Catholic propaganda by François de Chantelouve, *La Tragédie du feu Gaspard de Coligny* (1575).[4]

Shakespeare's pointed onomastic choices make the connections between love and religion, and the coding of religious antagonism as gender difference, inescapable. The real Henri of Navarre, ruler of the small kingdom bordering France and Spain, had founded an academy for the study of philosophy and was the leader of the Protestant Huguenot faction in France until he ascended to the French throne as Henri IV in 1589 after the assassination of his predecessor, Henri III. In 1593 he converted to Catholicism – arguably out of political necessity rather than mere expediency – famously remarking, "Paris vaut bien une messe" (Paris is worth a Mass). Such politically motivated conversion is also anticipated in *Love's Labour's Lost*: "Necessity will make us all forsworn . . . If I break faith, this word shall speak for me, / I am forsworn on mere necessity" (1.1.148–53). Political exigencies of this order continued to unfold in the years after Shakespeare's play when conversion had bought Henri some time, but ultimately could not save him. He was assassinated in 1610.

The unsuccessful marriage negotiations of the play had their historical analog in the disastrous marriage of Henri and Marguerite de Navarre. In 1572, while Navarre was still a Protestant, he had married the Catholic Marguerite de Valois, daughter of Henri II. The marriage, purely a dynastic alliance that sought to suture the bloody gash made by religious factionalism, did not fare well, and the pair lived separately in openly adulterous liaisons. Marguerite's entourage, which included her formidable mother, Catherine de Medici, visited her estranged husband in an attempted reconciliation in 1578. This was an extraordinarily elaborate event featuring a garden setting and fabulous courtly entertainments. The event was celebrated in a sumptuous Valois tapestry after François Quesnel the Elder (1543–1619). While the antagonism between the men of Navarre and the ladies of France transposes the bloody battles that constitute the real historical events to a few well-decorated skirmishes in the battle of the sexes – or more accurately, in this courtly context, a series of attempts at rapprochement between the sexes – this tendency towards ornament and artifice in the midst of an on-going bloodbath was also a well-documented facet of French history. Indeed, in her *Memoirs*, published in 1628, Marguerite de Navarre recounts of her sojourn in Navarre,

> We had only to lament that they [the gentlemen] were Huguenots. This difference of religion, however, caused no dispute amongst us; the King my husband and the Princess his sister heard a sermon, whilst I and my servants heard Mass. I had a chapel in the park for this purpose, and, as soon as the service of both religions was over, we joined the company in a beautiful garden, ornamented with long walks shaded with laurel and cypress trees. Sometimes we took a walk in the park

and on the banks of the river, bordered by an avenue of trees three thousand yards in length. The rest of the day we passed in innocent amusements, and in the afternoon, or at night, we commonly had a ball.[5]

While in the play, the death of the French king makes the immediate union between King Ferdinand of Navarre and the princess impossible, it does not mandate the delay and the conditions the princess imposes. Thus, the play's impending nuptials are ruptured not just by grief but also by a studied hesitancy on the part of the play's female characters that is, in complicated ways, bound up with religious differences. The women resist their suitors throughout the play on the grounds that the men are "forsworn," and thus ostensibly guilty of perjury. Yet, the trials the ladies make the suitors undergo are not so much chivalric ordeals as penitential rites. The king, for example, is sent to "some forlorn and naked hermitage, / Remote from all the pleasures of the world" (5.2.787–8), while Berowne will work in a hospital where he is charged to use his wit in service of others. These trials resonate with notions of heresy and apostasy that oath-taking and oath-breaking invariably summoned up in wake of the pan-European cataclysm of the Protestant Reformation: "It is religion to be thus forsworn" (4.3.359).

While the play unquestionably reflects the prominence of women in sixteenth-century French politics, it also examines – albeit from a safe distance at the other side of the Channel, Elizabeth's own power. This is quite remarkable given that the first recorded performance of the play was for the queen and her court during the Christmas festivities of 1597. The court as a political and social entity, both in France and in England, forged and brokered dynastic alliances between aristocratic families, and these sexual politics determined the distribution and exercise of power in the realm. Elizabeth herself was notorious for controlling the marriages of her courtiers, and the male members of her court were all expected to do something of the wooing dance in relation to her as the appropriate way of expressing deference and devotion. Furthermore, aristocratic decorum exercised in music, dance, and, above all, in literary production constituted the very *political* culture of the court. But one example of this is the poem *Ocean to Cynthia* by the courtier-poet Sir Walter Raleigh, in which he addresses Elizabeth as the chaste goddess of the moon. Amorous sycophancy, executed at a very high literary level, was thus the very language of Elizabethan court politics.

In the play, courtly entertainments abound. Shakespeare includes a bungled visit on the part of the suitors to the ladies in which they are disguised as Muscovites accompanied by Moorish minstrels, an episode indebted to the Christmas revels at Gray's Inn in 1594–5. There are too, the more lowly, aesthetic endeavors of the educated, Latinate, but non-aristocratic class that Shakespeare hailed from himself who ineptly attempt to perform the pageant of the Nine Worthies.

As in *A Midsummer Night's Dream*, aristocratic spectators are depicted as arrogant, rude, and boorish in their response to the honest efforts of those lower down the social ladder than themselves. Thus, as Holofernes remarks in wounded response to the guffaws of the male courtiers, "This is not generous, not gentle, not humble" (5.2.623). Thus, learned, courtly artifice is shown to be incapable of sympathy with those outside its well-ornamented enclosures.

*Love's Labour's Lost* demonstrates also that things can go wrong in both entertainment and in marriage. The aristocratic alliances around Elizabeth – those of Marguerite de Valois and Mary Queen of Scots – had been failures. On the entertainment front, Sir Philip Sidney's *The Lady of May* (published in 1598) also went awry. Performed for the queen at the Earl of Leicester's country estate, this entertainment was first recognized by Samuel Johnson as being reminiscent of *Love's Labour's* both on grounds of its pastoralism and because one of its characters is a Holofernes-like schoolmaster. The queen herself was asked, in this entertainment, to make an ostensibly free choice at the end of the masque between two suitors for the hand of the daughter of a woman who, in Sidney's fiction, has sought the queen's help. Elizabeth is permitted by the structure of the masque to exercise her sovereign power choice. For the masque to make sense, however, it was clear from the outset which suitor she must pick. Sidney had thus carefully tipped the queen's hand, and she did not like it. Stubbornly refusing to comply with Sidney's aesthetic design, Elizabeth chose contrary to Sidney's clear intent, thus completely deflating the proceedings. Her reasons for doing so may well have been that she saw Sidney making a veiled commentary on her own marriage prospects. In contrast, while Shakespeare deflates the expectations of comedy at the end of *Love's Labour's Lost*, what he retains is the political and personal power of the aristocratic lady to choose, to refuse, or to set the terms on which she will consider a suit.

Elizabeth herself certainly exercised this power in relation to the brother of the king of Navarre, François, Duc d'Alençon, whom she strung along with hopes of marriage until his death in 1584. Indeed, Elizabeth achieved her autonomy by developing the fine art of deferral. She may even have gone through a betrothal ceremony with Alençon, and one of her surviving poems, "The Doubt of Future Foes," seems to be a personal account of her sorrow in regard to this relationship. Shakespeare again evokes the power of a very Elizabethan stripe of virginity when the princess kills a buck in Act 4. This is, of course, a singularly courtly pastime, known as the noble art of venery – which was also the title of a contemporary book on the subject by George Turberville (1575). Deer were kept in parks as captive game, and Shakespeare alludes to the potentially erotic nature of this sport in *Venus and Adonis*, when the goddess of love tells her reluctant beloved, "I'll be a park, and thou shalt be my deer" (*l.* 231).[6] Hunting was a sport from which commoners were completely excluded because deer belonged to landowners and thus venison was meat consumed only by the wealthy. Although it is probably completely apocryphal, there is a story that has circulated since the eighteenth century that as a boy Shakespeare poached deer in Charlecote Park. However, a more plausible connection is with the image of Elizabeth standing over her kill, in the ritualistic slaughter of the deer in Turberville's book. This association of Elizabeth as huntress further aligned her with Diana (the Roman name for the Greek goddess Artemis or Cynthia), the deity of the hunt who had Acteon devoured by his own hounds because he had the misfortune to catch a glimpse of the goddess bathing. Even though this was mythologically rendered, no doubt this kind of treading on eggs around female power was all too familiar to Elizabeth's retinue. In fact, the image of Diana's potential for ferocious chastity was one Elizabeth was keen to cultivate. Far from being a passive condition in relation to the reigning monarch, then, virginity was an active, and potentially deadly force. This is precisely the feminine ending of *Love's Labour's Lost*, which ends, unresolved, with a song. The only rapprochement between the sexes achieved in the play is that between Costard and the country wench, Jaquenetta, whom he has impregnated. Among the lower orders, wooing may be about sex, but in the upper echelons, courtship is only about power.

The problematic conclusion of *Love's Labour's Lost*, which ends without closure, seems to demand a sequel. The sense that the end of the play is simply the anticipation of the next drama to follow would mean that Shakespeare had merely suspended the satisfactions of comedy rather than denied them altogether. Indeed, Shakespeare is believed to have written a sequel, the lost play, *Love's Labour's Won*. Certainly, this play is listed by Francis Meres in *Palladis Tamia: Wit's Treasury* of 1598, the same year that the quarto of *Love's Labour's Lost* appeared, as one of Shakespeare's achievements in comedy: "his Gentlemen of Verona, his Errors, his Love Labors Lost, his Love Labour's wonne, his Midsummer night dreame, & his Merchant of Venice."[7] Meres' reference was further corroborated in the twentieth century by the discovery of a bookseller's list from 1603 that also includes the now missing play. However, for some reason that we will probably never know, *Love's Labour's Won* was not included in the First Folio of 1623 with *Love's Labour's Lost*. There the trail runs dry, so we must take the play as it is, as a fragment in the exposition of a longer, more fully developed set of ideas.

## A Midsummer Night's Dream

I know a bank where the wild thyme blows,
Where oxlips and the nodding violet grows,

> Quite overcanopied with luscious woodbine,
> With sweet muskroses and with eglantine: . . . (2.1.249–52)[1]

An earlier generation of biographers never tired of pointing out that Shakespeare embodied the spirit of the English countryside. While that vein of commentary has gone into abeyance in recent years, it remains true that although *A Midsummer Night's Dream* is set in Athens and the woods outside it, it is a quintessentially English, and specifically Elizabethan, comedy.[2] However, what Shakespeare's Victorian and Edwardian commentators did not fully appreciate was the degree to which he took extraordinary risks in representing sex and power, albeit against the backdrop of the exquisite natural beauty of the rural English landscape.

The play's panorama of fairyland connotes the kingdom ruled by Gloriana, the allegorical figure for Elizabeth I in Edmund Spenser's imperial epic poem *The Faerie Queene* (1590–6). In a play about the perils and pitfalls of erotic attachment and marriage, Shakespeare includes an intensely lyrical and mythical paean of praise to her virginity as the "imperial vot'ress" (2.1.163). Cupid, flying between the moon and the earth, takes certain aim at the virgin, but her chastity is proof against his dart:

> That very time I saw . . .
> Flying between the cold moon and the earth
> Cupid, all armed. A certain aim he took
> At a fair vestal thronèd by the west,
> And loosed his love shaft smartly from his bow
> As it should pierce a hundred thousand hearts;
> But I might see young Cupid's fiery shaft
> Quenched in the chaste beams of the watery moon,
> And the imperial vot'ress passèd on,
> In maiden meditation, fancy-free.
> Yet marked I where the bolt of Cupid fell:
> It fell upon a little western flower,
> Before milk-white, now purple with love's wound,
> And maidens call it love-in-idleness (2.1.155–68)

The rather mystical reference to Elizabeth as *virgo vestal* derives from classical mythology. Vestal virgins were priestess devotees of the goddess Vesta and they played a key role in upholding the rituals of the Roman state. "Fair vestal" further alludes to the Christian idea of the appearance of a great sign in the heavens of "the woman clothed with the sun," the Mother of God, from the Book of Revelations, as well as to the lines from Virgil's *Fourth Eclogue*, which were believed to prophesy the coming of Christ and the return of the

Golden Age. The Golden Age, celebrated by painters and poets, was also promulgated by Elizabeth's progresses through the country, where she was lavishly entertained at the expense of the nobles she visited.

Here, Elizabeth as "imperial vot'ress" is not only inured to the vicissitudes of desire, she is impervious to the thing itself. This passage, in fact, deploys the central themes of Elizabeth's reign. By 1600, three years before her death, the queen's virginity had had become a commitment to perpetual chastity. This speech was, then, in concert with the ideological fast footwork of portraits and speeches where Elizabeth's virginity was sometimes represented as actual, physical impermeability. For example, the 1583 portrait by Quentin Metsys the Younger depicts her with a sieve that holds water. As the very paradigm of virginity, any and all representations of female chastity might be understood as allusions to, or reflections of, what had become the queen's defining characteristic. In a society that understood power and femininity to be mutually exclusive categories, Elizabeth's exalted virginity was one way of claiming that her sovereignty was a providential exception to the alleged evils of female rule, what the Calvinist minister John Knox had unwisely referred to as "the monstrous regiment of women"[3] (Elizabeth never allowed him to set foot in England again). All references to female autonomy and female government in *Dream* thus reflect the power dynamics of the period, and since they might have caused some offense to the sovereign, it was as well to identify Elizabeth in a very direct, unambiguous way as the vestal virgin of the west by way of an antidote to the other, unflattering images of female sovereignty in the play. Certainly, Edmund Spenser's many allegorical figurations of Elizabeth did not include anything approaching the Queen of the Fairies' *mésalliance* with an ass.

In *A Midsummer Night's Dream*, the world of the fairies is definitively under the patriarchal rule of Oberon, whose supremacy in the play is challenged by his consort, Titania. This world, infused with magic by Puck, also known as Robin Goodfellow, a familiar figure from English folklore, is juxtaposed with the world of everyday mortals, ruled by a character from the highly literary world of classical myth, Duke Theseus. He is betrothed to Hippolyta, the mythical Amazon queen. However, the image of Hippolyta is not an especially positive one. That the queen of the Amazons, a tribe vowed to sexual separatism, should cede her chastity to Theseus under threat of rape, "I wooed thee with my sword / And won thy love doing thee injuries" (1.1.16–7), is a reference to Greek mythology to which the Virgin Queen, who had herself been bullied toward marriage any number of times, might well have taken exception. The figure of the Amazon Hippolyta is further problematic in that this was a role Elizabeth herself assumed when she addressed the troops at Tilbury before the Spanish Armada in 1588.[4] Although there is some doubt about whether she actually donned armor for the occasion, there is a depiction of her in martial male attire with a raised sword in a Dutch engraving of 1598.

The impending nuptial celebration for Theseus and Hippolyta is to take place on the night of the next new moon. By that date, also, Hermia must decide whether to obey her father's will and marry Demetrius, whom she does not love, or she must go "to her death, according to our law" (1.1.44). Hermia in fact loves Lysander, and her best friend, Helena, loves Demetrius, who does not love her. While the collision between the worlds of mortals, myths, and the world of fairies generates the humor of the play, Shakespeare also engineers a clash of genres. For, embedded within the comedy is the story of Pyramus and Thisbe, derived from Book 4 of Ovid's *Metamorphoses*. This is the tragic tale of divided lovers – in this case literally divided by a wall – who come to their deaths after Pyramus commits suicide in the mistaken belief that the bloody napkin he finds is evidence of Thisbe's death. In reality, she has just had a close encounter with a lion, from which she has managed to escape. On seeing the body of her dead lover, like Juliet in the tomb of the Capulets, Thisbe follows suit and kills herself. Far from sounding a somber tragic note in the midst of comic action, however, the Pyramus and Thisbe interlude, rehearsed and performed by the bumbling "mechanicals," a group of Athenian workmen "which never labored in their minds till now" (5.1.73), is a hilarious send-up of dramatic tragedy. Because Pyramus and Thisbe constitutes a play within a play, it is also a reminder that Shakespeare knew how the conventions of tragedy, its implausible misprisions and multiple deaths, might bring audiences perilously close to mirth. Shakespeare takes full advantage of the propensity for things to go wrong on stage. Contrary to Henslowe's maxim in the film *Shakespeare in Love*, things did not always go "all right on the night."

Since, like other local administrations, Stratford Corporation also made its contribution toward "the Queen's provision" whenever she was in the region, Shakespeare possibly knew firsthand something of how royal entertainments could go awry. During his childhood, in 1575 when Elizabeth visited Robert Dudley, Earl of Leicester, at Kenilworth Castle, he may have witnessed the famous entertainment that went fabulously wrong. There are idealized echoes of this performance in Oberon's speech:

> Once I sat upon a promontory,
> And heard a mermaid on a dolphin's back
> Uttering such dulcet and harmonious breath
> That the rude sea grew civil at her song,
> And certain stars shot madly from their spheres
> To hear the sea-maid's music (2.1.149–54)

Oberon recounts a story indebted to classical myth of the drowning Arion who was rescued by means of the good offices of a dolphin who allowed him to ride upon his back. However, at Kenilworth, this impressive rescue did not go as planned. An eyewitness to the entertainment, Robert Laneham, reports:

> There was a spectacle presented to Queen Elizabeth upon the water, and amongst others Harry Goldingham was to represent Arion upon the dolphin's back, but finding his voice to be very hoarse and unpleasant when he came to perform it, he tears off his disguise, and swears he was none of Arion, not he, but e'en honest Harry Goldingham: which blunt discovery pleased the Queen better than if it had gone through in the right way.[5]

The mechanicals, the "hempen homespuns" (3.1.60), similarly feel the necessity of revealing their actual identities to their aristocratic audience because they cannot grasp the fictionality of theatre:

> You, ladies, you whose gentle hearts do fear
> The smallest monstrous mouse that creeps on the floor,
> May now perchance both quake and tremble here,
> When lion rough in wildest rage doth roar.
> Then know that I, . . . Snug the joiner, am . . . (5.1.210–14)

Snug's concern not to alarm women in the audience is touching and gentle as much as it is ludicrous. The mechanicals' inept performance, however, works to domesticate the realms of myth and magic with which Bottom, the weaver, and his fellow artisans have found themselves entwined. In this sense, their theatricals are at least as important as Oberon's magic to the creation of a cohesive community that is intrinsic to the generic purposes of comedy.

The aristocratic wedding is at the center of the play because it is the social celebration of a new conjugal union, that fundamental building block of community in the period. However, the bridal couple is juxtaposed with their already married counterparts in fairyland. Oberon and Titania are in the midst of a bitter custody dispute about an orphaned Indian boy, who, although he is not a character in the play, is ostensibly the source of their antagonism. In Shakespeare, already married characters rarely fare well. With the ingenious assistance of Robin Goodfellow, Oberon formulates outrageous revenge upon his wife: Robin will administer a love potion upon her eyes while she sleeps that will make her fall in love with the first thing she sees. What she sees is Bottom, the weaver. To compound Titania's humiliation when she falls in love with him, Puck first has poor Bottom "translated," that is, transformed, so that he is endowed with the head of an ass. The play thus literalizes the idea that love is blind and that people driven by desire behave in ways that are far outside the compass of rational behavior. *Dream* thus constitutes a comic perspective on the "violent desires" associated with the hot passions of midsummer that Shakespeare was writing at about the same time in the love tragedy *Romeo and Juliet*, where youthful intemperance leads to death.

The scenes in the fairy world are further paralleled by events in the human realm among the courting couples. The play follows comic convention in having Egeus obstruct his daughter's erotic choice, accusing Lysander of having deceived and enchanted her. Hermia, together with the play's other young folk, Lysander, Demetrius, and Helena, repairs to the woods, which as in *As You Like It*, is a green world where conventional order is suspended and reshaped. When Oberon attempts to cure Demetrius of his disdain for Helena by ordering Puck to anoint his eyes with a love potion, the plan goes comically awry, causing love and friendship to unravel as the couples switch and change their romantic allegiances. This confusion among the couples raises the questions about the nature and duration of erotic attachment, about why we prefer one partner over another. This problem is exacerbated by the fact that in the text (though obviously this may not be the case in performance) there is very little to distinguish Demetrius from Lysander. The play also asks whether such erotic preference can last a lifetime and whether romantic alliances can survive the competing demands of friendship. Importantly, the potentially erotic aspects of same-sex friendship are described in terms not dissimilar to the Protestant ideal of marriage:

> Like to a double cherry, seeming parted,
> But yet an union in partition,
> Two lovely berries molded on one stem;
> So, with two seeming bodies, but one heart . . . (3.2.209–12)

While the play demonstrates that all forms of human relationship pose difficulties, the ideal of union seems more fully realized, as well as more natural and less perverse, between persons of the same sex than it does in marriage.

Indeed, heteroerotic relations in the play are driven by dissident desire. This is most fully exemplified in the comically incongruous and adulterous coupling of Titania and Bottom. While, as we have noted, Shakespeare takes pains to praise Elizabeth's sovereignty, he treads on politically dangerous territory with the spectacle of Titania's comic humiliation, which is the result of her attempt to govern her husband. Shakespeare derived this part of the plot from the Roman writer Lucius Apuleius's story, *The Golden Ass*. In this fictional autobiography, Apuleius is transformed into an ass who is to perform sex with a Roman matron before the assembled multitude prior to being executed himself. Apuleius narrowly escapes death. The story offers on the one hand a grotesque exaggeration of the relatively benign idea of incompatible and incongruous unions. On the other hand, the Apuleius source also raises quite explicitly the spectacle of bestiality. Both aspects of mismatched sexual conjunctions are reflected in *Midsummer Night's Dream*, not only in the liaison between Bottom and Titania but even – or perhaps, especially – in the play's marriages. For these unions are also shadowed by exaggeratedly nightmarish configurations: the rapist and the Amazon queen; the potentially pederastic Oberon (after all, what does he want the Indian boy to attend him *for*?) who enjoys making a spectacle of his wife by having her commit bestiality. Nor are the more conventional courting couples insulated from the preposterous, monstrous aspects of desire. Spurned by Demetrius, Helena declares: "I am as ugly as a bear, / For beasts that meet me run away for fear" (2.2.100–1), while Demetrius leaves her to the "mercy of wild beasts" (2.1.228). These lines bespeak Helena's kinship with Bottom, who will, in bestial form, terrify and horrify the other mechanicals. In the woods, love very quickly turns to hate, and the choice of a mate becomes, albeit temporarily, an arbitrary matter of chance and caprice.

The play is in part about how human beings are transformed by sexual desire, but it is also about theatre as a space of transformation. Bottom represents the lower rungs of the social hierarchy, but he is also a *bad* actor who favors the thundering alliteration and crude rhythms of an earlier theatrical mode: "raging rocks," "shivering shocks" (1.2.24–5). His deficiencies as a performer are made all the more risible by his conviction that he is a great actor. Yet for all that, before the eyes of Peter Quince the carpenter, Snug the joiner, Snout the tinker, Flute the bellows-mender, and Starveling the tailor, the humble artisans who are onomastically defined by the manual labors they perform, Bottom undergoes a terrifying metamorphosis, yet one which gains him access to the very bower of the queen of the fairies. This type of transformation is at once suspect as a form of witchcraft, as Quince's reaction indicates: "Bless thee, Bottom, bless thee! Thou art translated" (3.1.97), and at the same time, a kind of divine magic. When Bottom recounts the "dream" of what happened to him in the fairy bower, he employs a mangled version of St Paul's words in 1 Corinthians 2.9: "Eye hath not seen, nor ear heard, neither have entered into the heart of man, the things which God hath prepared for them that love him"; "The eye of man hath not heard, the ear of man hath not seen, man's hand is not able to taste, his tongue to conceive, nor his heart to report, what my dream was" (4.1.203–5). With his senses thus confounded, the mesmerized Bottom represents something *almost* holy. Like the actors of Shakespeare's own company, many of whom, as we have seen, belonged to the livery companies of a variety of work-a-day trades, and who, like Shakespeare himself, came from households where those trades were exercised, Bottom, the bad actor, becomes the unlikely instrument of wonder. Shakespeare thus reminds the audience that it is the "mechanical" actor who is the improbable vehicle for this spectacular, fantastic theatrical vision they witness.

Oberon, the director of the play's magic, and Puck, the stage manager, finally restore order to the disrupted relationships of the play. Oberon is reconciled with Titania, the human couples are married, and the mechanicals perform their play. Shakespeare explores here the ways in which reality itself cannot exist independently of our dream-like perceptions. Rather, reality is amenable to, and perhaps even created by, the comic and tragic paradigms we willingly or unconsciously impose on it. Further, it is his insistence on the imagination, on fiction, on the fictional narratives theatre stages, that allows Shakespeare to represent astonishing, even subversive, images of sex and power, and to do so without incurring the wrath of the Virgin Queen.

Although it is mentioned by Francis Meres in 1598, we do not know exactly when Shakespeare wrote *A Midsummer Night's Dream*. However, it was probably written sometime around 1595, in the same period as *Romeo and Juliet*. The play was first published in quarto in 1600 (Q1) and again, in a slightly different version in 1619 (Q2), and in yet another variation in the First Folio (F) in 1623. The latter, is based on Q2 and a theatrical manuscript that is no longer extant. The principal differences between these textual variants are relatively minor, consisting of the introduction of printing errors, corrections, and stage directions.

## The Merchant of Venice

In Shakespeare's Sonnet 128, the poet says he envies the keyboard his mistress fingers, wishing that he could have the same intimate, sensual contact with her as the keys (the dancing "jacks" or "chips") that she plays:

> To be so tickled they would change their state
> And situation with those dancing chips,
> O'er whom thy fingers walk with gentle gait,
> Making dead wood more blessed than living lips.
>     Since saucy jacks so happy are in this,
>     Give them thy fingers, me thy lips to kiss. (128.9–14)[1]

On the grounds that the woman in this sonnet is a musician, and because she is later described as "colored-ill," the search for the "true identity" of the so-called dark lady of Shakespeare's *Sonnets* led A.L. Rowse, among others, to the poet Aemelia Lanyer, née Bassano, who was born into a family of Venetian

Jewish immigrants employed as court musicians and instrument makers who arrived in England in 1531.[2] Lanyer had been the mistress of Lord Henry Hunsdon but was married off to another musician, Alphonso Lanyer, after becoming pregnant with Hunsdon's child. More important than these personal circumstances, however, is that she was a poet whose work included an impressive long poem in celebration of divine mercy, *Salve Deus Rex Judaeorum* (Hail God, King of the Jews), published in 1611, just two years after the publication of Shakespeare's *Sonnets* in 1609. In it, Christ is the "Mercy of Mercies" (*l.* 646) who's "Mercy made way to make us highly blest" (*l.* 533). In the crucifixion, "Grace, Love, and Mercy did so much abound, / Thou entertaindst the Crosse, even to the death" (*ll.* 478–9). Having endowed the world with divine mercy, God now delights in acts of human kindness: "These workes of mercy are so sweete, so deare / To him that is the Lord of Life and Love" (*ll.*1361–2).[3] While the poem has a more specifically theological cast than the treatment of mercy in Shakespeare's *Merchant of Venice*, it nonetheless resonates with Portia's speech on mercy, which is one of the most famous in the canon:

> The quality of mercy is not strained:
> It droppeth as the gentle rain from heaven
> Upon the place beneath. It is twice blest:
> It blesseth him that gives and him that takes. (4.1.180–3).[4]

Portia's articulation of mercy as "gentle" and Gentile, that is, emanating from non-Jews (an incessant pun in this play), is situated as the power that supersedes all temporal authority. Femininity is thus allied with mercy in a way that coincides with Lanyer's emphasis on the empathetic women at the crucifixion. Such connections between Lanyer's *Salve* and Shakespeare's *The Merchant of Venice* are undoubtedly coincidental (especially given that Shakespeare's play and Lanyer's poem may be as much as a full decade apart). They remain interesting nonetheless. That there was in London a gifted, musical woman poet of Venetian-Jewish origins who wrote about the nature of Christian mercy in the context of Christ's passion and death complicates received ideas both about the paucity of Jews in England and about the demarcations between religious identities. There is no proof that Lanyer ever had an affair with Shakespeare, or that the performance of Shakespeare's plays at court ever led him to meet her there. Her significance in relation to him is rather that of her very presence in those circles. We cannot say that Shakespeare knew Lanyer, but given the extent of her connections both aristocratic and artistic, and given what we know of her and of her family, we can say that it is unlikely that Shakespeare could have failed to encounter Jews, both male and female, in London.[5]

Shakespeare gives considerable prominence in the play to Shylock's daughter, Jessica, who is, at least from our post-holocaust point of view, one of the least sympathetic characters in Shakespeare, and who has fallen in love with the Christian, Lorenzo. Masuccio Salernitano's *II Novellino* (1476) was Shakespeare's source for this part of the story, though in Salernitano the Jessica figure is merely the daughter of a miser, not the daughter of a Jew. Jessica tells Launcelot Gobbo, her father's servant, who himself flees the house, "Our house is hell" (2.3.2), but her meaning is ambiguous. She may mean that it is simply a miserably unhappy living circumstance, or alternatively that *because* it is a Jewish household where Jewish rites and rituals are practiced, it is damned; or perhaps some combination of the two senses. When she elopes, Jessica takes bags of gold and other valuables with her. We then learn that she has willfully squandered this wealth in an obscenely extravagant fashion, and her behavior seems to bespeak a form of vengeance on her father: "Your daughter spent in Genoa, as I heard, one night fourscore ducats" (3.1.98–9).

Shakespeare was not alone in foregrounding the figure of the Jewess. Christopher Marlowe's *The Jew of Malta* also concerns a Jew and his beautiful daughter. Marlowe's central character, Barabas, is a caricature of a Jew drawn from a crudely anti-Semitic perspective. Anti-semitism surged again in 1594 when Elizabeth's own physician, the Portuguese Jew Roderigo Lopez, who had been living in London since 1559, was accused of poisoning his patients and of plotting against the queen's life. His religious identity is complicated by the fact that he had been baptized by force in Portugal. His wife, Sarah, was born in England, the daughter of Dunstan Anes, a Jewish "purveyor and merchant" who was a member of the Grocers Company and a citizen of London. Like Sarah's father, Lopez also practiced Judaism in secret. At his trial, this crypto-Judaism was adduced as evidence of his guilt. He was hanged, drawn, and quartered at Tyburn on June 7, 1594 before a jeering and hostile crowd. In the wake of the Lopez affair, although by then an old play, *The Jew of Malta* was performed fifteen times to crowded houses.

Although Jews had been exiled from England in 1290 and were not officially readmitted until the Interregnum, there was still a Jewish synagogue in London, and Jewish visitors and even some émigrés worshipped there. There were also Jews who had converted to Christianity, since this was a requirement of residency in England, where Judaizing constituted a felony. While some may have indeed been genuine converts, a proportion may well have been crypto-Jews – that is, Jews who presented themselves as Christians and outwardly conformed to the established church in order to survive and work in England. Some Jews undoubtedly embraced their Christian identities wholeheartedly. However, converts were always under suspicion, whatever their true spiritual inclinations. The foundation for all anti-Semitism was the Christians' belief that the Jews

had murdered Christ. This conviction persisted despite being contrary to orthodox theology that held that all human beings, because of their sinfulness, had
participated in Christ's death on the cross, and further, that if he had not died,
there would be no salvation. The Christian hatred of the Jews, then, did not
even stand up to the rigorous application of doctrinal logic.

Shakespeare stages *The Merchant of Venice* amid the ethnic and religious
antipathies that were rife in Elizabethan London. The profligate Bassanio,
already in debt to Antonio, is keen to turn a profit by marrying Portia, "a lady
richly left" (1.1.161), and the need to borrow capital, three thousand ducats,
to invest in this marriage venture is what leads him to ask Antonio for this
further loan. Since the latter's investments are all at sea, he is compelled to ask
his loathed enemy, Shylock, for money. Shylock agrees, but the terms of the
bond are not financial, and he asks for no interest, but for a pound of Antonio's "fair flesh" (1.3.146). This is to serve as security, in the apparently
unlikely event that Antonio defaults on the loan. Bassanio succeeds in his suit
to Portia at Belmont, having passed a test devised by her deceased father in
which suitors must choose one of three caskets. When the black prince of
Morocco chooses the gold casket, Portia declares a relief that betrays some of
the other racial antipathies of this society: "Let all of his complexion choose
me so" (2.7.79). Bassanio correctly chooses the lead casket that contains her
portrait, the legend on which reads, " 'Who chooseth me must give and hazard
all he hath' " (2.7.16). Yet, is it really Bassanio who hazards all, or is he simply
profligate with other people's money? Bassanio's choice seems unmotivated by
greed, but he urges Antonio to give him the money with the gambler's logic
that this time he will "with more advisèd watch" (1.1.142) attend to the
investment:

> In my schooldays, when I had lost one shaft,
> I shot his fellow of the selfsame flight
> The selfsame way, with more advisèd watch
> To find the other forth, and by adventuring both
> I oft found both . . . (1.1.140–4)

Antonio may be Christ-like in his selfless willingness to undertake financial risk
and personal sacrifice for Bassanio, but he is also rabidly anti-Semitic:

> Signior Antonio, many a time and oft
> In the Rialto you have rated me
> About my moneys and my usances:
> Still have I borne it with a patient shrug,
> For sufferance is the badge of all our tribe
> You call me misbeliever, cut-throat dog,

And spit upon my Jewish gaberdine,
And all for use of that which is mine own. (1.3.102–9)

Shylock is a usurer. Though the practice of usury was officially prohibited by Christianity, it was, nonetheless, widespread, and the interest rate in Elizabethan England was ten percent. "Forbidden usury," as Shakespeare calls it in the *Sonnets* (6.5), was understood as "breeding" money – that is, using money to generate more money – and it is, in fact, one of the fundamental mechanisms on which capitalism is based. This is certainly how Antonio understands it: "A breed for barren metal of his friend" (1.3.129). While the Christians in the play purport to have nothing to do with such practices, when Portia expresses her love to Bassanio, she also deploys precisely the language of "usance":

I would be trebled twenty times myself,
A thousand times more fair, ten thousand times more rich,
That only to stand high in your account
I might in virtues, beauties, livings, friends
Exceed account . . . (3.2.153–7)

This language serves to demonstrate that, in fact, all the bonds – including ostensibly affective and emotional ties – in Venice are in some way or other, in the last resort, economic ones. Further, financial transactions far extend the nexus of relationships in the city and work to erase the boundaries of discrete identities. Thus, when Portia arrives at court and pretends not to be able to distinguish Antonio from Shylock, the audience is compelled to consider not just their fundamental similarity, but also the level at which they might be understood to be indistinguishable: "Which is the merchant here, and which the Jew?" (4.1.170). Antonio's code, however, is based instead on the absolute difference between himself and Shylock and on exchanges between "friends," an early modern term that is more comprehensive than our modern meaning. "Friends" were not just people one liked or spent time with; they were a network of associates, a cohesive group with shared economic interests with whom one sought to consolidate bonds – especially financial ones – that were already well established. It is Antonio's understanding of friendship that "brings down / The rate of usance here with us in Venice" (1.3.40–1). That is, Antonio damages Shylock's business by lending money without charging interest.

When he makes the agreement not to charge Antonio interest but to charge a pound of flesh, Shylock makes a joke of it, a "merry bond" (1.3.169). Whether he has sinister motivations at this point in the play is uncertain, and the play does not paint him as an innocent victim of oppression and racism. However, Shakespeare does humanize him, and his impact on the action is far in excess of the time he is on stage: he appears in only five scenes. Whatever his intentions at the time he made the bond with Antonio, he vows vengeance against all Christians once Jessica elopes with Lorenzo. Not only did Jessica steal money from her father but also a turquoise ring that her deceased mother had given her father before they married, which she has exchanged for a monkey:

> Thou torturest me Tubal. It was my turquoise:
> I had it of Leah when I was a bachelor.
> I would not have given it for a wilderness of monkeys. (3.1.109–11)

The bond between Shylock and Leah clearly transcends the financial – it was indeed priceless. Although Shylock's lament, "'My daughter! O, my ducats! O, my daughter!'" (2.8.15), implies that the two are equivalent, the contrast between the way Shylock cherishes his ring as a precious memory of his wife and the ring plot that Shakespeare appends to the courtroom scene is instructive. Bassanio and Gratiano easily part with the rings their wives have sworn them to keep. Rings are symbolic and suggest – or actually specify in the case of the "poesy" engraved on the one that Nerissa gives Gratiano, "'Love me, and leave me not'" (5.1.150) – the end of a circuit of exchange, a terminus incompatible even with the multiplying, promiscuous transactions of the market.

When Jessica elopes with a Christian she gleefully takes the opportunity to rob her father and squander his wealth. This cannot dispose him to be sympathetic when Antonio's ships fail to return. When Antonio cannot pay the loan, Shylock demands his pound of flesh. In this, Shylock reprises the role of the Old Testament patriarch, Abraham, whose obedience to God is tested when he is asked to slay Isaac. Seeing his willingness to adhere even to the most unfathomable of the deity's commands, an angel intervenes to save the boy. Shylock is further associated with the Jewish practice of ritual circumcision, which Christians believed constituted a racial predisposition toward murderous knife wielding. Antonio is saved only by Portia, who appears at the court in the disguise of a gifted young lawyer, attended by her waiting woman, Nerissa, who poses as Portia's clerk. Antonio may take his pound of flesh, but not one drop of blood because it was not specified in the bond.[6]

According to St Paul, the old law of the Old Testament gave way to the new dispensation of mercy in the New Testament, and the letter of the law to its spirit. While this transition is referred to repeatedly in the play, the Christians are nonetheless depicted as ruthless and merciless, even while they deploy the rhetoric of mercy. For his part, Shylock proves impervious to the simple idea of mercy, no matter how eloquently expressed. His outrage at being denigrated by Christians and his desire for justice do not have a monetary value: when he refuses Portia's offer to pay three times the sum to redeem Antonio, it is clear that, whatever else his motivations may be, murderous or villainous, they are not financial. He neither shows nor receives mercy. When, at the end of the play, Antonio's ships have come in, Shylock's execution is commuted to pauperization as all his goods are confiscated. There is little mercy for him – a fact relished by the main characters of the play. He is, moreover, deprived of his religion, forced under sore duress to do what his daughter has done by choice, namely convert to Christianity.

Whatever the fiction that Shakespeare created for the stage, there remained in England Jewish merchants, like the Anes family Dr Lopez had married into, as well as artists and musicians like the Bassanos. Jews continued to ply their trades and practice their creative arts, often very successfully, perhaps because in early modern London there was a sense of the necessity of economic and cultural interdependence. Indeed, in 1601 we find Dunstan Anes's son William, like a belated Shylock, entering into a bond for £3,000 at the high court of admiralty to enable a group of Amsterdam Portuguese Jewish merchants to recover their goods from six ships of Emden taken as prize in the queen's ships.[7] This was the new economic reality in London where, as in Shakespeare's Venice, "the trade and profit of the city / Consisteth of all nations" (3.3.30–1).

*The Merchant of Venice* was first published as a quarto in 1600 by the stationer Thomas Heyes. It appeared in 1619 with nine other plays printed by William Jaggard and again in the First Folio of 1623.

## Much Ado About Nothing

"These maidenheads . . . are so like nothing that there is nothing like them,"[1] offers a late seventeenth-century quip. The key word in Shakespeare's riddling title bespeaks the material and epistemological problems constellating the concept of "nothing" as well as the equation of that idea in early modern culture with female virginity. A maidenhead, "nothing," is the focus of the main plot where, just as they are about to be married, Claudio falsely and publicly accuses Hero of unchastity. He alleges that she has been unfaithful, not just with one man but with many, and that she engaged in this infidelity even on the very eve of their nuptials. Upon hearing Claudio's accusation, Hero immediately falls into a swoon and is presumed dead. Claudio's accusations against Hero are made plausible not only by evidence trumped up by the wicked Don John, the bastard half-brother of Prince Don Pedro of Aragon, but also because of the insubstantiality of female honor itself. Male honor, *virtus*, could be proven by valor in battle and other noble deeds, but female honor, because it consisted entirely of sexual integrity, could not easily be confirmed. A maidenhead (the hymen) is "like nothing," in so far as it is a far more symbolic than readily discernible physical attribute. Because a maidenhead was "nothing" real, physical or substantive, it was, to put this in more theoretical language, essentially a sign without a referent. Despite the problems of verification attendant on using hymenal rupture as evidence of virginity, however, the cultural fiction of physiological integrity remained.

*Much Ado About Nothing* was also a proverbial expression, and then as now, meant a lot of fuss about a trifling matter. In this play, Shakespeare explores the perils of the insubstantiality of female honor for women and explores the cultural and legal import of their chastity. "Nothing" was also an homonym in the period for "noting," that is, careful recording and observation, and several characters in the play overhear or observe critical events, which are significant motors of the plot. Overwhelmingly, however, the ultimate object of these observations is Hero's "nothing." For the discovery of Don John's plot serves to establish Hero's chastity as palpable reality. Shakespeare uses "nothing" more than once in relation to this obscene meaning – the female sexual organs. Famously Hamlet taunts Ophelia about the "nothing" that lies between a maid's legs:

> HAMLET: Lady, shall I lie in your lap?
> OPHELIA: No, my lord.
> HAMLET: Do you think I meant country matters?
> OPHELIA: I think nothing, my lord.
> HAMLET: That's a fair thought to lie between maids' legs. (3.2.109–15)[2]

Hamlet's paronomastic play on "cunt" and "country" also suggests a rustic, pastoral world, quite unlike Elsinore, where sex has not been entirely denatured. In the fantasy of pastoral, at least (although certainly not in the social reality of rural life), sex is less freighted with significance – and consequence – than it is at court, where aristocratic marital alliance depends, as it does in *Much Ado*'s Messina, upon female honor. In a world where property and power must be transmitted only to legitimate offspring, the female "nothing" also takes on a vast metaphysical significance. In *King Lear*, Cordelia's "Nothing, my lord" (1.1.87) in response to her father's demand that she quantify her love for him, is devoid of innuendo.[3] Cordelia's "nothing" bespeaks the philosophical sense of "nothing" as infinitely void and does so in defiance of Lear's misguided assertion that "nothing will come of nothing" (1.1.90). Again, in *A Midsummer Night's Dream*, "airy nothing" is the substance of specifically literary creativity: "the poet's pen . . . gives to airy nothing / A local habitation and a name" (5.1.15–6).[4] This image replicates prevailing understandings of biological reproduction, namely that men (as in the phallic "poet's pen" or "thing" – of which "no-thing" is the opposite) essentially created new life from "airy nothing," while the female matrix was merely a passive receptacle. "Nothing" here also references all that is beyond and prior to the signifying powers of language itself. What this greater significance serves to achieve, however, is not the separation of the bawdy from the profound meaning of "nothing," but rather the weighting of feminine sexuality with infinite significance – an infinite nothing. This, then, is the culturally complex paradox of "nothing" to which Shakespeare's apparently throwaway title alludes.

The song sung by Balthasar in *Much Ado* has as its refrain, "Hey nonny, nonny," a colloquial variant on the genital "nothing":

> Sigh no more, ladies, sigh no more,
> Men were deceivers ever:
> One foot in sea, and one on shore,
> To one thing constant never.
> Then sigh not so, but let them go,
> And be you blithe and bonny,
> Converting all your sounds of woe
> Into Hey nonny, nonny. (2.3.62–9)[5]

The lyric offers a counterpoint to the prevailing idea that it is women who are sexually suspect, but it also draws again on the central theme of the play's title. "These noninos of filthie ribauldry," as one disapproving commentator opined, referred to what John Florio called "a woman's pleasure-pit, non-nony, or palace of pleasure." Another observer noted that ladies taught to dance the volta, which involved a leaping motion, sometimes went "so high, that you may see their hey nony, nony, no."[6] While female genitals, by this account, could occasionally be seen in public places, the problem with chastity was that it could not be visually identified. Hero's beautiful exterior may bespeak her innocence, so Claudio's reasoning goes, but she is guilty all the same.

> Would you not swear,
> All you that see her, that she were a maid,
> By these exterior shows? But she is none. (4.1.37–9)

This was precisely the logic that allowed the invasive "searching" or examination of the bodies of women suspected of prostitution in early modern London. Overwhelmingly, extant records show that women whose virtue was suspect were arrested, examined, and indicted. Only very occasionally do records exonerate a woman who, like Anne Brooke, was imprisoned in Bridewell in 1604 for what she maintained was a false accusation. Her defense was that "she is a maide and hath lived honest ever hitherto," a claim that was, most unusually, corroborated by the matron.[7] In the fictitious world of the theatre, Shakespeare's comedy offers Hero a similar and equally unlikely reprieve.

At the end of the play, when Claudio accepts that he has wronged Hero and must, for his penance, marry a woman whose face he agrees *not to see* until after the conclusion of the nuptial rite, he agrees to marry even if his bride turns out to be "an Ethiope" (5.4.38). Because of the period's tendency to equate black skin with moral corruption, the suggestion here is that the genuinely penitent Claudio has learned his lesson and that he is willing to marry not only someone whose appearance does not please him but perhaps even someone whose virginity is in doubt, a woman who might actually be what he falsely accused Hero of being, namely "an approved wanton" (4.1.44). However, the language Claudio uses once his mystery bride is revealed as Hero in this second matrimonial event undermines this notion:

> Sweet Hero! Now thy image doth appear
> In the rare semblance that I lov'd it first. (5.1.243–4)

The language precisely echoes his accusation of Hero at their wedding: "She's but the sign and semblance of her honour" (4.1.33). In other words, Claudio's love remains superficial and preoccupied with appearances. The audience may recall that Claudio's intent to marry Hero first and foremost entailed discreet inquiries about her financial worth, when he tried to discover whether she was her father's only heir. Further, Claudio did not undertake the wooing himself but had a masked Don Pedro do it for him. By his own admission also, Claudio is something of a cold fish. When Hero's father, Leonato, tries to find a rational explanation for the accusations leveled against his daughter on her wedding day, he assumes it is Claudio who must have seduced Hero, and that she is being charged with ante-nuptial sex, which from Leonato's point of view would "extenuate the 'forehand sin" (4.1.50). Claudio, however, is quick to dismiss this possibility and firmly denies that he ever demonstrated any sexual feelings towards her: "But, as a brother to his sister, show'd / Bashful sincerity and comely love" (4.1.53–4). Since courtship is precisely *not* a species of siblinghood, there is something inescapably incestuous about the language of Claudio's unsettling disclaimer of all sexual interest in the woman to whom he was betrothed. The word "semblance" that Claudio uses in relation to Hero further suggests courtly artifice, the aesthetic and diplomatic skills of the courtier outlined by Baldassare Castiglione in *Il Cortegiano* (*The Courtier*), translated into English by Sir Thomas Hoby in 1561. When Don Pedro woos Hero and when their friends gull Beatrice and Benedick into an admission of love for one another, these are benign, comic illusions and deceptions – white lies. The other facet of the charade, like the little drama performed at Hero's window, is that it has the capacity to deceive and conceal. Shakespeare at this point is probing the problem of representation intrinsic to his own medium.

Fundamentally, indeed, the play poses the problem of truth – truth about people and the truth of images – as a judicial one. In a scenario that perfectly mirrors the original perfidy of having Claudio and Don John overhear staged falsehoods, the comic obfuscators – the constable, Dogberry, and his watch – come as close as anyone in the play to the apprehension of truth. These bunglers overhear the truth when they chance upon a conversation among the villains. Shakespeare's satire on the watch is taken directly from life, where needy men, often in ill-health and poor physical condition, undertook – sometimes under pressure – to stand watch or patrol the streets all night.[8] But just like Dogberry, the master of malapropisms *avant la lettre*, these unpromising fellows often made arrests and enforced the law quite effectively.[9] That Dogberry and Verges grasp Don John's plot is a miracle in itself, since they take Borachio's quip about fashion: "What a deformed thief this fashion is" to refer to a malefactor: "I know that Deformed; a has been a vile thief this seven year; a goes up and down like a gentleman: I remember his name" (3.3.122–4). Once again, Shakespeare insists on the moral and practical problems in his own medium – the tendency for language to be taken to mean something it does not say. However, Dogberry's words reverberate with the historical record of what went on in the streets of London. Martha Mammoth, a "common nightwalker," told a constable who tried to arrest her that he was "a man of fashion" and offered to go home with him, although this particular officer proved resistant to flattery and seduction.[10]

Ostensibly, the play ends happily ever after despite the string of misprisions that comprise the action. Yet there remains an unshakable sense that Claudio was always too willing to believe Hero's betrayal, from the very first moment he heard the trumped up accusation. Claudio leaves an aftertaste that the play's formal comic resolution does not dispel. Further, the public humiliation of his calumny against Hero *could* indeed have killed her: "Thy slander hath gone through and through her heart"; "she is dead, slander'd to death by villains" (5. 1.68–9; 88). Only Hero's mock death spares her the shame and social shunning that she would otherwise have endured. In this, the play prefigures the murder of the slandered Desdemona by Othello, and the defamation of Hermione in *The Winter's Tale*. The latter is, like Hero, resurrected from apparent death.

The action of the play occurs in a period of homecoming from the military campaign against the now ostensibly reconciled Don John and represents a shift from combat to court where warfare gives way to courtship, love, and marriage. In the case of Hero and Claudio, however, a new "war" is begun that is still deadly. Indeed, this so pressures the bounds of conventional comic resolution that these characters are only awkwardly and uncomfortably contained within the decorum of the genre.[11]

What serves to leaven the essentially tragic coupling of the main plot is the comic couple of the subplot, Beatrice and Benedick, between whom the antagonisms of war are not so much suspended as transferred to the perennial battle between the sexes. Beatrice and Benedick are sparring partners in the game of love, and the play works to reveal their reticence and apparent hostility towards one another as thinly disguised sexual passion. Beatrice vows spinsterhood because submission to a husband, a son of Adam, made of clay, is unthinkable: "Would it not grieve a woman to be overmastered by a piece of valiant dust?" (2.1.56–7). She, of course, revokes this vow as soon as she is convinced of Benedick's genuine love for her: "I will requite thee, / Taming my wild heart to thy loving hand" (3.1.111–12). This is an outcome worthy of comedy simply because Beatrice retains her agency, and it is she who tames her heart, and not her husband. The erotically charged exchanges between these lovers are in the spirit of mutual belligerence, alive with the wit of "a merry war" (1.1.56).

However, when Beatrice engages Benedick to "Kill Claudio" (4.1.288) in her outrage at the injustice done to her kinswoman, this only serves to intensify the sense of tragic wrong done to Hero. Beatrice's indignation at the powerlessness of women in the face of such injuries ("O, God that I were a man. I would eat his heart out in the market-place!" (4.1.304–5)) also demonstrates that slandered female honor has no recourse to justice, even what Francis Bacon called the "wilde justice" of revenge.[12] Hero is, after all, decried by the sovereign himself, Don Pedro, as "a common stale" (4.1.65). Early modern culture's profound anxiety about legitimate paternity made all women sexually suspect because men could not prove that their children, their heirs, were in fact their own. As Benedick declares when he pledges bachelorhood, "Because I will not do them the wrong to mistrust any, I will do myself the right to trust none" (1.1.225–7). The kind of "wrong" of which he speaks is, of course, exactly that which Claudio commits in his violent, public shaming of Hero: "Give not this rotten orange to your friend" (4.1.31). Claudio's accusations have furthermore all the flavor of the courtroom:

> CLAUDIO:  What man was he talk'd with you yesternight,
>              Out at your window betwixt twelve and one?
>              Now, if you are a maid, answer to this.
> HERO:  I talk'd with no man at that hour, my lord. (4.1.83–6)

Based on the erroneous belief that it was Hero who was seen to "Talk with a ruffian at her chamber-window" (4.1.91), she is judged guilty. The woman at the window was not, of course, Hero but her maidservant, Margaret. For all that, like the women at Bridewell, Hero has fallen under suspicion on the grounds of being in the wrong place at the wrong time. For a woman to be seen at night in London was good grounds for suspicion that she was a "night-walker," a prostitute touting for customers. Hero's arraignment, then, is indeed "much ado about nothing" – a trumped up charge, a groundless accusation.

The double meanings of "nothing" have received much more critical attention than "ado." Like "nothing," however, "ado" also had strongly sexual connotations. When, for example, on April 25, 1530 at St Ives in Huntingdonshire Joan Martyn of Owton alleged that Robert Blundell had made an informal contract of marriage with her before making her pregnant, the term "ado" was used to express the consummation of the relationship: " 'I will mary thee and if thou wilt let me have *adoo* with thee and she said certain I will never have noon but you,' and upon that they had *adoo* together" (my emphasis). The pair were judged lawfully married and ordered to solemnize their marriage before the following August, or else suffer excommunication.[13] In 1609, Anne Eliffe was arraigned for "playing the queene" [prostitute] with a youth but "confidently den[ied] that she ever had *to doe* with him or he with her" (my emphasis).[14] "Ado," or "to do" was thus a common colloquialism for sexual intercourse, and records from Bridewell and the "bawdy courts" (the trials held in the ecclesiastical courts that dealt so often with cases of sexual misconduct) frequently use it. For all that "ado" remains subordinate in the play to "nothing," whose verification, in the form of Hero's virginity, is the play's *terminus ad quem*.

Even during the most critical junctures of the action, the punning insistence on the multiple meanings of "nothing" is unrelenting. Thus, in Act 5 Don Pedro tells Leonato: "She [Hero] was charg'd with *nothing* / But what was true, and very full of proof" (5.1.104–5, my emphasis). In the case of aristocratic marriages, blood from a ruptured hymen was typically adduced as evidence of not only of consummation but also of the woman's virginity. Wedding sheets were sometimes publicly displayed after the wedding night, and Catherine of Aragon was able to produce her bloodstained wedding sheet as evidence of consummation almost thirty years after her marriage to Henry VIII when he sued for divorce. This evidence was crucial since she had been previously married to Henry's late brother, Arthur. He died aged fifteen after only a few months of marriage, though, and she maintained that they had shared a bed for only seven nights during that period and that she married Henry "as intact and incorrupt as when she emerged from her mother's womb."[15] Shakespeare was to dramatize this episode from recent Tudor history in *Henry VIII*, where the queen challenges Henry to deny that she was "a true maid" at the time of their marriage in evidence of its legality. Queen Catherine was on much more solid ground than the scores of women who were "searched" by midwives when they came before the courts for sexual misconduct. The records for Bridewell, for example, show matrons examining women's bodies to find out whether female suspects were "maids" or "noe maids."[16] Many of these women were not charged with any specific crime, but were rather, as we have noted, in the wrong place at the wrong time, and most after the ordeal of being searched were found to be "noe maid," "light," "loose," "unhonest," "untrue," "otherwise," "contrary," "faulty," or "harlots."[17] Such was the kind of evidence brought against women in the harsh reality of London's streets.

Hero, as "an approved wanton" (4.1.44), is the aristocratic version of the woman who has had physical evidence marshaled against her. When the prince, Don Pedro, hears Hero deny that she spoke to a ruffian out her window on the night before her wedding – something he erroneously believes he has witnessed with his own eyes – he utters precisely the same language of judgment used in the Bridewell records: "Why then you are no maiden" (4.1.86). There is a very much related kind of wordplay on negatives in *Measure for Measure* when Mariana is brought before the duke after the bed trick in which she has consummated her betrothal to Angelo. She is asked a series of questions by the duke about her marital status – is she a maid, a married woman, or a widow? When she replies: "Neither my Lord" (5.1.182), the duke pronounces: "Why, you are *nothing*" (5.1.185. my emphasis). Mariana is thus not only devoid of social status, but, at least in the eyes of society, of any subjective existence at all. Women in early modern England could be married or widowed, but they could not be simply *unmarried*. Rather they were either unmarried virgins, "maids" or *not*, "*no* maids." Of the words for this condition, "rotten" (4.1.31) and "stale" (4.1.65) are applied to the defamed Hero, but there were many more: whore, drab, doxy, and trull among them. These words were also part the lexicon of early modern prostitution, which made no distinction between women who received payment for sex with men to whom they were not married and women who did not.

To fall outside the acceptable parameters of womanhood, then, is to become a kind of social negative. Intriguingly, there is another "nothing" woman, a phantom character in the first printed version of the text of *Much Ado* in the figure of Innogen, who is the wife of Leonato, and therefore, presumably, Hero's mother. She appears in the stage directions for the first scenes of both Act 1 and Act 2. That a character who never appears is nonetheless named early on in the play adds an additional layer of complexity since the name Innogen derives from a Celtic word *inghean*, which means "maiden."

*Much Ado* was probably written in 1598, and the quarto was printed in 1600. Shakespeare's source for the plot of the woman falsely accused of unchastity is Italian Matteo Bandello's twenty-second *Novella*, which Shakespeare either read in the original Italian or in French in the third volume of Belleforest's *Histoires Tragiques* (1559). Other sources include Spenser's *Faerie Queene* (2.4) and Ludovico Ariosto's *Orlando Furioso* (1516). The latter had been translated in 1591 by the queen's godson, Sir John Harington, and printed by another of Shakespeare's contemporaries from Stratford-Upon-Avon, Richard Field. The rendition of this theme in *Much Ado*, however, poses one of the most radical questions in Shakespeare: Can the law protect a slandered woman? Despite all misgivings about Claudio, that the play answers this question in the affirmative is what finally makes *Much Ado* a comedy in spirit as well as in form.

## As You Like It

*As You Like It* was first printed in the First Folio of 1623. The exact date of its first performance is unknown. However, in a recent edition of the play, Juliet Dusinberre suggests that this occurred not in the public theatre, but at court, only ten days after the queen and her retinue had moved to Richmond Palace on Shrove Tuesday, February 20, 1599.[1] For this momentous opening, Shakespeare used a recently published and popular story (it had seen four editions by 1599) as his source for the plot, namely Thomas Lodge's pastoral romance *Rosalynde* (1590), which is written in prose interspersed with lyric. Once again there is a connection with the ubiquitous Robert Greene, who may have ushered Lodge's book through publication while its author was away at sea. *As You Like It* is almost an early modern musical – there are more songs than in any other play in the canon, and its overall tone, despite a few melancholy notes, is that of "a holiday humour" (4.1.63). The most ebullient of those plays designated by critics as Shakespeare's festive comedies – although, of course, that term does not mean that such plays are sunshine without shadow – this comedy emphasizes the way that, as the critic C.L. Barber put it, festivity "organizes experience."[2]

The play is premised on a juxtaposition of the country and the court, on the contrast between the restrictions of civility, especially those imposed by unjust rulers, and the freedoms of rural life. Duke Frederick has usurped his domain from his older brother, the rightful Duke Senior, while Oliver, the eldest son of Sir Rowland de Boys, and the inheritor of his entire estate, abuses his younger brother, Orlando, and attempts to have him killed in a wrestling contest with Charles, the duke's own herculean wrestler, who has already grievously injured the three sturdy sons of an old man. Yet, Orlando miraculously defeats Charles and does so immediately after having met and fallen in love with Rosalind, daughter of the banished duke. Orlando soon learns that he must escape the usurper duke's wrath, despite his victory, while Rosalind is ordered to flee because Duke Frederick fears that if she remains her popularity will remind the people of her father. She makes her escape dressed as a man, accompanied by her companion since childhood, Celia, Duke Frederick's daughter, who is disguised as a maid of humble origins, Aliena. The evils of their society compel these characters to seek refuge in a world beyond civilization, the green world of the forest. There the play uses the license of comedy, exile, and displacement to explore some of the most profound political questions of Shakespeare's day – and indeed of ours – about the nature of political liberty.

The central action of the play takes place in the forest utopia to which the "old Duke" has been exiled:

> They say he is already in the Forest of Arden
> and a many merry men with him, and there they live
> like the old Robin Hood of England. They say many
> young gentlemen flock to him every day and fleet the
> time carelessly as they did in the golden world. (1.1.109–13)

In popular culture, Sherwood Forest in Nottinghamshire, which borders on Shakespeare's own native county of Warwickshire, was the mythic location of Robin Hood and his Merry Men, whose transgressions against the prevailing social order were motivated, according to popular tradition, purely by an attempt to rectify its injustice. Arden echoes Eden, as well as the classical convention of pastoral derived from Theocritus, and in England recently popularized by Edmund Spenser's *Shepheardes Calendar* (1579). The profoundly literary nature of the forest is disclosed also in the play's evocation of a Golden Age derived both from Ovid's *Metamorphoses* and Virgil's *Eclogues*. The courtly art of literature paradoxically crafts the dominant discourse of the natural world. *As You Like It* is also marked, like *Much Ado About Nothing*, by the influence of the Italian Ariosto's *Orlando Furioso*, translated in 1591 by the queen's godson, Sir John Harington, and by Sir Philip Sidney's prose romance *Arcadia* (1590), as well as Robert Greene's *Menaphon* (1589), subsequently reprinted in 1598 as *Greene's Arcadia*. Pastoral in these literary renditions is the natural world rendered via artifice, and Shakespeare's similarly unnaturalistic green world harbors a lion, a snake, as well as an olive tree and a palm tree. By means of these conventions, Shakespeare's audience is allowed an escape from the pressures of urban life along with the play's exiles into an improved and idealized version of the rural world for which many of them may have had nostalgic longings.

Arden was certainly freighted with personal and literary nostalgia for Shakespeare. The name Arden harks back to the Arden Forest of his Warwickshire childhood. Arden was his mother's name, and although her father, Robert, was

only a yeoman from Wilmcote, the family claimed connection with the aristocratic Ardens of Castle Bromwich, and indeed, Shakespeare applied to have that
relationship represented on his coat of arms. The French forest, the Ardennes
of Lodge's novella, becomes in the play the idyll of rural England, albeit one
which also registers the ills of rural life, such as dearth, absentee landlords, and
the scourge of the 1590s – the enclosure of common land. The play is also, in
some sense, a eulogy for Christopher Marlowe, who wrote one of the most
exquisite pastoral lyrics of the Elizabethan age, "Come live with me and be my
love," and who is twice referred to in the course of the play: "Dead shepherd,
now I find thy saw of might: / 'Who ever loved, that loved not at first sight?'"
(3.5.82–3). The "saw," or saying, is a quotation from Marlowe's *Hero and
Leander*. The second reference to Shakespeare's great rival points explicitly
to the circumstances of his death in 1593 in what was reported in depositions
from the time to be the consequence of a violent altercation concerning "the
reckoning," that is, his account at a tavern: "It strikes a man more dead than
a great reckoning in a little room" (3.3.12–13).

Most importantly, however, the forest conforms to the pervasive Renaissance
notion of the world-upside-down, an inverted world where all the prevailing
social hierarchies are turned on their heads. Such topsy-turvy behavior was a
crucial feature of popular festivals, and temporary inversion served as a safety
valve to ensure that repressive hierarchy would be less vulnerable to assault from
those whom it oppressed. However, there was always the danger that once
unleashed on these occasions, popular discontent might not be contained again
and that social elites could not right the world once it had been up-ended. This
is the disorderly world of carnival, in which normal social restraints are not only
held in abeyance but also are potentially undone altogether; the inherently
transgressive structure of revelry frequently offered the convenient occasion for
riot and disorder as well.

The political implications of the inverted world were profound, and they are
emphasized from the very opening of the play when Orlando laments his condition as an orphaned younger son who is denied the education and treatment
befitting his rank. The play thus begins with a critique of one of the foundational institutions of the English social structure, namely that of primogeniture,
according to which, inheritance, and especially land, was kept together by
passing estates on in their entirety to the eldest son:

> The
> courtesy of nations allows you my better in that you are
> the first-born, but the same tradition takes not away my
> blood, were there twenty brothers betwixt us.

> I have as much of my father in me as you, albeit I confess your
> coming before me is nearer his reverence. (1.1.43–8)

This is a particularly important part of the plot because it is not to be found in Shakespeare's source, where Thomas Lodge's characters are not subject to the English law of primogeniture. Orlando represents the principle of Natural Law – a complex term in the period, but one which broadly underwrites arguments for freedom of conscience and the right to survival. It encapsulates the conviction that "law and justice are innate to human beings as part of their very nature."[3] Possessing an innate sense of justice, Orlando is identified with unschooled virtue, and with charity, when he takes with him to Arden the aged servant Adam, who has been turned out of doors by his brother. This is in marked contrast to Oliver, who describes himself as Orlando's "natural brother" (1.1.136). Oliver slanders his brother in order to persuade Charles that he should kill him in the ring:

> It is the
> stubbornest young fellow of France, full of ambition,
> an envious emulator of every man's good parts, a secret
> and villainous contriver against me his natural brother. (1.1.133–6)

Oliver appropriates Natural Law to his own ends, but in this context, "natural" also suggests illegitimacy, and thus casts a shadow, however subliminally, on his own claim to rightful inheritance. In contrast, twice acknowledging the legitimacy of Oliver's claim to supremacy, the "tradition" and "courtesy of nations" that upholds it, Orlando nonetheless insists on his rightful entitlement, which has been legally ratified by his father's will (1.1.61–3). The cleverly implied criticism in Orlando's speech is that the law of primogeniture did not take into account the incidence of bad elder brothers. Church and state urged obedience to all superiors, whether in the family or civic hierarchy, and did so regardless of the particular character of the individual who held authority. Further, disobedience at any point in the chain of hierarchy was understood to have consequences that would undermine the social structure as a whole. Obedience to God was to be expressed by submission to the magistrate, and where the law of God and the ruler were in conflict, exile appeared to be the only solution. Thus, wives were charged to obey even brutal husbands, servants to endure tyrannous masters, subjects to obey evil rulers, and, as in *As You Like It*, younger brothers to submit to "tyrant brother[s]" (1.2.277). William Tyndale's *Obedience of a Christian Man* (1528) and John Ponet's *A Short Treatise of Politike Power, and of the True Obedience which Subjects Owe to Kings and other Civill Governours* (1556) are, in their different ways, English attempts to discern the nature of political submission. While this doctrine served those in power, it did not serve subordinates, especially when they were subject to either political or familial tyranny. One of the most radical texts of this period, published anonymously because of the incendiary nature of its arguments, was the infamous *Vindiciae Contra Tyrannos: Or Concerning the Legitimate Power of a Prince Over the People, and of the People over a Prince* (1579). The publishing imprint of this text is Edinburgh, but it was subsequently printed in England in 1581 and 1589, and in partial translation from Latin in 1588 and 1622.[4] The *Vindiciae* urges limitations on sovereign power. Though notorious all over Europe, it was written in France and not fully translated into English until 1648.

The problem of the people's allegiance to their rulers had been exacerbated by the religious strife that plagued Europe during this period. The pope, upon excommunicating Elizabeth I in 1570, had essentially required all English Catholics to abjure fealty to the Crown. Orlando's argument with his brother is phrased, then, in the language of legal and political treatises: "The courtesy of nations." Similarly arguing that the power of kings should be tempered, the *Vindiciae* urges that the "practice of almost all nations," *ius gentium*, lays down the limits of political office.[5] In *King Lear*, the wicked and illegitimate Edmund, another "natural brother," whose rallying cry is "Now gods, stand up for bastards!" (1.2.22), utters a similar phrase, "the curiosity of nations" (1.2.4), that is, the strange customs of nations, in his compelling critique of the structure and transmission of political power.[6] Orlando's protest against "the courtesy of nations" is then phrased in the language of political radicalism.

When Orlando vanquishes Charles in the wrestling contest, he has not only successfully overthrown his brother's tyranny, he has also reenacted one of the most sublime moments in biblical pastoral, the story of the "comely" shepherd boy, David, whose route to kingship was also keenly investigated by the *Vindiciae*. David, like Orlando, was the youngest son. Wearing neither sword nor armor, David vanquished the Philistine giant, Goliath, after three of his brothers (paralleling Charles's three earlier victims) have already gone into battle against the Philistine army but without success. Like Orlando's, David's victory was against all odds: "Thou art a boy, and he is a man of war from his youth" (1 Samuel 17.33). David's prowess repudiates the English law of primogeniture because it derives from the fact that he is God's anointed and is destined to become the king of Israel and the founder of the lineage which achieves its fulfillment in the birth of Christ, "a perpetual light from the line of David," as the author of the *Vindiciae* puts it.

Those who promulgated orthodox notions of hierarchy and obedience did so in the belief that it was God given: God anointed kings and God appointed all temporal rulers and magistrates. That Shakespeare inserts the David and

Goliath motif at the beginning of the play unsettles this hierarchy because David is the youngest and the least of his father's house. David is anointed, as the Geneva translation of 1560 puts it, "in the middes of his bretheren" after all his older brothers have been rejected as leaders of Israel. When it is clear that none of his brothers have been chosen by God to lead the people of Israel, David's father, asked if he indeed has no other sons but these, admits: "There remaineth yet a little one behind, [that] keepeth sheep" (1 Samuel 16.11). The "little one behind," small and belated, is the chosen one, and the very epitome of his kingship in that he is, in what was to become one of the most radical Christian refigurations of sovereignty, a shepherd. While classical pastoral is above all a genre populated by shepherds, it took on new resonances within the Judeo-Christian tradition. Above all, in the New Testament, Christ figures as a radically alternative form of authority and power: Jesus is the Good Shepherd who leads his flock, and who asserts not power and might but claims instead an inverted order, proclaiming that, like younger sons, "So the last shall be first, and the first last" (Matthew 20.16). In the play, the rightful Duke Senior is signally figured as the good shepherd: "They say many young gentlemen *flock* to him every day and fleet the time carelessly as they did in the golden world" (1.1.111–13, my emphasis). Further, when Rosalind becomes the mythological Ganymede, she takes on the role of a beautiful Trojan shepherd boy.

This is quite the "dainty dish" – a spectacle that interrogates established authority – to set before the queen. Fortunately, at Richmond Palace, the queen might choose to identify with rusticated sovereignty. (Edmund Spenser referred to her as "Elisa, Queene of shepheardes all" in the April Eclogue of the *Shepheardes Calendar* published in 1579.) Further, Elizabeth more than once expressed these fantasies herself. When recounting her imprisonment at Woodstock Castle by her sister, Mary Tudor, she confessed she "wished herself to be a milkmaid."[7] And, at the closing of Parliament on March 15, 1576, she said, "If I were a milkmaid with a pail on mine arm, whereby my private person might be little set by, I would not forsake my single state to match myself with the greatest monarch."[8] Elizabeth played both roles, of course – that of the beneficent and just sovereign and the tyrannical ruler – while fantasizing about an escape to a simpler, rustic life. A good example of this contrast between competing figurations of female sovereignty is to be found in Hans Eworth's painting, *Elizabeth I and the Three Goddesses* (1569).[9] Susan Doran has observed of this painting, "The central contrast in the painting is not between Elizabeth and Venus, but between the dark, enclosed, formal world of the Tudor court, where the queen and her two gentlewomen are placed, and the bright pastoral world inhabited by the goddesses . . ."[10] Her entire reign as the Virgin Queen was promulgated in the period as a return to the Golden World prophesied in

Virgil's Fourth Eclogue, but for many early moderns it was also a violation of the proper order of male rule and was rather ungodly than festive.

The world-upside-down is also a world where women are on top, and *As You Like It* foregrounds the transvestite stage as the central motor of its plot. Modern performance, which has traditionally used a female actor to play Rosalind, has thus downplayed the outrageously transgressive homoeroticism that is key to the play's humor. That the actor playing Rosalind is usually a woman in modern productions is a more conservative performance choice. Typically, as in Peggy Ashcroft's paradigmatic performance at the Old Vic in 1932, Rosalind is rigged out in fetching thigh-high boots and tights, that is, in a stylized and very feminized version of masculine attire that foregrounds her specifically feminine allure rather than the ambivalence of her gender identity.

Deep ties of friendship bind Celia to Rosalind despite their fathers, and the lyrical language describing their amity lends the play hope from the beginning. However, from a metatheatrical point of view, two cross-dressed young men are voicing their indivisible union in language that was often used to describe marriage, where the "two become one." As Ganymede, the boy abducted by Jove to become his cupbearer, Rosalind takes on a specifically homoerotic role, and plays it out in her interviews with Orlando, in which she purports to play, like a catamite, the woman's part, in order to teach him how to woo. This enchanting courtship serves to emphasize the artificial language of love – especially that derived from the Petrarchan love lyric – with which Orlando papers the forest – and at the same time, the way even such rhetorical posturing can be invested with real emotion. Gender roles are presented as relatively arbitrary throughout the play – Rosalind can play her part as man or woman, and Phoebe, who falls in love with the male Ganymede and sends "him" love poems, can switch her desire instead to her besotted suitor, Silvius, when the impossibility of a union with Ganymede is revealed to her. Long before Judith Butler articulated the notion of identity as performance, Jacques argued not dissimilarly: "All the world's a stage, / And all the men and women merely players. / They have their exits and their entrances, / And one man in his time plays many parts" (2.7.140–3). Theatre, in other words, is the perfect analogy for life, and the roles – including sexual roles – which human beings enact in the course of it, are multiple and various.

Most radically, in the forest of Arden, political liberty is associated with the unrestrained erotic possibilities of the rural life. Rosalind is one of the liveliest of Shakespeare's heroines, and at the end of the play she orchestrates the play's concluding nuptial rites officiated by Hymen, the god of marriage. Conjugality exalts even the most comic of these pairings, namely that of the goat herder, Audrey, and the courtier Touchstone. In other words, the play returns to the values of civility to sanctify these couplings. These conjunctions are not the disorderly matches Touchstone has earlier condemned as "betray[ing] a she-lamb of a twelvemonth to a crooked-pated old cuckoldly ram, out of all reasonable match," when he has accused the shepherd Corin of pimping sheep (3.2.78–80). However, this principle of natural, animal generation is still registered in the final scene by the melancholy Jacques when he evokes the procession of the animals two-by-two into Noah's Ark: "There is sure another flood toward, and these couples are coming to the ark. Here comes a pair of very strange beasts . . ." (5.4.35–7). Early modern audiences would have known that in the medieval mystery plays, despite this orderly procession, the one troubled coupling was that of Noah, whose shrewish wife, Uxor, was the single greatest impediment to her husband's project of saving the human race. She is unnamed in the Bible, but was subsequently given this name, which is simply the Latin for "wife." As the representatives of civility on the Ark, Noah and Uxor were far outclassed by every animal couple on the face of the earth. *As You Like It*, too, insists on the complex relationship between people and animals as the primal instance of human domination over the "natural" world by taking the license of comedy to explore the consequences of that imposition.

## Twelfth Night, Or What You Will

"We'll have the bear again, and we will fool him black and blue"
                                        *Twelfth Night* (2.5.9–10)[1]

Built on the order of Henry VIII in 1526, the Paris Garden bear pit was almost next door to the Globe, but physical proximity was not its only connection with London theatre. Like the Fortune and the Rose, the bear pit was "at the heart of a business empire" and run by theatrical entrepreneur Philip Henslowe and his son-in-law, Edward Alleyn.[2] They were also actively engaged in staging bearbaiting spectacles as a form of entertainment and in James's reign acquired the lucrative offices of the Mastership and Sergeantship of the Bears by the king's privilege.[3] After an accident at Paris Garden in 1583 that resulted in the deaths of several people, hotter Protestants (that is to say, those with Puritan sympathies who tended to disapprove of all forms of public entertainment and not just those involving cruelty to animals) interpreted the accident as God's providential punishment on the spectators. Most Elizabethans, however, appear to have found this kind of cruelty not only unobjectionable but also a source of immense amusement. In this, they have much in common with Sir Toby Belch, Maria, Sir Andrew Aguecheek, and Fabian, the characters of the subplot of *Twelfth Night* who pursue their delight in tormenting the Puritan steward, Malvolio, to cruel and unusual extremes. They are moved to do so in part by his disapproval of bearbaitings on the property of the mistress of the household, Olivia, who is also Sir Toby's niece: "You know he brought me out o' favour with my lady, about a bear-baiting here" *Twelfth Night* (2.5.8). Clearly, Olivia does not condone the sport either, but Sir Toby decides that it is better to substitute Malvolio for the bear, and he gleefully anticipates the brutality they can inflict upon him: "We will fool him black and blue" (2.5.10).

The bear pit was, at least from a playwright's point of view, in competition with the stage, and the bears themselves were called "beasts of recreation." It is as if in *Twelfth Night* Shakespeare was contemplating the nature of "festive" entertainment, and did so in what is essentially a musical. If the subplot addresses the way spectators take pleasure in brutality inflicted on others, the main plot considers the elements of theatricality that its Puritan detractors most took issue with in "lewd plays," specifically the bawdy and ribald elements of comedy and the cross-dressing that was an inescapable feature of the all-male stage.

The play was first performed to celebrate the feast of Twelfth Night, on Candlemas Day, February 2, 1602; however, the location of this first performance was not the public theatre but one of the Inns of Court – the hall of Middle Temple. Middle Temple was also the Inn to which Sir John Davies belonged (he had been called to the bar in 1595), and it is he who composed the following verse description of the bearbaiting proclivities of students from the Inns of Court:

> Publius student at the common law,
> Oft leaves his books, and for his recreation:
> To Paris Garden doth himself Withdrawe,
> Where he is ravish[ed] with such delectation
> As downe amongst the dogges and beares he goes,
> Where whilst he skipping cries To Head, To head,
> His satten doublet and his velvet hose,
> Are with sputtle from above be-spread . . . .
> And rightly too on him this filth doth fall,
> Which for such filthie sports his books forsakes . . .
>
> John Davies, *Epigrammes* (c.1594)[4]

Neither his education nor his fine attire of satin and velvet deter this young man from going down among the dogs in what is presented as a filthy but also quasi-comically reprehensible recreational activity. Thus, baiting Malvolio like a bear was probably something that many of the law students in Shakespeare's first audience could have identified with.

This bearbaiting vignette is important because at the end of the play Malvolio remains enraged by his mistreatment and leaves the stage unreconciled to his mistress and her household. Further, his parting promise of vengeance indicates that he is fully conscious that he has been baited like a bear by a pack of curs: "I'll be reveng'd on the whole *pack* of you" (5.1.377, my emphasis). Through Malvolio's defiance of comic reconciliation and restored harmony, Shakespeare insists on the complexities of laughter, and that the genre of comedy encompasses not only all that is festive and delightful, such as marriage and the reunion of lost siblings, but also the vicious spectacle of a blood sport.[5]

Malvolio's gulling, of course, is ancillary to the story of separated twins and confusion of identity. This was mainly based on an Italian comedy called *Gl'Ingannati* (*The Deceived*, 1537) that was also treated in a novella by Bandello in 1554. Shakespeare may have accessed Bandello's Italian version via the French translation by Belleforest, *Histoires Tragiques* (1571), and he read Barnabe Riche's story of *Apolonius and Silla* in a volume titled *Farewell to Military Profession* (1581). While Shakespeare's incurs these clearly identifiable literary debts in the main plot, the subplot concerning Olivia's household is completely original to him. Interestingly too, the only surviving contemporary account of the play, by another law student, John Manningham, focuses not on the main plot but on the cruel game played at Malvolio's expense:

> At our feast wee had a play called "Twelve Night, or What You Will," much like the Commedy of Errores, or the Menechmi in Plautus, but most like and near to that in Italian called Ingnanni. A good practice in it [was] to make the Steward believe his Lady . . . in love with him, by counterfeiting a letter as from his Lady in general terms, telling him what she liked best in him, and prescribing his gesture in smiling, his apparel, &c., and then when he came to practice making him belive they took him to be mad.[6]

That Manningham mentions Shakespeare's earlier play *The Comedy of Errors*, which features two pairs of twins, makes it clear that he is fully aware of the classical antecedents and contemporary sources for the main plot whose central character, Viola, believes herself to be (like Shakespeare's daughter, Judith), a surviving twin. Viola and Sebastian, orphaned and improbably "identical" fraternal twins, are separated after a shipwreck. Believing that her brother is drowned, Viola dons male clothing to present herself under the name Cesario at the court of Duke Orsino, where she gains employment as a page. Orsino charges her to woo the wealthy Lady Olivia on his behalf. Olivia has vowed a life of celibacy in response to the death of her brother, but in spite of it, she falls in love with the disguised Viola. Only when Sebastian arrives later in the play does this dilemma resolve itself, although, up until the final denouement, Olivia believes she has married Cesario/Viola, who is in turn in love with her employer, Orsino. The romantic tangles of the play are untied, but the antagonisms generated in the subplot are never resolved. Malvolio is the enemy to revelry, to "cakes and ale" (2.3.115), and eventually to comedy itself. This play explores the perversity and absurdity of desire understood both as erotic longing and social aspiration. At the same time, the play seems to glance tantalizingly at Shakespeare's own life: the title *Twelfth Night, or What You Will* encodes a pun on the playwright's own Christian name, and may even register a certain self-consciousness about his own painstaking and expensive pursuit of social recognition at the College of Arms, which was the subject of Chapter 4.

The comedy begins, quite literally, on a sad note. The opening scene reveals not the shipwreck, which is saved for the second scene of the play (even though modern productions often reverse the order), but Orsino, who is listening to music that feeds his melancholy: "That strain again, it had a dying fall" (1.1.4). The "dying fall" is a melancholy decrescendo appropriate both to Orsino's character, as Duke of Illyria (a place name that suggests discordance and disharmony, the un-tuned or ill-lyrical) and to a play that begins with Orsino and Olivia, whose melancholy and grief finds them in retreat and isolation. The sparkling comic vitality of the play subdues – but does not entirely dispel – these qualities in the conjugal unions of Act 5. Yet, the play's title references the close of the Christmas festivities, an occasion frequently celebrated by the carnivalesque inversion of order in the everyday world – the world-turned-upside-down. Thus it is a world where women dominate, a fantasy world where wishes can be fulfilled.

In the musical setting of Illyria, the shipwrecked Viola takes an identity upon herself, which is not, as modern audiences often imagine, that of a young man, but rather that of a eunuch, Cesario. Despite the many songs in *Twelfth Night*, we never actually hear Viola sing, although she tells us quite specifically that it is her vocal gifts that lead her to select this particular disguise and to present herself as "an eunuch" (1.2.56) to the duke and seek employment at his court. "Viola" is itself the name of a musical instrument and that name is echoed anagrammatically, like a musical variation, across the identities of the other characters, Olivia and Malvolio. When Malvolio describes "Cesario," newly arrived as the emissary from Orsino's court, the emphasis is once again on her vocal qualities, her "pipe." This is also a joke about her diminished genital equipment, since in early modern English "pipe" was a synonym for penis. Orsino, too, remarks upon Viola's vocal characteristics:

> For they shall yet belie thy happy years,
> That say thou art a man; Diana's lip
> Is not more smooth and rubious: thy small pipe
> Is as the maiden's organ, shrill and sound,
> And all is semblative a woman's part. (1.4.30–34)

The conventional obscene equivocation on "pipe," "organ," and "woman's part" serves to confuse even genital identity, since the hermaphroditic suggestion here is that Viola/Cesario is possessed of both the male "pipe-organ" *and* the female "part." That she is a eunuch also suggests the Continental theatrical practice of using castrati, that is, singers who had been castrated before their voices had broken. Castration was not, however, practiced in England except for medical reasons. Just as in *As You Like It*, where Rosalind becomes the definitively homoerotic Ganymede, that Viola is a eunuch adds a layer of complexity, but also of erotic allure to the disguise. The suggestion is that in the theatre, as in Illyria, the satisfaction of all manner of erotic choices, "what you will," can be delivered.

Disguise, confusion about sexual identity, and about appropriate sexual objects and objectives, is the engine of the play's comedy, as is to be expected of the licensed misrule of a festive holiday, and everything in the play tends toward its ultimate resolution – to the return of proper order and hierarchy:

> How will this fadge? My master loves her dearly,
> And I, poor monster, fond as much on him,
> And she, mistaken, seems to dote on me:
> What will become of this? As I am man,
> My state is desperate for my master's love:
> As I am woman (now alas the day!)
> What thriftless sighs shall poore Olivia breathe?
> O time, thou must untangle this, not I,
> It is too hard a knot for me t' untie. (2.2.32–40)

Neither man nor woman, Viola indeed constitutes, at least by early modern lights, a "poor monster," a freak of nature. Engaged as a page to woo Olivia in his stead, Cesario instantly conquers Olivia's heart. Modern productions often fail to capture the genuinely transgressive aspect of this courtship even though it has been the topic of much feminist criticism of the play.[7] Olivia is an heiress, the ruler of her own household, what early moderns would have understood as a "woman on top," and from the outset, she is determined, in ways highly reminiscent of the Virgin Queen's own refusal to cede dominion to a man, not to marry anyone who is "*above* her in degree." Initially, this resolution seems synonymous with the desire not to marry at all. For it seems inconceivable that Olivia would eschew marriage *up* the ladder of social hierarchy out of a desire to marry several rungs *down* it. She falls in love with a decidedly unmanly youth who is also a servant, albeit s/he is a gentleman: "Yet my state is well; / I am a gentleman" (1.5.294–5). We might pass over this except that the steward, Malvolio, is mercilessly vilified for his fantasies about marrying up the social scale with his mistress Olivia, even as he recounts instances in which such transgressive matches have occurred: "The Lady of Strachy married with the yeoman of the wardrobe" (2.5.39–40). For early modern audiences, this would have resonated with the real-life incidences in which social hierarchy was thus turned on its head.

Onomastically coded as "ill-will," Malvolio is indeed "a kind of Puritan" (2.3.140) who believes there should be "no more cakes and ale" (2.3.115), as well as no more bearbaiting, and is set in opposition to the essentially carnivalesque spirit of the play. Traditionally, early modern carnivals featured the corpulent, ruddy-faced figure of Carnival, associated with meat and all the pleasures of the flesh, while his dour counterpart, "Jack O'Lent," embodied the lean, self-abnegating principle of the traditional period of fasting in the six weeks preceding the Easter celebration. Malvolio is precisely this latter figure, and he is set in opposition to the aptly named Sir Toby Belch, who is taking money from Sir Andrew Aguecheek ostensibly for forwarding his suit to Olivia. Olivia's lady in waiting, Maria, is described as Penthesilia, the Queen of the Amazons, and thus serves as another figure for female sovereignty in this topsy-turvy world, though she too is eventually domesticated by marriage to Sir Toby. Maria writes a cryptic letter in her mistress's handwriting, which, as she correctly surmises, gulls Malvolio into the mistaken belief that Olivia loves and desires him. The audience looks on with the perpetrators of this practical joke as Malvolio's wishful thinking leads him further and further down the blind alley of misinterpretation. At this point in the play, Malvolio's own folly, hypocrisy, and especially his social aspirations, are primarily responsible for his ridicule. He genuinely believes that Olivia wishes to see him wearing the ridiculous attire of yellow stockings and cross garters, and his own crazed imagination has him fill in the blanks of the letter: "M. O. A. I. doth sway my life" (2.5.109). Though the letter is unsigned, he concludes, in one of the most outrageously bawdy passages in Shakespeare, that "these be her very C's, her U's, and her T's" (2.5.88). This joke is often lost on modern audiences, but it would not have been lost on the male law students of the Middle Temple that "cut" was an obscene reference to female genitalia.

Malvolio is indeed responsible for his egregious misinterpretation of the letter and for the weaknesses of character that make him vulnerable to it in the first place. What is less clear is that he deserves the cruelty of imprisonment that ensues on the trumped up grounds of insanity. To be locked away in a dark cell does not strike most modern audiences as a fitting punishment for having told a drunken aristocrat that his behavior is unacceptable. On the other hand, Malvolio's hypocrisy does seem to merit punishment, and his status as a "Puritan" aligns him with religious fanaticism. How such zealotry should be dealt with is as much a problem in our own society as it was in Shakespeare's.

Yet, while Malvolio remains outside the enchanted circle of erotic attachments with which the play concludes, he is not alone. Feste, the clown, and Antonio, the sea captain and companion to Sebastian, are similarly unmated, and some losses, such as that of Olivia's brother, cannot be repaired. While the very name of the clown Feste (a role probably played by Robert Armin) bespeaks the world of festivity, his humor is always tinged with melancholy even as his jokes and his songs serve to bind the play together and to mark it as a comedy. The clown is often the outsider, and his distanced status permits him a fool's eye on the world, a perspective that those too thoroughly immersed in its machinations cannot possess. Antonio, in contrast, is quite another matter. He has risked his life for Sebastian, and he seems to have the kind of homoerotic attachment to him that the melancholy character of the same name displays toward Bassiano in *The Merchant of Venice*. That the play seriously proposes such a homoerotic prospect is also indicated when Orsino takes Viola's hand while she is still dressed in male attire. Indeed, she never actually returns to her "woman's weeds" at any point in the play (5.1.271).[8]

In an important reading of the play, Indira Ghose argues that Malvolio's unassimilablility to the social consensus of comedy constitutes Shakespeare's critique of the notion that laughter is a social corrective. Ghose also points out that Sir Toby and his entourage are not included in the final reconciliation of the play and that Puritans and Puritan-haters are equally subject to satire. What is clear, however, is that certain types of laughter – the baiting of a human being like a bear, for instance – are "no longer acceptable." The central characters unanimously reject the type of humor shared by the roisterers, Sir Toby, Andrew Aguecheek, and Fabian."[9] In other words, Shakespeare's sympathies seem to have been with the bears. An image of its torment may have been imprinted even from his earliest days. The emblem of the "bear and ragged staff" had been used by the earls of Warwick for generations on their coat of arms (it later became incorporated into the arms of the county) and thus Shakespeare, like everyone in Stratford would have been very familiar with it.

As for Malvolio, finally released from his imprisonment, he leaves the stage with his bitter vow of vengeance. Of course, with the benefit of historical hindsight, the Puritanism represented by Malvolio did exact its vengeance on the disorderly license of the theatres when they were closed by the new regime in 1642.[10]

## Measure for Measure

In *Measure for Measure*, the overzealous Angelo has temporarily taken the reins of the government of Vienna from Duke Vincentio. Under Angelo's stringent regime, Claudio has been arrested for fornication, a crime for which he is to be decapitated. If, in Stratford in the 1580s, there had been the severe penalties for sexual transgression that are the subject of *Measure for Measure*, Shakespeare, who married Anne Hathaway five months after making her pregnant, might have found himself in the same position as Claudio: "within these three days his head to be chopped off" (1.2.53–4).[1]

Of course, in England, penalties for sexual incontinence were not so severe. Elsewhere in Europe, however, it was quite another matter, especially in the strict Protestant theocracy of John Calvin's Geneva, whose government much resembled Angelo's Vienna. The citizens of Geneva had taken an oath in May of 1536 to live by the law of God, and had invited Calvin, the great French reformer, to help them do it. Calvin's legislative efforts were not aimed at changing hearts but at reforming human nature from the outside in. His first attempts met with failure, but he was later invited back into the city to take up the cause once more. Calvin's Geneva was scoured of temptations and vice – whether heinous or harmless: drinking, dancing, and dicing were prohibited, along with ostentatious dress.[2] In 1543, for example, François de Bonivard was summoned to justice for the crime of playing a game of "trique-trac" (tic-tac) with the poet Clément Marot, and in 1562, even though he was impotent, he was compelled by the magistrates to marry a young woman, formerly a nun, who had been his housekeeper. Within three years of the marriage, the woman had drowned herself, and Bonivard's servant was beheaded for having committed adultery with her.[3] There is a striking resonance here with Shakespeare's play, where Lucio, who regards sex as a harmless recreational activity, dubs it "a game of tick-tack" (1.2.162–3). Whether or not Shakespeare knew the Bonivard case in particular, such stories of Genevan justice would surely have made their way to England because there had been an English community in exile there during the reign of Elizabeth's Catholic sister, Mary Tudor. These exiles returned after the accession of the Protestant queen in 1558 and brought with them, in addition to the English Bible they had published in French-speaking Geneva in May 1560, a renewed zealotry for the Protestant cause. This particular community was likely to have applauded severe punishments for moral failings and to have pressed for them to be upheld on English soil when they returned. Shakespeare's knowledge of Calvin's theocracy is even more likely because, during the time of writing *Measure for Measure*, he was living on Silver Street in the community of French Huguenot refugees.

If England was no Geneva, neither was it a safe-haven for adulterers and fornicators. Adultery and fornication were offenses that had always been punishable by the ecclesiastical courts. Brothel keeping, however, the offense for which Pompey is indicted, was never under ecclesiastical jurisdiction but was always a matter for the secular authorities, as it is in Shakespeare's Vienna where Angelo orders that "All houses in the suburbs of Vienna must be plucked down" (1.2.77). These are the "naughty house[s]" (2.1.67), or bawdy houses, that in real life in the London suburb of Southwark stood cheek by jowl with the Globe, but also potentially playhouses and alehouses as "houses of resort" (1.2.81).

The playhouses were geographically proximate to the Bankside brothels, known as the "stews," and to many other forms of vice – gaming, cockfighting, bearbaiting, and drinking. Sexual misdemeanors were everywhere. In some towns there were battles about whether justices or the church had proper jurisdiction over whoremongers, fornicators, and adulterers, particularly when zealous local magistrates regarded clerical punishments as too lenient. Prostitution on the scale depicted in *Measure For Measure*, however, was an issue that essentially concerned only London.

*Measure for Measure* ends with a series of legitimate, if highly problematic, unions. These marriages are what place it under the genre heading of comedy, along with the fact that despite all threats to the contrary, in the end, the play's only death is one of natural causes. The play's main plot lines, the Disguised Ruler and the Corrupt Magistrate, were already well known to early modern audiences. Shakespeare's sources for the plot include Giovanni Battista Giraldi Cinthio's novella *Gli Hecatommithi* (1565) and his posthumous play *Epitia* (1583). He also drew on George Whetstone's *The Right Excellent History of Promos and Cassandra* (1578) and his story in *Heptameron of Civil Discourses* (1582), republished as *Aurelia* in 1592.

*Measure for Measure* presents the social comedy of city life lived within and outside the law, as well as the administration of justice from the highest office in the land down to the seamy urban landscape. Yet, despite the comic structure and comic types, such as the awkwardly inept Constable Elbow, the madam, Mistress Overdone (married nine times and "overdone" by her last, and now deceased husband), the pimp, Pompey, and the recalcitrant drunken prisoner, Barnardine, the play's comedy does not eschew the bitter, joylessly sordid and potentially tragic dimensions of life that must accompany the world of brothels, prisons, and corrupt government. This problem of tone, deliberately exacerbated by the unpromising conjugal alliances at the play's conclusion, is why critics often refer to the play as a "problem comedy."

Claudio's transgression consists of having impregnated his lover, Juliet. Later in the play, Claudio protests that they are in fact married, albeit not yet in church:

> upon a true contract
> I got possession of Julietta's bed.
> You know the lady; she is fast my wife,

Save that we do the denunciation lack
Of outward order. (1.2.118–22)

A verbal promise between the couple, known as a *de presenti* agreement, especially one to which there were witnesses, was a legitimate and legally binding
conjugal contract in Shakespeare's time, despite endeavors in the period to
enforce ecclesiastical ratification. Claudio's initial response to his imprisonment,
however, was an admission of guilt, not only to the charge of fornication, but
also to sexual "surfeit" or gluttony, a kind of raging lust (1.2.103). Meanwhile,
Isabella, Claudio's sister, who has recently joined a convent as a novice, goes
to Angelo to plead for her brother's life. Angelo, who is repeatedly aligned with
Puritanism, professes himself immune to sexual temptation and believes that
sexual misdemeanors merit the harshest punishments. Yet, overcome by Isabella's passionate plea on her brother's behalf, Angelo tries to coerce her into
sex: if she sleeps with him, Claudio's life will be spared. Unbeknownst to
Angelo, Isabella enlists Mariana, his former, spurned, lover, to take her place
in his bed. Yet even though he believes the sexual bargain to have been fulfilled,
Angelo still orders Claudio's execution. Through the clever substitution of
Claudio with the corpse of a man who has died in prison from natural causes,
his life is saved. The play ends in the unions of Claudio and Juliet, Angelo and
Mariana, and most astonishingly, with the Duke Vincentio's proposal of marriage to Isabella – in response to which she is strangely mute. Shakespeare's
major alterations from his source are significant. In Whetstone's version the
sister of the condemned man is not an acolyte and, unlike Isabella, she cedes
her virginity to the deputy in order to save her brother's life.

Like London, the Vienna of the play is rife with moral and physical corruption. The play's numerous references to venereal disease are symptomatic of
political decay. In the context of this metaphorically and literally diseased urban
landscape Shakespeare poses disturbing questions about the relation between
political and sexual subjection and about whether, or rather to what degree,
maintenance of political authority depends upon the control of sexuality. Above
all, *Measure for Measure* is a play about moral hypocrisy – the private vices of
public persons, and it asks one of the most urgent questions of its time: do
sexual transgressions merit censure by the state?

St Paul's famous dictum "Better to marry than to burn" (1 Corinthians 7.9)
had been used for centuries as scriptural proof of the superiority of celibate life
over the married state. From the Pauline perspective, since sexual incontinence
would be punished with everlasting damnation, those persons who were inca-

pable of keeping chaste should marry. Marriage was thus a second-rate alternative to the higher state of life which renounced sex altogether. Partly in response to the astonishing promiscuity that sometimes prevailed in medieval monastic communities – vows of celibacy not withstanding – and a monastic rule that favored severe asceticism, Protestantism raised marriage to the highest state of life, the preferred path of the Christian on his or her journey to God. After Henry VIII's dissolution of the monasteries, the ideal of married chastity and conjugal felicity in the secular world replaced that of cloistered, consecrated celibacy.

While the verbal contact entered into by Juliet and Claudio could be upheld in the courts, it was often difficult for a pregnant woman to prove that the father of her child had undertaken such an agreement before the child was conceived. This led to all manner of disputes in the church courts about what had and had not been agreed upon, and indeed a "verbal contract" might achieve a woman's consent even though the man's real objective was the immediate one of seduction and not the long-term one of marriage. Romeo's Juliet, quick to issue the conditions under which she will pursue the relationship, provides an interesting comparison with Claudio's: "Thy bent of love be honourable, / Thy purpose marriage" (2.2.143–4), and when Romeo proves reluctant to leave, she inquires rather sharply, "What satisfaction canst thou have tonight?" (2.2.126).[4] The notion of a private contract, a verbal agreement between the couple, also conflicted with the new understanding of marriage that occurred in the period. Marriage was a mark of social maturity, and to enter into it was to change one's estate in a definitive and public way. Clandestine marriages that were not in some way publicly ratified singularly failed as such a public marker. Whether or not Shakespeare and Anne Hathaway had an informal contract prior to their church wedding, we do not know. But we do know that as marriage accrued greater religious and social importance under Protestantism, the legal and clerical regulations governing marriage underwent a major transformation. There was thus much more pressure to have marriages solemnized in church. Particularly egregious was for the woman's body to start showing visible evidence of consummation without the sanction of church or community.

If early modern England did not execute fornicators, it did exact strict and sometimes severe penalties for sexual misconduct. These penalties did not extend to decapitation, unless like Elizabeth I's mother, Anne Boleyn, the alleged miscreant happened to have had the misfortune of being married to Henry VIII. Shortly before Shakespeare died, his son-in-law Thomas Quiney, newly married to his daughter Judith, was ordered by the ecclesiastical court to do public penance in a white sheet for three successive Sundays, a sentence that was commuted upon payment of a fine of five shillings. Quiney had fathered a child on a woman named Margaret Wheeler, who was buried with her baby on March 15, 1616. Wheeler and her infant suffered the saddest consequences of an illicit sexual liaison. As was often the case with ante-nuptial sexual offenses, Shakespeare's own illicit sexual liaison resolved by wedlock what would otherwise have brought censure from an ecclesiastical tribunal, popularly known (as we noted earlier) as the "bawdy court."

Sexual transgression was also an urgent political matter. Virtually every Parliament in the period entertained legislation pertaining to it. Shakespeare probably knew at least one of the alternative renditions of his story, especially Thomas Lupton's *The Second Part and Knitting up of the Boke entitled Too Good To Be True* (1581). The woman who pleads with the magistrate in this version is married to the accused (the Claudio figure) and thus coerced into adultery, another of the sexual transgressions about which there was heated debate. In 1626, the "precise" member of Parliament for Exeter, Ignatius Jordan, tried to have the death penalty instituted for adultery. His bill did not pass, but undeterred, he tried again in 1628, hoping for success this time with the more moderate proposal of a hundred marks' fine for gentlemen and a whipping for all others. Another member of the house, John Pym, urged support for the bill by arguing that "since the sin required the judgement of God on this land, they should commit it," that is, assign it to a committee for further examination. Pym's proposal was met with uproarious laughter and members shouting out, "Commit it! Commit it!" Ignatius Jordan, however, was not amused and made known his disdain for the outburst of mirth to the Speaker of the House: "I did always look that this bill should find many opposers, but Mr. Speaker, this is no laughing matter." Sir Edward Coke took the opportunity to unpack the matter a little further by claiming that the House had not actually opposed the bill, urging only that they "commit it." "It is the bill not the sin which we would have committed," said Coke.[5] Needless to say, the bill was not ratified. For all that, proposals for increased sexual legislation were a constant feature of both Elizabeth and Jacobean Parliaments, with Puritan members keeping the pressure up for moral reform despite repeated rejection of their attempts to push the legislation through.

For many of the men in the House of Commons, discussion of sexual impropriety struck close to home. In 1625, Coke's own daughter, Frances, was found guilty of adultery, albeit in the extenuating circumstances of having been coerced into marriage by Coke himself when she was only fourteen. She had been matched with Sir John Villiers, the lunatic half-brother of the most powerful nobleman in the land, the Duke of Buckingham. Her co-adulterer was a member of Parliament, Sir Robert Howard, who was excommunicated, while Frances was fined five hundred marks and ordered to do public penance.[6]

When Pompey asks, "Does your worship mean to geld and splay all the youth of the city?" (2.1.191–2) his question speaks to the impossibility of legislating desire despite the repeated attempts of the authorities to do so. Interestingly, "geld and splay," an expression relating to animal husbandry, refers to both sexes even though "youth" usually refers only to males. Taken literally, Pompey's question suggests castration as the only real, but unthinkable, solution. For all that, some of Shakespeare's contemporaries urged physical mutilation – literally, the "most biting laws" (1.3.19) – as an appropriate penalty. William Lambarde, in *A Perambulation of Kent* (1576), for example, advocated cutting off the noses of transgressors. This form of punishment is echoed again in *Measure for Measure* when Claudio observes that in seeking his sister's chastity in exchange for his life, Angelo is attempting to "bite the law by the nose" (3.1.110), that is, to mutilate the law itself. Finally, in 1650, in the Puritan-dominated English Republic of Oliver Cromwell, strict penalties against sexual misconduct were passed into law in the "[Act] for suppressing the detestable sins of incest, adultery and fornication." As R.S. White points out, this was not some Puritan aberration, but rather the outcome of more than a century of political pressure.[7]

Both Angelo and Isabella represent sexual repression in the play. Isabella has chosen the life of a nun, "wishing a more strict restraint / Upon the sisterhood" (1.4.4–5). Prior to being aroused by her, Angelo has been celibate, and the duke expresses confidence in him, in part based upon the belief that it is impossible that "the dribbling dart of love / Can pierce a complete bosom" (1.3.2–3). This line, like so many in the play, is a thoroughly sexual image, in this case one of impenetrability and the highly phallic, "dribbling dart." Isabella's own language is even more sexual. She rejects Claudio's plea that she accede to Angelo's desires and save his life with irresistibly erotic imagery:

> "Th'impression of keen whips I'd wear as rubies,
> And strip myself to death as to a bed
> That longing have been sick for, ere I'd yield
> My body up to shame. (2.4.101–4)

Whips, rubies, stripping, the bed, longing, yielding, shame, and the body, all vividly elaborate the very sexual act Isabella is at pains to renounce. Her words bespeak what Freud called the return of the repressed. She offers the masochistic and pornographic spectacle of her naked body ("strip myself") aroused to erotic martyrdom at the prospect of stringent repression. The perverse austerity of her resolution to remain chaste is like the language of the period's punitive measures against sexual license in that it inescapably reiterates what it seeks to eradicate. Isabella also offers the mirror image of Angelo's sadistic language earlier in the play when he tells Escalus that he is "Hoping you'll find good cause to whip them all" (2.1.117). From this point of view, Angelo is already partnered with Isabella in a punitive, erotic discourse that suggests the natural alignment of their desires rather than the more straightforward antagonism between perpetrator and victim.

Shakespeare's language here is telling in other ways, too. Whipping was especially prominent in the many legislative attempts to curb immoral behavior. In 1579 in Bury St Edmunds, a committee of justices of the peace determined the penalties for fornication, adultery, and incest: twenty-four hours tied to the whipping post, the hair cut off, and "thirty stripes well laid on till the blood come."[8] These, then, are Isabella's "rubies." She refers to the conventional, public punishment of "whipping and stripping," with an erotically masochistic relish that is not very different in tenor from the sadistic language of the justices of the peace for Bury St Edmunds. Whipping was the routine punishment for women found guilty of fornication, but it was not typically administered to men.[9] When the provisions against bastardy in the Poor Relief Act of 1567 were revisited in 1596, a dispute arose about whether the original act intended corporal punishment for male miscreants or merely imprisonment. One member of Parliament noted in his diary that "many thought too liberall to leave it to the discretion of a Justice of Peace to have power to whipp one that should offend the law."[10] Some members of Parliament were concerned that whipping was "slavish," and thus an inappropriate punishment for gentlemen who had, at least from their point of view, like Lucio, but sown their wild oats. In 1593 objections were made to a proposal that the fathers of bastards be whipped along with their mothers. The concern was that the penalty "might chance upon gentlemen or men of quality, whom it were not fit to put to such a shame."[11] The bawd Pompey is threatened with whipping by the duke's magistrate, Escalus, in Act 2 (2.1.207), but he is certainly not a man of quality. The concupiscent Lucio, however, relies on precisely the protection of his class status, and has suffered no consequences for fathering a bastard, "Mistress Kate Keepdown was with child by him in the Duke's time; he promised her marriage. His child is a year and a quarter old . . ." (3.2.160–1). Lucio reflects utter contempt for women, and reserves particular loathing for prostitutes. More sensibly, some members of Parliament thought that innocent men might be falsely accused and that malicious or corrupt justices might be inclined to have them whipped anyway: "Uppon ill will might geve this correction to one not offendinge if he were accused by a whore."[12] In the end, the proviso for whipping was not enacted, but an anonymous diarist summarized this perplexing matter that "Much a doe was made how a question [resolution] should be made of this."[13]

Although Shakespeare's biographers have speculated that he himself frequented brothels, *Measure for Measure* certainly does not set any scenes there. He did, however, use brothel scenes in *Pericles* when he began collaborating with another denizen of Silver Street, the brothel-keeper-cum-playwright, George Wilkins.[14] Nor is there anything of the cheerfully sordid pornography of Thomas Nashe's *Choyse of Valentines*, which also refers to the impact of law on "the trade." In that poem, Frances, the young whore of Thomalin's fancy, has been removed by the authorities to a "house of venery in upper ground." Upper Ground Street was in the theatrical neighborhood, the South Bank's "sinfully polluted suburbs," as Thomas Dekker called them in *The Wonderfull Yeare* (1603).

Claudio, as we have noted, does not immediately plead his innocence upon arrest, and in this he contrasts with the one apparently happily married man in the play, Constable Elbow. The latter vigorously denies, albeit in malapropistic language that runs counter to his intent, that he had sexual relations with this wife ("respected her") prior to their wedding: "I respected with her before I was married to her? – If ever I was respected with her, or she with me, let not your worship think me the poor Duke's officer" (2.1.145–8). Although Elbow's "honest" wife does not appear as a character in the play, the dialog in Act 2, Scene 1, in which he unsuccessfully tries to report the nature of the offense Pompey committed against her, offers a delightful vignette. Mistress Elbow, being heavily pregnant, had been compelled by her cravings for stewed prunes to stop off at Pompey's house of ill repute. One of his customers, Master Froth, then did some indefinable thing that caused her to spit in his face. Elbow's awkwardness with language prevents him from elaborating further, and he is finally dismissed by Escalus, who ends their interview by trying to replace him with a more competent officer. Elbow's wife may be a rather rare Shakespearean example of female sexual fidelity among the lower orders, but of that we cannot be certain. Her husband's bungled and inarticulate account of events render the circumstances of her visit to this disreputable premises somewhat murky, in every sense, and make Elbow himself foolish enough to be a gullible cuckold, that is, a man who is ignorant of his wife's infidelity even as it is well-known to everyone else. On the other hand, in the event that the Elbows' marriage is indeed happily monogamous, it would seem that virtue and intelligence do not go hand in hand.

This episode is important in the play because it details the reality of justice on the ground and in the streets, rather than in the rarified abstractions of the law. Further, in the midst of drabs, knaves, whores, and bawds, there is (potentially) the image of the virtuous, fertile wife resisting the contaminating sexual disorders of the city, and of a protective husband conscious of his domestic felicity. In contrast, although Claudio and Juliet are of a more elevated social status, and although they are married, in some technical, legal sense, the impression of their liaison is one of sexual voracity, "immoderate use" (1.2.104), rather than contented conjugality.

Crucially, when Claudio acknowledges his culpability and says he is but paying the price for "too much liberty" (1.2.102), his statement is freighted with political meaning indicative of the belief in early modern Europe as a whole that "liberty" was a greater danger than restraint. The problem, as many legal thinkers saw it, was not the law itself, which was already severe, but that its implementation might give way to lenience. (English sodomy statutes, for instance, were very rarely enforced.) Angelo's "tyranny" (1.2.136) is likewise that he seeks to revitalize defunct legislative powers:

> This new governor
> Awakes . . . all the enrolled penalties
> Which have, like unscoured armor, hung by the wall
> So long that nineteen zodiacs have gone round
> And none of them been worn . . . (1.2.138–42)

The analogy Claudio makes here is between unused legal mechanisms and rusty armor, which Angelo now seeks to "scour" with legislative zeal. The sense of legislative cleansing applied to moral filth is culturally pervasive. In Simion Grahame's *The Anatomie of Humors* (1609), the bedrooms of slatternly women are also described as "unscoured." This language is reminiscent of that used by Hamlet to upbraid his mother when he visits her in the room she now shares with her second husband: "the rank sweat of an enseamed bed / Stewed in corruption" (3.4.83–4).[15]

One of the most fascinating aspects of Calvin's legislative achievements in Geneva is that he did not so much *change* the laws of the city as simply *enforce* them to the full.[16] In England, William Lambarde, who was appointed Keeper of the Records of the Rolls Chapel in 1597 and Keeper of Records at the Tower in 1601 (the Tower was both a library and a prison), only three years before the royal performance of *Measure for Measure*, argued in a very Angelo-like vein, that judicial authority needed to be wrested from the bishops because they had failed to uphold "the Prince's commodity," and as a direct result of their laxity in enforcing the law "incontinency in his subjects [is] intolerably augmented."[17] Lambarde stressed the rule of law as the bedrock of social order, "the outward guides and masters of our lives and manners."[18] "Incontinency," particularly uncontrolled sexual behavior, threatened the rule of law itself for Lambarde and others like him.

This was, of course, the same Lambarde to whom the queen had complained about performances of *Richard II* and who advocated nose-clipping as a punishment for sexual impropriety. Lambarde is, indeed, an interesting figure. In the late 1930s, it was thought that one of his treatises contained a genuine Shakespeare signature – a fact still in dispute. Further, some biographers have claimed that Shakespeare might have known Lambarde either through John Shakespeare's legal affairs at the Court of Chancery, or because he was in charge of entertainments while a law student at Lincoln's Inn.[19] The former seems highly speculative, but since Lambarde remained attached to the Inns of Court and became a "bencher," a senior lawyer at Lincoln's Inn, the latter is quite possible. Lambarde's work certainly engages the key debates of his era, and since it is into these discussions that *Measure for Measure* is a cultural intervention, Shakespeare might well have read it, although its relevance to the play does not depend on that fact.

Interestingly, another of Lambarde's works has significance in relation to the questions of legislation and liberty that Shakespeare addresses. In 1584 he wrote the influential "Notes on the procedures and privileges of the House of Commons," a treatise which supported the tradition of free speech in parliament. This circulated in manuscript until it was finally published in 1641, when Puritanism had achieved its ultimate victory. For Lambarde, then, like many early moderns, political liberty did not extend to sexual behavior. In fact, even Lambarde's defense of political liberty in the form of parliamentary privilege was aimed at freedom to discuss the succession crisis (the question of who would become the unmarried Elizabeth's heir) in order to forestall the possibility of a Catholic ruler. This brings us to the other key theme of the play, namely that of the disguised ruler.

The well-known trope of the disguised ruler promises to situate the plot firmly in the world of fiction and not in the reality of early seventeenth-century London, this theme seeming more remote from Shakespeare's historical reality than the theme of the corrupt magistrate and the issue of sexual control. In fact, however, when James I and Queen Anne made their first royal progress through London on March 15, 1604, they planned a secret visit to the Royal Exchange, the enormous indoor market erected by Thomas Gresham. The royal couple had hoped to watch the merchants unobserved, but reports of their visit leaked, and they were beset with crowds hoping to catch a glimpse of them.[20] The significance of the disguised ruler as a plot device, whereby disguise gives the ruler the advantage of clandestine and voyeuristic observation of his subjects, however, does not reside primarily in this specific, local context. Much more important, in the context of the play's first recorded performance at court on St Stephen's Night, December 26, 1604, and the most salient political issue of the day, was the transfer of power that had just occurred between the Elizabethan regime and the Jacobean one. Despite the incidental significance of James's visit to the Exchange, what is crucial about the *disguised* ruler trope is that it raises the problem of how to assess the unknown quantity that is a new ruler and how to achieve the transfer of power between rulers. Throughout her long reign, the queen had stubbornly persisted in her refusal to choose a successor. Only on her deathbed did she name James as her "heir." James, although a Protestant, was the son of Elizabeth's Scottish cousin, Mary, whose sexual misadventures were regarded as integral to her Catholic misrule as queen of Scotland, and whose scandalous life was brought to a premature conclusion when Elizabeth ordered her beheaded at Fotheringay Castle in 1587. Thus, the eminently literary theme of the disguised ruler reframes a political problem by circumventing succession entirely: the problem of a new ruler is taken care of by having the old one on hand, just in case things go wrong. The return of the duke in disguise is thus a rehearsal of a transition of power that must come one day as an inevitable function of the ruler's mortality.

With the return of the duke as rightful ruler comes the return of justice, which he dispenses, like the magistrates of Geneva, by ordering Lucio to marry his "stale," Angelo to marry Mariana (whose promise to marry he had reneged upon when her dowry was lost at sea), and Claudio to marry – again – Juliet. Essentially, too, he orders Isabella to marry him, and it is not clear to what degree she has the right to refuse a proposal uttered in the context of this list of ducal conjugal decrees. He also orders Barnardine, who has been impervious to all law, both ecclesiastical and civil, to go with the friar for instruction on how to mend his ways. In this rather unsatisfactory dispensation of justice, the duke exhibits clemency, which was a facet of royal prerogative that served to enhance sovereign power by emphasizing those instances in which subjects were utterly dependent upon their ruler for liberty. James exercised this prerogative in 1604, and at every parliament between 1584 and 1601, Queen Elizabeth had also granted her "most gracious and free pardon."[21] In 1593, Queen Elizabeth was in attendance at the House of Lords when the bill was read on a general pardon concerning those subjects suffering the just penalties for their offences, "from which they cannot any way be freed or delivered but by her Majesties great Mercye."[22] In fact, the duke's dispensations go beyond those of the late queen whose pardon did not extend to "fornication and adultery," just as it did not cover high treason or homicide.[23] Like murderers in Elizabethan England, fornicators and adulterers were required to pay the penalty for their misdeeds in full. That sexual misdemeanors were understood to be as unpardonable as treason and murder, bizarrely suggests their equivalence. In a sense, the play suggests that marriage *is* a kind of penalty – Lucio certainly has always understood it as a curb on *his* liberty.

Originally published in the First Folio of 1623, the very title of *Measure for Measure* refers to a cryptic and complex biblical passage about the mechanisms of divine justice, rendered in the 1587 edition of the Geneva Bible as follows:

And he said vnto them, Take heede what ye heare. With what measure ye mete, it shall be measured vnto you: and vnto you that heare, shall more be giuen. For vnto him that hath, shall it be giuen, and from him that hath not, shall be taken away, euen that he hath. (Mark 4.24)

The play explores the spectrum of sexual behavior from renunciation and repression to unbridled sexual license without resolving the problem one way or the other. That the only happily married person in the play is the potentially deluded Constable Elbow is sad comedy indeed.

# Notes

## The Comedy of Errors

1 Samuel Schoenbaum, *William Shakespeare: A Documentary Life* (New York: Oxford University Press, 1975), p. 23.

2 Schoenbaum, *Documentary Life*, p. 25.

3 Frances E. Dolan, ed., *The Comedy of Errors* (New York: Penguin, 1999), p. xxxi.

4 Aristotle, *Poetics*, trans. Stephen Halliwell (Cambridge, MA: Harvard University Press, 1995), p. 1449a.

5 All citations from *The Comedy of Errors* are from William Shakespeare, *The Comedy of Errors*, ed. R.A. Foakes (London: Methuen & Co. Ltd., 1962).

6 All references to *Hamlet* are from William Shakespeare, *Hamlet*, ed. Ann Thompson and Neil Taylor (London: Methuen, 2006).

7 T.S. Dorsch ed., *The Comedy of Errors*, updated edition, revised with a new introduction by Ros King (Cambridge: Cambridge University Press, 2004), p. 12.

8 George Redmonds, *Christian Names in Local and Family History* (National Archives: Kew, Surrey, 2004), p. 48. See also, Scott Smith-Bannister, *Names and Naming Patterns in England 1538–1700* (New York: Oxford University Press, 1997).

9 J.L. Vivian, ed., *Visitations of Devon* (Exeter: H.S. Eland, 1895), p. 856.

10 On this kind of "disguised" duplication of names, see Redmonds, *Christian Names*, pp. 48–9.

11 Walter C. Metcalfe, ed., *The Visitations of Essex* (Harleian Society, London, 1878), pp. xiii, 321–2.

12 Charles Whitworth, ed., *The Comedy of Errors* (New York: Oxford University Press, 2002), pp. 7–9.

13 Laurie E. Maguire, *Studying Shakespeare: A Guide to the Plays* (Malden: Blackwell, 2003), p. 15.

14 See Stephen Greenblatt, *Will in the World* (New York: W.W. Norton, 2004), pp. 130–1.

15 Montaigne was afflicted with gallstones, a condition from which his father also suffered. Michel de Montaigne, "Of the Resemblance Between Children and Fathers," *The Essayes or Morall, Politike and Millitarie Discourses: of Lo: Michaell de Montaigne*, trans. John Florio (London: 1603, STC / 18041), p. 447.

16 Montaigne, "Resemblance," p. 450.

17 For an inspired reading of the problem of marriage in Ephesus, a place whose name bespeaks its own complex Christian and pre-Christian history, see Laurie Maguire, *Shakespeare's Names* (Oxford: University Press, 2007), pp. 164–72.

18 Whitworth, *The Comedy of Errors*.

19 In contrast, Stephen Greenblatt makes the case for *Errors* as "one of the

earliest of Shakespeare's plays." Stephen Greenblatt *et al.* eds, *The Norton Shakespeare*, 2nd edn (New York: Norton, 2008), p. 719.

#### The Taming of the Shrew

1  All references to *The Taming of the Shrew* are from William Shakespeare, *The Taming of the Shrew: A Norton Critical Edition*, ed. Dympna Callaghan (New York: W.W. Norton, 2009).
2  William Shakespeare, *King Lear*, ed. R.A. Foakes (Walton-on-Thames: Arden Shakespeare, 1997).
3  William Shakespeare, *Pericles*, ed. Stephen Orgel (New York, Pelican, 2001).
4  *Ovid's Metamorphoses: The Arthur Golding Translation 1567*, ed. John Frederick Nims with a new essay, "Shakespeare's Ovid," by Jonathan Bate (Philadelphia: Paul Dry Books, 2000).
5  John Donne, Letter to Sir George More, in Dympna Callaghan, ed., *Romeo and Juliet: Texts and Contexts* (Boston: Bedford/St. Martin's, 2003), p. 296.
6  British Library, Additional MS 15227, f. 16.
7  See Lynda E. Boose, "Scolding Brides and Bridling Scolds: Taming the Woman's Unruly Member," in *Shrew*, ed. Callaghan, pp. 174–86; and Frances E. Dolan, "Household Chastisements: Gender, Authority, and 'Domestic Violence'," in *Shrew*, ed. Callaghan, pp. 164–73.

#### Love's Labour's Lost

1  Sig. S3r.
2  William Shakespeare, *Love's Labour's Lost: The Arden Shakespeare* (London: Methuen, 1983; 1st edn. 1951).
3  Quoted in James M. Dutcher and Anne Lake Prescott, eds, *Renaissance Historicisms: Essays in Honor of Arthur F. Kinney* (Newark: University of Delaware Press, 2008), p. 79.
4  Richard Hillman, *Shakespeare, Marlowe and the Politics of France* (New York: Palgrave, 2002), p. 5.

5  Robert Codrington, translated the *Memoirs* in 1651; two years after England had been rid of its own glittering royals. *Memoirs of Margaret de Valois, Queen of Navarre, Containing the Secret History of the Court of France for Seventeen Years, viz., from 1565 to 1582, During the Reigns of Charles IX and Henry III, Written by Herself, in a Series of Letters* (London: H.S. Nichols, 1895), pp. 226–7.
6  References to Shakespeare's poems are from William Shakespeare, *Shakespeare's Poems: Venus and Adonis, The Rape of Lucrece and the Shorter Poems*, ed. Katherine Duncan-Jones and H.R. Woudhuysen (London: Arden Shakespeare, 2007).
7  Francis Meres, *Palladis Tamia: Wit's Treasury* (1598), p. 282.

#### A Midsummer Night's Dream

1  All citations from *A Midsummer Night's Dream* are from William Shakespeare, *A Midsummer Night's Dream: Texts and Contexts*, ed. Gail Kern Paster and Skiles Howard (Boston: Bedford/St. Martin's, 1999).
2  See A.D. Nuttall, *Shakespeare the Thinker* (New Haven: Yale University Press, 2007), p. xi.
3  See Jane Dawson, "Knox, John (c. 1514–1572)," *ODNB*.
4  See Susan Frye, "The Myth of Elizabeth at Tilbury," *Sixteenth Century Journal* 23 (1): 95–114.
5  BL Harley MS 6395; quoted Katherine Duncan-Jones, *Shakespeare's Life and World*, p. 48.

#### The Merchant of Venice

1  William Shakespeare, *Shakespeare's Sonnets: The Arden Shakespeare*, ed. Katherine Duncan-Jones (London: Methuen Drama, 2010).
2  David Bevington, "A. L. Rowse's Dark Lady," in Marshall Grossman, ed., *Aemilia Lanyer: Gender, Genre, and the Canon* (Lexington: University Press of Kentucky, 1998), pp. 10–28.

3 Aemilia Lanyer, *The Poems of Aemilia Lanyer*, ed. Susanne Woods (New York: Oxford University Press, 1993).

4 All references to *The Merchant of Venice* are from William Shakespeare, *The Merchant of Venice: The Arden Shakespeare*, ed. John Drakakis (London: Methuen Drama, 2010).

5 For a splendid contextualization of Jews in the play, see M. Lindsay Kaplan, ed., *The Merchant of Venice: Texts and Contexts* (Boston: Bedford St. Martin's, 2002), especially pp. 248–9.

6 See James Shapiro, *Shakespeare and the Jews* (New York: Columbia University Press, 1996), ch. 4.

7 Samuel Edgar, "Anes, Dunstan (*c*.1520–1594)," *ODNB*.

### Much Ado About Nothing

1 Gordon Williams, *A Dictionary of Sexual Language and Imagery in Shakespearean and Stuart Literature* (London: Athlone Press, 1994), p. 961.

2 William Shakespeare, *Hamlet: The Texts of 1603 and 1623*, ed. Ann Thompson and Neil Taylor (London: Arden Shakespeare, 2006).

3 William Shakespeare, *The Arden Shakespeare: King Lear*, ed. R.A. Foakes (London: Thomas Nelson and Sons, 1997).

4 William Shakespeare, *A Midsummer Night's Dream: Texts and Contexts*, ed. Gail Kern Paster and Skiles Howard (Boston: Bedford/St. Martin's, 1999).

5 All references to *Much Ado About Nothing* are from William Shakespeare, *Much Ado About Nothing: The Arden Shakespeare*, ed. A.R. Humphreys (London: Methuen Drama, 1981).

6 Williams, *Dictionary of Sexual Language*, p. 954.

7 Paul Griffiths, *Lost Londons: Change, Crime, and Control in the Capital City 1550–1616* (Cambridge: Cambridge University Press, 2008), p. 273.

8 Griffiths, *Lost Londons*, p. 353.

9 Griffiths, *Lost Londons*, p. 353.

10 Griffiths, *Lost Londons*, p. 356.

11 Leo Salinger classifies *Much Ado* along with *Merchant of Venice*, *All's Well That Ends Well*, and *Measure For Measure* as problem comedies. Carol Neely points out that what clearly places it in this category is its "broken nuptials": Carol Thomas Neely, *Broken Nuptials in Shakespeare's Plays* (Urbana: University of Illinois Press, 1993, 1st edn 1985), p. 39.

12 Michael Kiernan, ed., *Sir Francis Bacon: The Essayes of Counsels, Civill and Morall* (Cambridge, MA, 1985), p. 16.

13 Paul Hair, ed., *Before the Bawdy Court: Selections from the Church Court and Other Records Relating to the Correction of Moral Offences in England, Scotland and New England, 1300–1800* (London: Elk, 1972), pp. 55–6.

14 Griffiths, *Lost Londons*, p. 274.

15 Quoted in, C.S.L. Davies and John Edwards, "Catherine of Aragon (1485–1536)", *ODNB*.

16 Griffiths, *Lost Londons*, pp. 270–1.

17 Griffiths, *Lost Londons*, p. 272.

### As You Like It

1 William Shakespeare, *As You Like It: The Arden Shakespeare*, ed. Juliet Dusinberre (London: Methuen, 2006) pp. 7, 37. All quotations are from this edition.

2 C.L. Barber, *Shakespeare's Festive Comedy: A Study of Dramatic Form and Its Relation to Social Custom* (Princeton: Princeton University Press, 1990).

3 R.S. White, *Natural Law in English Renaissance Literature* (Cambridge: Cambridge University Press, 1996), pp. 72, xvi, xiii, 104–6.

4 On its impact in Shakespeare's England, see Andrew Hadfield, *Shakespeare and Republicanism* (Cambridge: Cambridge University Press, 2005), p. 33; Junius Brutus, *A Defence of Liberty Against*

*Tyrants*, ed. Harold Laski (London: Bell and Sons, 1924).

5  *Vindiciae Contra Tryannos*, ed. and trans. George Garnett (Cambridge: Cambridge University Press, 1994), p. xliii.

6  All references from *King Lear* are from William Shakespeare, *King Lear: The Arden Shakespeare*, ed. R.A. Foakes (Walton-on-Thames: Thomas Nelson and Sons, 1997).

7  John Foxe, *Acts and Monuments*, ed. Stephen Reed Cattley (London: 8:619, 1837). This narrative first appeared in Foxe's 1570 edition.

8  Leah S. Marcus, Janel Mueller, and Mary Beth Rose, ed., *Elizabeth I: Collected Works* (Chicago: University of Chicago Press, 2000), p. 170.

9  Hans Eworth, *Elizabeth I and the Three Goddesses*, "The Royal Collection: Royal Palaces, Residences and Art Collection."

10  Susan Doran, "Virginity, Divinity, and Power: The Portraits of Elizabeth I," *The Myth of Elizabeth*, ed. Susan Doran and Thomas S. Freeman (New York: Palgrave Macmillan, 2003), p. 176.

## *Twelfth Night, Or What You Will*

1  All references to *Twelfth Night* are from William Shakespeare, *Twelfth Night: The Arden Shakespeare*, ed. J.M. Lothian and T.W. Craik (London: Methuen Drama, 1981).

2  Barbara Ravelhofer, " 'Beasts of Recreacion': Henslowe's White Bears," *ELR* 32(2002): 287–323, at 288.

3  Ravelhofer, " 'Beasts of Recreacion,' " p. 288.

4  Quoted in Ravelhofer, " 'Beasts of Recreacion,' " p. 290.

5  Ralph Berry argues that blood sport is intrinsic to festive comedy, " *Twelfth Night*: The Experience of the Audience," in *Shakespeare and the Awareness of the Audience* (London: Macmillan, 1985), p. 74.

6  John Bruce, ed., *The Diary of John Manningham* (Westminster: Camden Society, 1868), p. 18.

7  See, for example, Valerie Traub, *Desire and Anxiety* (1992), pp. 130–43; Jean Howard *The Stage and Social Struggle in Early Modern England*, Ch. 5 and Dympna Callaghan, *Shakespeare Without Women: Representing Gender and Race on the Renaissance Stage*, Ch. 1 (New York: Routledge, 2000), pp. 26–48.

8  Stephen Orgel, *Impersonations: The Performance of Gender in Shakespeare's England* (Cambridge: Cambridge University Press, 1996), p. 64.

9  Indira Ghose, *Shakespeare and Laughter: A Cultural History* (New York: Manchester University Press, 2008), p. 117.

10  Ravelhofer, " 'Beasts of Recreacion,' " p. 292.

## *Measure for Measure*

1  References to *Measure for Measure* are taken from William Shakespeare, *Measure for Measure*, ed. Ivo Kamps and Karen Raber (Boston: Bedford/St. Martin's, 2004).

2  A.W. Ward, G.W. Prothero, and Stanley Leathes, *The Cambridge Modern History: The Reformation* (Cambridge: Cambridge University Press, 1903) Vol. 2, p. 368.

3  E. William Monter, *Calvin's Geneva* (New York: John Wiley and Sons, 1967), p. 17.

4  References to *Romeo and Juliet* are taken from William Shakespeare, *Romeo and Juliet*, ed. Dympna Callaghan (Boston: Bedford/St. Martin's, 2003).

5  Conrad Russell, *Parliament and English Politics 1621–1629* (Oxford: Clarendon Press, 1979); see also Chris R. Kyle, *Theater of State: Parliament and Political Culture in Early Stuart England* (Stanford: Stanford University Press, 2012).

6  Russell, *Parliament*, p. 277.

7  R.S. White, *Natural Law in English Renaissance Literature* (Cambridge: Cambridge University Press, 1996), p. 170.

8  Keith Thomas, "The Puritans and Adultery: The Act of 1650 Reconsidered," in Donald Pennington and Keith Thomas, eds, *Puritans and Revolutionaries: Essays in Seventeenth-Century History Presented to Christopher Hill* (Oxford: Oxford University Press, 1978), p. 266.

9  Thomas, *"Puritans and Adultery,"* p. 267.

10  David M. Dean, *Law-making and Society in Late Elizabethan England* (Cambridge: Cambridge University Press, 1996), p. 268.

11  Dean, *Law-making*, p. 268.

12  Dean, *Law-making*, p. 268.

13  Dean, *Law-making*, p. 268.

14  See Charles Nicholl, *The Lodger Shakespeare: His Life on Silver Street* (New York: Penguin, 2007), p. 223.

15  References to *Hamlet* are from William Shakespeare, *Hamlet*, ed. Ann Thompson and Neil Taylor (London: Methuen, 2006).

16  Monter, *Calvin's Geneva*, p. 152.

17  Quoted in White, *Natural Law*, p. 171.

18  Quoted from (Lambarde, *Ephemeris*, p. 76) by J.D. Alsop, "Lambarde, William (1536–1601)" *ODNB*.

19  See Peter Ackroyd, *Shakespeare: The Biography* (New York: Nan A. Talese, 2005).

20  J.W. Lever, ed., *Measure for Measure* (London: Methuen, 1965), p. xxxiv.

21  Dean, *Law-making*, p. 55.

22  Quoted in Dean, *Law-making*, p. 56.

23  Dean, *Law-making*, p. 55.

# 7

# ENGLISH AND ROMAN HISTORIES

## Shakespeare's Politics

*Richard II*
*1 Henry IV*
*Henry V*
*Richard III*
*Julius Caesar*
*Coriolanus*

### *Richard II*

One of the central historical and theological concepts of Shakespeare's era was that of divine providence. As opposed to the arbitrary occurrences of fate or luck, Providence was the manifestation of God's often punitive will, which could be tracked throughout history in the narrative of how God chose and, in the case of *Richard II*, deposed his anointed kings. A providential view of history incorporated and transformed the ancient pagan idea of fortune, represented by the Roman goddess Fortuna, who turned her wheel so that human beings might be brought high or low depending upon her capricious whim. However, the idea of fortune had been Christianized since the Middle Ages in collections of moral exempla in the genre known as *de casibus* tragedy, from Boccaccio's *De Casibus Virorum Illustrium* (Of the Fall of Illustrious Men). This was popularized in England in the early fifteenth century in John Lydgate's *The Fall of Princes*. After the Protestant Reformation, such tales took on a singularly providential cast. God was understood to bring down those

*Who Was William Shakespeare?: An Introduction to the Life and Works*, First Edition.
Dympna Callaghan.
© 2013 John Wiley & Sons, Ltd. Published 2013 by John Wiley & Sons, Ltd.

whose standing in the world rested upon a sinful foundation. One of the most popular books in Shakespeare's time, *The Mirror for Magistrates* (1555), was an unapologetically didactic verse collection of exempla in which the high and mighty fell from grace to providentially appointed punishment. These were stories of rulers and other persons in public office whose triumphs were invariably followed by a spectacular fall when their sins caught up with them. In alignment with the new and specifically Protestant Elizabethan agenda, the 1559 edition of *The Mirror* was compiled by William Baldwin under the title *A Myrroure for Magistrates* (London, 1559) only a year after Elizabeth ascended the throne. Indeed, with the advent of the Protestant Reformation, and especially the promulgation of the Calvinist doctrine of predestination, according to which God's design for human history had been formed before the beginning of time, providentialism gained new scope and momentum as the single most important paradigm through which historical events could be viewed and understood. When Shakespeare wrote *Richard II* in 1595, all prior historical events were understood to have conspired with the aid of divine providence to place Elizabeth on the throne. Needless to say, this fortuitous outcome was one the Elizabethan state had every reason to endorse.

Convenient as it was as a justification for Elizabeth's Protestant sovereignty, providentialism was nonetheless a notion riven with deep contradictions, especially since even the acts of evil people could be construed as part of the grand providential design. Thus, a tyrannical ruler could be understood, from the providential point of view, as a punishment visited upon a sinful people. Similarly, rulers raised up by God could always be brought low. Indeed, for the Protestant martyrologist John Foxe, monarchs chosen by God's providence were to be held to higher standards, and his *Actes and Monuments* (1563), a copy of which, as we noted earlier, was chained to the furnishings of every church in England, harangued Elizabeth toward a more radical Protestant agenda under the guise of promoting the providential nature of her succession. *The Mirror for Magistrates* was rather more cautious, and all Elizabethan editions of the volume were careful to avoid dealing with rulers who were within living memory. Though informed by a providential point of view, like other extant chronicle histories, Shakespeare's primary source for *Richard II*, Raphael Holinshed's *Chronicles of England, Scotland and Ireland* (1587), did not share *The Mirror*'s crudely ideological agenda.

In a very significant way, even though all of history, good and bad, led up to the glorious Protestant reign of the present time, *all* recorded history was potentially an admonition to the reigning sovereign. In *The Mirror for Magistrates*, the figure of Richard II consents to have his story told as a cautionary tale:

> Sith thou wilt declare
> How princes fell, to make the living wise,
> My vicious story in no point see thou spare,
> But paint it out, that rulers may beware
> Good counsel, lawe, or virtue to despise.[1]

Unlike other genres of history, far from being required to resolve or take a position on the political and ethical problems presented in the chronicles, drama's propensity was to stage them for debate. There were two Elizabethan plays that, more than any others, confronted the volatile problem of power and its justification. These were Christopher Marlowe's *Edward II* (published in 1592) and Shakespeare's *Richard II*. In Marlowe's play, the weak, effeminate king – swayed by favorites, especially his paramour, Piers Gaveston – meets a spectacularly gruesome death, albeit one the play does not specify in any detail: he was anally penetrated with a hot iron. In a society that proposed femininity and power as mutually exclusive, the reign of Elizabeth notwithstanding, the effeminacy of the womanish male ruler was potentially, in conceptual terms at least, dangerously proximate to the female ruler. Yet, for all that, there is no record that this particular play fell afoul of the Elizabethan authorities.

Like *Edward II*, *Richard II* is also a play about a weak and vacillating king who rejects the sound counsel of his uncles in favor of frivolous and foolish advice. The outcome of his folly is that he is compelled to abdicate by a usurper before being imprisoned and eventually murdered. It is clear from the fact that Sir Edward Hoby presented the play as an entertainment to Elizabeth's privy councilor Sir Robert Cecil in December 1595 that it was not then thought to be seditious. It was only six years after its first performance, in the context of subsequent events, when the Earl of Essex's supporters commissioned a performance of the play on the afternoon of February 7, 1601, the eve of the Essex Rising (an ill-conceived plan to capture Whitehall and the queen), that it accrued a potentially treasonous cast. Elizabeth herself feared that its depiction of a ruler forced to abdicate was a mirror of what might befall her if the dashing Robert Devereux, Earl of Essex, her former favorite, succeeded in his ill-fated rebellion. Some months after Essex had been discreetly beheaded in the Tower on February 25, 1601, Elizabeth famously remarked that "this tragedy was played 40tie times in open streets and houses" and protested to the antiquarian William Lambarde: "I am Richard II. Know ye not that?"[2] The play demonstrates all too clearly that God's anointing confers neither infallibility nor indestructibility, despite Richard's eloquent assertion to the contrary: "Not all the water in the rough rude sea / Can wash the balm off from an anointed king" (3.2.54–5).[3]

Indeed, the interest of *Richard II* lies not only in its political theme but also in the characterization of Richard, especially in the lyrical eloquence with which Shakespeare endows him:

> For God's sake let us sit upon the ground
> And tell sad stories of the death of kings –
> How some have been deposed, some slain in war,
> Some haunted by the ghosts they have deposed,
> Some poisoned by their wives, some sleeping killed –
> All murdered. For within the hollow crown
> That rounds the mortal temples of a king
> Keeps Death his court; and there the antic sits,
> Scoffing his state and grinning at his pomp,
> Allowing him a breath, a little scene,
> To monarchize, be feared, and kill with looks . . . (3.2.155–65)

Richard here captures the fallibility and mortality of rulers, and in a sense recapitulates the fates not only of historical monarchs but also of Shakespeare's own kings – Richard himself is deposed, Henry IV will be haunted by his usurpation of Richard's crown, Macbeth is slain in battle, and both Duncan and King Hamlet are killed while sleeping. The personified figure of Death is the real power in Richard's abbreviated chronicle, where all monarchs, even the most powerful, are actors – as they certainly are in Shakespeare's second tetralogy (the sequence of *Richard II*, *1* and *2 Henry IV*, and *Henry V*) – who are permitted but "a little scene." As David Kastan argues, "The histories expose the idealizations of political power by presenting rule as role, by revealing that power passes to him who can best control and manipulate the visual and verbal symbols of authority."[4] Thus, Richard's metatheatrical emphasis on the histrionics of sovereign power cannot serve to make him an effective king, though they render him a sympathetic figure of "Proud majesty [made] a subject" (4.1.252). Nor does the exquisite lyricism of a line like "For God's sake let us sit upon the ground / And tell sad stories of the death of kings" (3.2.155–6) make Richard someone who would have been better suited to the life of a poet than to that of a ruler. As Peter Ure explains, "the poetry in Richard is there because he is a character in a poetic drama, not because Shakespeare thought that Richard II lost his kingdom through a preference for blank verse over battles . . ."[5] This is especially true in this play, which is the only one of Shakespeare's histories written entirely in verse, where even the symbolically charged lower-class gardeners are given verse speeches. Richard is elegiac, then, because in poetry, this is the language of loss.

The chronological period covered by the play is 1397–1399, when Henry Bolingbroke, the future Henry IV, deposed Richard II. This usurpation goes on to haunt not only Bolingbroke himself in the *Henry IV* plays but also the reign of his son, Henry V, who, the night before the battle of Agincourt, fears that even though Providence brought about his father's victory, he may now have to pay for his father's sin in deposing God's anointed king. *Richard II* opens when Bolingbroke challenges the Duke of Norfolk about his role in the death of the king's uncle, the Duke of Gloucester. A tournament is set to resolve the matter, but the ever-vacillating Richard decides instead to banish Norfolk for life and to exile Bolingbroke for a limited term of six years. Key to establishing the providential momentum gathering behind Bolingbroke here is the presence of his father, the famous John of Gaunt, Duke of Lancaster, whose virtue is unimpeachable and who ultimately dies broken-hearted as a result of his son's exile. When Richard appropriates Gaunt's lands and uses the revenue to fund an expedition to Ireland, Bolingbroke returns with an invading army and is greeted with popular support. After being cornered in Flint Castle, Richard finally agrees to go to Westminster where he is persuaded to abdicate in favor of Bolingbroke. The latter's power remains insecure as Aumerle, one of Richard's most trusted advisors, plots against the new king. In a demonstration that family loyalty cannot come at the expense of treason, Aumerle's own father, the Duke of York, uncovers this treachery and supports Henry IV's rightful kingship. Richard is then imprisoned in Pontefract Castle where Piers of Exton, misinterpreting Henry's directives, murders him. Henry does not condone this assassination and vows to make a pilgrimage to the Holy Land as an act of penitence for Richard's death.

One of the play's most interesting stagings of power is the depiction of the Parliament in Westminster Hall. While there was a safe chronological distance between the 1390s and the 1590s, this was a location with which everyone in Shakespeare's London was familiar. As one of the major shopping areas of the capital and the home of the courts of justice, Shakespeare's audience would have had particularly vivid, present-tense points of reference for an event which otherwise might have remained unthinkable in the present Elizabethan context, namely what the title page of the Third Quarto calls "the pageant" in which Richard literally cedes the scepter and crown, great symbols of sovereign power, to his adversary.

Denuded of his majesty, "plume-plucked Richard . . . his high sceptre yields" (4.1.109–10) in an act of submission no anointed king was ever intended to make. After he has parted with the crown, like the all characters in *The Mirror for Magistrates*, Richard asks for a looking glass:

> An if my word be sterling yet in England,
> Let it command a mirror hither straight,
> That it may show me what a face I have,
> Since it is bankrupt of his majesty. (4.1.264–8)

One hundred and sixty-five lines from this scene, in which Richard physically hands over his crown, were omitted from the Elizabethan quartos of 1597 and 1598. However, they were included in the text in the 1608 printing when Elizabeth was safely dead: "With new additions of the Parliament Scene and the deposing of King Richard." Whether the lines in question from Act 4, Scene 1 were added in 1608, or were always part of the play but simply omitted from the printing, is still a matter for scholarly debate.[6] A fourth quarto appeared in 1615, which again included the scene.

*Richard II*, perhaps more than any other play, indicates both the degree of license Shakespeare took in handling politically sensitive themes, and the degree of caution he was also required to exercise if he were to survive as a person and as a playwright in early modern England.

# 1 Henry IV

Although all of *The First Part of King Henry the Fourth* is ostensibly set in the period 1402–3, much of the play is recognizably located in Shakespeare's London. The parts of the play that are far less medieval than early modern in flavor concern the habitués of a recognizably Elizabethan tavern located in what was, in Shakespeare's London, the major market thoroughfare of Eastcheap. The tavern is frequented by the Prince of Wales, the madcap Hal, whose life of dissipation seems ill-fitted to his position as heir to the throne. The play moves between the high politics of medieval aristocracy rendered in blank verse to much less conventional matter for a history play, namely, the concerns of ordinary and low-life characters (typically the subjects of comedy) whose speech is represented in the everyday language of prose. *1 Henry IV* is fundamentally structured by generic hybridity and by a shift in temporality. The latter would not, however, have struck Elizabethan audiences as unpardonably anachronistic and may even account for the play's popularity. Probably written in 1596, *The First Part of King Henry the Fourth* was twice printed in quarto in 1598, and before the play appeared in the First Folio, it had appeared in no fewer than five further quarto editions.

The play is unique among Shakespeare's ten English histories, and is markedly different from *Richard II* and *Henry V* with their much tighter focus on the monarch as protagonist. It is like Shakespeare's earliest histories, the three parts of *Henry VI*, in so far as it is about *the reign* of Henry IV rather than Henry himself. That is to say, the focus of *1 Henry IV* is on the way power operated, was contested and transmitted. However, *1 Henry IV* differs markedly from the episodic structure of the *Henry VI* plays. In addition, its dramatic amplification of characters other than the monarch, especially Prince Hal and his fat-gutted drinking companion, the irrepressible aristocrat-turned-larcenist, Sir John Falstaff, is unique. The conventional topics of history are still addressed: power and sovereignty, rebellion and treason, together with the battles that provide resolution of conflict, at least until the next challenge to the status quo. In an important sense, when addressing historical events, there is always potential for a sequel, and, of course, *Henry IV* has a second part, even though it is far from clear that Shakespeare conceived the play as a first installment while he was writing it.[1] Questions about legitimate succession and how to hold onto power once you have it dominate the high politics of the play. However, Shakespeare allows these dynamics to play out among diverse consistencies from tavern dwellers to the king's rivals for control in other parts of the nation: in the North, the fiery Hotspur (Henry Percy), son of the Earl of Northumberland; in Wales, Owen Glendower; and, Edward Mortimer, Earl of March, who hails from the border, in the far west of the country.

Shakespeare relied on specifically historical sources to probe the operations of power across the social and geographical contours of England. Chief among them was his primary chronicle source, Raphael Holinshed's *Chronicles of England, Scotland, and Ireland* (second edition, 1587), although he also took cues about how to set off Hal and Hostpur as worthy opponents of equal age (as they were not in historical fact) from Samuel Daniel's verse account of *The Civil Wars Between the Two Houses of Lancaster and York* (1595). In addition, Shakespeare clearly knew popular accounts of the transformation of the dissolute Hal into the great and victorious monarch, Henry V, most notably an anonymous play from the 1580s, *The Famous Victories of Henry the Fifth*. The influence of Machiavelli's *The Prince* (printed in 1532) is also evident in both Hal's carefully considered strategy to achieve power and his rival Hotspur's relentless pragmatism in the face of his co-conspirator Glendower's occult powers (he claims to be able to summon demons).[2] However, in this history play, Shakespeare went further. He did away with the more conventional frameworks of *de casibus* tragedy and the model which attributed the events of human history to God's grand providential – and often punitive – design. The conventional treatment of the fall of great men was, anyway, ill-suited to the material on hand about the rise of a great king, and he employed, instead, a more freely imaginative structure of causation. His rendition is infused with the types of images, genealogies, and temporalities – the past made present in ways that defy linear chronology – that belong to Ovidian mythology, or to what Ovid referred to in his great book on the theme of change, the *Metamorphoses*, as "the registers of things . . . made to be."[3] The *Metamorphoses*, Shakespeare's favorite poem, is also "a kind of history" (*The Taming of the Shrew*, Induction 2.135), a book that measures the culmination of sequences of actions within a life and across generations and thus looks both forward into the future as much as it looks back into the past.[4] For all that the comic antics of Falstaff may threaten to steal the show, the fulcrum and centrifuge of the play's action is Hal's transformation from prodigal youth into the glorious prince who saves his father, vanquishes the rebels, and crucially, in so doing, averts a potential crisis of succession.[5] This is a play that is, above all, about metamorphosis.

The play opens with King Henry IV expressing the burdens of sovereignty in a perfectly poised line of iambic pentameter: "So shaken as we are, so wan with care" (1.1.1). In the wake of civil war, he now hopes to secure his position strategically, to "busy giddy minds/ with foreign quarrels" (2 Henry IV, 4.5.216–17),[6] as he puts it in Part 2, by sending an army to join the crusades. This intention is also motivated by his guilt about having usurped the throne of his predecessor, Richard II. Henry's is the insecurity of the usurper: the hand of Providence, was, according to this way of coming to terms with historical events, always ready to strike those who unseat God's anointed kings. Thus, even though Henry is now himself anointed, his tenure as sovereign remains inherently vulnerable. This seizure of power is figured, however, not just through the lens of the providentialism Henry believes in but also symbolically, especially in Hotspur's language, as a metamorphosis. Here, metamorphosis is a form of degeneration, it is the diminishment of sovereignty from the legitimate King Richard II, "that sweet lovely rose," who has been "put down" only to "plant this thorn, this canker, Bolingbroke." (1.3.137). Hotspur's repeated insistence on the king's former identity as "this ingrate and canker'd Bolingbroke" (1.3) bespeaks his refusal to acknowledge the legitimacy of Henry's sovereignty.

The immediate pressure of these events dashes any hopes Henry might have cherished about assuaging the deity for his usurpation by means of a crusade. While Harry Percy has won a victory over the Scots at Holmedon, in Wales, the English led by Edmund Mortimer are defeated by the "rude hand[s]" (1.1.41) of Owen Glendower, who has taken Mortimer prisoner. While captive, Mortimer has married Glendower's daughter, and thus, Henry contends, has betrayed the troops slaughtered in the conflict: "A thousand of his people butchered" (1.1.42). The king therefore refuses to ransom Mortimer from Glendower. In anger about this state of affairs, Hotspur stubbornly still refuses to turn over prisoners to Henry whom he had previously failed to release to the king on the grounds that they were first demanded of him by a "popinjay" (1.3.50) of a courtier on the battlefield. Hotspur is now irremediably at odds with his sovereign and, along with his father, the Earl of Northumberland, and his uncle, Westmoreland, foments rebellion. Ironically, the conspirators who helped Henry to the crown are now challenging him for it and forming alliances with England's erstwhile enemies, the Scots and the Welsh. The hot-headed, valiant warrior and devoted husband, Hotspur, joins with the Scottish earl, Douglas, while Mortimer is allied with the Welsh opposition to Henry's rule through his marriage to Owen Glendower's daughter.

Among the king's troubles, his heir, Prince Hal, is a wastrel whom his father believes may be a providential "revengement and a scourge" (3.2.7) bred out of his own blood in payment for his previous transgressions:

> Thou dost in thy passages of life
> Make me believe that thou art only marked
> For the hot vengeance and the rod of heaven,
> To punish my mistreadings. (3.2.8–11)

Henry's is a variation on the idea that the sins of the fathers might be visited upon successive generations – an idea that was certainly deployed to explain his grandson Henry VI's disastrous reign. The Bible, however, contained contradictory statements on this point: "I the Lord thy God am a jealous God, visiting the iniquity of the fathers upon the children unto the third and fourth [generation] of them that hate me" (Exodus 20.5). Clearly, God's vengeance could persist through a fairly lengthy period of history. In contrast, the Old Testament later assures, "A son doth not bear of the iniquity of the father, And a father doth not bear of the iniquity of the son, The righteousness of the righteous is on him, And the wickedness of the wicked is on him" (Ezekiel 18.20). In Henry's speech, however, the prince is God's rod of correction upon Henry himself. These ideas are important because they speak to the key problem of succession – the point of transmission, where power was at its most vulnerable. In Book 10 of the *Metamorphoses*, succession is described as the accretion of ever-more glorious deeds down the generations of classical heroes, concluding with the example of Jove (Jupiter) outshining his father, Saturn. Since throughout the previous books of the poem Jove has been shown to be a serial rapist and abuser of power, we may suspect a heavy dose of Ovidian political irony about the current regime of the emperor Augustus in this idealized account of patrilineal descent:

> So Atreus gave way to Agamemnon,
> Aegeus to Theseus, Peleus to Achilles,
> so Saturn, in the later light of Jove:
> for Jupiter rules kingdoms up above
> as well as air and sea and earth below;
> on earth Augustus rules, and like great Jove
> he is our father and our governor.
>
> (*Metamorphoses*, 10.1076–82)[7]

Thus Shakespeare knew from his Roman predecessor how patriarchal genealogy might be integral to the very concept of metamorphosis as well as to its politics. In Hal's ultimate metamorphosis into Henry V he follows this Ovidian trajectory in historical as well as in literary fact.

However, just as in Ovid's critique of power in this genealogy, Shakespeare too always allows some room for suspicion about power itself in the creation of his warrior hero, so that Hal's transformation is, in the end, more than just a saccharine glorification or a hagiography – a predictable tale of sin and redemption – and this is because of the very nature of metamorphosis itself that Shakespeare inherited from Ovid. In *2 Henry IV*, the prince explicitly aligns himself with Jove in the story of the rape of Europa from Book 2 of the *Metamorphoses*. Here, Jove seduces Europa by transforming himself into a bull. Only when he has enticed her to ride on his back into the ocean and abducted her to Crete does he reveal his divinity: "From a god to a bull – a heavy declension – it was Jove's case. From a prince to a prentice, a low transformation – that shall be mine" (*2 Henry IV*, 2.2.165–7). In this recapitulation of his mythic narrative, the first step is descent, "heavy declension." This pattern of divine descent that precedes glorification is one that this Ovidian schema has in common with Christian eschatology. For a pre-condition of the Savior's resurrection and ascension to glory is incarnation – coming to earth, becoming flesh – and obscuring divine identity with human form, particularly in the lowly circumstances of the stable at Bethlehem. This is the mythic trajectory that Hal follows, and it is one Henry cannot comprehend, seeing the image of his own youth (quite correctly since he is a usurper) in Hotspur: "And even as I was then is Percy now" (3.2.96).

While biblical and mythic notions of generational succession subtend the play's father–son relationship, it remains the case that, from a purely practical point of view, regal succession depended on the reliable transmission of power between father and son. Infant successors like Henry VI, for example, were invariably weak and vulnerable to those who governed until their majority. Henry IV, however, simply fears that his son is incapable of assuming the mantle of sovereignty. This is an assessment with which Hostpur contemptuously concurs: "this sword and buckler Prince of Wales" (1.3.229). The rivalry between contemporaries that Shakespeare sets up between these two makes sharply apparent the degree to which Shakespeare's inclinations as a dramatist towards the narrative structure of myth caused him to alter historical fact to suit his dramatic purposes. When the Earl of Westmoreland pointedly remarks that Hotspur's subjugation of Douglas "is a conquest for a prince to boast of" (1.1.76) Henry speaks regretfully of his own paternity and fantasizes being "the father to so blest a son" (1.1.79) as Hotspur, who is "the theme of honor's tongue" (1.1.80), rather than his own dissipated progeny, who seems more like a changeling, an infant exchanged at birth for the valiant young Harry Percy:

> Whilst I, by looking on the praise of him,
> See riot and dishonor stain the brow
> Of my young Harry. O that it could be proved
> That some night-tripping fairy had exchang'd
> In cradle clothes our children where they lay,
> And called mine Percy, his Plantagenet!
> Then I would have his Harry, and he mine. (1.1.83–9)

In historical fact, as we have noted, the prince and Hotspur's cradles never came near one another – Henry Percy was older than Henry IV. Yet, this association, early in the play, of babes who have the same name and who in Henry's wishful fiction seem to share the same cradle like twins, is an image of transformed, exchanged identity. This image serves as preparation for Hal's appropriation of his rival's "glorious deeds" (3.2.146) in the final battle at Shrewsbury.

This condensed myth of exchanged identity also resonates with the metamorphosis that ignites the play's action, namely Hal's plan to redeem his reputation. His soliloquy at the end of Act 1, Scene 2 discloses that this dissolute life has been merely a strategy so that when he reveals himself in true, regal demeanor he will be all the more spectacular. In this he instigates the metamorphosis that constitutes the play's main action:

> I know you all, and will awhile uphold
> The unyok'd humor of your idleness.
> Yet herein will I imitate the sun,
> Who doth permit the base contagious clouds
> To smother up his beauty from the world
> That when he please again to be himself,
> Being wanted he may be more wondered at. (1.2.148–55)

Like Jove in the *Metamorphoses*, change does not befall the prince; rather, he determines the moment "when this loose behavior I throw off," (1.2.161), when he will discard his disguise, and it is his subterfuge in exercising his regal will that marks him as both a cunning tactician and a great future king:

> By so much shall I falsify men's hopes;
> And like bright metal on a sullen ground,
> My reformation, glittering o'er my fault,
> Shall show more goodly and attract more eyes

> Than that which hath no foil to set it off.
> I'll so offend to make offense a skill,
> Redeeming time when men think least I will. (1.2.164–70)

The soliloquy shows Hal to be endowed with the introspective intelligence that his rival lacks. For Hotspur is perpetually bent on action and has no time for rumination or carefully prepared strategy. This soliloquy recapitulates fundamentally Ovidian themes: the intrusion of the all-powerful into the lives of unsuspecting mortals and the transformation and shape-shifting that is the prerogative of Jove. On this speech hangs the connection between the realm of high politics and the tavern world, and Shakespeare forges the connection in a way that is indebted for its expression to Ovidian metamorphoses. Like Jove's power over lesser mortals, Hal's is similarly morally questionable. Even though, unlike his mythic antecedent, Hal is not a sexual predator, he is, nonetheless, potentially just as sinister. While the alignment of sovereignty with the sun is conventional, this description of his current companions, who seem here to provide nothing more than a convenient screen, has long troubled critics. Certainly this soliloquy is a prelude to the prince's later ruthless rejection of his companions, especially Falstaff, whom he publicly repudiates in *Part Two*, a repulse that kills his corpulent former companion, as we learn in *Henry V*.

> FALSTAFF:   Banish not him thy Harry's company – banish plump Jack, and banish all the world
> PRINCE:   I do I will. (2.4.380–3)

This is an unsettling moment for audiences and readers who by this stage in the play may prefer to see Prince Hal as "sweet wag" (1.2.19) and the "rascalliest, sweet, young prince" (1.2.62), as Falstaff endearingly calls him, than as the calculating Machiavel. More benignly, Hal can also be seen as a role player, an actor capable of multiple personae. This is in part also what differentiates Hal from Hotspur. The latter is committed to a static, single identity to the extent that it becomes a caricature, as his rival recognizes: "The Hotspur of the north: he that kills me some six or seven dozen of Scots at a breakfast, washes his hands, and says to his wife, "Fie upon this quiet life! I want work" (2.4.84–8).

   "A very valiant rebel" (5.4.62), Hotspur is a great warrior who cannot escape his role and is not even aware he is playing one. In contrast, when Hal is summoned to appear before his father, he and Falstaff role-rehearse the interview. This is a fascinating vignette because amateur theatricals did sometimes occur in Elizabethan taverns, and indeed some inns served as theatres late into the sixteenth century.[8] This episode both demystifies high politics and brings them

down to earth, putting them into startling contact with the present, Elizabethan, moment in which the play was originally performed.

This decision, announced in his soliloquy, to throw off his current role and
to spurn Falstaff represents the decisive moment of transformation from dissolute Hal to valiant Prince Harry who will defend his father's throne against
the rebels. This is the resolve of someone who knows he can change history.
However, this is not the will applied for the purpose of repression or self-
discipline because his is self-transformation, not just a conversion to virtue. The
latter is simply how it appears to those onlookers the prince plans to dazzle.[9]
In this there is a marked contrast with Falstaff, who earlier in the scene has
jestingly promised reformation. Here his vow is inflected with specifically religious notions of repentance when he attests, that, "I must give over this life,
and I will give it over . . ." (1.2.73–4). Later, he adopts the mask of pious
Puritan rhetoric, echoing St Paul (1 Corinthians 4.20) to claim that purse-
snatching is "my vocation, Hal. 'Tis no sin for a man to labour in his vocation"
(1.2.81–2). So we must assume his professed amendment is not serious. In any
event, it is clear that where Hal achieves metamorphosis, Falstaff merely promises reformation in a fashion that may be indebted to the fact that Shakespeare
initially named Falstaff's character Sir John Oldcastle. Hal even refers to him as
"my old lad of the castle" (1.2.34), an appellation that appears to be the residue
of this earlier circumstance. The historical Oldcastle, later Lord Cobham, was
a Lollard, a proto-Protestant religious dissident who was burnt as a heretic in
1417. Shakespeare was forced to change the name, possibly because Cobham's
descendants objected or because of broader Protestant objection to making a
comic spectacle of someone who died a martyr.

Whichever of these scenarios is the case, Falstaff is no doubt the most dense
of the clouds that hide Hal's radiance. During the episode at Gadshill, when
Falstaff, Bardolph, and Peto rob pilgrims on the road, only to be relieved of
their spoils by Hal and Poins in disguise, Hal remarks: "Falstaff sweats to death
/ And lards the lean earth as he walks along" (2.2.89–90). After the escapade,
Falstaff predictably rewrites events in grossly exaggerated terms so that he is
the hero of the hour: "If I fought not with fifty of them, I am a bunch of
radish" (2.4.151–2). At the same time, he accuses Hal and Poins of cowardly
running away. When cornered in his lie, he claims that he recognized Hal as a
"true prince" (2.4.215) and therefore would not fight him for the booty. Falstaff's body may be slow and fat, but his wit is nimble enough to fit a new
narrative to suit a changed circumstance. In the tavern, these lies are harmless,
entertaining, but on the battlefield they become profoundly troubling. After
Percy has been killed by the prince, Falstaff desecrates the corpse in order to
claim the honor. More egregious than his outrageous mendacity, however, is
his use of the order to muster troops as an opportunity to profiteer. His men

are those only in the most wretched circumstances and state of health who could not buy their way out. Though, as he also so points out, with coldly cynical if subversive acuity, they will serve just as well as their betters as "food for powder, food for powder" (4.2.49–50). What is disquieting here is that, apparently without qualms, he has led these men straight to the slaughter: "I have led my ragamuffins where they are peppered" (5.3.34–5).

The prince, at least, ought to have Falstaff's unqualified allegiance. Yet, it is very clear at the level of the play's imagery that he does not. Instead, in his mythologized identity as a thief, he is a votary of the moon and not the sun, which is the symbol of kingship: "we that take purses go by the moon and the seven stars, and not 'by Phoebus . . .' " (1.2.10–11). While not actually a rebel, neither is he fully in alignment with the prince's party, as his fanciful rhetoric about a footpads' utopia in England when Hal ascends the throne reveals:

> When thou art king, let not us that are squires of the night's body be called thieves of the day's beauty: let us be Diana's foresters, gentlemen of the shade, minions of the moon; and let men say we be men of good government, being governed as the sea is, by our noble and chaste mistress the moon, under whose countenance we steal. (1.2.19–24)

Since Diana as the chaste goddess of the hunt and the moon was also a figure for Elizabeth I, the implications here are potentially dangerous. Further, Falstaff's familiarity with "the night's body" implies at the very least a form of trespass and at worse, violation.[10] Further, every fiber in Falstaff's all too substantial being is, as Hal well knows, inimical to "good government." Falstaff is, of course, not like the rebels in their desire to abolish the established order only to put themselves (or at least Mortimer who had a claim to the throne) in its place. Such aspirations would take more ambition and energy than he possesses. He is however, associated with them in so far as Hotspur also declares, "To push against a kingdom, . . . / We shall o'erturn it topsy-turvy down" (4.1.81–2). This is because Falstaff is a figure of carnivalesque misrule associated with the body and its pleasures that are catered to in the tavern and the bawdy house. The popular image for licensed and therefore temporary festive disorder was the world turned upside down that prevailed in periods of holiday. However, as Hal has also pointed out, it would not do to have everyday a day of licentious disorder: "If all the year were playing holidays, / To sport would be as tedious as to work" (1.2.157–8).[11] Yet this is precisely what Falstaff proposes (albeit in jest) – the world would be turned upside down so that the thief in the night would be as respectable as the day laborer.

Such ideas may not be treasonous, but they are subversive, and we see the extent of Falstaff's capacity to upturn the status quo in his scathing interrogation of the idea of honor as merely "a word" (5.1.132). The intrinsic virtue of honor has gone unquestioned for the entire duration of the play up until the moment on the battlefield at Shrewsbury in the last act of the play when Falstaff inquires: "Can honor set to a leg?" (5.1.130). He feigns death in his bout with Douglas, citing the maxim, "The better part of valour is discretion" (5.4.117). Falstaff's is indeed the view from the underside of this world, from "the shade." His demystification of honor is the antithesis of both Hotspur and Hal's ambition. What his father has called "never-dying honour" (3.2.106) remains for Hal a glittering prize, and for Hotspur it is the trophy that inspires his vaulting ambition: "By heaven, methinks it were an easy leap/ To pluck bright honor from the pale-faced moon," (1.3.201–2).

Before the contending forces meet for the culminating battle at Shrewsbury, Shakespeare inserts a gathering of the rebels and their wives. Jean Howard and Phyllis Rackin have pointed out that on the king's side of the quarrel, so to speak, the only female character is Mistress Quickly, the hostess of the tavern, whose name implies the sexual services that may also be performed there.[12] Only the rebels have wives: the lyrical Welshwoman married to Mortimer and the feisty Kate, Hotspur's wife, whom he has with him at Glendower's castle. That women are regarded as something of a liability among the king's supporters is arguably evidenced by Hal's parody of Lady Percy's communication with her husband: " 'O my sweet Harry,' says she, 'how many hast thou killed today?' " (2.4.87–8). The wives in this play signal the rebels' weakness as they contend against the overwhelmingly masculine forces of the king.

However, there is a mythic femininity associated with the king's party, which is that of England itself. At the beginning of the play, when Henry hopes that these "intestine broils" (civil wars) have ceased: "No more the thirsty entrance of this soil / Shall daub her lips with her own children's blood" (1.1.5–6). Cannibalistically devouring (and possibly menstrual) femininity, then, is one of the things to be constrained by proper sovereignty so that England can become the good mother who can provide soldiers who will kill abroad rather than at home:

> Forthwith a power of English shall we levy,
> Whose arms were moulded in their mother's womb
> To chase these pagans in those holy fields . . . (1.1.22–4)

At Shrewsbury, chasing rebels rather than pagans, Prince Harry demonstrates that he is made exactly of this mettle. Hotspur is expecting a report of "The nimble-footed madcap Prince of Wales" (4.1.95), but instead the prince is, as he promised, "Glittering in golden coats . . . / And gorgeous as the sun at midsummer" (4.1.100–2.). He is equipped with the accouterments of knighthood – a beaver (helmet with the face guard) and cushes or cuisses (leg armor). Presumably, this apotheosis is what he had in mind when he promised his father that he would now "Be more myself" (3.2.93).

Indeed, the supernatural or magical dimensions of metamorphosis are what most distinguish it from reformation or conversion. At Shrewsbury, these aspects are emphasized by reference to figures associated with flight, namely Pegasus, the winged horse and Mercury, the winged messenger, from Greek and Roman mythology respectively. The prince has left the mundane and merely terrestrial behind him:

> I saw young Harry with his beaver on,
> His cuisses on his thighs, gallantly armed,
> Rise from the ground like feathered Mercury,
> And vaulted with such ease into his seat
> As if an angel dropp'd down from the clouds
> To turn and wind a fiery Pegasus,
> And witch the world with noble horsemanship. (4.1.104–110)[13]

To complete the picture of magical transformation there is the image of a bewitching ("witch the world" *l.* 110 ) angel (*l.*108).[14] Not only has the prince finally revealed himself but he has also achieved the very image of sovereignty delineated by his father by securing among his beholders that "extraordinary gaze, / Such as is bent on sun like majesty" (3.2.78–9). For he is not just the perfect prince; he is the perfect heir to the throne. This is the politics of metamorphosis.

## Henry V

When Hamlet describes bad acting as the histrionic, overblown style of some performers, the very antithesis of naturalism, the figure he uses is that of Herod, the infanticidal king of the Jews whose ranting tyranny had been a staple of medieval religious drama: "It out-Herods Herod. Pray you avoid it" (3.2.13–14).[1] By the time Shakespeare composed that line, he had already written *Henry V*, where his representation of England's heroic warrior king is to be found in flagrant violation of Hamlet's advice. Before the besieged town of Harfleur, Henry V terrifies the mayor and his citizens into capitulation with the specter of indiscriminate slaughter:

> Your naked infants spitted upon pikes,
> Whiles the mad mothers with their howls confused

> Do break the clouds, as did the wives of Jewry
> At Herod's bloody-hunting slaughtermen. (3.3.38–41)[2]

It may be objected that Henry V is a warrior king rather than a performer, but he is, too, the mirror of all Christian kings (2.0.6), and we might be expected to assume that he does not truly intend to make good his threats. We might be expected to assume, in short, that he is acting, and that his bluff needs to be sufficiently good – sufficiently horrific – that it will not be called. Yet, Henry's speech refers to horrors that would have had specifically theatrical connotations for early modern audiences. The massacre of the innocents, Herod's murder of all male children in Bethlehem under two years of age in an endeavor to kill the Christ child, was an infamous atrocity familiar from the recently proscribed mystery cycles (performed, of course, prior to the advent of professional acting). These dramatizations were based on Matthew's Gospel (2.16–18) where Herod, duped by the wise men who fail to return to him after visiting the infant Jesus because they have been forewarned against him in a dream, becomes "excedyng wroth" (Bishops' Bible, 1568). It is Herod's wrath and rage that became the basis for the ferocious ranting Herod the plays depicted. That drama also portrayed an element of the story derived from a prophesy in the Old Testament book of Jeremiah: "A voice was heard in Ramah, lamentation, and bitter weeping; Rachel weeping for her children refused to be comforted for her children, because they were not" (31.15). These are the howling "wives of Jewry" to whose lamentations Henry refers and who were always included in the mystery plays on this theme.[3] The horrific spectacle Henry summons up both establishes and complicates his martial and rhetorical prowess. Invoking Herod aligns the king not only with the infamous biblical monarch, but also with the role of Herod, the staged enactment of tyranny rather than its actuality. This would clearly convey to an early modern audience that Henry is self-consciously playing a role. On the one hand, this role-playing suggests that he is offering the strategic presentiment of evil despite his intrinsic virtue, even though, as an adept politician, Henry is careful to lay the responsibility for horrors he proposes to unleash upon the denizens of Harfleur themselves by claiming that only their obdurate resistance will provoke him to it. On the other hand, the allusion to Herod conveys the potentially disquieting information that there is something inherently histrionic about the nature of sovereignty itself. That is, the performance of power becomes a species of dissimulation at which Henry is supremely adept, and as such it cannot be morally neutral. In contrast to Hamlet's experience of inept stage tyrants, then, Henry's performance is the perfect part, and his threats prove to be precisely calibrated to secure the surrender of Harfleur.

Although early modern political orthodoxy essentialized anointed sovereignty, this play presents sovereignty as a *performance* of power rather than as a quality intrinsic to the monarch whom God had elected to govern. The issue of "acting" like a king is crucial in relation to *Henry V* because it is the last play of the second series of four chronicle plays (*Richard II*; *1* and *2 Henry IV*; and *Henry V*) in which Shakespeare examined the nature of sovereignty. (Importantly, "second" here refers to the order in which Shakespeare wrote the history plays – he wrote *Henry VI* and *Richard III* first – and not to the chronological order in which the historical events he depicts occurred). In this final play of the second tetralogy, Henry, the formerly dissolute Prince Hal, has fulfilled the promise no one who knew him in his wild youth would have dreamed him to possess. In *1 Henry IV*, Shakespeare demonstrates that Prince Hal's metamorphosis is not merely the effect of natural maturation, but rather a carefully strategized performance of power. Shakespeare thus reveals Prince Hal as "Harry," King of England in *Henry V* – arguably not without criticism – in the fullest and finest expression of his power as a sovereign and as a leader of men at arms.

Henry has identified always, even from his youth, with the symbol of kingship, the sun, and staging the spectacle of his sovereignty is an integral aspect of his success as a warrior king. At Harfleur, "the contagious clouds" (*1 Henry IV*, 1.2.190) make another appearance when Henry promises the metamorphosis of his men:

> Therefore, you men of Harfleur,
> Take pity of your town and of your people
> Whiles yet my soldiers are in my command,
> Whiles yet the cool and temperate wind of grace
> O'erblows the filthy and *contagious clouds*
> Of heady murder, spoil and villainy. (3.3.27–32, my emphasis)

These clouds are literally the smoke from cannon fire, but they are also of a piece with the meteorological conditions stage-managed by the sun/sovereign. The clouds that revealed Hal's sovereignty can just as easily unveil hell. As Hamlet recognized, this kind of omniscient, periodically enraged grandiosity has its theatrical limits. However, what makes it appropriate for Henry V to thus contravene the rules of plausible, naturalistic stage representation is that he is the hero of an epic in the grand sweep of historical events considered over a span of many generations, a poetic genre that Shakespeare transposed to the medium of theatre. *Henry V* begins with a conventional epic invocation: "O for a muse of fire" (Prologue 1), and the play ends the history cycle on a relatively triumphant note. Whatever the play's much-debated interrogation of war and its related sufferings, Henry is victorious rather than vanquished. The chorus reminds the audience that Henry, "This star of England" (Epilogue 6), bequeathed his kingdom to an infant son in whose reign all that was won would be lost with much bloodshed, "Which oft our stage hath shown" (Epilogue 13). This allusion reminded the audience of Shakespeare's first and immensely popular histories, the three parts of *Henry VI*, and thus they knew the disastrous future of which Henry in his triumph is blissfully unaware.

The time was ripe for epic grandiosity in the theatre when Shakespeare wrote the play (first printed in 1600) because the dashing Robert Devereux, Earl of Essex, "the General of our gracious Empress" (5.0.30), had been sent to Ireland by Elizabeth in March 1599 to contain the rebellion of Hugh O'Neill, second Earl of Tyrone. A topical reference of this specificity is very unusual in Shakespeare and suggests that he was writing not at the dictates of his own muse but for the requirements of his company, and thus for the tastes of his London audiences who, elite and common alike, were fascinated by the chivalric magnificence of the Earl of Essex. However, the reference also suggests the degree to which the anticipated Earl of Essex was a matter of national preoccupation:[4]

> But now behold,
> In the quick forge and working-house of thought,
> How London doth pour out her citizens.
> The Mayor and all his brethren in best sort,
> Like to the senators of th'antique Rome
> With the plebeians swarming at their heels,
> Go forth and fetch their conquering Caesar in;
> As, by a lower but as loving likelihood,
> Were now the General of our gracious Empress,
> As in good time he may, from Ireland coming,
> Bringing rebellion broached on his sword,
> How many would the peaceful city quit
> To welcome him! Much more, and much more cause,
> Did they this Harry. (5.0.22–35)

In a line that echoes the impaled infants of the Harfleur speech, rebellion in Ireland is "broached," or spitted, on Essex's sword. Essex here is a modern epic hero, though only a general and not a king or an emperor. The analogy with the imperial triumphs of Caesar returning to Rome also serves to forge a connection between the epic aspirations of the play and classical epic poetry. In fact, history itself demonstrated the hyperbole of this analogy since Essex failed miserably in Ireland and subsequently plotted against the queen, only to be beheaded in 1601.

Shakespeare found much safer ground in epicizing the past, turning back the clock to medieval politics and to the lives of the English kings rather than miring himself in the dangerous terrain of the present. He dramatized the far from objective history he found in the chronicles of Raphael Holinshed and Edward Hall, and, upon this occasion, the anonymous play *The Famous Victories of Henry V* (1598). Shakespeare's play is grounded in the historical reality of the war Henry waged in France in 1414 in order to make good his claim to the French throne. As in the play, massively outnumbered, he nonetheless led the English to victory in the battle of Agincourt in 1415. When Charles V declared Henry his heir over his own son, the dauphin, the future of English sovereignty in France seemed secure. A dynastic marriage with the French king's daughter, Catherine de Valois, further sealed the victory.[5] In the disastrous reign of Henry VI, of course, as we have already noted, all his victories would be undone. For all that, the play's overwhelming appeal is its treatment of victory against all odds, first at the besieged town of Harfleur and then at the decisive battle of Agincourt.

Shakespeare does not, then, propose an entirely revisionist history of Henry's glorious reign but essentially tries to have it both ways – and succeeds in doing so. Without in any way impugning his record as a war hero or denying the reality of Henry's triumphs, Shakespeare also succeeds in posing crucial questions about the justification and cost of war. These costs are seen not only from Henry's point of view and from that of his nobles but also from the lives of the lower orders: Mistress Quickly, who dies while her new husband, Pistol, is away in France; the common soldiers John Bates, Alexander Court, and Michael Williams; the English boys slaughtered as they guard the luggage; the French prisoners whose throats are cut because their leaders rally their remaining forces. Most poignant of all is the off-stage death of Sir John Falstaff, heartbroken in being spurned by his former royal intimate in the taverns of Eastcheap. Henry's ruthless erasure of his past is an emotional cost that weighs heavily on the play, although it does not seem to weigh on Henry himself at all.

Critical opinion remains divided as to whether Henry is a manipulative Machiavel or a great leader, and about whether these are mutually exclusive. On the one hand, the spurned Falstaff, and Bardolph, a friend from those early days whom Henry nonetheless has executed for stealing ritual artifacts from a church, may be seen as the casualties of his power; but on the other, they constitute the sacrifice of all aspects of his life to the single purpose of playing the role of king. In the wake of his dissolute youth, the French grossly underestimate Henry's leadership, and the scene in which the play opens, with its very lengthy discussion of Salic law – that is, Henry's claim to the throne through his maternal line – is leavened by the delivery of a gift of tennis balls from the dauphin. The gift is not Shakespeare's invention but was a real historical event, a French jibe at Henry's frivolity. An outraged Henry claims in the first scene that he will indeed play the game, and he announces the start of the war with, "The game's afoot" (3.1.32).

His rhetorical powers of persuasion, so evident at Harfleur, are used to a different effect when he rouses his troops to victory before battle at Agincourt. These are the great set of speeches of the play. The St Crispin's Day speech even takes the radical position of absolute social equality in the pursuit of a national victory:

> He today that sheds his blood with me
> Shall be my brother; be he ne'er so vile,
> This day shall gentle his condition . . . (4.3.61–3)

National identity here subsumes distinctions as profoundly differentiated as the "vile" and the "gentle," the commoner and the gentleman. In death, in the self-sacrifice of heroic combat, the common soldier is of Henry's fraternity: "We few, we happy few, we band of brothers" (4.3.60). In other words, in order to create a cohesive national identity, other identities become irrelevant, superfluous, or at least temporarily suspended. When Henry goes incognito about the camp before Agincourt, wrestling with the moral burdens of kingship, he also addresses the divisions of class and nationality that could potentially undermine an English victory. When he engages the common soldier, Michael Williams, about whether the king's lot is the same as that of a man in the ranks, he is still "acting" because he is in disguise, and while his own identity remains "clouded" and occluded Williams is allowed to reveal his true opinions to the king. In defeat, Williams says, the king will be ransomed, but the soldier will be killed. The argument between the two ends with a challenge that is to be met after the battle. The play works over what it means to be part of Henry's fraternity in scenes with the Scottish Captain Jamie, the Anglo-Irish (that is, descended from English settlers rather than being one of the much disparaged, indigenous Irish) Captain McMorris, and Fluellen, the Welshman. The friction between these potentially competing designations is brought to cohesion and unity under Henry's charismatic leadership.

Henry's predominant characteristic as a king is his unassailably masculine, heroic identity, and what characterizes the French is their overwhelming effeminacy. The joke about the French is especially pointed in relation to the dauphin, who writes a love sonnet to his horse. Importantly, however, no such jokes about sexual objects, or indeed about weaknesses of any kind, are indulged in at the expense of the French king. Yet, the real Charles V suffered from severe mental infirmities that are signally *not* alluded to in the play. The French king needs to be beyond reproach because he is the grandfather of an English king, Henry VI.

One of the problems of sovereignty, however, and one not considered in Henry's ruminations before the battle, is that in order to make an appropriate, royal alliance, marrying the enemy was often required. The scenes with Katherine and her lady in waiting, Alice, are ones in which Shakespeare demonstrates his own command of the French language and serve to domesticate the enemy. Katherine's English lesson is essentially a list of bawdy puns on female body parts. The French may be effeminate, but actual French women serve as ballast to Henry's own bluff, straight-talking masculine style rendered in prose, rather than the high-blown verse of Henry's magnificent performances of battle rhetoric. Wooing Katherine is a formality, since the only marriage negotiations that count, namely those between Henry and the French king, have already taken place. This is a glimpse of Henry the soon-to-be-married man, as opposed to Hal the wastrel and Harry the warrior. Because these scenes return the audience to an intimacy with Henry that they had not enjoyed since *2 Henry IV*, there is the sense that he is *not* performing sovereignty here but rather being his private self "a fellow of plain and uncoined [natural] constancy" (5.2.152–3). Yet the scenes with Katherine are further a reminder that one of the burdens of sovereignty, one which had bedeviled the reign of Henry VIII, was to produce a male heir and to secure the succession of the crown, or else potentially throw the country into civil war in the power struggle for the throne that would probably ensue. Elizabeth, while she avoided taking this particular burden upon herself was nonetheless acutely aware of it. When news arrived of the birth of James to Mary Queen of Scots she is reported to have said to her ladies in waiting: "The queen of Scots is this day lighter of a fair son, and I am but a barren stock."[6]

The play ends, however, with amatory, dynastic, and military triumph, and much – though not all – of the play's performance history has been invested in exaggerating the already hyperbolic heroism of Henry and the epic grandiosity of the play. For example, during World War II, Laurence Olivier's film version successfully endowed the text with the rousing chauvinism of Henry's St Crispin Day's speech. In order not to undermine the war effort Olivier omitted the depiction of the treachery of aristocrats Cambridge, Grey, and Scrope that Henry uncovers just before setting sail for France. However, the inclusion of these traitors in Shakespeare's text is indicative of the play's nuanced, complex treatment both of war and of victory. Both he and his audience knew that in the reign of Henry's successor England would not escape ignominy and defeat.

## *Richard III*

In the histories, Shakespeare's story of politics, power, and national identity is largely concerned with what those deviant Scottish historians, the weird sisters of *Macbeth*, refer to as the on-going narrative of battles "lost and won" (1.1.4).[1] Out of time, beyond the vagaries of mortal life, beyond the urgent power struggles and the political ambitions of those involved, for the sisters it does not seem to matter much precisely *who* is vanquished and who is victorious in the martial engagements that punctuate the historical record with such appalling regularity. Like the dramatist, the weird sisters take the long view of history, seeing both the past and the future, although the witches possess a license for a supernatural indifference to history's specific outcomes that is scarcely permitted to the mortal playwright. Shakespeare's English histories are not disinterested surveys of the glorious triumphs and ignominious defeats of their protagonists, even while the overall effect of the tetralogies is that of panoramic perspective. In the case of Richard III's hunchbacked charisma, however, Shakespeare demonstrated that defeat could be turned into glorious theatrical triumph. Such were the early indications of the play's success that not only was *Richard III* the most frequently printed Elizabethan play, but also the actor who played the title role, Richard Burbage, apparently conveyed sufficient erotic appeal that, according to the diarist John Manningham, writing in 1601, at least one woman arranged an assignation with him after the show.[2]

The deformed Richard is an ebulliently histrionic character who is not yet king when the play opens, and we see his rise to power by means of what were in reality the not entirely unusual routes of machination and assassination, but which in Shakespeare's rendition make him one of the most colorfully wicked characters in the canon. Since history is not written by the vanquished, the material Shakespeare had to work from in the chronicles was already a version of events skewed so far in favor of the Tudors that it might be said to constitute fiction. For all that, the play engages fundamental political realities such as factionalism, the problem of succession, the corruption of dynastic politics, the capacity of ruthless politicians to cover their tracks, and, long before the advent of televised political campaigning, the relationship between political power and personal magnetism. Throughout, Shakespeare insists on the sheer power of Richard as an actor, a "dissembler" in the theatre of state.[3]

Richard III was the last king from the Plantagenet line of the House of York. He was defeated at the battle of Bosworth Field on August 22, 1485 by Elizabeth I's grandfather, Henry Tudor, who then became King Henry VII, the first Tudor monarch. Henry's victory represented the end of the Wars of the Roses, that is, the civil conflict between the houses of York and Lancaster that had engulfed England for the better part of thirty-two years. The conclusion of these hostilities represented the demise of feudal power, the rise of a much more centralized state, and the advent of the relatively stable Tudor regime under which Shakespeare and his contemporaries were now living. However, the Tudor monarchy required for its legitimacy a version of the past that justified the current regime. If, for example, Henry VII was seen to have been wrong to seize power from Richard III, the entire dynasty would be imperiled. Regicide under any circumstances always required some fast footwork by way of justification, and in this instance the rationale for Henry VII's ascendency was that he had freed England from the yoke of a tyrant. For this reason, the extant chronicle histories of the period were, at least by modern standards, propaganda for the Tudor state. Shakespeare's historical sources were Edward Hall's *The Union of the Two Noble and Illustrious Families of Lancaster and York* (1548); Raphael Holinshed's *Chronicles* (1577; revised in 1587), which was, in turn, indebted to Sir Thomas More's *History of King Richard the Third* (1543); and Polydore Vergil's *Historia Anglica* (1534).[4] Far from attempting to provide an objective account of Richard's government, More succeeded in painting the Yorkist monarch as an outright villain. In this, the play follows More's lead, attributing no fewer than ten murders to Richard. However, the play opens with the imprisonment of the Duke of Clarence in 1478, only to revert in the next scene to the funeral of Henry VI in 1471. By such tricks with temporality, Shakespeare vividly enlivens rather than slavishly follows Tudor history. This, for example, is More's account of Richard's personality: "He was close and secret, a deep dissembler, lowly of countenance, arrogant of heart, outwardly companionable where he inwardly hated. . . . He spared no man's death whose life withstood his purpose."[5] That More's Richard is a "dissembler" was particularly suited to Shakespeare's purposes. A dissembler was, in early modern English, not only a liar but also an actor, a player. In the opening soliloquy Richard affirms that since he "cannot prove a lover," he is "determined to prove a villain" (1.1.28–30). Like an actor considering the possible parts he might play, Richard, all too conscious of his physical limitations and his repellent physiognomy, selects the role most suited to his type. He self-consciously embraces his affinity with two medieval dramatic types: the devil of the mystery plays ("I play the devil," 1.3.337) and Vice of the morality plays and interludes ("the formal Vice," 3.1.82). The mystery cycles have a particular connection with Shakespeare's chronicle plays in that they were also essentially historical panoramas seeking to represent events in the world, albeit from a strictly scriptural point of view, from Creation till Doomsday. In these plays, the devil, the arch-dissembler and father of lies, was the character audiences most loved to hate and whose ever-thwarted ambition was to usurp the throne of the supreme ruler. In the interludes, the vice and the devil were often a comic duo, the vice beating the devil (who served as a comic sidekick) about the stage with a cudgel. Buckingham represents this role in Shakespeare's play, serving as Richard's adjutant in iniquity.

Shakespeare's audience first met Richard in *3 Henry VI* when he made his marvelously wicked declaration that he would "set the murderous Machiavel to school" (*3 Henry VI*, 3.2.193). God's mission statement is never so succinctly articulated, and unlike God in the mystery plays, who was quite literally remote from the audience, the devil came downstage to its level, equipped with a vastly more realistic, on-the-ground knowledge of human nature than that possessed by the deity. God may be omnipotent and omnibenevolent, but those qualities do not serve to endow him in the theatre with a sense of humor. In dramatic terms, this is a fatal flaw, allowing Lucifer always to upstage him. Further, the deity's penchant for ponderous consideration makes him seem slow on the uptake in comparison to his scheming cosmic adversary with his rapid-fire acuity. It is, then, within these dynamics, inherited from the tradition of religious drama, that Shakespeare brings the devil's closest secular counterpart into being. Further, like the devil and the vice in the medieval tradition, Richard addresses the audience directly from a position of downstage intimacy; not in spite of his wickedness, but precisely because of it, the audience *like*s him.

Lucifer's paradigmatic fall from a high place is also, of course, the founding structure of tragedy. Richard's trajectory, his rise to power and then, by virtue of Shakespeare's temporal compression, his swift and spectacular descent merited the play's classification as a tragedy in the First Quarto of 1597: *The Tragedy of King Richard the Third Containing, His Treacherous Plots Against his Brother Clarence: The Pittiefull Murther of his Iunocent [sic] Nephewes: His Tyrannicall Vsurpation: With the Whole Course of His Detested Life, and Most Deserued Death. As It Hath Been Lately Acted by the Right Honourable the Lord Chamberlaine his Seruants*. Whereas in medieval drama the audience does not feel much sympathy for Satan – and nor does he ask for any – Shakespeare generates a certain audience commiseration for Richard. The only character in Shakespeare to begin a play with a soliloquy, Richard explains how his physical disabilities have destined his villainy:

> I, that am rudely stamped, and want love's majesty
> To strut before a wanton ambling nymph;
> I, that am curtailed of this fair proportion,
> Cheated of feature by dissembling Nature,
> Deformed, unfinished, sent before my time
> Into this breathing world, scarce half made up,
> And that so lamely and unfashionable
> That dogs bark at me as I halt by them . . . (1.1.16–23)

Elizabethans tended to regard deformity as evidence of sinfulness, but Richard's opening speech blames Nature herself as the true dissembler, the confidence trickster who has short-changed him with the disfigurement attendant upon a premature birth. He thus persuades the audience that he is not the author of his circumstances but rather their victim.

In an uncanny convergence between art and life, Richard's deformity was historically analogous to that of the humped-backed, splay-legged Robert Cecil, later Earl of Salisbury (1563–1612), son of William Cecil Lord Burghley and thus the other member of the political dynasty contemptuously referred to by contemporaries as *regnum Cecilianum*. Despite all physical impediments, Robert or "Robin" Cecil, who was "a dissembling, smooth-faced dwarf"[6] according to his detractors, was intellectually gifted and was appointed to Elizabeth's privy council when he was only twenty-eight years old. He was one of the most important ministers under both Elizabeth and James, and after his death a spate of libels made the connection with Richard III quite explicit: "Here lieth Robin Crooktback, unjustly reckoned A Richard the Third: he was Judas the second."[7] Further, libelers claimed his final physical disintegration from scurvy and cancer was the consequence of unbridled sexual depravity.

While the hunch-backed Richard has disclaimed any capacity for capering "nimbly in a lady's chamber" (1.1.12) or "amorous," "sportive tricks" (1.1.15; 14) he nonetheless claims his own abilities as a dissembler endow him with seductive powers that overwhelm even his physical deformity. In the second scene of the play, Richard attempts a seemingly impossible suit – to seduce Lady Anne Neville, the widow of the man he has murdered. Further, he makes his play over the coffin of her deceased father-in-law, Henry VI. (In reality, Anne was not Henry's daughter-in-law, having been merely betrothed, rather than married, to his son). There is something grotesque but also comic about his implausible success in this wooing scene. At its start, the romance seems distinctly unpromising. Anne calls him "fiend," "hedgehog," "dissembler," and "homicide" (the latter is yet another allusion to Richard as a theatrical type) who has murdered both her husband and her father-in-law (1.2.34, 104, 187, 128). She spits at him when he claims that all his evil has been committed out of love for her. Yet, by the end of the scene she has accepted his ring. Richard confides in the audience his delighted surprise at his own success: "Was ever woman in this humour wooed? / Was ever woman in this humour won?" (1.2.230–1).

At this point in the play, Richard is credited with the deaths of Henry, Anne's husband Neville, and his own brother the Duke of Clarence, who had a dream he would be drowned and whose body is disposed of in a butt of Malmsey wine. Richard goes on to kill King Edward, Rivers, Grey, Vaughan, Hastings, and his own wife. Engaging though he is, Richard loses the audience's complicity in his evil designs when he has his nephews, "the gentle babes" (4.3.9), murdered in the Tower of London. Indeed, the imprisonment of the little boys in Act 3, Scene 1 is a turning point in the play, and all his other murders pale in comparison. The princes draw even the remorse of Dighton and Forrest whom James Tyrell had sent to dispatch them, a scene reported in Act 4: "They were fleshed villains, bloody dogs / Melted with tenderness and mild compassion" (4.3.6–7). By the time Richard achieves the summit of his powers the audience is willing him to destruction rather than to success. He achieves the crown by having Buckingham intimate in a eulogy for King Edward before the Guildhall in the City of London that the deceased monarch was illegitimate. This not only impugns his own mother's honor but also makes Edward's heirs bastards and thus ineligible to govern England. The audience has witnessed Richard cover up heinous crimes, and now he feigns reluctance when he is pressed by the Lord Mayor to take the crown.

Richard's power at this point is undercut by one of the most powerful all-female vignettes in Shakespeare. Remarkably, Shakespeare shows women, and especially older women who are the detritus of patriarchal rule after their reproductive functions are exhausted, as possessed of a moral power beyond masculine dominion. Anne is interrupted in her visit to the Tower of London where the Duchess of York and Queen Elizabeth are confined. She is summoned to Westminster in order to be crowned Richard's queen. The women are horrified at the news, especially as they suspect the little princes have been murdered. The women's power in opposing Richard is essentially the power of privileged forms of speech: the power to curse and the power to prophesy. This power of female vocality is most potently embodied in Queen Margaret, the widow of Henry VI. Margaret may not possess political power, but her long and devastating invective against Richard in Act 1 is indelibly engraved on the minds of its auditors. Richard's victims, the Duke of Buckingham, Rivers, Grey, and Hastings, go to their deaths remembering Margaret's words. That Margaret was not actually even in England during most of the events depicted by the play demonstrates Shakespeare's deliberate decision to make feminine rage the primary vehicle for truth. Margaret is not simply a woman, she is also, at the mythological level, the expression of the enraged goddess.

Given that history plays are by their very nature about patriarchal succession, Shakespeare greatly amplifies the role of women, and especially the ways in which they become victims of a system that requires their male progeny in order to transmit power down the generations but prevents them from holding it themselves. The Richard these women know, especially his own mother, the Duchess of York, is a much darker monstrosity than the man who has earlier seduced not only Anne but also the audience. "Thou toad, thou toad," says the Duchess of York: "Where is thy brother Clarence, / And little Ned Plantagenet his son?" (4.4.145–6).

Queen Elizabeth, King Edward's wife, is driven to distraction by the murder of her young sons and she seeks to protect her daughter from Richard, who, once he has dispatched Anne, incestuously seeks his niece's hand in marriage as a way of consolidating his position. Richard, at this point deluded about his sexual and political prowess, attempts to replay his earlier success with Anne. In an important deviation from Shakespeare's source in Hall, which charges her with inconstancy, Richard is outmaneuvered by Queen Elizabeth, who merely feigns consent to the marriage of her daughter, the young Elizabeth, in order to protect her.[8] The latter is an important figure in the play, even though her part does not appear in the cast list and she speaks no lines. In a world that regarded women's chastity as synonymous with their silence, Shakespeare may be carefully observing the protocols of decorous female behavior. Elizabeth is, after all, the future wife of Henry VII, and thus the grandmother of Elizabeth I. Two women, both Elizabeths, both blood relatives of the present queen, outwit Richard, as no man in the play is capable of doing.

The Richard uncovered by modern historians is not nearly as interesting as that depicted in More, Holinshed, Hall or in Shakespeare. His reign was not unduly marked by evil or tyranny. Further, according to the most recent entry in the *Oxford Dictionary of National Biography*,[9] there is very little in the way of verifiable historical evidence, for example, about what transpired at the battle of Bosworth, except that Richard probably led the final charge that ushered in his defeat. Polydore Vergil's account records that he died "fighting manfully in the thickest press of his enemies."[10] In Shakespeare, of course, Bosworth is the culminating conflict. The night before battle, Richard is visited by the ghosts of his enemies, including his murdered wife, while Henry Tudor experiences the consolations of God, who is, unquestionably, on his side. Henry's inevitable, preordained success evacuates his agency of the energy of human interest, so that once again, knowing he will be defeated, the audience is back on Richard's side. Having lost his mount in the battle, he cries out with what is one of the most famous lines in Shakespeare, "A horse, a horse my kingdom for a horse!" (5.4.7). This is the line that audiences took home with them, rather than the more pious pronouncements of Henry.

The inherently dramatic paradox of *Richard III* is that he is a much more compelling character than the future Henry VII, who is backed to the hilt by the providential deity whose visitations before battle assure him of victory. A recent historian, Steven Gunn, has observed that the influence of Shakespeare's protagonist is such that there are three books on Richard III for every one on the man who defeated him.[11] In the world of theatre, the decisive victory goes to Richard III.

## *Julius Caesar*

Famous in England as he had invaded the country at the head of a Roman army in 55 and 54 BC, Julius Caesar was a figure readily recognizable even to those members of Shakespeare's audience who had not had the benefit of reading his *Commentarii de Bello Gallico* (*The Gallic Wars*) in the grammar school. However, England also bore a significant connection with Caesar's republican antagonist, Brutus. Indeed, the very name "Britain" was believed to derive from its founder, Brutus. This Brutus was an ancestor of the character of the same name who appears in Shakespeare's play as well as a great grandson of Aeneas who, according to Geoffrey of Monmouth's twelfth-century *Historia Regum Britanniae* (*The History of the Kings of Britain*), sailed from Rome to establish Londinium in response to a directive given to him in a dream by the goddess Diana. In the mythology of ancient Britain, the trajectory of the great cities of empire ran from the mythic Troy, through Rome to London, the New Troy or "Troynovant." So while contemporary Rome was "other," the very lair of the pope, "the whore of Babylon" vilified by Protestants, classical Rome was revered as having sown the seeds of English nationhood that were rapidly being nurtured into fruition during the Elizabethan period.

England's imperial status went back only as far as the Reformation. Always geographically isolated from the rest of Europe, England achieved the status of empire when Henry VIII broke from Rome during his divorce from Catherine of Aragon. By severing England's ties with the pope, he acquired sovereign power over every aspect of English life, spiritual and temporal, and thus met the definition of imperial monarchy. The events depicted in Shakespeare's play represent the cataclysmic disintegration of the republicanism that Brutus and his co-conspirators aspire to save.

Set at the (relatively) safe distance of the ancient world, Shakespeare's play investigates the question of who and what exactly confers power on individual leaders, poses radical questions about the nature and extent of political authority, and examines the potency of rhetoric as possibly a more dangerous instrument than martial prowess. The play does not condone the murder of the autocratic, epileptic Caesar, but neither does it condemn the conspirators. Indeed, Shakespeare elaborates their motivations with some sympathy and, via the pivotal figure of Brutus, depicts the political and psychological struggles of the republican faction. The language of Caesar's supporter, Mark Antony, is without equal in the play. His is the power to manipulate rhetoric, but he will not finally govern Rome. That task will be left to Caesar's nephew, Octavius, who gets the play's last word and celebrates the defeat of his enemies as what he calls, rather chillingly, "the glories of this happy day" (5.5.82).[1]

Not published until the First Folio of 1623, *Julius Caesar* continued Shakespeare's interest in the ancient world first evinced in the gory revenge tragedy *Titus Andronicus*. Shakespeare's plot, taken from Sir Thomas North's 1595 translation of Plutarch's *Lives*, concerns the events leading up to and following the assassination of Julius Caesar on the Ides of March (March 15) 44 BC by

Brutus and his fellow conspirators, first of whom is the "lean and hungry" (1.2.3) looking senator, Cassius. Rome is a republic but Caesar's popularity is such that, on his return from a decisive victory in the civil war against Pompey the Great and his faction, he is urged by the people to be king. Caesar has been offered the crown three times, but this demurral has only further excited popular support: "the rabblement hooted, and clapped their chopped hands" (1.2.243–4). Despite his having thus rejected the crown, Caska (another conspirator) reports that the senate intends "to establish Caesar as a king" (1.3.86). Cassius urges Brutus to quell this possibility and put an end to Caesar's autocratic behavior. Inwardly tortured by his anticipation of the murder, Brutus is reluctantly driven to the conclusion that Caesar must be assassinated. A key factor in this carefully reasoned decision is that his ancestor had driven the tyrant Tarquin from power in 510 BC to establish the republic. Caesar goes to the Capitol against the admonition of the soothsayer, who has told him to "Beware the Ides of March" (1.2.23), and against the advice of his wife, Calphurnia, who has had a prophetic dream that he will be harmed on this day. Fearful tempests, hideous prodigies, and terrifying portents (1.3) also presage Caesar's death.

Directly prior to the moment of his assassination, at the beginning of Act 3, reacting to the petitioner Metellus, who seeks reprieve on behalf of his banished brother, Caesar arrogantly refuses clemency: "Know, Caesar doth not wrong, nor without cause / Will he be satisfied" (3.1.47–8). Ben Jonson famously mocked this line, but since he reports it differently – "Caesar did never wrong, but with just cause" – it seems likely that Shakespeare revised the offending phrase prior to publication, perhaps in response to Jonson's criticism. In fact, the allegedly risible line exactly mirrors the logic of the conspirators who commit the murder as an act of righteousness. Not only does Caesar claim he never errs, however; he also claims that, despite being deaf in one ear, subject to foaming at the mouth, and "falling sickness" (1.2.253), he is "Unshaked of motion" (3.1.70). He is implacable, he tells Cassius, because "I am constant as the northern star" (3.1.60). This insistence on his uniquely "true-fixed," "unassailable" nature (3.1.61, 69), on his possession of perfect constancy, "Always I am Caesar" (1.2.211), echoes Elizabeth's personal motto: *Semper eadem*, that is, always the same. When Shakespeare wrote *Julius Caesar* in 1599, the increasingly decayed body of the aged Virgin Queen – "the imperial vot'ress" of *A Midsummer Night's Dream* (2.1.163)[2] and "our gracious Empress" in *Henry V* (5.0.30)[3] embodied English national identity. Despite the unchanging image depicted in her state-sponsored portraits, Elizabeth's hair and teeth had fallen out, in part from the use of cosmetics containing mercury, and in old age she was prone to outbursts of irrational rage.

The play demonstrates the fragility of Elizabethan absolutism when Brutus delivers the final, fatal blow, to which Caesar responds with his last breath, "*Et tu, Brute?* – Then fall, Caesar" (3.1.77). "*Et tu, Brute,*" or "Even thou, Brutus," a phrase that does not belong to any Latin author, conveys an astonished sense of betrayal in a remarkable moment of what we might call homicidal intimacy. This proximity between Brutus and Caesar is immediately reversed by the emblematically ironic public display that follows. Brutus urges his fellow con-spirators to wash their hands "Up to the elbows" in Caesar's blood and to smear their swords in it so that they can go into the market place, weapons aloft, crying, "Peace, Freedom and Liberty" (3.1.10). Cassius is similarly con-fident in claiming violence as a political virtue and assumes that subsequent ages will approve the murder:

> How many ages hence
> Shall this our lofty scene be acted over
> In states unborn and accents yet unknown? (3.1.111–13)

Cassius's metatheatrical statement (he reminds the audience that they are in the theatre watching a re-enaction) may also work as a kind of safety device for the playwright, insisting that this astonishing political violence is "only a play" and one whose reiteration of historical events is far from being unique to Shakespeare. In *Hamlet*, for example, Polonius speaks of his acting experience at the university: "I did enact Julius Caesar. I was killed i'th' Capitol. Brutus killed me" (*Hamlet* 3.2.99–100).[4]

One of the most pressing issues of the play is how far history is a safe haven from which to ponder issues even as weighty as conspiracy and assassination, which would have been treasonous to discuss in other, more contemporary contexts. Certainly, the crisis of *Julius Caesar*, in some respects at least, danger-ously resembled Elizabeth's predicament as an increasingly autocratic ruler without an heir, who might, like her Roman predecessor, be readily dispatched by a disgruntled faction. All monarchs feared regicide, and there had been several plots against Elizabeth. In 1585, for example, the Catholic Anthony Babington conspired to murder Elizabeth and place Mary Queen of Scots on the throne. The play's "secret Romans" (2.1.124), the conspirators, might be analogous to England's seditious crypto-Catholics, were it not for the fact that members of this same faction look quasi-Protestant when they denounce popular festivity in the feast of Lupercal and remove the ornaments from Cae-sar's standards. Antony's funeral oration positions the plebeians as "Roman Catholics" when he predicts their veneration of Caesar's body as if it were a crucifix, the image of the crucified Christ. He also imagines them, like relic collectors at the execution of a martyr, mopping up the blood in their hand-kerchiefs: "They would go and kiss dead Caesar's wounds / And dip their napkins in his sacred blood" (3.2.133–4).[5] Time and again, the play seems to move deliberately in and out of contiguity with the present.

While Brutus and the conspirators proclaim the victory of liberty over tyranny, Mark Antony openly mourns Caesar. In a characteristic political misstep, Brutus, who has urged that Antony's life must be spared, not only permits him to deliver a funeral oration but also insists the populace stay to hear it. This decision, rather than the assassination itself, proves to be his downfall. Antony has, in Roman fashion, hidden his rage at Caesar's murder, confiding only in soliloquy to the audience his plan to unleash "the dogs of war" (3.1.273) by way of vengeance for Caesar's murder. With "Friends, Romans, countrymen, lend me your ears: / I come to bury Caesar, not to praise him" (3.2.74–5), Antony's masterful oration, a Roman genre, wins over the fickle populace, who now fall to riot against the conspirators, killing Cinna the poet merely because he bears the same name as Cinna the conspirator.

Crucially, the power of Roman leaders is, albeit in rather undefined ways, related to, if not dependent upon, the people in the streets, the plebeians, like the carpenters and cobblers with whom the play begins. In *Coriolanus* Shake-speare calls them the "many-headed multitude" (2.3.17),[6] yet they have little power, and like the mechanical laborers of the play's first scene, "They vanish tongue-tied" (*Julius Caesar*, 1.1.63) at the reproachful rhetoric of their social superiors. In *Julius Caesar* these many heads wear "sweaty nightcaps" and have "stinking breath" (1.2.244, 245). Unlike the conspirators who with Cassius are characterized by stoic rationalism and cerebral activity – "Yond Cassius has a lean and hungry look: / He thinks too much: such men are dangerous" (1.2.193–4) – the heads of the multitude are occupied with somatic activity: sweat and stink. They are the "common herd" (1.2.263), the "rabblement" (1.2.243). But the collectives that define the populace change, and they are at times a murderous mob and a congregation – the funeral orations for Caesar are delivered from a pulpit. Even more importantly, they are an audience. "The tag-rag people" responded to Caesar as to "the players in the theatre" (1.2.257, 259). As auditors, the people are completely malleable and at the mercy of what they hear. Thus, before they are swayed by Antony, the plebeians receive Bru-tus's prose defense of the murder with unqualified adulation, having at that point reached the "certain" conclusion that they are "blest that Rome is rid of" Caesar (3.2.70–1). Further, their enthusiasm for Brutus – who has just defended republicanism – is ironically expressed as a desire to make *him* Caesar. The "base," "rude," and "vile" populace (3.2.29–32) thus willingly surrender their power to rhetorical eloquence. Brutus's string of rhetorical questions in his funeral oration, beginning "Who is here so base, that would be a bondman?" (3.2.29), is answered in the affirmative by the third plebian, who shouts out "Let him be Caesar" (3.2.51). All those stinking, sweating heads merely seek another, bigger head. Shakespeare seems, however, also to understand his own audience with its inherent class stratifications as an entity possessed of power, albeit power that has not yet achieved its fullest political articulation. When he forges the parallel between the political histories of England and Rome in *Henry V*, the citizens of London are described in that English history play as greeting their anointed king like the "swarming" masses of ancient Rome:

> Like to the senators of th'antique Rome,
> With the plebeians swarming at their heels,
> Go forth and fetch the conqu'ring Caesar in . . . (*Henry V*, 5.0.26–8)

As in *Julius Caesar*, power in this passage consists of three elements: the conquering leader, the senatorial class whose English equivalent consists of the "citizens. / The Mayor and all his brethren" (5.0.25–8), and the rest.

After Caesar's death, the struggle for Rome ensues between the republican faction of Brutus and Cassius and Caesar's supporters, Mark Antony and Octavius, Julius Caesar's nephew who will become the future Emperor Augustus. During the engagement between their respective forces at Philippi, Brutus accuses Cassius of accepting bribes. The quarrel is eventually settled and Brutus discloses that he has had news that his wife, Portia, a woman who earlier slashed her thigh (2.1.297–300) in an attempt to demonstrate feminine stoicism, has committed suicide by swallowing hot coals. Yet after this revelation in Act 4, Scene 2, when a messenger arrives with the news again, Brutus does not reveal that he already knows of Portia's death, but reacts with the public face of stoic response that is apparently only permitted by his foreknowledge. Shakespeare shows here, as he does over and over again in his career, the terrible human cost of the unequivocal fact that history is made by men often at the expense of women. The undoing of the conspirators continues when Cassius, the victim of erroneous information about the progress of the battle, commits suicide. Brutus, who has been visited by Caesar's ghost before the combat began, subsequently dies, in the appropriately Roman manner, by falling on his sword, saying he kills himself more willingly than he killed his friend Caesar. Antony, Octavius, and their followers find the body, and Brutus is lauded as "the noblest Roman of them all" (5.5.69), who acted entirely from a conviction of public "common good" (5.5.73) and not from baser personal motivations.

Shakespeare, then, does not attempt to resolve the arguments he unfolds in *Julius Caesar*, but merely presenting them before the heterogeneous audience at the Globe was surely radical enough. The play's themes of government, autocracy, and tyranny were immensely relevant to Shakespeare's audience, even though, under the imperious government of Elizabeth, the prevailing ideology maintained that England was in its Golden Age and that tyranny and autocracy were but fables from so very long ago. But if Shakespeare treads dangerous ground here, it was lost on the Swiss visitor Thomas Platter, whose diary records the play's performance at the Globe in 1599. What Platter most enjoyed was that the two wives, Calphurnia and Portia, danced with their husbands after the play. Theatre does indeed appear to have license to present even the most dangerous and potentially seditious of political ideas.

*Julius Caesar* is also a crucial play in terms of the history of Shakespeare's on-going engagement with antiquity in the course of his career. His first dramatic representation of the ancient world, printed in 1594, though not based on actual events, was *Titus Andronicus*, whose gory revenge violence followed the tradition of Senecan tragedy. *The Rape of Lucrece*, also printed in 1594, was a verse foray into the realms of antiquity, and addressed how the violation of that chaste Roman matron and her subsequent suicide ended the tyrannous rule of the Tarquins in Rome. He took up the themes of politics and power in the ancient world in his later Roman plays, *Antony and Cleopatra* and *Coriolanus*, and in *Troilus and Cressida* represented the heroes of classical Greece.

However, *Julius Caesar* is additionally significant because it immediately precedes and thematically anticipates *Hamlet*, a play about whether or not to kill the king. *Julius Caesar* prepared the ground by assessing the dilemma, already debated for hundreds of years by the time Shakespeare wrote his play, about whether or not to kill Caesar, the man who *would be* king.

## Coriolanus

Some commentators, especially in the nineteenth century, argued that Shakespeare must have been a soldier because his accounts of military action were so vivid and lifelike, and more recently, Jonathan Bate's play *Being Shakespeare* (2011; performed at the Trafalgar studios), explores the idea that Shakespeare was a soldier during the "lost years." However attractive such creative speculation may seem, it is an incontrovertible fact about Shakespeare's life that he made his reputation as a writer, a poet, and player, and not as a man of action or as a war hero. In the quest for novel information about Shakespeare's life, it is too easy to forget that the pursuit that arguably occupied most of Shakespeare's time as a writer, and one that was indeed integral to the process of literary composition itself, was the corollary activity of reading.

In *Coriolanus*, Shakespeare demonstrated his tremendous capacities as a reader, a reader, moreover, who was able to process and vivify what he had read for a new medium – the public theatre. The play is a biography of its eponymous hero, Caius Martius, who is later endowed with the honorific surname Coriola-nus. He lives for martial honor and is the product of both the Roman culture of militarism, and, even more importantly, his mother, Volumnia, a patriotic Roman matron who would rather see her son dead than dishonored by defeat. Shake-speare's source, "The Life of Caius Martius Coriolanus" was from a book he turned to repeatedly in his writing career, Plutarch's *Lives of the Noble Grecians and Romans* translated by Thomas North (printed in 1579 and again with new lives in 1595). *Coriolanus* reveals the way that Shakespeare, first and foremost as reader, but also as player and as a writer, brought the history he had read of the ancient world to life in the Jacobean theatre.

*Coriolanus* opens with the rioting of the Roman plebeians, and while in Plutarch they protest usury, in Shakespeare they are the victims of a scourge very familiar to his audience, namely dearth. An aristocratic class inured to their needs exac-erbates their sufferings, and the arrogance and contempt of their superiors is, as far as the populace is concerned, exemplified and embodied by Caius Martius. For this reason, they revile him even as, under the generalship of Cominius, he leads Rome into battle against the Volsces. Caius Martius is all the things of which the populace accuse him, but they are themselves a fickle conglomeration of opinions and are easily manipulated by their corrupt representatives, the Tribunes: this is not a play that simplifies class struggle. Coriolanus wins a glori-ous victory for Rome against the Volsces when he is trapped in the walls of the town Corioli and single handedly vanquishes its denizens, including their noble warrior Aufideus. It is as a reward for this that Caius Martius is endowed with the honorific "Coriolanus." In the wake of his victory, his mother, Volumnia, hopes to see him awarded the ultimate honor of becoming consul. Essential to this process is a political dynamic familiar to us but quite alien to Shakespeare's world, namely the participation of the plebians – "neither will they bate / One jot of ceremony" (2.2.139–40).[1] Yet, Coriolanus dismisses their role as "need-less vouches" (2.3.116). While the populace initially give their assent to his consulship, Coriolanus's refusal to display his wounds to them in the required Roman manner, along with the conniving of their representatives, makes them turn against him. Initially they call for his execution, but ultimately, they demand the lesser penalty of exile from Rome.

Furious about his rejection by the people of Rome, with the magisterial declaration, "There is a world elsewhere" (3.3.136), Coriolanus ultimately joins with his former enemy Aufidius and marches towards his native city, whose destruction is now inevitable. His greatest supporter, Menenius, a man for whom Coriolanus is like a son, goes to the Voscian camp to implore him to have pity on Rome, only to find that Coriolanus is impervious to his pleas. Only when the party of women (Volumnia, Virgilia, and Valeria) along with Young

Martius arrive to implore him to desist does Coriolanus relent. Here, a remarkable moment occurs between mother and son, a pause, for which the Folio offers unusually full stage-directions, instructing that Coriolanus "*Holds her by the hand silent*" (5.3.182). This short but telling hiatus in the play's action represents the decisive moment of his change of heart, when begins the tragic headlong descent towards the hero's death. The suasive powers of his mother have in effect sealed Coriolanus's death warrant. Already disgruntled by the fact that Coriolanus's popularity with the Volscians so far outshines his own, Aufidius finds new reason to be enraged now that Volumnia has successfully dissuaded her son from razing Rome to the ground. The play ends with Coriolanus stabbed to death by Aufidius but with no sense of what ensues thereafter.

*Coriolanus* is a dramatization of Plutarch's account of the Roman general, and in the play, Shakespeare offers a reading of his source to create the tragic hero as a man of action and the greatest warrior in Rome. As such, he has no tolerance for politics and no respect for social inferiors, and the play essentially poses the question: what, or rather *who*, has made him thus? The answer is Volumnia, Coriolanus's formidable mother (the character Shakespeare most elaborates upon from his source), who claims possession of him because she has, both literally and metaphorically, made him: "Thou art my warrior / I holp to frame thee" (5.3.62–3). "Frame" has, in addition, an architectural and a political sense here that refers back to the social structure of Rome, specifically the body politic that is the subject of the Fable of the Belly told by Menenius in Act 1, a well-worn political analogy whereby the privileged belly gorges all, ostensibly for the good of all the members of the body. That Volumnia is the source and architect of the warrior body is also a reverse of conventional hierarchy that assumes the male as the ground of generation and the female as simply a passive receptacle. However, Coriolanus himself evokes the more conventional primacy of males in relation to his wife when he addresses her as "Best of my flesh" (5.3.42), an echo of Genesis 2.23 where Adam calls Eve "flesh of my flesh" because, derived from his rib, "she was taken out of man."

While the audience is not directly privy to Coriolanus's boyhood, we are offered its indirect representation through his son, whose identity with his father is insisted upon in the opening of the play and again as the play veers irrevocably towards tragic catastrophe. For Young Martius is "O' my word, the father's son!" (1.3.57), the miniaturized replica of his father:

> This is a poor epitome of yours,
> Which by th'interpretation of full time
> May show like all yourself. (5.3.68–70)

Young Martius is a "*poor* epitome" not because he is a botched copy of Coriolanus but simply because he is a pitiable emissary who attends the women who have come to sue his father for peace. Shakespeare emphasizes this resemblance between father and son in his most conspicuous departure from North's translation. Set among the women of the play, Act 1, Scene 3 is a scene entirely of his own invention. Here, Shakespeare focuses and amplifies Plutarch's account of the extraordinary bond between Coriolanus and his widowed mother:

> . . . Martius thinking all due to his mother that had been also due to his father if he had lived, did not only content himself to rejoice and honour her, but at her desire took a wife also, by whom he had two children; and yet never left his mother's house.[2]

While Plutarch merely intimates the degree of control that Volumnia has over her son, Shakespeare vividly elaborates upon and enlivens the nature and extent of her influence. Caius Martius is away fighting for Rome, and Shakespeare takes the opportunity to turn the audience's attention towards the women who await news of his fate in battle and who are ostensibly marginal to Roman power. The exchanges between Volumnia and her daughter-in-law, Virgilia, and their visitor, Valeria, do not reveal Volumnia as the source of either her son's valor or his arrogance, but rather demonstrate an inbred, thoroughly masculine propensity towards aggression. Valeria accounts approvingly how, with a "confirmed countenance" (1.3.59–60), a determined look, the child raced after a butterfly, only to tear it to pieces when he caught it:

> I saw him run after a gilded butterfly, and when he caught it, he let it go again, and after it again, and over and over he comes, and up again, catched it again; or whether his fall enraged him, or how 'twas, he did so set his teeth and tear it. Oh, I warrant how he mammocked it! (1.3.60–5)

The butterfly symbolizes all that must be destroyed within human nature to make a war-machine of a warrior like Coriolanus. There is something profoundly disturbing about the violence of this child who directs his rage upon a fragile, beautiful living thing that Shakespeare conveys especially in word "mammocked" (torn to pieces). Further, this destructive tendency is precisely where Young Martius shows not just resemblance to his father but rather complete identity with him. As Volumina points out when she hears Valeria's account of the boy's murderous playtime: "One on's father's moods" (1.3.66).

The butterfly episode contains the prescription for tragedy: ambition, frustration, violence, and then, inevitably, death. Crucially, this process occurs with female oversight and even approbation.[3]

It is especially significant that the first vivid description of battle also occurs in this early domestic scene (1.3). However, this is not a war story told by an old soldier, but an account given by Volumnia herself:

> Methinks I hear hither your husband's drum;
> See him pluck Aufidius down by th'hair,
> As children from a bear, the Volsces shunning him,
> Methinks I see him stamp thus, and call thus:
> "Come on you cowards! You were got in fear
> Though you were born in Rome." His bloody brow
> With his mail'd hand then wiping, forth he goes,
> Like to a harvestman that's tasked to mow
> Or all or lose his hire. (1.3.29–37)

The repetition of "Methinks" suggests Volumnia's senses are fully engaged by the image she creates. Since she cannot go to war, she must, perforce, use her imagination to participate vicariously in her son's battles: "Methinks *I hear*," "Methinks *I see*." Imagination allows her to enter her son's consciousness to hear his rallying cry: "Come on you cowards." Volumnia clearly enjoys war stories that involve her son's illustrious acts as her daughter-in-law, fearful of his safety, does not. In "Methinks I *h*ear *h*ither your *h*usband's drum," the alliterative "h" makes the sound Volumnia imagines hearing echo down the line. Coriolanus, in contrast, has never had to learn to use his imagination. In the deftly inserted flashback to his childhood via his son and diminutive duplicate, Shakespeare discloses the forces that have shaped his worldview: "He had rather see the swords and hear a drum than look upon his schoolmaster" (1.3.55–6). Young Martius attends neither to his schoolmaster, nor, by implication, to the arts of reading and writing.

Action heroes (or anti-heroes) in Shakespeare don't have much time for books. In *1 Henry IV*, Hotspur, the leader of the rebels, is (literally) not a reader. As he is about to go into battle, he does not even take the time to see if letters delivered to him contain pertinent intelligence about how the rebellion proceeds, and when the messenger arrives with them he brushes them aside: "I cannot read them now. / O gentlemen, the time of life is short" (5.2.81–2).[4] Reading and rumination require time, patience, and stillness that are anathema to Hotspur. Similarly, in *Coriolanus* Shakespeare's amplification of his source material discloses, via the refracted glimpse of his decidedly unbookish tragic hero's childhood, that the Roman general is someone whose life reading has *not* shaped.

Unlike Volumnia's reactions, which are characterized by imaginative engagement, even the boy's attention is a form of action rather than of cognition – as in Volumnia's "methinks." Short phrases that create action in the line – "see the swords," "hear a drum" – give the sense is that he is completely alert, poised for engagement, every animal instinct honed to attack. This disposition serves to identify him even more firmly with his father, whose definitive characteristic is his relish for the unmediated experience of war.

While Coriolanus is a belligerent man of action, Volumnia sounds, if one may be permitted to say such a thing, more like Shakespeare – a woman capable of using her excited imagination to picture the bloody battle with the Volsces. Volumnia may be a frustrated warrior but she is also, paradoxically, like both the author and the audience, and like all those who hear and read war stories: she is a bystander. It is Volumnia, more than anyone else in the play, who demonstrates this fully engaged, vicarious participation in the events of war, even though her visceral pleasure in the story she tells repels her daughter-in-law. However, Volumina's speech may also convey Shakespeare's awareness of the enormous power of the *mediated* experiences of reading and theatre-going. It might be quite correctly objected that reading about the Trojan War, for example, is not the same as actually having fought in it. The *experience* of reading, however, is every bit as real as the *experience* of armed conflict – they are simply different experiences.[5] Further, the mental impression of battle imparted by reading is as intimately real as sharpening one's quill or quarreling with one's mother.

Shakespeare was extraordinarily attentive to the impact of war stories on those who heard them. In *Cymbeline*, a play about the quasi-fictional history of Ancient Britain, Guiderius, together with his younger brother, listens with rapt attention to stories of battle.

> When on my three-foot stool I sit and tell
> The war-like feats I have done, his spirits fly out
> Into my story: say, "Thus mine enemy fell,
> And thus I set my foot on's neck," even then
> The princely blood flows in his cheeks, he sweats,
> Strains his young nerves, and puts himself in posture
> That acts my words. (3.3.96–102)[6]

Guiderius attends with the desire to act that is the primary characteristic of a warrior hero and future king. This description also brings to mind the image of two acting styles in response to a script. The younger prince, Arviragus, embodies the narrative in a way that does not simply enact or imitate the story but rather reanimates the tale by, if you will, inhabiting the narrative: "In as like a figure, / Strikes life into my speech and shows much more / His own conceiving (3.3.103–5).[7] These children represent, then, two distinct but related forms of attention. In both cases, of course, their vicarious involvement in battle is necessarily removed from warfare itself in a way that makes the boys' immersion in the story of battle closer to that of readers, audiences, or actors than to actual combatants. Through the young princes, Shakespeare depicts the possible range of response to the narrative excitement generated by a compelling war story. The princes are, of course, auditors rather than readers, and they are being told a story from direct experience rather than from a book. However, in a world where literacy had not yet outstripped orality as people's primary means of accessing cultural information, the listener, the play-goer, and the reader were arguably more closely conjoined categories than they are today.

Volumnia's depiction of what the battle must be like, is, as we have seen, vivid, characterized by an almost cinematic action, and of a piece with her earlier argument that it served no purpose for Coriolanus to be simply a beautiful young man – as he was in his youth – but that his beauty must be animated by action, by war, and by the honors martial engagement could bring him:

> When he was yet but tender-bodied, and the only son of my womb, when youth with comeliness plucked all gaze his way, when for a day of kings' entreaties a mother should not sell him an hour from her beholding, I considering how honor would become such a person – that it was no better than picture like to hang by th'wall, if renown made it not stir – was pleased to let him seek danger where he was like to find fame. To a cruel war I sent him, from whence he returned, his brows bound with oak. (1.3.5–15)

Static beauty is worthless, mere ornament, like a picture hanging on a wall, and Volumnia describes her son's youthful physical charms in language almost identical with that of Shakespeare's Sonnet 20: he "steals men's eyes and women's souls amazeth." The *Sonnets* were published in 1609, only a year after *Coriolanus* was first performed, so the proximity of the descriptions here is understandable. Action, valor, and victory animate beauty. It is the renown from glorious deeds in battle that makes beauty "stir" or come to life. Volumnia has taken the malleable flesh of her "tender-bodied" son and made him battle hard. This does not make her wicked or invariably a bad mother. On the contrary, Volumnia represents the form of motherhood the Roman state requires. Indeed, this early battle is recalled again in the play by Cominius who remembers seeing a girlish looking Coriolanus defeat seasoned warriors when "with his Amazonian chin he drove / The bristled lips before him" (2.2.90–1). As yet unmarked by mature masculinity, unbearded, he looks like one of the mythic race of warrior women, the Amazons, in an image than invariably summons up his mother as a feminine version of himself.

She may have molded Coriolanus, but Rome had formed her in the model of warrior mothers like the women of Sparta, would tell their sons to return from war victorious or else dead and borne on their shields. Thus, when Virgilia inquires about Volumnia's decision to thrust him into battle at such an early age with "But had he died in the business, madam, how then?" (1.3.19), Volumnia responds with chilling patriotism: "Then his good report should have been my son" (1.3.20–1). In language that echoes Lady Macbeth's invocation to the "murdering ministers" to "take my milk for gall" (*Macbeth*, 1.5.41), Volumnia dismisses out of hand her daughter-in-law's fears of Coriolanus returning from the current conflict covered in bloody wounds:

> Away you fool! It more becomes a man
> Than gilt his trophy. The breasts of Hecuba,
> When she did suckle Hector, looked not lovelier
> Than Hector's forehead when it spit forth blood
> At Grecian sword, contemning. (1.3.39–43)

Blood is like the gilding on a victory monument, a war decoration. However, this passage takes an extraordinary turn when, in a single line, Shakespeare takes us from the public display of martial honor to the intimate – and in this instance, erotic (these are beautiful breasts), scene of Hecuba's breastfeeding.

Hecuba is, of course, wife of Priam, King of Troy, and mother of numerous sons, including Hector, the great leader of the Trojan army. It would seem logical to expect the comparison to be between Hector's forehead wounded in an engagement with the Greeks and Hector's unblemished infant brow. But this is not where Shakespeare takes the imagery. Instead the comparison he makes is between Hecuba's *breasts* and Hector's wound, between mother's milk, and the emission of milk in lactation with the blood that "spit forth" from Hector's face. Members of the audience may have remembered Hector's fate not only from ancient stories but also from Thomas Kyd's *The Spanish Tragedy*, which recounts his fate in the "martial fields" of the afterlife, "where wounded Hector lives in lasting pain" (1.1.47–8). Mother's milk is an inferior form of the spurting blood that sustains empire.

What Volumnia does not mention, but what Shakespeare's audiences and readers would have known (especially since Hector was one of the Nine Worthies, popular from the Middle Ages), is that in the *Illiad* Hecuba implores her son not to fight Achilles. As she had feared, Achilles indeed kills him and then drags the body behind his chariot below the walls of Troy until Priam himself meets with him in order to ransom Hector's desecrated corpse and return it to Troy for proper burial. Jacobean audiences might also recall that Shakespeare himself had earlier represented Hecuba's grief both in *Lucrece* and in *Hamlet*. Hecuba's motherhood is a tragic story of loss and desolation, but it is also merely a prelude to what is ultimately the epic destruction of Troy.

Intimations of this tragedy lie in Volumnia's willingness to sacrifice her son, which is prefaced by an incestuous fantasy of how she would feel if she were in Virgilia's place: "*If my son were my husband*, I should freelier rejoice in that absence wherein he won honor than in the embracements of his bed where he would show most love" (1.3.2–5, my emphasis). Of course, since she is his mother, not his wife, the incestuous coloring of this passage is somewhat qualified: she would rather have him win honor than have sex with him. (There's a relief.) This is Shakespeare's elaboration on Plutarch's intimation that for Coriolanus, his mother was always more important than his wife: "At her desire took a wife also, by whom he had two children; and yet never left his mother's house."[8]

The source and root of Coriolanus's tragedy is seen to reside in his mother. Coriolanus, however, shows preference for his relationships with men over women at key moments in the play. While twice in the play the nuptial night is described as the epitome of bliss, it is cited at all only in order to show how a relationship with a man surpasses even that anticipation of sexual pleasure with a woman:

> Oh! Let me clip ye
> In arms as sound as when I woo'd; in heart
> As merry as when our nuptial day was done,
> And tapers burned to bedward! (1.6.29–32)

There is an inescapable homoeroticism in the fact that these lines are addressed to another man. Similarly, in Act 4, Aufidius feminizes his former antagonist[9] and implies that Coriolanus, not his wife, is the great love of his life:

> Know thou first,
> I lov'd the maid I married; never man; never man
> Sigh'd truer breath; but that I see thee here,
> Thou noble thing, more dances my rapt heart
> Than when I first my wedded mistress saw
> Bestride my threshold. (4.5.117–22)

The analogy is a telling one, and the very physical relationship between the two men is heightened even further by the following request: "Let me twine / Mine arms about thy body" (4.5.110–11). Even actual combat between Coriolanus and Aufidius is a quasi-sexual encounter in which Coriolanus mounts Aufidius and grasps him by the throat. The image is that of a wrestling contest, but their connection is, nonetheless, far more passionate, far more physical and visceral than in any other relationship in the play:

> I have nightly . . .
> Dreamt of encounters 'twixt thyself and me.

> We have been down together in my sleep,
> Unbuckling helms, fisting each other's throat,
> And waked half dead with nothing. (4.5.126–30)

"Nothing" is nearly always a sexual pun, and the connotations here are those of nocturnal emission and sexual depletion.

In fact, a great deal of fantasy attaches itself to Coriolanus. Volumnia has "lived / To see my very wishes / And the buildings of my fancy" (2.1.194–5), that is, to see her dreams for her son fully realized. She has, however, raised a warrior, not a politician or a diplomat. Even with the Consulship at stake, Coriolanus cannot swallow his pride and appease the plebeians. Menenius asks in disbelief: "Could he not speak 'em fair?" (3.1.264). For Coriolanus, however, such persuasive rhetoric would constitute emasculation: "My throat of war be turned . . . into a pipe / Small as an eunuch, or the virgin voice / That babies lulls asleep!" (3.2.112–15). Notably, the comparison is with a eunuch and a virgin, *not* with a mother's voice, and indeed one cannot imagine that even in his earliest infancy, Volumnia sung him any lullabies. In an image that refers back once again to the Trojan War and the infant Hector, Volumnia takes credit for her son's aggression: "Thy valiantness was mine, thou suck'st it from me," (3.2.129). In this way, Shakespeare imbues his reading of Plutarch with the fraught and complex dynamics of the mother–son relationship in a single parent household.

However, *Coriolanus* is also a complex political play that draws in part upon analogy between government in England and government in Rome and on the cultural memory of the fact that ancient Britain had been under Roman rule for four hundred years.[10] While in the Italy of Shakespeare's time, more and more of the art and artifacts of Roman civilization were being recovered every day,[11] few physical traces of Roman rule in England remained, and instead, knowledge of the classical past was accessible primarily through books. In *Coriolanus*, Shakespeare combed North's translation of Plutarch to create, in this the last of his tragedies, a hero who is arguably the very antithesis of himself, even as he catered to those in his audience who "had rather see the swords and hear a drum" than look upon a book.

# Notes

### Richard II

1 Lily B. Campbell, ed., *The Mirror for Magistrates* (Cambridge: Cambridge University Press, 1938), p. 112.

2 E.K. Chambers, *William Shakespeare: A Study of Facts and Problems*, 2 vols (Oxford, Clarendon Press, 1930), Vol. 2, pp. 326–7. For a comprehensive historical account of the play's relation to the Essex

Rising, see Paul E.J. Hammer, "Shakespeare's *Richard II*, the Play of 7 February 1601, and the Essex Rising," *Shakespeare Quarterly* 59 (2008): 1–35.

3   All references to *Richard II* are from William Shakespeare, *King Richard II: The Arden Shakespeare*, ed. Charles R. Forker (London: Thomson Learning, 2002).

4   David Scott Kastan, *Shakespeare after Theory* (New York: Routledge, 1999), pp. 110–11.

5   William Shakespeare, *King Richard II: The Arden Shakespeare*, ed. Peter Ure (New York: Methuen, 1982), p. xix.

6   See Forker, ed., *Richard II*, pp. 515–6; Hammer, "*Shakespeare's Richard II*," pp. 1–3; Cyndia Susan Clegg, "'By the Choise and Inuitation of al the Realme': *Richard II* and Elizabeth Press Censorship," *Shakespeare Quarterly* 48 (1997): 432–48; David M. Bergeron, "*Richard II* and Carnival Politics," *Shakespeare Quarterly* 42 (1991): 33–43; Janet Clare, "The Censorship of the Deposition Scene in *Richard II*," *Review of English Studies* 41 (1990): 89–94; and J. Leeds Barroll, "A New History for Shakespeare and His Time," *Shakespeare Quarterly* 39 (1988): 441–64, esp. 444–9.

*1 Henry IV*

1   All quotations in this chapter are taken from Barbara Hodgdon, ed., *The First Part of King Henry the Fourth: Texts and Contexts* (Boston: Bedford Books, 1997). In his edition of the play, David Scott Kastan suggests that the second part was probably written only after the first had achieved success. William Shakespeare, *King Henry IV Part I* (Arden, third series, London: Thompson Learning, 2002), ed. David Scott Kastan, p. 21.

2   See Phyllis Rackin, *Stages of History: Shakespeare's English Chronicles* (Ithaca: Cornell University Press), p. 37.

3   *Ovid's Metamorphoses: The Arthur Golding Translation 1567*, ed. John Frederick Nimms, with a new essay, "Shakespeare's Ovid," by Jonathan Bate (Philadelphia: Paul Dry Books, 2000), 15.911.

4   See Raphael Lyne, *Ovid's Changing Worlds: English Metamorphoses, 1567–1632* (Oxford: Oxford University Press, 2001), p. 269.

5   See Stephen Greenblatt, *Shakespearean Negotiations: The Circulation of Social Energy in Renaissance England* (Berkeley: University of California Press, 1988), pp. 40–57.

6   William Shakespeare, *The Second Part of King Henry IV*, ed. A.R. Humphries (London: Methuen, 1981).

7   Ovid, *Metamorphoses*, trans Charles Martin (New York: Norton, 2005).

8   Barbara Hodgdon ed., *Henry the Fourth: Texts and Contexts*, p. 211.

9   For a discussion of the problems of reformation and redemption, see Jonathan Crewe, "Reforming Prince Hal: The Sovereign Inheritor in *2 Henry IV*," *Renaissance Drama New Series* 21 (1990): 225–42.

10   Harry Berger, "Food for Words: Hotspur and the Discourse of Honor" in Harold Bloom ed., *William Shakespeare Histories*, Bloom's Modern Critical Views (New York: Chelsea House Publishers, 2009), p. 152.

11   There have been a number of important discussions of carnival in the play, including Michael Bristol, "The Battle between Carnival and Lent," in *Carnival and Theatre: Plebian Culture and the Structure of Authority in Renaissance England* (London: Methuen, 1985) and David Ruiter, *Shakespeare's Festive History: Feasting, Festivity, Fasting and Lent in the Second Henriad* (Burlington VT: Ashgate, 2003), ch. 3.

12   Jean Howard and Phyllis Rackin, *Engendering a Nation: A Feminist Account of Shakespeare's English Histories* (New York: Routledge: 1997), pp. 160–76.

13   On the complexities of the mythological imagery here, see Jonathan Bate,

*Shakespeare and Ovid* (Oxford: Clarendon Press, 1993), p. 125.

14   See Peter J. Gillett, "Vernon and the Metamorphosis of Hal," *Shakespeare Quarterly* 3 (Summer, 1977): 351–3 at 353.

## Henry V

1   All references to *Hamlet* are from William Shakespeare, *Hamlet*, ed. Ann Thompson and Neil Taylor (London: Methuen, 2006).

2   All references to *Henry V* are from William Shakespeare, *Henry V*, ed. T.W. Craik (New York: Routledge, 1995).

3   See Craik, ed., *King Henry V*, p. 218.

4   This was a shorter quarto version, and was reprinted in 1602 and 1619. This text differs markedly from the longer version that appeared in 1623 in the First Folio.

5   The character's name is spelled Katherine.

6   June 1566, in Sir James Melville, *Memoirs of His Own Life* (1827 edn).

## Richard III

1   All citations from *Macbeth* are from William Shakespeare, *Macbeth: The Arden Shakespeare*, ed. Kenneth Muir (London: Methuen, 1997).

2   See William Shakespeare, *King Richard III: The Arden Shakespeare*, ed. James R. Siemon (London: Methuen, 2009), pp. 82–3. All references are to this edition.

3   Jean E. Howard and Phyllis Rackin observe, "Richard's identity as a master performer becomes the structural principle of the dramatic action," *Engendering a Nation: A Feminist Account of Shakespeare's English Histories* (New York: Routledge, 1997), p. 111.

4   In his edition of the play, Siemon points out both that Elizabeth I's tutor, Roger Ascham, thought that More avoided "flattery and hatred" and did not view

Henry VII in an uncritical light. *Richard III*, ed. Siemon, p. 53.

5   Excerpted in Henry Norman et al., eds, *William Shakespeare: The Complete Works*, (New York: 1909), Vol. 1, p. xviii.

6   Quoted in *Richard III*, ed. Siemon, p. 38. I have modernized the spelling.

7   Pauline Croft, "Cecil, Robert, first earl of Salisbury (1563–1612)," *ODNB*.

8   See Howard and Rackin, *Engendering a Nation*, p. 108.

9   Rosemary Horrox, "Richard III (1425–1485),"*ODNB*.

10   *Three books of Polydore Vergil's "English history,"* ed. H. Ellis (London: Camden Society, 1844), pp. 29, 224.

11   Steven Gunn, "Henry VII in Context: Problems and Possibilities," *History* 92 (2007): 301.

## Julius Caesar

1   All references to *Julius Caesar* are from William Shakespeare, *Julius Caesar: The Arden Shakespeare*, ed. David Daniell (London: Thomson Learning, 2004).

2   All references to *A Midsummer Night's Dream* are from William Shakespeare, *A Midsummer Night's Dream: Texts and Contexts*, ed. Gail Kern Paster and Skiles Howard (New York: Bedford/St. Martin's, 1999).

3   All references to *Henry V* are from William Shakespeare, *Henry V*, ed. T.W. Craik (New York: Routledge, 1995).

4   All references to *Hamlet* are from William Shakespeare, *Hamlet*, ed. Ann Thompson and Neil Taylor (London: Methuen, 2006).

5   See Richard Wilson, *Secret Shakespeare: Studies in Theatre, Religion and Resistance* (Manchester: Manchester University Press, 2004), p. 171.

6   William Shakespeare, *Coriolanus: The Arden Shakespeare*, ed. Philip Brockbank (London: Thomson Learning, 1976).

*Coriolanus*

1 All quotations are from William Shakespeare, *Coriolanus*, Pelican Shakespeare, ed., Jonathan Crewe (New York: Penguin, 1999).

2 T.J.B. Spencer, ed., *Shakespeare's Plutarch* (1964; London: Penguin, 1968), p. 300.

3 For a fuller account of Volumnia's role, see Janet Adelman, *Suffocating Mothers: Fantasies of Maternal Origin in Shakespeare, Hamlet to "The Tempest"* (New York: Routledge, 1992), ch. 6.

4 William Shakespeare, *1 Henry IV* ed., A.R. Humphries (1960; London: Methuen; 1974).

5 For an account of how this phenomenon has been important to Shakespeare biography, see Catherine Belsey, *A Future for Criticism* (Oxford: Wiley-Blackwell, 2011), ch. 3.

6 William Shakespeare, *Cymbeline*, ed., Roger Warren (Oxford: Oxford University Press, 1988).

7 Harold Goddard long ago pointed out that neither of the boys "is a mere passive receptacle for the narrative. Each participates in, contributes to it." *The Meaning of Shakespeare* (1951; Chicago: Pheonix Books, University of Chicago Press,1960), Vol.1, p. 2.

8 Spencer ed., *Shakespeare's Plutarch*, p. 300.

9 Alan Sinfield, *Shakespeare, Authority, Sexuality: Unfinished Business in Cultural Materialism* (New York: Routledge, 2006), p. 106.

10 Of the play's politics, Mark Kishlansky notes: "It is the people's role, and Shakespeare's attitude toward it, that has so perplexed modern commentators. Certainly, there was nothing democratic about their participation; nor was there anything antidemocratic in Shakespeare's depiction of it." Mark A. Kishlansky, *Parliamentary Selection: Social and Political Choice in Early Modern England* (Cambridge: Cambridge University Press, 1986), p. 6. Oliver Arnold makes the case for Roman politics as the English Parliament in disguise: "There were serious impediments, then, to representing the English Parliament in its proper shape, but the Roman republic was much more than a safely alien screen for Shakespeare's critique of parliamentary rhetoric and practices." Oliver Arnold, *The Third Citizen: Shakespeare's Theater and the Early Modern House of Commons* (Baltimore: Johns Hopkins University Press, 2007), p. 19.

11 Leonard Barkan, *Unearthing the Past: Archaeology and Aesthetics in the Making of Renaissance Culture* (New Haven: Yale University Press, 1999), ch. 1.

# 8

# TRAGEDIES
## Shakespeare in Love and Loss

*Romeo and Juliet*
*Hamlet*
*Othello*
*King Lear*
*Macbeth*
*Antony and Cleopatra*

### *Romeo and Juliet*

While we might well expect all of Shakespeare's tragedies to be "excellent" and "lamentable," only *Romeo and Juliet* of all the titles in the First Folio is accorded these additional adjectives: *The Most Excellent and Lamentable Tragedie of Romeo and Juliet*. (Shakespeare's only other love tragedy is titled simply *The Tragedy of Antony and Cleopatra*). The adjectival indication is that this play possesses more than the typical quotient of tragic pathos. Crucially, the title admits no possibility that the fate of the Veronese lovers could be otherwise than tragic. Even without the title's amplifications, extant versions of the story at the time Shakespeare was writing had already established the definitively tragic trajectory of this love affair. These included the popular English narrative poem (and Shakespeare's primary source), Arthur Brooke's narrative poem *The Tragicall Historye of Romeus and Juliet* (1562); William Painter's "Rhomeo and Julietta" in his collection of prose translations, *The Palace of*

*Who Was William Shakespeare?: An Introduction to the Life and Works*, First Edition.
Dympna Callaghan.
© 2013 John Wiley & Sons, Ltd. Published 2013 by John Wiley & Sons, Ltd.

*Pleasure* (Vol. 2, 1567); François Belleforest's *Histoires Tragiques* (1576); Luigi da Porto's Italian novella, *Historia novellamente ritrovata di due nobili amanti* (A Story Newly Found of two Noble Lovers, 1530); and Matteo Bandello's *Giulietta e Romeo* (1554). The inevitability of the lovers' deaths was thus predestined by literary precedent and, at the very opening of Shakespeare's play, as if to allay any doubt on this scene, the Chorus offers a compact summation of the plot and announces the tragic conclusion: "A pair of star-crossed lovers take their life" (1.0.6).[1]

Romeo has a foreboding of his astrologically predestined fate shortly before he meets Juliet at the Capulet ball: "Some consequence yet hanging in the stars / Shall bitterly begin his fearful *date*" (1.4.107–8, my emphasis). His premonition echoes the famous lyrical moment when the Italian poet Francesco Petrarch first set eyes on Laura, an event (real or imaginary) which precipitated both his exquisite misery and the best known sonnet sequence in Europe, the *Canzoniere* (Lyrics, or Songs), which includes 317 sonnets in all, together with poems in a number of other verse forms. The date of this event was Good Friday, April 6, 1327:

> It was the day the sun's rays had turned pale
> with pity for the suffering of his Maker
> when I was caught (and I put up no fight),
> my lady, for your lovely eyes had bound me.
>
> (*Canzone* 3)

Here, the crucifixion, the passion of the cross, when the daytime sky turns dark at Christ's death, is the appropriately dolorous backdrop to the secular passion that will engulf the poet now that he is captured, bound, captivated, and enthralled (he cannot resist) by Laura's eyes. The rest of Petrarch's sequence recounts the poet's tortured, unrequited love for Laura. Of course, even though the poet was stabbed by Cupid's arrow at the start of Petrarch's sequence, the *Canzoniere* was not literally a tragedy in terms of generic designation, but its pervasive tragic ethos (the poet's love is never reciprocated and Laura dies) nonetheless infused Shakespeare's love tragedy at every level.

A sudden turn to happiness was neither expected nor desired by Petrarch's readers any more than it was by Shakespeare's audiences. That the form of Shakespeare's Prologue is itself a sonnet gives a further signal not only that the play's events can end only in tragedy, so too does the way in which the play utilizes to supreme tragic effect the powerfully destructive forces so deeply rooted in the tragic *amour* of Petrarchan tradition: "the numbers [metrical count] that Petrarch flowed in" (2.4.33). The power of *Romeo and Juliet*, so heavily indebted to Petrarchan convention, then, paradoxically depends, this chapter will argue, on the predictability of its unhappy conclusions and the inevitability of its lamentable outcome.

*Romeo and Juliet* may deploy and manipulate Petrarchan conventions in service of the play's tragic ending, but Shakespeare does so without slavishly imitating them. His departure from Petrarch is evident above all in the way that *Romeo and Juliet* is about a relationship, whereas the *Canzoniere* is not. Indeed, Petrarch's sonnets are not so much about Laura (who may have been a real person or an imaginary conglomeration of women, ideal and real) but about the obsessive idea of Laura in the heart of the poet-lover. Whoever Laura was, she certainly was not the real woman who bore Petrarch two illegitimate off-spring. Laura is occasionally glimpsed from afar, but without any endeavor to convey her feelings, desires, or concerns. Indeed, the entire course of Petrarch's love is presented wholly from the male point of view. The popularity of Petrarch's sonnets was such that they became a dominant paradigm for love in the Western world. Even in Shakespeare's time, the sighing, weeping poet-lover was so familiar as to be risible. Thus Mercutio undercuts the play's roman-tic lyricism by bawdily punning that Romeo is "Without his roe" (2.4.32), that is, the first part of his name. The paronomastic joke here is on sexual depletion. In other words, all that remains of Romeo is his "meo," – his trademark self-absorbed Petrarchan "deep sighs" (1.1.118–20), his "Me- Oh." As Romeo himself says, "Love is a smoke raised with the fume of sighs" (1.1.177).

Romeo's first love, Rosaline, follows the pattern of the Petrarchan lady. She is cold, chaste, and distant, and she causes him to behave in entirely predictable Petrarchan manner – worrying his parents by staying up all night and locking himself in his room all day. Petrarchan love in its most conventional form is presented in the play as fickle. Romeo quickly trades his love for Rosaline for that of Juliet. In contrast, while the tropes that describe their love remain emi-nently Petrarchan, both Romeo and Juliet participate in this discourse; their love is reciprocal, something unheard of in Petrarch. At their first meeting, in Act 1, Scene 5, they speak fourteen lines of the sonnet form, not as dejected introspection but as a joyful duet:

ROMEO:  If I profane with my unworthiest hand
         This holy shrine, the gentle sin is this:
         My lips, two blushing pilgrims, ready stand
         To smooth that rough touch with a tender kiss.
JULIET:  Good pilgrim, you do wrong your hand too much,
         Which mannerly devotion shows in this;
         For saints have hands that pilgrims' hands do touch,
         And palm to palm is holy palmers' kiss.

ROMEO:   Have not saints lips, and holy palmers too?
JULIET:  Ay, pilgrim, lips that they must use in prayer
ROMEO:   O, then, dear saint, let lips do what hands do.
         They pray; grant though, lest faith turn to despair.
JULIET:  Saints do not move, though grant for prayers' sake.
ROMEO:   Then move not, while my prayer's effect I take. (1.5.90–103)

The sonnet, in which Romeo has professed that love is his religion, ends with a kiss. Shakespeare here engineers a paradigm shift, changing the nature of the relationship between the Petrarchan lover and the beloved from one of the latter's frosty indifference to warmly reciprocated love whose end, as Juliet is quick to point out, is marriage: "If that thy bent of love be honorable, / Thy purpose marriage" (2.2.143–4).

The fundamental mutuality of the lovers' relationship is further expressed in the theme of complementary opposites, especially in its insistently lyrical, celestial themes. For Romeo, "Juliet is the sun," as is appropriate to her onomastic association with the summer month of July and with her birthday: "Come Lammas Eve at night shall she be fourteen" (1.3.18), Lammas is August 1, making her birthday the last day of July. Romeo, in contrast, is like the stars:

> Give me my Romeo, and when I shall die
> Take him and cut him out in little stars,
> And he will make the face of heaven so fine
> That all the world will be in love with night
> And pay no worship to the garish sun. (3.2.21–5)

This image is developed in the course of Juliet's epithalamium, or wedding poem, where she urges time onward toward night and the consummation of her marriage with the imagery of Phaeton's chariot as analogous to uncontrolled, careening desire. The rash charioteer in this myth was allowed to drive the chariot of the sun for a day, but he lost control of the horses and was killed by a thunderbolt:

> Gallop apace, you fiery-footed steeds,
> Towards Phoebus' lodging! Such a wagoner
> As Phaëton would whip you to the west
> And bring in cloudy night immediately. (3.2.1–4)

That this epithalamium is spoken as a soliloquy in the middle act of the play gives Juliet a dramatic and lyrical centrality that constitutes a significant departure from the one-sided Petrarchan emphasis on male suffering.

Indeed, Shakespeare devoted a great deal of the play to Juliet – we know the story of her life from infancy via the garrulous nurse, from when she was weaned to when she is buried, and we see her eager anticipation of the marriage bed and her deep misgivings about taking the potion the friar has given her to put her in a state that resembles death: "What if it be a poison which the Friar / Subtly hath ministered to have me dead [?]" (4.3.24–5). In other words, there is a significant emphasis on female desire and female interiority in the thoughts and feelings of Juliet, rather than, as in the Petrarchan model, simply on her beauty, her external features, as an object of Romeo's desire: "She hangs upon the cheek of night / As a rich jewel in an Ethiop's ear" (1.5.42–3). This is in part Shakespeare's response to the new post-Reformation emphasis on marriage as the highest vocation in life, as opposed to the celibate asceticism of the medieval monastic tradition. Even clergy were now encouraged to marry, and numerous advice books of the period emphasize the importance of choosing the right marriage partner in order to achieve that newly exalted condition of connubial felicity.

Whatever his modifications of the Petrarchan paradigm, crucially, Shakespeare retains from it the inherently tragic idea that the beloved is also the enemy. In the Petrarchan schema, the lady is the poet's foe because she is cruelly indifferent to his sufferings and even takes pleasure in them. Mercutio voices this sense of the homicidal propensities of the Petrarchan lady when he declares that Romeo has been "stabbed with a white wench's black eye" (2.4.13–14). The lady's indifference toward the poet-lover is his ruin, his torture, and the cause of his intense melancholy, his sighs, and his tears. Shakespeare literalizes the idea that the beloved is the instrument of the lover's destruction but makes it the gender-neutral condition of internecine struggle in Verona, where it is Juliet who says she "must love a loathèd enemy" (1.5.138). This reversal of the gender roles in the Petrarchan dynamic is evident again when Romeo describes his beloved as the sun whom he enjoins to rise and outshine Diana, the goddess of the moon and of chastity, even though as a virgin, Juliet is metaphorically her "maid" or votary:

> But soft, what light through yonder window breaks?
> It is the east, and Juliet is the sun.
> Arise, fair sun, and kill the envious moon,
> Who is already sick and pale with grief
> That thou her maid art far more fair than she. (2.2.2–6)

In this image Juliet retains the association with the killing power of Petrarch's Laura, even though her ire is no longer directed at the man who loves her. This clever conceit embeds even the highest praise of the beloved with the murder of a rival but lesser beauty, who, although dying not of unrequited love but of envy, is nonetheless imaged as a kind of melancholic, the female equivalent of the male Petrarchan lover, a role that both Romeo and Benvolio occupied at the beginning of the play.

Romeo and Juliet are enemies not because their passion is unrequited – it is wonderfully mutual – but because of forces external to the lovers themselves. Because theirs is married love, Romeo's and Juliet's romance is intrinsically social – not set apart from social forces but deeply enmeshed in them. This social dimension is appropriate to drama as an inherently more social genre than lyric sequence, definitively setting Shakespeare's lovers apart from Petrarch and Laura. So while the poetic causations of fate are the overarching cause of the lovers' deaths, more locally, the outbreak of plague – a real and present danger to Shakespeare's audiences – prevents Romeo from receiving the message sent to him in his exile in Mantua. Thus, he does not know that Juliet's apparent death on the eve of her enforced marriage to Paris is but the result of the potion prescribed by Friar Lawrence. More than anything, however, it is the inexplicable enmity of the Montagues and the Capulets that dooms their relationship, just as much as it blights the urban landscape of Verona. Strangely, these families are divided not by their differences from one another but by their very similarities. They are, as the play's first line announces, "Two households *both alike* in dignity" (1.0.1, my emphasis). This is an irrational and ancient hatred, whose cause is never revealed, that positions Romeo and Juliet, despite their love, as enemies just as it sets them firmly within – rather than outside – the social structure of Verona.

Like the ending of *Henry V*, where Henry cements his conquest of France with marriage to its princess, a marital alliance could make a natural ending to the feud; but to "Deny thy father and refuse thy name!" (2.2.34) is not an available option in Verona, and it is for this reason that the marriage must be clandestine. Capulet's rage when he is confronted with Juliet's refusal to marry Paris is demonstration enough of why this secrecy is necessary. On the verge of striking his daughter, "My fingers itch" (3.5.164), he merely threatens to evict her from the house, drag her through the streets like a malefactor on a hurdle, and, finally, his wife wishes her daughter dead: "I would the fool were married to her grave!" (3.5.140). Capulet's tirade reflects real-life rage that many couples experienced when they contravened parental dictates in the choice of a spouse. When John Donne eloped with Anne, the sixteen- (or at most seventeen-) year-old daughter of Sir George More in 1601, the poet wrote to his new father-in-law imploring that although "I know this letter shall find you full of passion," he might refrain from unleashing violent rage on his daughter: "I humbly beg of you that she may not to her danger feel the terror of your sudden anger."[2]

Capulet's rage, however, not only mirrors such slices of reality, it simultaneously conforms him to the literary type of the *senex iratus*, the old man who objects to a love match, like Egeus in *A Midsummer Night's Dream*, who was determined to have his daughter Hermia punished with execution should she reject his choice of a husband for her. *Romeo and Juliet* begins similarly to *A Midsummer Night's Dream* with the comic scenario of young lovers who face parental obstacles to their unions; and in the comic scenario the problems will dissolve in the course of the play so that the end can achieve the happy resolution of the lovers' marriage.[3] On the social register, the sheer emphasis on mutuality in Elizabethan Protestantism, and on the spouse as "an help-meet," a fellow adventurer in the journey through life, offered an alternative ending to the solitary misery envisaged by Petrarchan lyricism. Henry Smith's *A Preparative to Marriage* (1591), for example, envisages the kind of conjugal felicity that might have been enjoyed by Romeo and Juliet had they lived:

> In all Nations the day of marriage was reputed the joyfullest day in all their life. And is reputed still of all, as though the sun of happiness began that day to shine upon us, when a good wife is brought unto us. Therefore one sayeth, that marriage doth signify *merriage*, because a playfellow is come to make our age merry.[4]

Shakespeare's lovers, however, as the Chorus insists, cannot survive their obdurate parents' "ancient grudge" (1.0.3) or the dictates of fate, "the stars." It is as if Shakespeare wanted to draw attention not so much to the idea that this story *could* have ended happily, but rather that it *could not* – it is lamentable, but unavoidable.

Shakespeare's audience is enjoined to take the lovers' part from the outset by the words of the Chorus, which make it clear that it is the ancient enmity between the houses of Montague and Capulet that is the fatal instrument of their children's violent and untimely death, an idea that is later corroborated by Paris: "And pity 'tis you lived at odds so long" (1.2.5). Shakespeare's huge innovation, even though modern audiences take this element of the play so much for granted, is that the play is unequivocal about the innocence of the lovers and the guilt of their parents. What is remarkable about this play and what – its immense literary merits aside – distinguishes it so markedly from Arthur Brooke's version of the story, is its overwhelming sympathy for the young lovers. Brooke found his lovers entirely culpable in the tragedy that befell them because they had not only consorted with dubious members of the Catholic clergy (Friar Lawrence who marries them) but had also deceived and disobeyed their parents in marrying one another in the first place. In Elizabethan England, one of the most pressing social problems of the day was enforced marriage where monetary considerations made families seek profitable alliances for their offspring. Questions of religious allegiance might also play a part, although the ubiquitous admixture of residual Catholicism alongside state Protestantism meant that there were invariably alliances between partners and families of both parties. These concerns are certainly registered in Brooke's poem where he adduces as evidence of the lovers' culpability the fact that Juliet has received the Catholic sacrament of "auricular confession." This seems a little unjust, to say the least, given that lovers are Italian and therefore, perforce, Catholic. The case that Shakespeare made in this play for freedom of choice and freedom from coercion in the selection of a mate is one that has become so much the norm that we can scarcely conceive of the idea that when Shakespeare wrote *Romeo and Juliet* this was a notion that was far from being universally accepted. The relationship between the lovers represents the period's new ideas about marriage – but they are, tragically, ideas that, because of the inflexibility of the old order, cannot be fully lived out.

It is the young men who must enact the violence of their elders. When, in Act 3, Romeo accidentally kills Tybalt, the comic structure with which the play begins suddenly ruptures. From that moment, the play is transposed from a comic register to a tragic one. The deaths of Mercutio and Tybalt irrevocably alter the play's course.[5] Indeed the dying Mercutio strikes an ominous note when he curses both sides of the feud with "A plague o' both your houses!" (3.1.87–8). Mercutio is the glittering figure who, as critics have often noted, had he been permitted to survive, might have taken over the whole tragedy. His "wit" as the early moderns would have called it lies in his capacity to spin fantastical images out of thin air, as Romeo says: "Peace, peace, Mercutio, peace! / Thou talk'st of nothing" (1.4.95–6). In Mercutio's "talk," his images of Queen Mab, the diminutive "fairies' midwife . . . Drawn with a teem of little atomi," are indeed so insubstantial that they defy both logic and gravity, but they are also a demonstration of lyrical virtuosity (1.4.54–7).

When we see Romeo with Mercutio he is in the world of the young men of Verona as they take to the streets, and this world is sharply opposed to the domestic interiors in which Shakespeare presents Juliet: at home with her parents or nurse, on the balcony or in her bedroom, or at church. In contrast, even when we glimpse Romeo with his concerned parents in Act 1, he is out of doors, "underneath the grove of sycamore" (1.1.108). In Verona, the heat of passion, which in the love affair of Romeo and Juliet is appropriately channeled into love and marriage, more often finds its outlet in the public and overwhelmingly male world of the streets. In summer time, the "dog days," that is the period when the constellation of Canis Major (the big dog) is in the sky and when temperatures and tempers are hottest, the "fiery Tybalt" (1.1.96) from the house of Capulet goads Benvolio into combat, which will eventually prove fatal to Mercutio. By this stage in the play, Romeo has wed Juliet, although the marriage remains to be consummated. On these grounds, he acknowledges his kinship with Tybalt – "the reason that I have to love thee" – as his motivation to make peace (3.1.53). Tybalt's inflamed belligerence is, however, not to be assuaged: "Boy, this shall not excuse the injuries / That thou hast done me; therefore turn and draw" (3.1.57–8). While this street fight offered a convenient way of staging swordfights that had become immensely popular with the arrival of Italian fencing masters in England like the famous Vincentio Saviolo and Geronimo, swordplay also resonates with the violent urban landscape of London itself.[6] When the dying Mercutio asks, "Why the devil came you between us? I was hurt under your arm" (3.1.90), his remarks are astonishingly similar to the account of how Shakespeare's fellow playwrights Thomas Watson and Christopher Marlowe came to kill an inn-keeper's son, Thomas Bradley, in 1589. The coroner's report on that occasion records that the combatants, who had a well-documented history of animosity, were in Hog Lane, close by the Theatre in Shoreditch. Marlowe and Bradley drew swords, and Watson drew in an attempt to separate them and "to keep the Queen's peace." But Watson's intervention further infuriated Bradley, who felt it was now a case of two against one. He then wounded Watson, who stabbed him with a fatal blow six inches deep into his chest. By the time Shake-speare wrote *Romeo and Juliet*, Marlowe had himself been stabbed in a tavern. The witty, mercurial playwright, who was, as Michael Drayton put it, all "ayre and fire,"[7] and whose talent had been a glorious match for Shakespeare's own, was perhaps the kind of ferocious eruption of life that, like Mercutio, does not seem to be set for any significant duration.

*Romeo and Juliet* is one of the works that established Shakespeare's fame during his own lifetime. Probably written in 1595, the play was printed in three dif-ferent versions in 1597, 1599, and 1623, and that the Bodleian Library's copy of the First Folio was worn through at the pages covering the balcony scene attests to the popularity of this tragic love affair between 1623 and 1664, at which point the Library replaced the First Folio with the Third Folio. Evidence of another reader's engagement with the text has also survived, namely that of the Scottish poet, William Drummond, who overscored the most intensely lyrical passages of the copy he purchased in 1599. Indeed, it is the complex lyricism of Shakespeare's rendition of the story of star-crossed lovers, so densely wrought with conceits and laden with puns, that made the play so overwhelm-ingly successful with audiences and readers alike.

I have argued above that the outcome of Petrarchan lyricism is as fixed as the historical circumstances of the feud. Petrarchanism structures this tragedy and assures its "lamentable and piteous" ending, even though typically, as a love story gathers momentum toward union, its logical, generic conclusion is that of comedy. As we have noted, the Petrarchanism of *Romeo and Juliet* requires its tragic ending. Yet, when William Davenant revived the play after the Restoration in 1662 it did not suit the tastes of the time. The diarist Samuel Pepys described it as "the worst [play] that ever I heard in my life." Following

this trend, James Howard produced a new version of the play, which, in complete defiance of Shakespeare's text, kept the lovers alive.[8]

## Hamlet

> Farewell, thou child of my right hand, and joy;
>   My sin was too much hope of thee, lov'd boy.
> Seven years thou wert lent to me, and I thee pay.
>   Exacted by the fate, on the just day.
> Oh, could I lose all father now! For why
>   Will man lament the state he should envy?
> To have so soon 'scaped world's and flesh's rage,
>   And, if no other misery, yet age?
> Rest in soft peace, and asked, say here doth lie
>   Ben Jonson his best piece of poetry;
> For whose sake, henceforth, all his vows be such,
>   As what he loves may never like too much.[1]

"On My First Son" was written not by Shakespeare, but by his friend and fellow
play-wright, by Ben Jonson. In the spring of 1603, Jonson left his family behind
in London for Robert Cotton's country estate in Huntingdonshire, where he
experienced a spectral visitation. The seven-year-old son who had been named
after him appeared before him in "Manlie shape" with "the Marke of a bloodie
crosse on his forehead as if it had been cutted with a sword."[2] Jonson was
convinced that the vision was a premonition of the child's death. That his son
had reached adulthood in the dream was, Jonson reasoned, because he was "of
that Growth . . . he shall be at the resurrection."[3] A fellow guest at Conington,
the immensely learned William Camden, Jonson's former schoolmaster and
friend, tried to persuade him that the vision was "but an apprehension of his
fantasie at which he should not be disjected." Letters soon arrived from Jonson's wife in London, however, confirming his worst fears: his son, Ben, had
died of bubonic plague.

The experience of childhood mortality was pervasive in early modern England,
and children were especially vulnerable to outbreaks of pestilence and other
diseases. As an infant, indeed, Shakespeare himself had narrowly escaped an
outbreak of plague in Stratford. In the year that young Ben died, in one London
parish alone, St Giles in Cripplegate, of the three thousand people resident in
July of 1603, only six hundred survived until the following December.[4] Although
Jonson's touching elegy argues that the poet's bitter grief makes him regret the
depth of his paternal attachment, grief for the departed was not subsumed by
the ubiquity of loss. Jonson's "Oh, could I lose all father now!" is at once the

desire not to be a father and thus no longer experience this suffering, but is also tacitly embedded with the idea that it would be better to lose a father (Jonson's own father had died while the poet was still an infant) than to suffer the death of a first-born son.

The lines of Jonson's poem that question why he should lament death, "the state he should envy" (*l.* 6), given the miseries of life, follow the logic of Hamlet's suicidal contemplations in his most famous soliloquy, "To be, or not to be" (3.1.55).[5] There, Hamlet ponders the "calamity" of "long life" (3.1.68) and the inevitable burdens of existence, such as "The pangs of despised love" (3.1.71), and the anxieties attendant upon protracted litigation, "the law's delay" (3.1.71). Despite the thematic congruence between Jonson and Shakespeare's representation of death as potentially a desired state, when viewed from the perspective of extraordinary grief and despair, there is little else to connect them. Further, although Jonson's vision reprises some of the central issues of Shakespeare's most famous tragedy – the relationship between fathers and sons and the visitation of a specter – the incident bears, nonetheless, only an oblique if uncanny correlation with *Hamlet*, written in 1600, some three years before the death of young Ben. More compelling, rather, is the *disjunction* between Jonson's poem and Shakespeare's play. Shakespeare himself lost his first and only son, Hamnet, the eleven-year-old twin brother of Judith, in August 1596, four years before he wrote *Hamlet*. Yet, no elegy marks Hamnet's passing. Shakespeare did, however, write a play, a profound meditation on death, whose title bears such close onomastic proximity to Hamnet (and the names were interchangeable at this period)[6] as to be almost identical. For all that, *Hamlet* is not a play about lost children unlike, for example, *The Winter's Tale* or *The Comedy of Errors*. It is, however, a play very much concerned with parents and progeny and with a father's legacy to his son. Shakespeare's own father died in 1601, and since *Hamlet* was most likely written the year before, there is a sense in which the play is also an anticipation of that loss. These, albeit elusive, biographical connections demonstrate the premise of this chapter, namely that as a genre tragedy performs the cultural work of processing the meaning of grief and death. Shakespeare, who lost his son, wrote his greatest tragedy about a son who lost his father, and in this he may well have bequeathed the world "his best piece of poetry."

In *Hamlet* Shakespeare foregrounds the cultural work of tragedy by making death the fulcrum of the play. *Hamlet*, in other words, is *about* death. That is to say, in *Hamlet* Shakespeare chose to make death his central, driving theme rather than letting it serve simply, as he does in other tragedies, as the climax of a series of tragic events that may not be specifically or directly related to it – for example, ambition in *Macbeth*, whose first scene reveals the witches; old age in *King Lear*, which begins with Gloucester and his illegitimate son and the division of the kingdom; and interracial marriage in *Othello*, a play that begins with news of the elopement of Othello and Desdemona.

All Shakespeare's tragedies end in death, but only *Hamlet* also begins so insistently with a loss that is immediately personal to the protagonist and with the apparition of the deceased, namely the ghost of Hamlet's father on the battlements before the terrified sentinels. When Hamlet himself meets the ghost, he is charged to "Revenge his foul and most unnatural murder!" (1.5.25). The object of the ghost's vengeance is his brother, Claudius, who "won to his shameful lust / The will of my most seeming-virtuous Queen" (1.5.45–6) and poured poison, a "leperous distilment" (1.5.64), into his ear one day as he lay sleeping in the garden. Michael Neill and Stephen Greenblatt have rightly drawn attention to the fact that, in concluding his interview with Hamlet, the ghost does not cry "Revenge me" but "Adieu, adieu, adieu, remember me" (1.5.91).[7] These words do indeed recall, as these critics suggest, the words of eucharistic sacrifice of the Mass: "Do this in memory of me," as well as the Catholic practice of praying for departed souls in purgatory – a liminal state between damnation and celestial bliss to which Protestant theology no longer gave credence. However, "remember me" may also reflect the more secular dimensions of the culturally accepted sense that the dead – especially those who die from natural and mundane causes – wish to be remembered by the living – with elegiac verses, tomb stones, memorial rings, and bequests for the dispersal of their property, as well as the conventional and appropriate sartorial markers such as those Hamlet wears in acknowledgement of his father's death: "customary suits of solemn black" (1.2.78), an "inky cloak" (1.2.77) and "suits of woe" (1.2.86). Despite Gertrude's protestations to the contrary, that "all that lives must die" (1.2.72), the play is *not* about death from *natural* causes. Paradoxically this serves to strengthen the idea that death in all its manifestations, whether as the ordinary consequence of corporeal atrophy or as sudden, abrupt, or violent cessation of life, is profoundly and inherently *unnatural*, an aberration, what Hamlet calls "The undiscovered country from whose bourn / No traveller returns" (3.1.78–9).

The ghost, however, has returned. Despite having received the proper Christian rite of interment, Old Hamlet's "canonized bones" (1.4.26) "have burst their cerements" (1.4.27). Interestingly, Hamlet does not here address his father as a ghost, but as a revivified corpse whose skeletal structure is still intact. Editors have been puzzled by an apparently clumsy repetition of the word "burst" in the multiple surviving texts of the play. "Burst" occurs three times in five lines in the First Quarto of 1603:

> O answere mee, let mee not *burst* in ignorance,
> But say why thy canonized bones hearsed in death

> Haue *burst* their ceremonies: why thy Sepulcher,
> In which wee saw thee quietly interr'd,
> Hath *burst* his ponderous and marble jawes . . . (C.3.v)

Whatever the deficiencies of the First Quarto text (a topic of long-standing critical argument), the reiteration nonetheless indicates Shakespeare's degree of emphasis on a kind of violent rupture from both sides of the grave. There is an uncanny symmetry here between Hamlet and his father's bones. He is "bursting in ignorance," bursting, that is, to know how his father's skeleton exhumed itself – how the bones "Have burst their cerements." The macabre image conveys the sense that graves are more often broken *into* rather than out of. Indeed, the figure of the burst grave resonates with the many instances of tomb breaking in Elizabethan England by those who thought that funeral monuments "erected up as well in churches as in other public places within this realm only to show a memory to the posterity of the persons there buried"[8] were idolatrous. The problem was sufficiently severe that Elizabeth issued a "Proclamation Prohibiting Destruction of Church Monuments" (1560). The inscription on Shakespeare's own funeral monument seems also to anticipate such violation: "Curst be he that moves my bones."[9]

Both the desecration of the dead by the living and the spectacular reanimation of Old Hamlet involve the unearthing of "the dead corpse" (1.4.52) and are attended by the disclosure of the horrors that the grave should hide. As Susan Zimmerman has argued, in *Hamlet*, "Shakespeare comes brilliantly close to representing the unrepresentable . . . the corpse itself."[10] Within Christian teleology there was a similar expectation – albeit a *slightly* less grisly one – that the dead who "shall not die forever" would be disinterred and rise at "the last trump."[11] Indeed, the Elizabethan funeral service reminded congregants of what lay in their distant future: "I shall rise out of the earth in the last day, and shall be covered again with my skin."[12] Although this is clearly meant to be a glorious occasion, the Prayer Book nonetheless offers the rather disquieting image of an exhumed skeleton suddenly sprouting flesh that resonates with Hamlet's image of his father disgorged from the mouth of death:

> The sepulchre,
> Wherein we saw thee quietly interred,
> Hath oped his ponderous and marble jaws
> To cast thee up again. (1.4.48–51)

While to be thus violently disinterred is clearly a supernatural event, in Act 5, there is a much more prosaic rendition of unearthed bones as the jocular gravedigger, who, Hamlet suggests, has "no feeling of [sensitivity to] his business" (5.1.61), throws up skulls (one of which famously belongs to Yorick, a former court jester) as he blithely disturbs old burial plots while digging Ophelia's grave. Neither the recently deceased, like Hamlet's father, nor the long interred, like Yorick, are ever safely out of sight and under the earth. Interestingly, the body of a tanner, whose trade is contiguous with that of Shakespeare's own father, persists undecayed, preserved like the leather he worked on all his life. With the gravedigger, Shakespeare returns to the ordinary and mundane practices, specifically the manual labor rather than the religious rites and rituals that surround the horror, the gaping jaw that is mortality.

Throughout *Hamlet*, Shakespeare examines death from both sides of the grave, that is, from the point of view of the deceased king and from that of his grief-stricken son, whose despair the audience is privy to even before he sees his father's ghost and even before Horatio tells him about the apparition. Already appalled by his mother's remarriage, in his first soliloquy Hamlet expresses a profound desire for oblivion, for the annihilation of the self, "O that this too sullied flesh would melt, / Thaw, and resolve itself into a dew" (1.2.129–30). For Hamlet, the meaning or import of death is that life is futile and meaningless, "weary, stale, flat and unprofitable" (1.2.133); only ethical scruples – "Conscience does make cowards" [3.1.82] – which will later prevent him from killing Claudius and, at this point in the play, prevent him from taking his own life: "the Everlasting had not fixed / His canon 'gainst self-slaughter" (1.2.131–32).

Because something is indeed "rotten in the state of Denmark" (1.4.90), Hamlet's mourning is made to seem unseasonable and mysterious. Claudius reports that Polonius "tells me, my sweet Queen, that he hath found / The head and source of all your son's distemper" (2.2.54–5). However, the cause of Hamlet's malady is perfectly transparent to his mother – "I doubt it is no other but the main – / His father's death, and our hasty marriage" (2.2.56–7) – even though she implores him to cheer up with the conventional platitudes about mortality that ordinarily conceal death:

> QUEEN:  Thou knowst 'tis common all that lives must die,
>       Passing through nature to eternity.
> HAMLET:  Ay, madam, it is common.
> QUEEN:             If it be,
>       Why seems it so particular with thee? (1.2.72–5)

Indeed, Act 1, Scene 2 is the first time the audience sees all three of King Hamlet's surviving family members: Hamlet, Gertrude, and Claudius. The dialog echoes the Elizabethan Prayer Book's words about the universality of death in the prayers said as the body was brought to the graveside:

Man that is born of a woman hath but a short time to live, and is full of misery: he cometh up, and is cut down like a flower; he flieth as it were a shadow, and never continueth in one stay. In the midst of life we be in death.[13]

Claudius, too, follows the Prayer Book's direction that "the earth shall be cast upon the body by some standing by"[14] when he all but orders Hamlet to cease mourning his father: "We pray you *throw to earth* / This unprevailing woe" (1.2.106–7, my emphasis). Those who survive him thus stand metaphorically around the dead king's grave in a way that is a parody of the proper rites of death that have been so abruptly curtailed by the wedding of Gertrude and Claudius.

By 1600, when *Hamlet* was written, the playwright himself may have been plundering a kind of theatrical grave in his reanimation of a "mouldy tale,"[15] that is, an anonymous earlier version known as Ur-*Hamlet* that does not survive. As John Kerrigan puts it, "Why, the Prince wonders, should obedience to revenge make his life conform to the shape of some old pot-boiler (the audience will be thinking of the Ur-*Hamlet*)? Why is he in this play?"[16] Yet, after the ghost departs from Hamlet, the play diverges from the typical trajectory of revenge tragedy. Indeed, critics have long noted that *Hamlet* is not so much about the pursuit of vengeance as its belated achievement. This deferred action is fitting for a play about death, when, in a sense, nothing happens. Death is, paradoxically, a state of oblivion and one of massively active biological degeneration.[17] That is, even without the Catholic concept of purgatory, the early modern idea of death involved a certain amount of suspended animation, a post-mortem vitality, as Hamlet rather gruesomely puts it: "We fat ourselves for maggots" (4.3.22).

As is entirely appropriate to this paradox of death, the play's *action* essentially concerns Hamlet's *inaction*. For all that, like Hamlet's image of decay, the "convocation of worms" (4.3.20), the plot is also an animated site of intricate complexity. Hamlet is distracted from revenge primarily by a preoccupation with his mother's culpability in spite of the ghost's instruction to "Taint not thy mind nor let thy soul contrive / Against thy mother aught; leave her to heaven" (1.5.85–6). This obsessive focus on maternal guilt evolves into misogynist antipathy towards women in general, especially his erstwhile love, the hapless Ophelia. A variety of incidents in the plot serve as substitutes for the murder of Claudius. These include botched vengeance (Hamlet stabs Polonius hiding behind the arras instead of Claudius); attempted murder (Claudius tries to do away with the ostensibly mad Hamlet by sending him on a voyage to England with Rosencrantz and Guildenstern, whose letters to the English king ordering his execution are discovered by Hamlet who forges a new letter ordering Rosencrantz and Guildensterns' executions before himself returning to Denmark on a pirate vessel); insanity (Hamlet's own "antic disposition" (1.5.170); and Ophelia's loss of reason after Hamlet inadvertently murders her father, Polonius); Hamlet's own contemplation of suicide and Ophelia's actual suicide by drowning. Most surprising of all, however, in the genre of revenge tragedy is that when a company of players arrives in Elsinore, in a strategy that surely tests the received boundaries of revenge as a genre, Hamlet decides not to kill the king but to test his guilt with a performance of "The Mousetrap" (3.2), a play that rehearses a murder much like the one Claudius has committed. Claudius' reaction confirms his guilt, and Hamlet, presented with an ideal opportunity to kill Claudius while he is praying ("Now might I do it," 3.3.73), still does not take action. On this occasion, the most telling hesitation in the play, he rationalizes his procrastination with the idea that unlike his father, who died "With all my imperfections on my head" (1.5.79), a praying Claudius might avert perdition: "in the purging of his soul, / When he is fit and season'd for his passage" (3.3.85–6).

The play is thus replete with eventful delay, which allows Claudius to survive until the denouement when he conspires with Laertes to have Hamlet murdered with a poisoned foil in a fencing contest. Hamlet is wounded; Gertrude drinks from a poisoned chalice. In the midst of the swordplay, the rapiers are switched and Laertes, too, becomes victim to the poison. As the venom takes its time to work, Laertes then reveals Claudius's plot to Hamlet, causing him at last to kill Claudius, to forgive Laertes, and to enjoin Horatio to live on "to tell my story" (5.2.303). Indeed, the story Hamlet bequeaths seems more important than the fact that Hamlet has at last taken his revenge.

While the plot of *Hamlet* has rightly been the object of intense fascination since it was first written, so has the play's language. It is important to consider the play if not as Shakespeare's "*best* piece of poetry," (since such comparisons between Shakespeare's masterpieces probably are invidious) then at least *as* poetry. There is a rich eloquence to the language – even in the prose. When Hamlet, unaware of Ophelia's death, asks whose grave is being dug, the clown replies with a quibble on death as the obliteration of identity – here specifically gender identity:

HAMLET:   Who is to be buried in't?
GRAVEDIGGER:   One that was a woman, sir; but, rest her soul, she's dead.
   (5.1.126–7)

The alacrity of the gravedigger's wit seems to heighten the early modern distinction between "the quick" (the living) and the dead. Even in these two short prose lines, then, Shakespeare is able to recast the riddle of mortality and its separation of soul from body.

Far from having been a prosaic demise, however, Ophelia's death, described by Gertrude, is arguably the most lyrical in literature:

> There is a willow grows askant a brook,
> That shows his hoary leaves in the glassy stream.
> Therewith fantastic garlands did she make
> Of crowflowers, nettles, daisies and long purples,
> That liberal shepherds give a grosser name
> But our cold maids do dead men's fingers call them;
> There on the pendent boughs her coronet weeds
> Clambering to hang, an envious sliver broke,
> When down her weedy trophies and herself
> Fell in the weeping brook. Her clothes spread wide
> And mermaid-like awhile they bore her up . . .
> Till that her garments, heavy with their drink,
> Pulled the poor wretch from her melodious lay
> To muddy death. (4.7.164–81)

Even here in the pastoral lyricism of this description, additional corpses of the deceased appear in the form of "cold maids" (chaste girls who avoid vulgar language, but also dead ones), "dead men's fingers" (the popular name of the flowers) and, by implication, dead men's genitals. The maids and the "liberal" shepherds are both described in terms of their speech (respectively restrained and lewd) and their sexuality (variously frigid and lascivious, pure or sexually energetic). Like figures from the *danse macabre* that illustrated prayer books published by John Day in 1590, even in the midst of their youth and fertility, death is hovering over these young people who, when they had occasion to name the flowers, seem almost to have been enjoying summer blossoms in some idyllic rural landscape. Meanwhile, Ophelia, the corpse herself, has metamorphosed into a mermaid before sinking into to the earth of the streambed.

The all-too common decimation of populations as a result of plague and other epidemics, did not, of course, mean that people in the late sixteenth and early seventeenth centuries were spared the accidental deaths that Gertrude seems to imply or the profound despair whose culmination was suicide. In December 1579, when Shakespeare was a youth of fifteen and only months after the death of his eight-year old sister, Anne, a young woman called Katherine Hamlett was drowned in the river Avon at Tiddington, a mile away from Stratford, while attempting to fill her pail with water. Like Ophelia, "Her death was doubtful" (5.1.216), that is, it might have been suicide. The drowning, so reminiscent of Ophelia's "muddy death" (4.3.181), was judged accidental (she was thought to have slipped) rather than *felo de se*, the legal term used to denote "self-slaughter" (1.2.132). That there is but one consonant difference between the name of this real-life Ophelia, Katherine Hamlett, and the name of the prince of Denmark compels our attention once again to the intersection between real life, or more accurately, real deaths, and Shakespeare's dramatic reworking of them.

As the most canonical of Shakespeare's works, we might well expect *Hamlet* to have a certain textual solidity – a clear sense of what constituted Shakespeare's final and finished version of the play, but nothing could be further from the truth. *Hamlet* is a textual minefield. The first printing of the play, the First Quarto (Q1) of 1603 is so different form the other surviving versions, so inferior in its versification and so much shorter, that it is often referred to as "the bad Quarto." The suspicion is that Q1 is an unreliable version of the play put together by someone other than Shakespeare, possibly one or more actors who had the play transcribed from their imperfect memory of the performance. The most famous example of the qualitative difference between the lines we associate with *Hamlet* and their rendition in Q1 is that "To be or not to be – ; that is the question" (3.1.55) becomes, "To be or not to be, ay there's the point." However, Q1 has had its defenders especially since it has proved to be surprisingly moving and effective in performance. There have been numerous theories about the status of Q1, and some speculation about whether it is simply Shakespeare's earliest version of the play. However, as John Jowett points out, "If Q1 *Hamlet* is an early draft, it represents a strange and otherwise unknown aspect of Shakespeare's writing."[18] In 1604, Q2, another version of the play, appeared with the claim that it was printed "according the true and perfect Coppie." This text does indeed seem to have been prepared from Shakespeare's own manuscript or "foul papers," and it was reprinted in 1611 (Q3). In the First Folio of 1623 a third version of the play was printed that is substantially different from all the previous ones. To confuse matters even further, there appears to have been, as we noted earlier, an anonymous play called *Hamlet* (usually referred to as the Ur-*Hamlet*), possibly written by Thomas Kyd, that predates all of these other versions. Scholarly debate on this textual conundrum is complex and contentious.[19] This situation does, however, compel us to consider that our own ideas about textual authority and the fixity of a text once it has been printed may well be quite different from those of Shakespeare and his contemporaries.

Of course, the plot of *Hamlet* did not originate with Shakespeare or with the earlier play, the Ur-*Hamlet*, but with Saxo Grammaticus's *Historiae Danicae*, which dates from the twelfth century although it was not printed until 1514. Shakespeare no doubt derived the story from François de Belleforest's *Histoires Tragiques* (1570).[20] The story of Shakespeare's play, convoluted as it is, offers evidence of a milieu where ideas, stories, texts, and stage-plays circulated in ways that it is now almost impossible to reconstruct. Shakespeare did not, then, compose *Hamlet* in isolation, but rather in dialog with his culture.

## *Othello*

According to her epitaph in Holy Trinity Church in Stratford-Upon-Avon, Susanna Shakespeare was a pious and virtuous woman: "Wise to salvation was good Mistris Hall." As we noted in Chapter 2, she was a person of lively intelligence, "Witty above her sex," but she is also described as practicing, in ready and down-to-earth fashion, the exemplary Christian quality of mercy. In life, she had shown ready empathy toward the grieving and offered them kind consolation:

> Then, Passenger, has ne're a tear,
> To weep with her that wept with all;
> That wept, yet set her self to cheer
> Them up with comforts cordiall.
> Her love shall live, her mercy spread,
> When thou hast ne're a tear to shed.

Susanna had made a good marriage to the physician John Hall in 1607, and since Shakespeare designated the couple as executors to his will and made Susanna the principal heir to his property, it must have been a match that very much pleased her father. Judging by the inscription on John's gravestone describing Susanna as "fidissima conjux" (faithful wife), she and her husband seem to have been a happy couple. Yet, in 1613 this scene of conjugal felicity was briefly shattered by the slanderous accusation that Susanna had rampant venereal disease and had committed adultery with a thirty-five-year-old man called Rafe Smith, the son of a vintner who was employed in Stratford as a hatter and haberdasher. Smith had strong connections with the Shakespeares as he was the nephew of Hamnet and Judith Shakespeare's godfather, Hamnet Sadler. Susanna responded to these accusations on July 15, 1613 when she brought a defamation suit against her detractor, John Lane, to the consistory court at Worcester Cathedral: "About 5 weekes past the defendant reported that the plaintiff had the runinge of the raynes [gonorrhea] & had bin naught with Rafe Smith."[1] To have been "naught" with someone was a euphemism for sexual intercourse, but Lane had a record of drunken and disorderly behavior, and Susanna won her suit.

This incident postdates *Othello* (first performed sometime between 1600 and 1604)[2] by almost a decade, but it is an interesting juxtaposition nonetheless because that play is similarly about a daughter's marriage and a slandered wife. Othello, whose past military prowess has made him a general, has eloped with the much younger Desdemona, the beautiful daughter of a Venetian citizen, Brabantio. Despite having regularly invited Othello to his home, Brabantio is horrified when Iago and Roderigo rudely awaken him in the middle of the night with news of the marriage. As part of his malevolent design, Iago manipulates the gullible Roderigo, falsely promising him sexual access to Desdemona in return for cash. Further, jealous at the fact that Othello has made Cassio his lieutenant instead of himself and knowing Cassio's unusual susceptibility to alcohol, Iago gets him drunk in the garrison at Cyprus and starts the brawl that leads to his demotion. Iago then cunningly suggests that Cassio appeal to Desdemona to intercede for his reinstatement with Othello, which Iago then uses as evidence that she is Cassio's lover. Cassio himself is beloved of a prostitute, a woman ironically named Bianca (white), and Iago uses Cassio's contempt for Bianca's infatuation with him as part of the web of deception that ensnares Othello into the conviction that his beloved and virtuous wife is unfaithful. Iago stages a conversation for Othello to overhear so that Cassio's derisory jests about Bianca are understood by Othello to refer to Desdemona. Iago's wife, Emilia, who is also Desdemona's servant, steals her mistress's handkerchief at his insistent behest. Iago plants it in Cassio's chamber and then presents Cassio's possession of it as irrefutable evidence of Desdemona's sexual betrayal. Iago, who has tried to arrange for Roderigo to murder Cassio, kills Roderigo while appearing to assist him. Cassio escapes with only a leg-wound, which occasions a moving demonstration of Bianca's love for him despite Iago's attempt to blame her for the injury. Othello strikes his wife, heedless to her pleas of innocence publically defames her as a whore, and ultimately smothers her in their bed. Emilia, horrified by Iago's perfidy, reveals it to Othello, Cassio, and the Venetians Lodovico, Gratiano (Brabantio's brother), and Montano, the Governor of Cyprus, and upon doing so is vilified by Iago as a "whore" and "filth" before being murdered. Othello kills himself, falling on the bed on which the dead Desdemona also lies in a final poignant emblem of consummation: "I kissed thee ere I killed thee: no way but this, / Killing myself, to die upon a kiss" (5.2.356–7). Iago is taken to prison to be tortured to death while Cassio is left to defend Venetian interests in Cyprus.

We need not rely on the dates alone to know that it is not an incredible coincidence that connects Susanna Hall's case and the plot of *Othello*. Cases like Susanna's were not, of course, unique to Shakespeare's family, and indeed their incidence increased in the litigious climate of late sixteenth- and early seventeenth-century England. What they demonstrate is that even the good marriage of a virtuous woman might not be enough to protect her reputation. In addition, the merciful, sympathetic nature that she shares with Mistress

Hall (she agrees to intercede on behalf of the demoted lieutenant Cassio) makes "the gentle Desdemona" (1.2.25)[3] especially vulnerable to slander. What Desdemona does not share with Shakespeare's daughter, however, is society's approval of her marriage: according to the popular social mores of both the play's Venice and early modern England, she has not made a good match but, in marrying a Moor, has made one so terrible that it kills her father despite its being ratified by the Venetian Senate: "Thy match was mortal to him" (5.2.203).

Shakespeare's imagination took his audience very far away from England in this tragedy to exotic landscapes ("antres vast and deserts idle, / Rough quarries, rocks and hills whose heads touch heaven" (1.3.141–2)) populated by extraordinary inhabitants ("the cannibals . . . The Anthropophagi, and men whose heads / Do grow beneath their shoulders" (1.3.144–6)), and to great adventures ("feats of broil and battle" (1.3.88); "moving accidents by flood and field"; or "hair-breadth scapes i'th' imminent deadly breach" (1.3.136–7)). These are the stories Brabantio has in the past elicited from Othello: "He bade me tell it" (1.3.134). The canvas whereon the play's tragic events unfold is magnificent and momentous: the great conflict between West and East, between European Christianity and Islam, but Shakespeare brings that conflict home in *Othello*, which is a household drama about the tragic course of the relationships comprised therein. In this, the play conforms to the subgenre of domestic tragedy. For more than anything, *Othello* is a tragedy of marriage.

Making an appropriate match was a very serious business in early modern England. Conduct books of the period continually urge marrying someone of similar "Age, Estate, Condition [and] Pietie,"[4] that is, someone as like oneself as possible in terms of social status and religious beliefs, as well as someone at a comparable stage of life. Desdemona, however, marries someone completely different, an older black man whose life experience as a soldier could not be more different from her own sheltered experience in Venice. Yet their incongruity is precisely what generates the erotic intensity of the relationship between Othello and Desdemona. When Brabantio arrives to appeal to the senate, charging that Othello has stolen and bewitched his daughter, Desdemona's frank and heart-felt confession of specifically sexual love for her husband shocks her father. He believed that it was impossible for his daughter, who had turned down "the wealthy, curled darlings of our nation" (1.2.68), to love what he assumes "she feared to look on" (1.3.99). Her testimony further contradicts him when she asks the senate to allow her accompany Othello on his mission against the Turks in Cyprus so that she can enjoy "the rites for which I love him" (1.3.258).

In eloping with Othello, in the eyes of many early moderns Desdemona would have violated the fifth commandment: "Honor thy father and thy

Mother." For some, like the Puritan leaning John Stockwood, the case was clear; his treatise, *A Bartholemew Fairing for Parents* (1589) states in its subtitle that *Children are not to marry, without the consent of their parentes*.[5] One of Stockwood's central concerns was that children observe their parents' choice in relation to the religion of a future spouse. While Catholicism was officially proscribed and Puritanism was simply a tendency within Protestantism rather than a completely separate religion, such differences remained obstacles to harmonious unions. This is one form of transgression – the crossing of sectarian boundaries – that Desdemona does not, on the face of it, commit in marrying Othello, who as a servant of the Venetian state is a convert to Christianity. Rather, Desdemona contravenes implicit assumptions about the sexual segregation of Africans and Europeans. Although there had been a black presence in England since Roman times, when an African regiment was posted at Hadrian's Wall, and although there was a tiny, if conspicuous minority of Africans in Shakespeare's London, unlike Brabantio, the English did not have to worry about their daughters running away with "blackamoors." Yet when Stockwood made his argument for religious homogeneity in marriage, and especially in marrying in alignment with the religious predilections of fathers, he used the biblical prohibition against marrying pagans by way of evidence:

> As for . . . not granting unto the father's choice in the cause of contrary religion, it is confirmed flatly by the counsel of the Apostle, where he willeth that we should not draw the yoke [marry] with infidels, which if it hold in other cases of the affairs of this life, much more ought it to be of force in marriage matters, marriage (I mean) hereafter to be made and not such as are already made, for where the knot is once already knit, there disparity, or unequalness in religion is no just cause of separation . . . [6]

For Stockwood, unlike Brabantio, whose plea to the senate is an attempt to annul the marriage, once the "knot" of matrimony is tied even "disparity, or unequalness" in matters of religion cannot be used as justification for untying it. That is, the marital bond, once entered into, is indissoluble. However, the case that Stockwood argues from is not the marriage between people who profess different brands of Christianity but, following St Paul ("the Apostle"), between Christians and those who do not profess any form of Judeo-Christian belief at all – "infidels": "Be ye not unequally yoked together with unbelievers: for what fellowship hath righteousness with unrighteousness? And what communion hath light with darkness? And what concord hath Christ with Belial [the devil]? Or what part hath he that believeth with an infidel? . . . Wherefore come out from among them, and be ye separate, says the Lord" (2 Corinthians 6.14–17).

"Yoke-fellow" was a common early modern term for spouse, and it referred to the pairing of draught animals whose necks were put through a wooden frame so that they could join their strength in pulling the plow, where incongruous coupling would prove an impediment to efficient tillage. In *Othello*, Shakespeare poses precisely St Paul's question about these yoke-fellows: "And what communion hath light with darkness?" The play answers by showing that in terms of racial difference within this particular marriage, the conjoining of light and dark could be that of complementary opposites rather than the irreconcilable antithesis of good ("Christ") and evil ("Belial"). This is not, however, Brabantio's interpretation. While Othello and Desdemona's marriage is ratified by the state, Brabantio predicts that it bodes the downfall of order and civility: "If such actions may have passage free / Bond-slaves and pagans shall our statesmen be" (1.2.98–9). Othello is not, of course, currently a slave, but Shakespeare's largely Protestant audience is reminded that he has been one and is referred back to the time before his conversion, when he was indeed a pagan. Now, however, Othello is charged by the Venetian Senate to defend Cyprus against the encroaching infidel forces of the Turkish fleet, an assault that, in historical fact, began in 1569. This transgressive marriage and the political insecurities it brings to the surface become the convenient peg on which the ensign, Iago, can hang his elaborate scheme for revenge upon Othello for promoting the Florentine Michael Cassio.

Once the action shifts from Venice to Cyprus, the play focuses entirely on Iago's destruction of the marriage. Since Desdemona is innocent of all wrongdoing, Iago cannot demonstrate that she has committed adultery with Cassio, but he can slanderously manipulate appearances. The "ocular proof" Othello demands of his wife's infidelity is provided in the form of the handkerchief Iago, "her first remembrance from the Moor" (3.3.295). Writing at the end of the seventeenth century, Thomas Rymer, in *A Short View of Tragedy* (1693), felt that *Othello* was a trivial play about laundry that should have been titled, "The Tragedy of the Handkerchief": "This may be a warning to all good Wives, that they look well to their Linnen."[7] Too much in the play, he argued, hinges on the theft of Desdemona's handkerchief: "Had it been *Desdemona's* Garter, the Sagacious Moor might have smelt a Rat: but the Handkerchief is so remote a trifle, no Booby on this side [of] *Mauritania*, cou'd make any consequence from it . . . Yet we find, it entered into our Poets' head, to make a Tragedy of this *Trifle*."[8] Rymer is certainly correct in observing that Shakespeare did not choose an object of proof that had specifically erotic connections. Yet, the handkerchief serves in the play both as the bridge and between the magically exotic ("there's magic in the web of it" (3.4.71)) and, not to put too fine a point on it, the laundry – the mundanely domestic. The "lost" handkerchief, taken by Emilia at her husband's persistent instigation, becomes the play's symbolic core, the repository of mythic symbolism. Further, far from being "so remote," as Rymer charges, the handkerchief is profoundly intimate. Already precious in that it was Othello's first gift to Desdemona, something "she reserves . . . evermore about her / To kiss and talk to" (3.3.299–300), in his suspicion, Othello embellishes it, so that it becomes a talisman of terrifying potency:

> 'Tis true, there's magic in the web of it.
> A sibyl that had numbered in the world
> The sun to course two hundred compasses,
> In her prophetic fury sewed the work;
> The worms were hallowed that did breed the silk,
> And it was dyed in mummy, which the skilful
> Conserved of maidens' hearts. (3.4.71–7)

Whether this mesmerizing tale of fantastic and gruesome origins is a true history or merely an attempt to terrify Desdemona is arguably beside the point. For Othello has from the very beginning been the exotic storyteller of his own hero's journey, "my travailous history" (1.3.140), "even from my boyish days" (1.3.133) to "being taken by the insolent foe / And sold to slavery" (1.3.138–9). Now, in relation to the handkerchief, he becomes a mythmaker, the fabricator of narrative, and in myth there are often competing stories of origin. Thus in Act 5, Scene 2, the handkerchief is "an antique token / My father gave my mother" (5.2.214–15), while earlier, in Act 3, Scene 4, the handkerchief was given to his mother as a talisman to "subdue" his father (3.4.61). Yet it is in the very act of "subduing" Othello – in this instance, tending to his afflictions – to a headache induced by the cuckold's horns he believes he is wearing – that Desdemona loses the handkerchief. Rebuffing his wife's attempt to bind his head with it, Othello thrusts the handkerchief away: "Your napkin is too little" (3.3.291).

The "domestic" is represented above all in the play by the world of women, the world of handkerchiefs and linens that links the virtuous Desdemona with the sexually incontinent Bianca. (It is not clear that she is actually a prostitute even though Cassio refers to himself as her "customer"). Bianca is also an embroiderer, and clearly an embroiderer of some considerable skill. Unaware that the object has been planted in his chamber by Iago as part of his plot to defame Desdemona, upon discovering the handkerchief Cassio charges Bianca to copy or "take out" the strawberry pattern on the handkerchief: "I like the work well: ere it be demanded, / As like enough it will, I'd have it copied. / Take it, and do't" (3.4.189–91). This skill in needlework is something Bianca (whose name, despite her unchastity, connotes purity) shares with Desdemona. Even in throes of jealousy Othello acknowledges Desdemona's facility with the feminine arts of needlework: "Hang her, I do but say what she is: so delicate with her needle" (4.1.184–5).

What Iago fully appreciates – and what Rymer does not – is the fact that in a marriage and in a household, "Trifles," that is, petty, and especially feminine, domestic matters loom large: "Trifles light as air / Are to the jealous confirmations strong / As proofs of holy writ" (3.3.325–7). Indeed, the world of linen becomes increasingly prominent as Iago's plot unfolds. Before the tragic catastrophe, Desdemona undresses, allowing the audience a glimpse of the world of women from within, a domestic interior, a scene of textiles, of sheets of garments unpinned and of nightwear, textiles that are the product of women's labor and quite literally the fabric of their world. It is not just Iago's machinations that have undone Othello but also his unfamiliarity with this world. Othello announces that he is not used to the "*soft* phrase of peace" (1.3.83, my emphasis) and that hitherto, as a warrior, he had been "unhoused" (1.2.26), used to the makeshift accommodations of military campaigns rather than the sensuous furnishing of Venetian domestic interiors:

> The tyrant custom, most grave senators,
> Hath made the flinty and steel couch of war
> My thrice-driven bed of down. (1.3.230–2)

He views feather beds ("thrice-driven" beds were the very softest available, having had their feathers sifted no fewer than three times), ordinary domestic luxuries, and by implication, the connubial intimacy they afford, with suspicion.[9] However, Othello's predicament is in many ways merely an exacerbated version of what is nonetheless a very familiar theme about the transformation of one's life upon entering the "estate of matrimony," the most momentous transition in the early modern life-cycle. In Shakespeare's unquestionably domestic *The Taming of the Shrew*, as we noted in Chapter 6, the newly married Petruchio sings a snatch of the popular song that voiced exactly this sentiment, "Where is the life that late I led?" (4.1.120), a refrain that echoes the bewilderment of the newly married man.

Crucially, the key stage properties of *Othello* are domestic objects specifically associated with consummation. The "napkin," or "handkerchief / Spotted with strawberries" (3.3.437–8), is emblematic of the post-coital wedding sheets that were traditionally used as evidence of the woman's virginity. Robert Burton's *Anatomy of Melancholy* (1621), which uses the words "napkin" and "sheet" interchangeably, points out that the "bloody napkin," the wedding undersheet, was preserved unlaundered by Greeks, Jews, and Africans. England's Queen

Catherine of Aragon, who was able to produce hers as evidence when Henry VIII sought to divorce her, also preserved it. When Desdemona requests that Emilia "Lay on my bed my wedding sheets; remember" (4.2.107), we, of course, do not know, in the interim between eloping with Othello and now, whether they have been laundered, or for that matter whether the marriage has been consummated at all. Back in Venice, Iago seemed in doubt of this when he asked Othello, "Are you fast married?" (1.2.11). This runs counter to his earlier taunts at Brabantio's window with a grotesque spectacle of consummation: "your daughter and the Moor are now making the beast with two backs"; "Even now, now, very now, an old black ram / Is tupping your white ewe!" (1.1.87–8). In Cyprus, too, when the couple are reunited, matters are not much clarified by Othello's ambiguous couplet: "The purchase made, the fruits are to ensue: / That profit's yet to come 'tween me and you" (2.3.9–10). The "purchase" is the marital bargain or agreement, but the fruits or the profit, could be either the enjoyment of sexual intimacy, or the birth of a child. If the marriage has indeed been consummated, Desdemona's subsequent request, "If I do die before thee, prithee shroud me / In one of these same sheets (4.3.22–3), perhaps argues for the fact that the wedding sheets are to serve as a reminder and as physical evidence of her virginity on their wedding night, and thus a sign of her subsequent marital chastity.

In marked contrast with Othello's perplexity in the face of domesticity and by extension women and sex, in Act 2, Scene 1 Iago boasts easy familiarity with the world of "huswifes" with a witty piece of misogyny that plays upon the connection between the housewife, the chaste, diligent household manager, and the "hussy":

> Come on, come on, you are pictures out of doors,
> Bells in your parlours, wild-cats in your kitchens,
> Saints in your injuries, devils being offended,
> Players in your housewifery, and housewives in . . .
> Your beds! (2.1.109–13)

Iago here purports to know what women really give their serious consideration to – not to their domestic duties but to their sexual pleasures, or, alternatively, they both neglect their household obligations and regard sex with their husbands as an unwelcome labor. Either way, Iago has left books of domestic conduct with their prim pronouncements about ideal, chaste behavior far behind.

In her petty pilfering, however, Emilia has, like a dutiful wife, obeyed Iago's command, but she has also violated the trust of her mistress. The early modern household, a more expansive unit than our own, was a hierarchy of a series of relationships ostensibly cemented by mutual fellow-feeling between the superiors and subordinates, whether in ties of marriage, blood, or simply employment. Crucially, however, these relationships were analogically related to those of the society as a whole, and thus rebellion and disorder in the household was widely understood, as it is in *Othello*, as not just analogous to civil unrest but as actively constitutive of it. Time and again, the play reiterates the language of proper hierarchy: "love," "service," and "duty." Othello himself insists both at the beginning and at the end of the play on his service to "my very noble and approved good masters" (1.3.78) in the senate. In the first instance, service is what protects his marriage from annulment despite Brabantio's complaints:

> Let him do his spite:
> My services, which I have done the signiory,
> Shall out-tongue his complaints. (1.2.17–19)

Othello's assessment of his credit with his masters proves to be completely correct and prefigures his claim in the tragic denouement that "I have done the state some service and they know't" (5.2.337). In the hierarchies of the early modern social order, the condition of the servant was one from which no one (not even the sovereign who was servant to God) was exempt. As William Gouge acknowledged in *Of Domesticall Duties* (1622), to be a servant in this broad sense was a universal condition and "applied to all such as by any outward civill bond, or right, owe their service to another."[10] However, those to whom the title "servant" applied in the rather less metaphorical way of labor exerted on behalf of another, accompanied by extensive gestures of deference, often shared Iago's disgruntlement about their "knee-crooking" (1.1.44) servility. As a subordinate, Iago bridles against the obligations of his employment as "the curse of service" (1.1.34) and disparages the man who faithfully discharges his duties as "much like his master's ass" (1.1.47). Instead, he adopts only the "forms and visages of duty" (1.1.49). In this, as Frances E. Dolan has shown, *Othello* is simply a variant on the plot of domestic tragedies such as the anonymous *Arden of Faversham* (1592), where a trusted manservant, like "honest Iago," conspires with others, including the master's wife, to murder him. In domestic drama, evil is close to home and perpetrated by "dangerous familiars" rather than by some readily suspect conspicuous "other."[11]

  In this, the slander-mongering Iago conforms to the stage-type of the Machiavel, the evil manipulator, which was the predominant English reading of Niccolò Machiavelli's *The Prince*, a handbook for rulers urging policy and pragmatism rather than virtue or ethical considerations to those who held the reins of power. But Iago's motivations exceed political aspiration. Not only is he jealous of Cassio's preferment, Iago also voices a suspicion, which

Shakespeare takes up from his source, the Italian novella by Giraldi Cinthio, *Gli Hecatommithi*, that there is a rumor, probably based on the cultural stereotype of the lascivious Moor, that Othello has slept with Emilia: "It is thought abroad that 'twixt my sheets / He's done my office. I know not if't be true, / But I for mere suspicion in that kind / Will do as if for surety" (1.3.386–9). At other times, Iago's evil is instigated by more abstract considerations: "He hath a daily beauty in his life" (5.1.19). These are rationalizations that generations of readers have felt do not quite add up to a motive as such. For the Romantic poet Samuel Taylor Coleridge, therefore, Iago was characterized by "motive-less malignity."[12] Only in the late twentieth century has Iago's motivation been seen as inescapably racist. Hitherto, the play's racial dimension was more easily marginalized because in the eighteenth and nineteenth centuries it was believed that Othello was not really black at all, or in Coleridge's infamous phrase, not "a veritable negro," but rather a North African Arab.[13]

The play's contest between good and evil is also figured in terms of the homegrown dramatic genre of the morality dramas. In the medieval tradition of the psychomachia, good and evil angels fought to win the Christian's soul. In *Othello*, these figures have their parallels in "that demi-devil" (5.2.298) Iago, "the blacker devil" (5.2.129) Othello, and the "the more angel she" (5.2.128) Desdemona. What complicates the scenario in *Othello* is that the real devil is a white man, whereas in the indigenous dramatic tradition, the devil was conventionally represented in blackface. Shakespeare further contorts the morality drama scenario by means of the culturally pervasive misogynist premise that women's beauty is a deceptive illusion designed to ensnare hapless men. This is the misogynist twist on the idea also to be found in *Hamlet* and which is proven true in the case of Iago, that "the devil hath power / T'assume a pleasing shape" (*Hamlet* 2.2.534–5).[14] Brabantio also articulates the idea that women are inherently deceptive when he discovers his daughter's clandestine marriage, and his admonition to Othello arguably plants the first seed of suspicion about his bride: "She hath deceived her father, and may thee" (1.3.294).

Shakespeare's Sonnet 144, a version of which was first published in a volume entitled *The Passionate Pilgrim* (1599) and in a revised version in 1609, also rehearses the triangulated contest of the morality plays: "Two loves I have, of comfort and despair" (*l.* 1).[15] However in this lyrical configuration, the angels and the poet constitute a love triangle, consisting of the poet, "a man right fair" (*l.* 3) who is "my better angel" (*l.* 6), and "a devil" (*l.* 7) who is "a woman coloured ill" (*l.* 4). This same language is echoed towards the end of *Othello* when Gratiano, Desdemona's uncle, seeing her dead body, avers that it is as well her father is dead:

> Did he live now
> This sight would make him do a desperate turn,
> Yea, curse his better angel from his side
> And fall to reprobance. (5.2.204–7)

These few lines recapitulate the drama of the human soul confronted with the choice between good and evil, and the end here is the ultimate tragedy in Christian theology of being cast utterly away from God. Here, as in the medieval morality dramas, the predicament is paradigmatic of the soul poised between salvation and damnation. This scenario is not, of course, an erotic one in the indigenous dramatic tradition, whereas in Shakespeare's sonnet it is profoundly sexualized. Despite this innovation, the poem still maintains the conventional associations of the devil with blackness and the angel with light, precisely the color-coding problematized in *Othello*.

In *Othello*, too, the central themes of the morality tradition are used to insist on the contiguity between the domestic and the exotic when they are transposed onto the military conflict between Western Christianity and the Ottoman Empire, the early modern world's greatest power. Shakespeare's contemporaries understood this conflict as nothing less than the battle for the soul of the world. As a convert, Othello straddles both the religion he was born into and the faith he has adopted, describing himself at the end of the play as a "circumcised dog" (5.2.353) and thus referring to the indelible trace of his former pagan identity. In this the play presents a model of religious difference that is at once ostensibly far removed from the internecine struggles in which English Christianity had been embroiled and yet at the same time disturbingly analogous to it. Not only, then, does Shakespeare very self-consciously displace an indigenous stage tradition onto a foreign context, but he also uses the lost handkerchief to reprise the central trope of the morality play, namely the ever-present threat of eternal damnation: "To lose't or give't away were such *perdition* / As nothing else could match" (3.4. 68–9, my emphasis). "Perdition" further connects the handkerchief with the global context of "the mere perdition of the Turkish fleet" (2.2.3) and with Othello's own tragic fall: "Perdition catch my soul / But I do love thee!" (3.3.90–1).

One of Shakespeare's most staged and popular plays, *Othello* was first published in quarto format in 1622, and printed again a year later, with significant textual differences, in the First Folio. *Othello*'s African protagonist was not the first black character on the early modern stage. Villainous Moors had featured in George Peele's *The Battle of Alcazar* (1588–9) and the authorially suspect *Lust's Dominion* (1598–9). Shakespeare had himself drawn on this tradition in his portrayal of the wicked Aaron the Moor in his early tragedy *Titus Andronicus*. Yet, even there, Shakespeare had begun to humanize the stage stereotype by having Aaron demonstrate touching paternal care for his illegitimate son. In contrast to Aaron, however, Othello's humanity is fully developed. Although when he at last falls from grace he could be argued to have reverted to the barbarism stereotypically attributed to black characters ("I will chop her into messes!" (4.1.197)), at no point in the play is he the villainous author of the evil that befalls him. We do not know if Shakespeare's amplification of Othello's character, despite the limitations of representing a black man via blackface, was the result of actual encounters with the small number of Africans in early modern London.[16] Certainly, Shakespeare's knowledge of far-flung places entirely depended upon an impressive range of reading, which included Sir Lewis Lewkenor's translation of Cardinal Contarini's *The Commonwealth and Government of Venice* (1599); Richard Knolles' *General History of the Turks* (1603); King James's *Lepanto* (first published in 1591); Pliny's *Natural History* (Shakespeare may have read Philemon Holland's 1601 translation); the *Travels of Sir John Mandeville* (republished in 1582); Sir Walter Raleigh's *Discoverie of Guiana* (1596); and Leo Africanus's *Geographical Historie of Africa* (1600). In *Othello* Shakespeare catered to the tastes of an audience increasingly interested in a world beyond England's shores and yet succeeded in making that decidedly un-English world recognizable by means of the play's thoroughly domestic themes.

Indeed, the play's tragic power derives precisely from the heady admixture of the ordinary and the exotic, the domestic and the foreign. What distracts from the intrinsically domestic nature of the play is that while perfidious subordinates, slandered wives, and lost linens were familiar and even mundane aspects of early modern life in England, black heads of household were not. Shakespeare uses the audience's appetite for the foreign and the exotic – their fear and revulsion as well as their attraction to racial and geographical difference – to explore, via the tropes of indigenous theatre, the major institutions of English domestic life.

## King Lear

*Hamlet*, as we have seen, is *almost* named after Shakespeare's deceased son. In *King Lear*, Shakespeare gave one of his greatest villains the name of his own much younger brother, Edmund, who was born in 1580 and who followed his illustrious older sibling into the theatre. Edmund had an illegitimate, but apparently acknowledged, son who, judging by the parish clerk of St Saviour's in Southwark's mistranscription of "Edmund" as "Edward," probably shared his father's Christian name.[1] The boy died on August 12, 1607: "Edward, son of

Edward Shackspeere, Player: base-born." We do not know how old Shake-speare's illegitimate nephew was, only that his father's death was recorded in the following in December: "Edmond Shakespeare, a player." By coincidence this was only a month after *Lear* (probably composed in 1604–5) was entered in the Stationers' Register on November 26, 1607 under the title *A Booke Called Mr William Shakespeare His Historye of Kinge Lear as yt was Played before the Kings Majestie at Whitehall upon St Stephans Night at Christmas Last by his Majesties Servants Playing Usually at the Globe on Banksyde.*

*King Lear* is alone among Shakespeare's tragedies in having a subplot. Derived from Sir Philip Sidney's *Arcadia* (1590), Shakespeare carefully wove in the story of two rival half-brothers – here called Leonatus and Plexirtus – with the tale of Lear and his daughters. Importantly, the play opens with that plotline. Shakespeare's brothers are the sons of Lear's great ally, the Duke of Gloucester. The elder is the legitimate Edgar, who is also Lear's godson: "My father's godson . . . / He whom my father named, your Edgar" (2.1.91–2).[2] The younger, Edmund, is Gloucester's energetically malevolent, illegitimate progeny. A patriarch with a checkered sexual history, Gloucester's downfall parallels that of Lear when he foolishly takes the part of his evil, illegitimate son against his virtuous, legitimate one. The audience, however, witnesses at the play's opening Gloucester jesting – in Edmund's hearing – about how "the whoreson" came into the world via some possibly adulterous, but certainly illicit, "sport" (1.1.22). Since Edgar is "some year elder" (1.1.18–19), Gloucester was either widowed at the time of what he euphemistically refers to as Edmund's "making" (1.1.22) or still married to the mother of his legitimate son and heir. For Gloucester, Edmund is a source of shame – "I have so often blushed to acknowledge him" (1.1.9) – so that when Edmund delivers his soliloquy on the injustices done to illegitimate offspring at the start of Scene 2, the traditional intimacy between the scheming Machiavel (the character everyone loves to hate) and the audience is colored by an unusual degree of sympathy.

The opening vignette about half-brothers, one begotten "by order of law" and one who "came something saucily to the world" (1.1.18–20), is key in some of the central themes of this tragedy, namely fathers, sibling rivalry, and the nature of authority, the "order of law." *Lear* is a play about two trou-bled, motherless families.[3] Kent's puzzled response to Gloucester's ambiguous acknowledgement of his paternity of Edmund, "I cannot conceive you" (1.1.11), provokes the only vividly realized maternal presence in this motherless play:

> Sir, this young fellow's mother could;
> whereupon she grew round-wombed, and had, indeed,
> sir, a son for a cradle ere she had a husband for her
> bed. Do you smell a fault? (1.1.12–15)

As the nameless mother of this "whoreson," is, by definition, a whore, her generative powers are trivialized, seen as disposable. Furthermore, "whore" was a word that might be applied not just to prostitutes but also to any woman believed to have had sexual contact outside the bonds of matrimony, or for that matter, to any woman at all.[4] Toward the end of the play, when Edmund's wickedness has become fully apparent and his father has been hideously blinded, Edgar tells his illegitimate brother that there is, nonetheless, a kind of cosmic justice operating even in this atrocious act:

> The gods are just and of our pleasant vices
> Make instruments to plague us.
> The dark and vicious place where thee he got
> Cost him his eyes. (5.3.168–71)

The "pleasant vice" in this case is the ostensibly harmless act of copulation with Edmund's mother. The "dark and vicious place," the sinister site of Edmund's conception, is his mother's womb and perhaps also a bawdy house or brothel where Gloucester may have sought sexual pleasure. This association between male sexual license as that which renders men vulnerable to contamination by feminine generativity is further enforced when a deranged Lear meets with the blinded Gloucester, whom he identifies via the image of blind Cupid that was used on brothel signs: "Do thy worst, blind Cupid, I'll not love" (4.6.134).

A play about the tragedy of generational conflict and filial antagonism set in a world almost out of time, the world of pre-Christian ancient Britain, *King Lear* offers an excoriating critique of patriarchy, even if one that shows powerful fathers to be some of its greatest victims: "They told me I was everything; 'tis a lie" (4.6.103–4).

In the main plot, a tragedy of fatherhood, an aging Lear has divided his kingdom among his three daughters and in return demands to know how much they love him. The wicked Goneril and Regan offer the expected flattering response. When Cordelia, Lear's youngest, favorite, and unmarried daughter, is asked what she can say to outdo her sister's fulsome declarations of filial adoration, she refuses the challenge, and her response to her father's imperious request is simply, "Nothing, my lord" (1.1.87). She subsequently protests: "Why have my sisters husbands, if they say / *They love you all?*" (1.1.99–100, my emphasis). In a tyrannical outburst, Lear casts Cordelia out of his heart and his kingdom, and as a further consequence, she is also rejected by one of her suitors, the Duke of Burgundy. Seeing her virtue despite her now dowerless condition, the king of France takes her as his bride. The Earl of Kent tries to defend Cordelia, but since he, too, only provokes Lear's ire, he disguises himself in order to stay to aid the sovereign who has banished him, while Goneril and Regan predictably go on to abuse their father.

Appearing in the play only after Cordelia has gone to France, Lear's fool alone has the license to speak truth to power. Lear finds himself driven mad and exposed on a heath during a storm, an experience that initially ignites his rage against the evils of women, but eventually lends him moral perspective on the plight of humankind. What most signals Lear's purification, his new understanding of how "the great image of authority" (4.6.154) tyrannizes the powerless, is his sympathy with prostitutes and the hypocrisy of those who punish them:

> Why dost thou lash that whore? Strip thine own back,
> Thou hotly lusts to use her in that kind
> For which thou whipp'st her. (4.6.157–9)

After he has achieved this extraordinarily humane level of insight, Cordelia arrives to rescue her father, but she is captured and hanged like a common criminal. The play's finale sees Lear embracing her corpse, holding up a mirror to her to see if she still breathes, in the futile hope of resuscitation.

The course of this plotline is also yet another Shakespearean meditation on the nature of authority and kingship. When Lear abdicates, the fool tells him, "thou mad'st thy daughters thy mothers; for when thou gav'st them the rod and putt'st down thine own breeches" (1.4.163–5). In *Richard II*, the king divided England into three parts so that he could become its landlord, and in his deposition scene takes a mirror to see if he can still discern sovereign qualities in his image. Richard's end is tragic, but while his moral frailty is the ruination of his dominion, his family relationships are not so devastated by his folly. Richard may "be o'erpow'r'd" (5.1.31) like Lear in the state, but unlike Lear, he is revered in his own household. His wife, Isabel, still loves him and wishes to "wash him fresh again with true-love tears" (5.1.10). Indeed it is Isabel, in words echoed by the fool in *Lear*, who warns him against submission: "Wilt thou, pupil-like, / Take the correction mildly, kiss the rod" (*Richard II* 5.1.31–2). Tellingly, it is the schoolmaster here, rather than the mother, who administers the punishment. Indeed, what allows *Lear* one of the most bleak and desolate outcomes in the history of tragedy is that the family and the state are so closely identified.

For Samuel Johnson, Shakespeare's eighteenth-century editor, the play's ending was "contrary to the natural ideas of justice,"[5] and indeed, for much of its theatrical history, the tragic outcome was shelved in favor of a happy ending. Shakespeare's tragic denouement is entirely unique to him and is shared by none of his sources. Indeed, the tragic catastrophe must have come as a surprise to Shakespeare's audience, who would have known either the folkloric origins of the main plot or its mytho-historical origins, including Holinshed's chronicle *History of England* (1577), in which King Lear is recorded as having reigned around 800 BC.[6] The main plot about three daughters who are commanded by their father to state how much they love him was part of folklore in which the wicked sisters profess lavish emotion for their father and the good daughter responds, rather cryptically, that she loves him as much as salt. The king and his daughter are happily reunited in folklore at the end of the story. This is similarly true of Geoffrey of Monmouth's twelfth-century *Historia Regum Britanniae* (The History of the Kings of Britain), where Lear dies of ripe old age and Cordelia becomes queen, even though there is a tragic addendum to that story: she is later imprisoned by rebellious nephews and commits suicide in prison. Other versions of this quasi-historical narrative appeared in a fictional verse complaint by John Higgins taking "Cordila's" point of view in the 1574 edition of *Mirror for Magistrates* and in William Warner's *Albion's England* (1586). In addition, there was a dramatic source for Shakespeare's text, a play performed at the Rose theatre in 1594 and printed in 1605 as *The True Chronicle History of King Leir and his three daughters, Gonerill, Ragan, and Cordella*. In this play, however, Leir's plan is to match Cordella with a man she does not desire.

The central problem of Shakespeare's play is not that, like Shakespeare himself, Lear has daughters and thus no son to whom he can bequeath the kingdom in its entirety, but that Lear's property is to be parceled up, not *after* he is dead, but *before* he deceases. In this, Shakespeare's plot may well have been influenced by another onomastic coincidence (in addition to that of the name "Edmund"), which seems to belong more to art than to life. A servant to Elizabeth I, Brian Annesley, made his will in 1600 bequeathing most of his wealth to his younger unmarried daughter, Cordell. Her married older sisters, Grace and Christian, challenged the will on grounds of their senile father's lunacy, but Cordell still prevailed. The similarity is conspicuous, but Shakespeare also had his own experience with aged parents: both having achieved their three score years and ten, his father had died in 1601 and his mother was buried in 1608, two years after Shakespeare wrote *Lear*. Goneril and Regan have already noticed Lear's decline: "You see how full of changes his age is. The observation we have made of it hath not been little" (1.1.290–1).

As the play progresses, the wicked sisters become as devoid of complexity as characters in a fairy story, yet at the beginning of the play, the audience is allowed some insight into their relationship with their father. There is a genuine poignancy about Goneril's assertion, the truth of which has already been amply demonstrated: "He always loved our sister most" (1.1.292). Goneril and

Regan's intimate knowledge of their erratic father is tellingly accurate: "He hath ever but slenderly known himself" (1.1.294–5); "The best and soundest of his time hath been but rash" (1.1.296–7). Thus, when Goneril complains that her father's riotous knights and squires are "men so disordered, so debauched," that they make her palace "like to a tavern or a brothel" (1.4.233–6), the audience is reminded of what Gloucester has revealed about his past at the very opening of the play. Like Goneril and Regan, Edmund, too, is a more sympathetic character at the start. He does what marginalized and countercultural groups do still; that is, he appropriates the derogatory labels applied to him – "natural" and "base-born" – and refashions them as a positive identity: "Now gods, stand up for bastards!" (1.2.22). He protests not only against the irrational "custom" and "curiosity of nations" that demean those conceived outside of wedlock, but also primogeniture itself, a condition that many perfectly legitimate younger sons in England had cause to lament: "I am some twelve or fourteen moonshines / Lag of a brother" (1.2.6).

Lear and Gloucester, then, may be indeed enfeebled and pitiable as a result of the cruelty inflicted upon them by their wicked offspring in the course of the play, but they begin as irascible, tyrannical parents whose response to any show of resistance to their power is met with a barrage of verbal violence. When Edmund deceives his father into believing that Edgar seeks to "manage the revenue" in his father's declining years, Gloucester's response is a tirade: "Abhorred villain! Unnatural, detested, brutish villain – worse than brutish!" (1.2.76–7). Lear's banishment of his "favorite" daughter includes even more terrifying invective:

> Or he that makes his generation messes
> To gorge his appetite, shall to my bosom
> Be as well neighboured, pitied and relieved,
> As thou my sometime daughter. (1.1.118–21)

Lear will befriend a child-eating cannibal sooner than Cordelia. Of course, ironically, Lear has become just like the thing he condemns, gorging his appetite for rage upon his own daughter. From this point on, good and evil diverge dramatically in the play, and evil intensifies. After Goneril and Regan disown him, Lear finally discovers them to be a more appropriate target for his ire than Cordelia. The tenor of his rage, however, is the same, although it is now amplified by vicious misogyny:

> Down from the waist they are
> centaurs, though women all above. But to the girdle do
> the gods inherit, beneath is all the fiend's: there's hell,

there's darkness, there is the sulphurous pit, burning,
scalding, stench, consumption! Fie, fie, fie! Pah, pah! (4.6.121–5)

Lear's language in respect of his two older daughters recapitulates the gynopho-
bic, misogynist subtext of all patriarchal order, acknowledging their humanity
as scarcely more than superficial. This was part of the everyday language of
Shakespeare's world, and although these words might be applied specifically to
prostitutes, whose associations with venereal burning, "the sulphurous pit," were
closest, they were also used in relation to all women since a fundamental premise
of misogyny is that all women are the same. The image of them here as half-
human, half-animal/demon reifies the polarized descriptions of Edmund's
mother as, on the one hand as beautiful, "yet was his mother fair" (1.1.21); and
on the other, "the dark and vicious place" of conception (5.3.170).[7]

Lear curses Regan's potential maternity when he begs the goddess Nature to
"convey sterility" to her womb. He refers to the fertility of "her derogate body"
as the capacity to "teem," a word not normally used in relation to human
reproduction, but typically part of the vocabulary of animal husbandry (1.4.270–
3). The cultural commonplaces Lear rehearses, such as the equation of the
vagina with hell's mouth, the sulphurous burning pit, were pervasive, and that
they come so readily to his tongue is perhaps indicative of some of his failings
as the father of daughters. However, this misogynist rhetoric was part of not
only the inheritance of classical and medieval misogyny, but also of the pan-
European debate about women known as the *querelle de femmes*, which, as we
noted in regard to *The Taming of the Shrew*, in England took the form of a
printed pamphlet war that began in the mid-sixteenth century. To take a notorious example, albeit one that post-dates the play, in 1615 Joseph Swetnam's *The
Araignment of Lewd, Idle, Froward, and Unconstant Women* opined, "betwixt
their [women's] breasts is the vale of destruction, & in their beds there is hell,
sorrow, and repentance."[8]

The apex of the play's violence, however, is not verbal but physical. It is when
Gloucester's eyes are plucked out on stage on Goneril's order. Gloucester is
tied down to a chair while Cornwall, husband to the evil Regan, mutilates him:
"Out, vile jelly" (3.7.82). The only voice raised in protest is that of a servant
who tries to stop the outrage. He is murdered by Regan, but his courage is
one of the only redeeming moments in the play:

> I have served you ever since I was a child,
> But better service I have never done you
> Than now to bid you hold. (3.7.72–4)

In terms of early modern hierarchy, the patriarch was in control not just of all
the women and children of his family but of *all* the members of his household.

In reminding his master that he "was a child," Cornwall's servant recapitulates Cordelia's resistance to Lear. Such disobedience is unequivocally demonstrated to be a virtue, as Lear himself becomes aware: "To say 'ay' and 'no' to everything that I said 'ay' and 'no' to was no good divinity [doctrine]" (4.6.98–100). Further, because of the pattern of analogical thinking that prevailed in Elizabethan England, resistance within the household had a political dimension as a species of specifically domestic treason.[9] We are shown over and again in the play that such treason *is* justified as a response to tyranny because all rulers, sovereign and domestic, are human, fallible, and vulnerable to frailty, old age, and the attenuation of rational capacity. Edgar, the son cast out and compelled to assume the disguise of Poor Tom, a Bedlam beggar, saves Gloucester from his intended suicide from Dover Cliff. As he leads his father by the hand, he is reminiscent of one of the most famous classical representations of filial compassion, namely that of Aneas who carries Anchises, his blind father, on his shoulders out of the burning city of Troy.

One of the most poignant images of the play, and the one which has been the source of the most debate, is that of Lear himself carrying the dead body of Cordelia: "*Enter Lear with Cordelia in his arms.*" (5.3.255). Critical discussion of the play has focused on whether this savagely bleak, arguably nihilistic ending, where "All's cheerless, dark, and deadly" (5.3.287), admits of anything redemptive. The play certainly opens up to a pagan or classical skepticism that would be impossible without its pagan setting, something akin to the sentiments of Marlowe's translation of Ovid's elegy on the death of the poet Tibullus: "When bad fates take good men, I am forbod / By secret thoughts to think there is a god" (3.8.35–6).[10] Indeed, at the end of the play, as the dead are borne offstage, the pair of rhymed couplets uttered by Edgar resorts to an audibly intensified artificiality that announces a conclusion to the play about lives already ended:

> The weight of this sad time we must obey,
> Speak what we feel, not what we ought to say.
> The oldest hath borne most; we that are young
> Shall never see so much, nor live so long. (5.3.322–5)

*King Lear* was performed at court in December 1605 and printed in 1608 as a quarto under the title, *The True Chronicle History of King Lear*. However, Shakespeare seems to have revised this play considerably, because in the First Folio of 1623 a version appeared under the title of *The Tragedy of King Lear* whose revisions and emendations from the badly printed First Quarto of 1608 are significant enough that some scholars have argued that these are not just different texts but essentially different plays.[11] Although there is considerable debate about whether the changes between the Quarto and the Folio are indeed Shakespeare's own, as Stephen Greenblatt points out, "there is a growing scholarly consensus that the 1608 text of *Lear* represents the play as Shakespeare first wrote it and that the 1623 text represents a substantial revision."[12] The two distinct yet authoritative versions remained in circulation throughout the seventeenth century, creating an editorial minefield for subsequent generations. From the eighteenth century until the publication of *The Oxford Complete Works* in 1986, editors opted to conflate the two texts. Most editions are a hybrid of the 1608 text and the subsequently revised play printed in the Folio. What is fascinating about this textual story is that Shakespeare clearly worked over ideas, perhaps responding to company pressure, to audience response, or simply to his own change of mind on the issues at hand. We see more clearly with this play than perhaps with any other that the play text, the script, even if already printed, was not understood by its author to be set in stone, but rather something more organic that could be reshaped according to changing circumstances or ideas. Life, in other words, had never quite finished with art.

## Macbeth

As Muriel Bradbrook long ago pointed out, unlike Ben Jonson, Shakespeare "was never asked to write a court masque, either by James or by anyone else."[1] Court masques were extravagant celebrations of aristocratic values, especially of the absolute power, wealth, and magnificence of the sovereign. Jonson's masque in celebration of Prince Charles's creation as Duke of York cost an astounding £2,100, but the court's investment in the masque was not merely financial. As Stephen Orgel notes, the masque "gave a higher meaning to the realities of politics and power, their fictions created heroic roles for the leaders of society."[2] While he also wrote for the commercial stage, by 1603, already the poet of elite court entertainments, Jonson had secured the powerful patronage of the king's cousin, Esmé Stuart, Seigneur d'Aubigny.

Shakespeare, in contrast, was definitively a poet of the public theatre, even when his plays were performed in court on royal command. Shakespeare's company had achieved new status as "the King's Servants" after James I's accession to the throne in 1603. They were now licensed "freely to use and exercise the art and faculty of Playing Comedies, Tragedies, Histories, Interludes, Morals, Pastorals, Stage Plays and such others like . . . to show and exercise publically to their best commodity."[3] There were, however, strictly circumscribed limits to the freedoms in "the art and faculty of playing," and when in that same year the company performed Ben Jonson's Roman tragedy *Sejanus*, with Shakespeare in its cast (probably in the role of the Emperor, Tiberius),

Jonson was summoned before the Privy Council on charges of popery and treason, and only intervention by the Lord Chamberlain spared him from punishment.[4] Thus Jonson's court connections did not give him carte blanche, but they did afford him at least some modicum of protection from the worst consequences of incurring the displeasure of the powerful. It is unlikely that Shakespeare, as much more of a court outsider than Jonson, would have been similarly shielded.

The very next year following the *Sejanus* debacle, the King's Servants were in trouble again, this time for performing a play depicting James I's alleged narrow escape from Alexander Ruthven, brother of the Earl of Gowrie, who it is generally agreed had tried to assassinate him in Scotland in 1600. The author of *The Tragedy of Gowrie* is unknown and the text lost to history. Although it was performed twice, the newsletter writer John Chamberlain reports that "some great Councillors are much displeased with it, and so [it] is thought [it] shall be forbidden."[5] Certainly, the play was never performed again. However, the council's concerns about depicting attempts to kill the king were not entirely misplaced. Only a year later, on November 5, 1605, the Gunpowder Plot, which would have blown up the Houses of Parliament at the very moment when James should have been giving his opening address, was narrowly averted.

*Macbeth*, a distinctly Jacobean play about regicide, then, seems an unlikely choice for Shakespeare and the King's Servants circa 1606 (although it was not printed until 1623 in the First Folio). Composed for a new ruler and a new regime, the play treats Macbeth's murder of the virtuous King Duncan urged on by his ambitious wife, Lady Macbeth. Taking Raphael Holinshed's *Chronicles* as his primary source, augmented by, among others, George Buchanan's *Rerum Scoticarum Historia* (1582), Shakespeare created an iniquitous, power-hungry character whose actions and motivations the audience nonetheless finds sympathetic. While the sense of royal audience does indeed shape the central themes and issues of the play, which treats Scottish rather than English history, and one of whose main characters, Banquo, is an ancestor of King James, *Macbeth* is anything but sycophantic. Shakespeare stages the very thing that James most feared – regicide at the instigation of witches, the "weird sisters," whose cryptic riddling prophecies about Macbeth as a future king encourage him to spill the "golden blood" of the reigning monarch. More than that, the play is an almost admonitory study in the excesses of power and the justice of rebellion in such instances. In *Macbeth* Shakespeare unflinchingly interrogates James's most cherished doctrine, the divine right of kings. The play probes even more deeply questions that interested Shakespeare from the very beginning of his career about who and what precisely constitutes, confers, and guarantees that right, and, more crucially, what threatens to undermine it. *Macbeth* betrays no aspirations to either the aesthetics or ideology of the masque.

As the son of the disgraced, executed Mary Queen of Scots, James VI of Scotland was named as Elizabeth's successor only on her deathbed. The question of who would inherit the English throne after Elizabeth had been one of the greatest unresolved problems for the majority of her forty-five-year reign. For, as Shakespeare showed repeatedly in his plays, the transmission of sovereign power was always its weakest link, and how that power was handed down would determine the degree to which, and the duration for which, it would be possible to hold and maintain it. For all that the succession crisis was decisively resolved upon James's accession, there remained a story to be told about what we might call his long genealogical path to sovereignty. How did a foreign, Scottish king come to sit upon the English throne? Although the play is set centuries before James's birth, Shakespeare engages this question of divine right – implicitly *to the English throne* as much as to the Scottish one – indirectly offering what we might think of as the Scottish pre-history of his anointing.

James himself was preoccupied with these matters. A scholar, learned though eccentric, he had written three treatises which bear direct relation to Shakespeare's play: the *Trew Law of Free Monarchies* (1598), *Basilikon Doron* (the first English edition was published in 1603), and *Daemonologie* (1597). The argument of *Trew Law* was that kings were, following the Old Testament model, anointed by God, and that God's providential plan required them to govern. *Basilikon Doron*, a study in the practical nature of kingship, was written for James's eldest son and heir, Prince Henry, a remarkable young prince who promised to be the ideal ruler, and, had he not died aged eighteen, certainly might have fared better than his younger brother, the future Charles I. *Daemonologie*, in contrast, rehearsed James's fears about the vulnerability of his sovereignty. Satan sought to overturn godly order, so the argument went, and thus witches – like the Scottish woman found with a wax doll representing James and stuck with pins – threatened God's established order, at the head of which was James himself. Indeed, women were the greatest enemies to James's reign, and he had himself examined the witches who had allegedly sought his death in Scotland. These included a woman who confessed under torture that she and two hundred others had each gone to sea in a sieve with the intent of bringing disaster to a royal vessel. James's own mother, popularly regarded as a witch by some English Protestants, had probably been his greatest impediment to ascending the English throne. He had been separated from her as an infant, but shortly after his arrival in England he commissioned Maximilian Colt to sculpt the effigy that he had installed in Westminster Abbey near to the tomb of Elizabeth I in the chapel built by their grandfather. In 1612, when the tomb was completed, his mother's remains, originally buried at Peterborough Cathedral after her execution, were reinterred.

In a telling refraction of these historical circumstances, the real flaw of Shakespeare's Macbeth as a leader is that he is under the government of women, the supernatural sisters and his own wife, Lady Macbeth. Macduff, the adversary who finally defeats Macbeth, is victorious because he demystifies the riddles of the feminine supernatural with masculine pragmatism. When Macbeth is surrounded at the end of the play and tries to take his last refuge in the fact that the witches have promised "none of woman born" (4.1.80)[6] can defeat him, Macduff retorts that he was the product not of natural birth but of a cesarian section. In some sense, the play can be seen to envisage a world in which the transmission of power in patriarchy can occur without resort to women at all – a motherless world, a system which can avoid using women as the "middlemen" in the system of patriarchal primogeniture. On the other hand, the play is remarkably insistent on the specifics of parturition and weaning – that is, the embodied physicality of motherhood.

If Macduff's revelation about his non-maternal origins seems like a curiously gynecological turn in the plot, it is one which nonetheless refers back to several earlier images in the play: the vision of a crowned babe; the "birth-strangled babe / Ditch-deliver'd by a drab" (4.1.30–1) that has found its way into the witches' cauldron. Most tellingly, there is the image of Lady Macbeth as someone who is by her own admission capable of the most violent infanticide:

> I have given suck, and know
> How tender 'tis to love the babe that milks me:
> I would, while it was smiling in my face,
> Have pluk'd my nipple from his boneless gums,
> And dash'd the brains out . . . (1.7.54–8)

Lady Macbeth's mistake is that when she renounces her capacity to reproduce, in an endeavor to seize power by force, she unwittingly relinquishes the only power she really possesses. She implores the "spirits that tend on mortal thoughts" to "unsex me here" (1.5.40), that is, to rid her of the supposedly weaker, more sympathetic qualities of women, and especially of women who are mothers. Thus, she becomes aligned with the bearded witches, whose androgyny is symbolic of their disorderly femininity – of womanhood in league with the powers of darkness. But as she renounces proper womanhood, Lady Macbeth summons up a powerfully domestic, yet sacrosanct, image of maternal care: "how tender 'tis to love the babe that milks me" (1.7.55). However, this memory of breastfeeding is also remarkable in this period on quite another account, namely that aristocratic and wealthy women typically did not breastfeed but, like Lady Capulet in *Romeo and Juliet*, employed a wet nurse to suckle their children. While contracting out such intimate labor is quite alien to modern audiences, it was a common practice up until World War I. The topic was controversial in the seventeenth century when arguments in favor of breastfeeding one's own children began to emerge. Churchman William Gouge's influential treatise *Domesticall Duties* (1622) included a lengthy section on the virtues of women breastfeeding their own offspring. In the same year, Elizabeth Clinton's treatise *The Countess of Lincoln's Nurserie* was published, which argued that "nursing, and nourishing of their own children in their own bosoms is God's ordinance." Clinton also emphasized the *natural* desire on the part of a mother to breastfeed her child: "The mother's affection is so knit by nature's law to her tender babe, as she finds no power to deny to suckle it, no not when she is in hazard to lose her own life, by attending on it." Women who "deny to give suck to their own children" "go against nature" and are "more savage than the dragons."[7] Lady Macbeth, of course, may be more savage than a dragon, but she *has* "given suck." Her argument that she would kill Duncan if she had sworn to do it is premised upon the fact that indeed she has been a diligent mother, and apparently also a good daughter. Her scruples about killing Duncan herself rather than urging her husband to do it arise from his resemblance to her father as he lies in bed sleeping.

Lady Macbeth's murderous resolve is more unnerving than the image summoned up by the witches of the prostitute who murders the child she has birthed in the ditch because those circumstances, one can at least imagine, might have been more extenuating. In the period, women did indeed commit infanticide: they abandoned and exposed infants, but court records rarely show the level of violence articulated by Lady Macbeth. The early seventeenth century saw a sharp rise in prosecutions for infanticide, and what is particularly fascinating about these statistics is that they correlate with a decline in witchcraft persecutions. In other words, women were indicted for being bad mothers rather than for being witches, and it is precisely the connection between these forms of female transgression and criminality that Shakespeare works through in *Macbeth*.

For although women are marginal to patriarchal history, they are necessary to its continuation, and Macbeth's own crisis is that he does not have an heir. Lady Macbeth has had a child, but what its fate has been, whether or not it has survived the play does not tell us. Lady Macbeth does, however, use a male pronoun, "*his* boneless gums" (1.7.57). Potentially, then, she is willing to murder an heir in order to secure power for the present moment. The play, and arguably early modern history itself, is more concerned with lineage than with present power, because present power becomes fragile as soon as it cannot secure its own continuity. This capacity to (re)generate power also constitutes Banquo's potency. He is the head of a line of kings even though he will not be king himself, and this is, of course, why Macbeth must have him killed. What is crucial is that Fleance, his young son, escapes; and his flight and survival ultimately permit James himself to be crowned king of England and Ireland as well as Scotland. Shakespeare does not make this explicit, simply because he does not need to: it is all too obvious in a world where power depends so heavily on progeny.

While *Macbeth*, from one perspective, is "a great man" tragedy as described by A.C. Bradley in *Shakespearean Tragedy* (1904),[8] that is, the story of the rise and fall of its eponymous hero, a great man with a fatal flaw, from another perspective *Macbeth* is, like *Othello*, the story of a tragic marriage. For Lady Macbeth and her husband have what is the dubious distinction of being (among his major characters) the closest couple in an established marriage in Shakespeare's canon. Macbeth hastens home to share the news of the sisters' prophesy; his wife is his co-conspirator and his confidant. But when his conscience causes him to waver at the point of regicide, she provokes him to commit murder by impugning his masculinity: "When you durst do it, then you were a man" (1.7.49). Of course, in "great man tragedy" the protagonist has to be shown to be great in the first place, prior to tragic decline. Shakespeare establishes Macbeth's prowess early on in the play, in the reports that come in about the battle between the king's forces and the rebels, led by the current Thane of Cawdor. Even before he appears on stage, Macbeth is described first and foremost as a married man, as the bridegroom of the goddess of war: "that Bellona's bridegroom, lapp'd in proof" (1.2.55). This mythic union might at first appear to be a much different marriage to the one he has beyond the battlefield; yet there is a sense in which Lady Macbeth is a domestic Bellona. Interestingly, the Roman goddess is the only strong, positive figuration of femininity in the play, and in contrast with the virtuous Lady Macduff, for example, she is neither a victim nor a mother but rather an agent of bloodshed.

Like the power of the witches as a threat to proper sovereignty, Lady Macbeth's power diminishes in the course of the play as the prospect of godly order and the end of tyranny approaches. The fiend-like queen becomes instead tormented by guilt and subject to the obsessive compulsion to wash her hands of the bloody stain of guilt for Duncan's murder. At the end of the play, we learn that she has "by self and violent hands / Took off her life" (5.9.36–7).

While the play's emphasis on evil and the supernatural has been the product of many theatrical superstitions, it is important to emphasize that witchcraft was a real, live issue in early modern Europe. Historians estimate that somewhere in the region of sixty thousand people in early modern Europe were victims of the so-called witch craze. Most victims of witch persecutions were old, crippled, powerless women, often already subjected to social ostracism. Literally marginalized, they nonetheless became symbolically central as the scapegoats for a range of social ills and everyday misfortunes. While some such women undoubtedly did seek to empower themselves by practicing black magic, most were harmless, old, and indigent. The threat such women were seen to represent was far out of proportion with social reality. The German witch prosecutors Heinrich Kramer and James Sprenger produced a compendious volume, *Malleus Maleficarum* (The hammer against witchcraft), used all over Europe that detailed witchcraft practice for the benefit of those searching out and prosecuting witches. But by the seventeenth century witch belief had diminished, and a healthy skepticism about the reality of witchcraft practice emerged. Most notable in England was Reginald Scot's *Discoverie of Witchcraft* (1584). James himself, who had in Scotland been a firm believer in the efficacy of *maleficium*, the evil wished on others by witches, became a skeptic sometime after he had ascended the English throne. Women who set sail in sieves seem to have lost their power over the new king.

Shakespeare never takes responsibility away from Macbeth for the murder of Duncan, but his susceptibility to female influence makes his actions, if not less culpable, at least explicable. His is not evil for its own sake but the result of ambition nourished by the witches and by his wife. That, especially in the early stages of his descent into brutality, he has a conscience – he hesitates about killing Duncan and he has to be persuaded and goaded into the murder because it does not come easily to him – reveals his potential to do other than evil. When Macbeth hallucinates "Is this a dagger, which I see before me [?]" (2.1.33) the audience witnesses the eruption of the conscience he is desperately trying to suppress. He makes a fatal choice in killing Duncan, but he chooses to continue on that course of evil quite independently of his wife and the sisters. What establishes his culpability beyond doubt is that he takes on the culturally coded female role of child killer, a murderer of "babes" (4.3.204) "pretty chickens" (4.3.218), attempting to have young Fleance murdered and ordering the dispatch of Lady Macduff and her precocious son. By this point, there are no more women to be blamed: "I am in blood / Stepp'd in so far, that, should I wade no more, / Returning were as tedious as to go o'er" (3.4.135–7). The irreversibility of an evil choice, despite the trouble in making it, and its consequences for the inner life of the individual are the ways in which Shakespeare brings an episode in Scottish history – no matter the dubious veracity of the Scottish chronicles – to life. This is history from within the bosom of its actors. From this point of view, only moral rectitude can secure the right of kings.

## Antony and Cleopatra

Although it is a perspective alien to our own, it remains the case that, from the point of view of Elizabethan and Jacobean hierarchy, Shakespeare's greatest achievement may have been the social status that his success in the theatre enabled rather than his means of achieving it. Having struggled to achieve a coat of arms on behalf of his father, as we saw in Chapter 4, Shakespeare had personal experience not only of the financial cost but also the cultural qualifications that were required by gentry status described in Henry Peacham's, *The Compleat Gentleman* (1622), a guide to everything a well-educated gentleman ought to know. Among them is one cultural test that we know Shakespeare passed with flying colors, namely the ability to recognize a representation of Cleopatra "by a viper," that is, the asp by means of which she committed suicide.

Interestingly, Peacham offers no parallel instructions about how Antony might be identified. This is because among the noble Romans of classical antiquity whose lives are recorded in Plutarch's *Lives of the Noble Grecians and Romans* (translated by Thomas North in 1579), Shakespeare's source for *Antony and Cleopatra*, even a life as remarkable as Antony's has nothing to render it so conspicuously symbolic as that of the Egyptian queen. Cleopatra was visibly distinct and readily identifiable. One might say she *has* an image, or rather that she possesses an inherent propensity to become one. Indeed, one of the most famous passages from Shakespeare's play, taken directly from North's translation, renders Cleopatra not with the specificity of individual description – for example, we do not know the color of her hair or eyes – but rather as a glittering image of sovereignty whose beauty exceeds even that of the most imaginatively idealized renditions of Venus in art:

> For her own person,
> It beggared all description: she did lie
> In her pavilion, cloth-of-gold of tissue,
> O'erpicturing that Venus where we see
> The fancy outwork nature . . . (2.2.207–11)[1]

When Antony predeceases Cleopatra in Act 4, his premature death (at least in terms of tragic structure) serves as a further concentration on the already over-whelming power of Cleopatra's presence. Her supremacy appropriately figures Venus subduing Mars, the pagan, mythological deities with whom Antony and Cleopatra are identified.

In his immensely popular narrative poem of 1593, *Venus and Adonis*, Shakespeare's Venus had boasted of this conquest that she had led Mars, her besotted consort, on "a red-rose chain" (*l.* 110), and in *Antony and Cleopatra*, Antony, identified with the armored ("plated") Mars from the very beginning of the play, is, like the audience, captivated by the sight of the dusky complexioned ("tawny") Cleopatra:[2]

> Those his goodly eyes,
> That o'er the files and musters of the war
> Have glowed like plated Mars, now bend, now turn
> The office and devotion of their view
> Upon a tawny front . . . (1.1.2–6)

Cleopatra, who unmans the "triple pillar of the world" (1.1.12), offers a spectacle not just of feminine beauty but also of female power. Shakespeare's England had its analogue in the carefully crafted image of the recently deceased Elizabeth I, who had died in 1603, three years before *Antony and Cleopatra* was written (it was not printed until 1623 in the First Folio). Elizabeth's power had been represented by the deified figures of Gloriana, Ceres, and Diana, and, like Cleopatra, she had been the mesmerizing focus of her English subjects. Not only Elizabeth but also Mary Tudor and Mary Queen of Scots had tested the patriarchal template that posited that power and femininity were mutually exclusive. Yet, what happened as a result of these accidents of history and biology – a veritable rash of female rulers – was that the male model had been stretched to accommodate female sovereigns without fundamentally altering women's status in society. *That*, indeed, remained to be changed primarily by shifts in economic conditions.

Elizabeth circumvented the patriarchal injunction against female sovereignty by espousing perpetual chastity, and thus accommodated herself to one of the prevailing paradigms of female virtue. This ideological maneuver allowed her to appropriate her subjects' ancient devotion to the now discredited Catholic cult of the Blessed Virgin, which had embodied the divine paradox of maternal virginity. Transposed onto pagan and secular symbols of female chastity and power, the cult of Elizabeth claimed a loyalty from her subjects that was tantamount to religious fervor. She also used the polarized construction of womanhood to her benefit. This understood women as *either* chaste *or* unchaste, with no middle ground to be had in between. Thus, Mary Queen of Scots, branded a Catholic whore, nicely played up the contrast with Elizabeth's unassailable sexual purity.

So while the English were well acquainted with women in power, they knew first-hand only Mary, the pious spouse of the Spanish king; Mary of Scotland, the deposed, disempowered strumpet; and the über-chaste Elizabeth. In contrast with these historical precedents, Shakespeare's Cleopatra is a woman of immense temporal *and* sexual power. The wanton, unmarried queen of Egypt, lover of Julius Caesar, Ptolemy, and then Antony, mother to offspring by both Caesar and Antony, fits no extant paradigm of women in power. She succeeds in embodying political power headily infused with exotic sensuality, and even when branded a "Triple-turned whore" (4.12.13) by Antony, she does not endure the humiliation that we might expect to accompany that role.

Crucially, *Antony and Cleopatra* is not only about an alluring, complex woman, but also, and most importantly, it is a play about a *goddess*. Cleopatra is identified repeatedly not only with Venus, but also with the great Egyptian goddess Isis, while Cleopatra's handmaiden, Charmian, is somewhat blasphemously identified with the Virgin Mary. As we have noted, Shakespeare had explored hyper-femininity much earlier in his career in the narrative poem *Venus and Adonis*, but a dramatic embodiment of divine femininity of Cleopatra's magnitude, her "immortal longings" (5.2.280), was much more challenging – and indeed, since the demise of the transvestite stage, actors and directors have certainly found this to be so. It might seem that on the early modern stage the most urgent challenge presented by the character of Cleopatra would be that of finding a young male actor with the dramatic wherewithal to pull off not just the convincing youthful passion required of the female lead in *Romeo and Juliet* but also the alluring spectacle of mature and exotic female sexuality before a Jacobean audience not wholly convinced of the emotional or intellectual capacities of women. Contrary to this expectation, however, the transvestite stage may have served to enable the depiction of such feminine complexity. Womanhood thus intensified by cross-dressing cleverly circumvented the need for a naturalistic representation. The play essentially concerns an endlessly described, disparaged, and worshipped species of hyperbolic, histrionic femininity that, paradoxically, may only have been dramatically viable in an all-male theatre. This is because the exaggeration of ordinary biological femininity on the all-male stage may well have been more plausible than if an actual woman played the role.

Shakespeare, then, confronts the particular predicament presented by the Egyptian queen in his all-male theatre and uses it as a vehicle to present not merely a human woman but a divine one. He posits the all-male stage not as a limitation but as an enabling, and arguably even a necessary structure for the depiction of the divine feminine. Further, he has Cleopatra herself disarm the audience of any uncertainty about the ability of the male actor who plays her to adequately execute the role:

> The quick comedians
> Extemporally will stage us and present
> Our Alexandrian revels; Antony
> Shall be brought drunken forth; and I shall see
> Some squeaking Cleopatra boy my greatness
> I'th' posture of a whore. (5.2.215–20)

Certainly, in the context of the early modern stage and its institutionally embedded practice of female impersonation, Cleopatra's fears about risible misrepresentation are well-founded. Whenever contemporaries complained about the representation of women it was not the failure of feminine appearance on the part of boy actors that they remarked upon but vocal failure – voices breaking or too low. Thus, when the players arrive in Elsinore, Hamlet's concern is about the voice quality of the boy actress who has grown so much since he last saw him that his voice may have broken: "Pray God your voice . . . be not cracked within the ring" (2.2.426–7).[3] Significantly, Cleopatra uses "boy" not as a noun but as a verb, as in "to boy greatness," meaning that the compact dimensions of youthful masculinity are incapable of extending their artistic range beyond some trivial comedy about a whore.[4]

Of course, representing Cleopatra's divine femininity was but one exacerbated problem of representation faced in early modern theatre. In *Henry V*, Shakespeare also confronts the difficulty of capturing the heat of battle within the confines of the "wooden O" (Prologue.13) of the stage.[5] The proportions of physical reality are necessarily reduced in the theatre, lacking, as it must, the technical capacity to convey with mimetic conviction the story it tells in any medium other than language. *Antony and Cleopatra*, much more than the "vasty fields of France" (*Henry V*, Prologue.12), requires, in defiance of all the rules of classical decorum, an unprecedented epic, panoramic scope in the depiction of the Roman territory from its epicenter to the vast reaches of its Egyptian periphery, "the wide arch / Of the ranged empire" (1.1.34–5). In order to grasp this territorial range, Shakespeare developed a dramatic structure characterized by rapid shifts of its forty-three scenes: thirteen in the third act and fifteen in the fourth act, for example.

In terms of the political history of the Roman Empire, the play follows *Julius Caesar* in addressing the era of the Roman Civil Wars, that is, the period after Caesar's death but prior to the establishment of the Roman Empire under Augustus, the erstwhile Octavius Caesar. The triumvirs, Antony, Octavius, and Lepidus, now govern the empire, although Pompey, the son of the dead Caesar's former adversary, now threatens their government. The play presents Antony in his "dotage" (1.1.1), that is, in the throes of his ungovernable passion for the Egyptian queen while his wife, Fulvia, remains in Rome. The plot could be summarized as the battle between the masculine, Roman, ideals of temperance, sobriety, valor and the feminine, Egyptian, world of pleasure and inebriated sensuality. Cleopatra reveals that in their moments of intimacy Antony has worn her garments, "tires and mantles" (2.5.22), and that she has donned his martial accoutrements, "his sword Philippan" (2.5.23). Antony is, of course, not the first to have fallen prey to Cleopatra's appropriation of phallic power represented by the sword: "She made great Caesar lay his sword to bed" (2.2.238). Antony, however, cannot recover and finds himself abandoned to carnal indulgence: "Let Rome in Tiber melt" (1.1.34). His fellow triumvirs charge him with neglect of his duties. Yet, Antony is also at war with himself. He knows that he "must from this enchanting queen break off" (1.2.135). He is, therefore, also in a sense at war with Cleopatra. He is "disposed to mirth," happily enjoying his lover's company, until "on the sudden / A Roman thought hath struck him" (1.2.87–8). In Rome lies duty while "I'th' East my pleasure lies" (2.3.39).

When Fulvia dies he returns to Rome. Cleopatra's expression of loss is one of the most poignant in literature: "Oh, my oblivion is a very Antony" (1.3.92). To Cleopatra's consternation, while he was away, Antony married Octavia, the sister of Octavius Caesar. Even this, however, cannot keep him from Egypt and from Cleopatra, with whom he is now crowned as joint ruler of the Eastern Empire. The three sons by their union are also created kings of lesser dominions. Outraged by this, Octavius engages Antony in a naval battle at Actium, but at a decisive moment Cleopatra turns her ships and sails off, leaving Antony to fight alone. Cowardly, he follows suit "like a doting mallard" (3.10.20). Even Enobarbus, Antony's trusted lieutenant, realizing his case is hopeless, finally defects to Octavius who vanquishes Antony. However, in an important sense, his defeat comes only after he has already willingly surrendered his Roman self – rational, martial, and dutiful – to the emasculating, sexual lure of Cleopatra. Cleopatra takes refuge in her monument and (falsely) sends word to Antony that she is dead.

At this point in the play, Antony fully enters the narrative of myth rather than the chronicle of Roman history, to which he has hitherto endeavored to cling. He imagines death as a nuptial rite and himself as an eager bridegroom, running "into't / As to a lover's bed" (4.14.101–2). In his revision of the myth of the African queen, Dido, and the Trojan warrior, Aeneas, who deserted her, the famous pair are now – as they never were in Virgil (where they pointedly remain unreconciled) – apparently happily reunited and wandering the Elysian fields together:[6]

> I come my queen [. . .] Stay for me.
> Where souls do couch on flowers we'll hand in hand
> And with our sprightly port make the ghosts gaze.
> Dido and her Aeneas shall want troops,
> And all the haunt be ours. (4.14.50–5)

Antony's pseudo-Virgilian fantasy of the afterlife is one where the ease and luxury of Egypt are transposed to a realm without gravity, "Where souls do couch on flowers" and where tripping through the Elysian glade ("the haunt") they both become the object of the gaze in a way that was, in terrestrial existence, the sole province of Cleopatra. Shakespeare's pun on "ghosts" and "haunt" (resort) further suggests transparent, ethereal versions of themselves unencumbered by the weighty pressures of incarnate existence. It is completely appropriate that Antony's mythos departs from that of Virgil, who had been, as the learned among Shakespeare's audience knew, the official poet of the Emperor Augustus's Roman regime. Thus, even in his death throes, Antony throws in his lot with Cleopatra and myth and turns tail on history and on Rome. He has now fully become the consort of the goddess.

When Antony falls upon his sword, in Roman fashion, however, his finale in Act 4 is not an ignominious one. Brought to the monument to die in Cleopatra's arms, he ends his life a great lover and a great warrior. His stature in death is established not only by his own testament – "a Roman by a Roman / Valiantly vanquished" (4.15.59–60) – but also by that of the guards who encounter him: "The star is fallen" (4.14.107). That Act 5 belongs to Cleopatra, who commits suicide with the emblematic viper at her breast before Octavius arrives to order that the lovers be buried together, is indicative that (even more conspicuously than in *Romeo and Juliet*) Shakespeare's emphasis in love tragedy is on his female character.

Although Antony and Cleopatra's passion is an adulterous one that ends in double suicide, theirs is still the most successful extant relationship in Shakespearean tragedy. Shakespeare's text follows North's closely; however, in an important change to Plutarch, where Fulvia is well dead and Antony already remarried when he begins his relationship with Cleopatra, Shakespeare changes the sequence to make the death of Fulvia and Antony's marriage to Octavia serve as a dramatic crisis in his relationship with Cleopatra. This is crucial in demonstrating the warrior Antony to be every bit as fickle as Cleopatra. For whatever the vagaries of her behavior, she is faithful and constant in her love for Antony. Thus, when Antony complains at Actium, "A right gipsy hath at fast and loose / Beguiled me to the very heart of loss" (4.12.28–9), one cannot help but feel that despite being the "triple pillar of the world" he does not have a leg to stand on.

That the play ends with Cleopatra and not with Antony follows the trajectory of myth rather than the orthodoxies of tragic structure, which require the hero's expiration in the last act. Because, as we have noted, Shakespeare makes a point of stressing throughout the play that Cleopatra is the avatar of Isis, the Egyptian goddess of the moon, in whose persona she dresses "In th'habiliments of the goddess Isis" (3.6.17), her survival into the final act is consistent with the mythos of the goddess. In Egyptian myth, Isis recovered the disintegrated body of her twin brother and lover, Osiris. Their story had been translated by Philemon Holland in 1603 from Plutarch's *Moralia*. So it is in her goddess identity that Cleopatra can embody all manner of contradictions. For example, even though she is sun-burnt and ageing "with Phoebus' amorous pinches black, / And wrinkled deep in time" (1.5.29–30), in a world which valued only fair youth, it remains the case that "age cannot wither her, nor custom stale / Her infinite variety" (2.2.245–6). Her serpentine nature is one with that of the goddess: "my serpent of old Nile" (1.5.26), and even when she is "riggish" (aroused, or promiscuous) she is blessed by "holy priests" (2.2.249–50). It is not, then, that misogynistic epithets do not apply to her; on the contrary, she is disparaged as a "gipsy" (4.12.28), a "grave charm" (4.12.25), "trull" (3.6.97), "whore" (4.12.13), "boggler" (3.13.115), "filth" (3.13.118), and even leftover food: "a morsel cold upon dead Caesar's trencher" (3.13.121–2). But in the vicinity of the Nile, where Isis reigns and in which the body of Osiris is dispersed, this mud does not stick. Shakespeare's Cleopatra remains "a lass unparalleled" (5.2.315).

# Notes

### Romeo and Juliet

1   All references from *Romeo and Juliet* are from William Shakespeare, *Romeo and Juliet: Texts and Contexts*, ed. Dympna Callaghan (Boston: Bedford/St. Martin's, 2003).

2   Reproduced in Callaghan, ed. *Romeo and Juliet*, pp. 296–7.

3   See, for example, Harry Levin, "Form and Formality in *Romeo and Juliet*," in *Shakespeare and the Revolution of the Times* (New York: Oxford University Press, 1976), pp. 103–20.

4   Callaghan, ed., *Romeo and Juliet*, 313–14.

5   Susan Snyder, *The Comic Matrix of Shakespeare's Tragedies* (Princeton: Princeton University Press, 1979), pp. 56–70.

6   See Callaghan, ed., *Romeo and Juliet*, pp. 196–8.

7   See Dympna Callaghan, "Marlowe's Last Poem," in *Marlowe the Craftsman*, ed. M.L. Stapleton and Sarah Scott (Aldershot: Ashgate, 2010), pp. 159–78.

8   See Jill L. Levenson, *Shakespeare in Performance: Romeo and Juliet* (Manchester: Manchester University Press, 1987), pp. 17–18.

### Hamlet

1   Ben Jonson, "On My First Son," in Richard Dutton, ed., *Epigrams; and, The Forest* (New York: Routledge, 2003).

2   Quoted in Richard Harp and Stanley Stewart, *The Cambridge Companion to Ben Jonson* (Cambridge: Cambridge University Press, 2000), p. 2.

3   Quoted in Harp and Stewart, *Ben Jonson*, p. 2.

4   David Riggs, *Ben Jonson: A Life* (Cambridge, MA: Harvard University Press, 1989), p. 97.

5   All references to *Hamlet* are from William Shakespeare, *Hamlet: The Texts of 1603 and 1623*, ed. Ann Thompson and Neil Taylor (London: Arden Shakespeare, 2006).

6   See Stephen Greenblatt, *Will in the World: How Shakespeare Became Shakespeare* (New York: Norton, 2004), p. 311.

7   Stephen Greenblatt, *Hamlet in Purgatory* (Princeton: Princeton University Press, 2001), p. 241; Michael Neill, *Issues of Death* (New York: Oxford University Press, 1997), p. 244.

8   Excerpted from *Romeo and Juliet: Texts and Contexts*, ed. Dympna Callaghan

(New York: Bedford/ St. Martin's 2003), p. 437.

9 Samuel Schoenbaum, *William Shakespeare: A Documentary Life* (Oxford: Oxford University Press, 1975), p. 250.

10 Susan Zimmerman, *The Early Modern Corpse and Shakespeare's Theatre* (Edinburgh: Edinburgh University Press, 2005), p. 18.

11 Book of Common Prayer (1559), excerpted from Callaghan, *Romeo and Juliet*, p. 430.

12 Book of Common Prayer (1559), excerpted from Callaghan, *Romeo and Juliet*, p. 430.

13 Quoted in Callaghan, *Romeo and Juliet*, p. 430.

14 Quoted in Callaghan, *Romeo and Juliet*, p. 430.

15 This was Ben Jonson's disparaging remark about *Pericles*.

16 John Kerrigan, *Revenge Tragedy: Aeschylus to Armageddon* (Oxford: Clarendon Press, 1996), p. 15.

17 See Michael Neill's observations on the cemetery as a location, "at once a place of oblivion and a site of memory" (*Issues of Death*, p. 234).

18 John Jowett, *Shakespeare and Text* (New York: Oxford University Press, 2007), p. 97.

19 For a thorough account of the textual issues see Thompson and Taylor, *Hamlet*, pp. 74–91.

20 These stories were published over a period of time, but 1570 is probably the date of the one that bears upon *Hamlet*.

## Othello

1 See Samuel Schoenbaum, *Shakespeare: A Compact Documentary Life* (New York: Oxford University Press, 1987), pp. 236–7.

2 Michael Neill, ed., *Othello* (Oxford: Oxford University Press, 2006), p. 2. Some scholars suggest that the later date, 1604, is probably more accurate on grounds that

Shakespeare seems to have read Richard Knolles, *History of the Turks*, which was not published until 1603.

3 All references to *Othello* are from William Shakespeare, *Othello*, ed. E.A.J. Honigmann (Walton-on-Thames: Thomas Nelson and Sons, 1997).

4 William Gouge, *Of Domesticall Duties* (London, 1622) STC / 12119, p. 188.

5 John Stockwood, *A Bartholmew Fairing for Parentes, to Bestow upon Their Sonnes and Daughters, and for One Friend to Give unto Another: Shevving that Children are Not to Marie, Without the Consent of their Parentes, in Whose Povver and Choise it Lieth to Provide Wives and Husbandes for Their Sonnes and Daughters* (London, 1589) STC / 23277, title page.

6 Quoted in Dympna Callaghan, ed., *Romeo and Juliet: Texts and Contexts* (Boston: Bedford/St. Martin's, 2003), p. 271.

7 Thomas Rymer, *A Short View of Tragedy* (London, 1693) Wing / R2429, p. 135.

8 Rymer, *Short View*, pp. 140, 145.

9 Dympna Callaghan, "Looking Well to Linens: Women and Cultural Production in *Othello* and Shakespeare's England," in Jean Howard and Scott Shershow, eds, *Marxist Shakespeares* (New York: Routledge, 2001), p. 59.

10 Gouge, *Domesticall Duties*, p. 160. See also David Schalkwyk, *Shakespeare, Love and Service* (Cambridge: Cambridge University Press, 2008), pp. 245–61. For full-length studies of servitude, see Mark Thornton Burnett, *Masters and Servants in English Renaissance Drama and Culture: Authority and Obedience* (New York: St Martin's Press, 1997) and David Evett, *Discourses of Service in Shakespeare's England* (New York: Palgrave Macmillan, 2005).

11 See Frances E. Dolan, *Dangerous Familiars: Representations of Domestic Crime in England, 1550–1700* (Ithaca: Cornell University Press, 1994), p. 67.

12  Honigmann, *Othello*, p. 34.

13  Samuel Taylor Coleridge, *Lectures and Notes on Shakspere and Other English Poets* (London: 1883), p. 386.

14  William Shakespeare, *Hamlet: The Texts of 1603 and 1623*, ed. Ann Thompson and Neil Taylor (London: Arden Shakespeare, 2006).

15  William Shakespeare, *Sonnet 144*, in Katherine Duncan-Jones, ed., *Shakespeare's Sonnets: The Arden Shakespeare* (London: Methuen Drama, 2010).

16  See Dympna Callaghan, "Othello was a White Man: Properties of Race on Shakespeare's Stage," in Dympna Callaghan, ed., *Shakespeare Without Women: Representing Gender and Race on the Renaissance Stage* (New York: Routledge, 2000), pp. 75–96.


### King Lear

1  See Samuel Schoenbaum, *William Shakespeare: A Documentary Life* (Oxford: Oxford University Press, 1975), p. 26.

2  Laurie Maguire points out that the anachronism of having a godparent in a pre-Christian play is typically Shakespearean: *Shakespeare's Names* (New York: Oxford University Press, 207) 189, fn. 25. All references to *King Lear* are from William Shakespeare, *The Arden Shakespeare: King Lear*, ed. R.A. Foakes (London: Thomas Nelson and Sons, 1997).

3  For a fuller discussion of absent mothers more generally, see Mary Beth Rose, "Where Are the Mothers in Shakespeare? Options for Gender Representation in the English Renaissance," *Shakespeare Quarterly* 42. 3 (1991): 291–314.

4  See Kay Stanton, "Made to Write Whore Upon? Male and Female Use of the Word 'Whore' in Shakespeare's Canon," ed. Dympna C. Callaghan, *The Feminist Companion to Shakespeare* (Oxford: Blackwell, 2000), pp. 91–2.

5  H.R. Woudhuysen, Samuel Johnson on Shakespeare (London: Penguin, 1989), p. 222.

6  See Catherine Belsey, *Why Shakespeare?* (New York: Palgrave, 2007).

7  Janet Adelman points out that Lear fantasizes that his daughters are bastards in an attempt to separate himself from them but that he ultimately cannot sustain the fantasy. See *Suffocating Mothers: Fantasies of Maternal Origin in Shakespeare's Plays, Hamlet to The Tempest* (New York: Routledge, 1992), p. 109.

8  Joseph Swetnam, *The Araignment of Lewde, Idle, Forward, and Unconstant Women: Or the Vanitie of Them, Choose You Whether* (London: STC / 23533), p. 16.

9  See Frances E. Dolan, *Dangerous Familiars: Representations of Domestic Crime in England: 1550–1700* (Ithaca: Cornell University Press, 1994), p. 12 on Lear's attempt to displace responsibility for familial disorder onto demonic agents.

10  *Ovid's Elegies in The Complete Works of Christopher Marlowe*, ed. Fredson Bowers, 2 vols. (1973; Cambridge University Press, 1981).

11  On the striking differences between the two texts in relation to the death of Cordelia see John Jowett, *Shakespeare and Text* (Oxford: Oxford University Press, 2007), p. 3.

12  Stephen Greenblatt *et al.*, eds, *The Norton Shakespeare* 2nd edn (New York: W.W. Norton, 2008), p. 2326.


### Macbeth

1  M.C. Bradbrook, *Shakespeare: The Poet in His World* (New York: Columbia University Press, 1978), p. 181.

2  Stephen Orgel, *The Illusion of Power: Political Theater in the English Renaissance* (Berkeley: University of California Press, 1975), p. 38.

3  E.K. Chambers, *The Elizabethan Stage* (Oxford: The Clarendon Press, 1974), Vol. 2, pp. 208–9.

4   The evidence for Shakespeare's role in Jonson's play survives in the list of actors that was published in Jonson, *The Workes* (1616).

5   John Chamberlain, *The Letters of John Chamberlain*, ed. Norman Egbert McClure, 2 vols (Philadelphia: American Philosophical Society, 1939), Vol. 1, p. 199.

6   All references to *Macbeth* are from William Shakespeare, *Macbeth: The Arden Shakespeare*, ed. Kenneth Muir (Walton-on-Thames, Surrey: Thomas Nelson and Sons, 1997).

7   Elizabeth (Knyvett) Clinton, Countess of Lincoln, From *The Countess of Lincoln's Nurserie* (Oxford: 1622).

8   A.C. Bradley, *Shakespearean Tragedy: Lectures on Hamlet, Othello, King Lear, Macbeth* (London: Macmillan, 1904). p. 377.

## Antony and Cleopatra

1   All references to *Antony and Cleopatra* are from William Shakespeare, *Antony and Cleopatra: The Arden Shakespeare*, ed. John Wilders (London: Routledge, 1995).

2   William Shakespeare, *Shakespeare's Poems: Venus and Adonis, The Rape of Lucrece and the Shorter Poems*, ed., Katherine Duncan-Jones and H.R. Woudhuysen (London: Arden Shakespeare, 2007).

3   William Shakespeare, *Hamlet: The Texts of 1603 and 1623*, ed. Ann Thompson and Neil Taylor (London: Arden Shakespeare, 2006).

4   See Juliet Dusinberre, "Squeaking Cleopatras: Gender and Performance in *Antony and Cleopatra*," in James C. Bulman, ed., *Shakespeare, Theory, and Performance* (New York: Routledge, 1996).

5   William Shakespeare, *King Henry V: The Arden Shakespeare*, ed. T.W. Craik (London: Routledge, 1995).

6   See Wilders, *Antony and Cleopatra*, p. 67; and Laurie Maguire, *Helen of Troy: From Homer to Hollywood* (Oxford: Wiley-Blackwell, 2009), p. 30.

# 9

# ROMANCES

## Shakespeare and Theatrical Magic

*The Winter's Tale*
*The Tempest*

### *The Winter's Tale*

Shakespeare most likely wrote *The Winter's Tale* in 1609–11, and it originally appeared in print in the First Folio of 1623, where it was listed on the contents page as the last of the comedies. However, like *Cymbeline*, *Pericles*, and *The Tempest*, *The Winter's Tale* is one of Shakespeare's late or last plays, whose episodic structure places it in the genre of romance. Shakespeare turned to the work of his former alleged antagonist, Robert Greene's popular prose romance *Pandosto or the Triumph of Time* (1588), as his primary source for the play, although he changed the names of the main characters. The avid playgoer Simon Forman, a physician and astrologer, saw the play at the Globe on May 15, 1611. Among Forman's clients were Marie Mountjoy, with whom Shakespeare lodged on Silver Street, and Jane Davenant, mother of the playwright William Davenant, who always liked to believe that Shakespeare was his real father. Most of Shakespeare's spectators are anonymous, and the kind of record that Forman left is one of the very few extant contemporary responses to Shakespeare's plays. Shakespeare's royal audience, however, is far from anonymous. *The Winter's Tale* was first performed at court in November 1611, and again over the period of the wedding celebrations of the only surviving daughter

*Who Was William Shakespeare?: An Introduction to the Life and Works*, First Edition.
Dympna Callaghan.
© 2013 John Wiley & Sons, Ltd. Published 2013 by John Wiley & Sons, Ltd.

of the royal couple, Princess Elizabeth, to the Elector Palatine, Frederick V during the Christmas period of 1612–13. Subsequent royal performances were in 1618, possibly again a year later in 1619, again in 1624, and for King Charles I in 1634. The play's strong dynastic theme (an idea which had necessarily lain in abeyance during Elizabeth's childless reign) no doubt appealed to the family of the Stuart court. We do not know their personal responses to the play, but because details of their lives are well recorded, we do know some of the life experiences they brought to it. This section will consider the play from the point of view of some of these known spectators – both Forman and the admittedly atypical audience of the Jacobean royal family.

*The Winter's Tale* begins with the visit of Polixenes, king of Bohemia to the court of Leontes at Sicilia. The two had once shared the idyllic world of childhood, and after reflecting upon their inseparable intimacy at that time, when they were "like twinned lambs" (1.2.67), Leontes notes, "which cannot chose but branch now" (1.1.24). He then becomes convinced that Polixenes has usurped the affections of his wife, Hermione. Convinced that Polixenes is the father of the child she is now carrying, he puts Hermione on trial even before the culturally sanctioned post-partum period of recovery has expired, "The childbed privilege denied" (3.2.101).[1] When his mother is taken away to prison these groundless accusations kill the couple's young son, Mamillius, the heir to the throne. Paulina, the queen's lady-in-waiting, fruitlessly defends her mistress throughout. Tyrannically enraged, Leontes commands that Paulina's husband, Antigonus, abandon and expose the infant daughter to whom Hermione has just given birth. Further, he orders the courtier Camillo, to poison Polixenes. Rather than commit murder, Camillo escapes with Polixenes, while Antigonus takes the babe, Perdita (a Latin name meaning "that which is lost") to Bohemia. He sets the child down in a basket just before being chased offstage to his death with the most famous stage direction in Shakespeare: "*Exit, pursued by a bear*" (3.3.57). Miraculously, a shepherd and his son (the clown) rescue Perdita. At this point, Shakespeare exuberantly violates the aesthetic decorum of the classical unities of time, space, and action by taking a surprising sixteen-year leap in time, announced by the chorus figure of Time himself. From this juncture on, the play shifts from its tragic mode to the resolutions of comedy.

Ignorant of her true royal identity, Perdita survives in rustic contentment in Bohemia, where she has fallen in love with King Polixenes' son, Florizel. She plays the queen in a sheep-shearing festival, a glorious pastoral interlude not found in Shakespeare's source material. A range of colorful rural characters attend this event, including Mopsa, Dorcas, and most notable of all, the ballad seller, peddler, and thief, Autolycus, who, as well as making off with the clown's money, provides much of the play's humor. The rustic ritual of the sheep shearing is also attended by Polixenes accompanied by Camillo. Both are in disguise because the king wishes to verify for himself the report that his son has fallen in love with a beautiful shepherdess. In an eloquent, philosophical set piece, Polixenes and Perdita debate the relative merits of nature and art. Perdita, figured in terms of the mythological figure of Proserpina, associated with the flowers and rites of spring, argues for nature, while Polixenes argues the merits of artifice and human ingenuity in grafting plants with one another. His philosophical position on plant life does not, however, extend to the social realm, where he believes royal blood must be kept free of the taint of lesser stock. Enraged that his heir would jeopardize the throne by marrying Perdita, Polixenes now takes his turn at patriarchal rage. Camillo, however, once again refusing to obey a tyrannical monarch and anxious to see his homeland once more, arranges for the young lovers to escape to Sicilia, where Perdita is to pretend to be Florizel's new bride, the Princess of Libya.

News of Hermione's innocence, pronounced by the Delphic Oracle, had already reached Leontes in the first part of the play. Remorse swiftly followed his initial rejection of the verdict, and he has lived the secluded life of a penitent for the intervening sixteen years. When the lovers arrive in Sicily, Perdita, followed by her rustic family, the shepherd and the clown, is revealed as the Princess of Sicilia. At this point, Shakespeare takes his most radical departure from his source. In Greene, the queen is well and truly dead and there are no prospects for conjugal restoration. However, in Shakespeare, at Paulina's invitation, Leontes, Perdita, and the other members of the court go to see a newly executed life-size statue of Hermione by the Italian artist Guilio Romano. Crucially, Hermione is supposed dead not only by all the other characters in the play but also by Shakespeare's audience. Thus, those who knew *Pandosto* would have been anticipating a tragic ending. In an astonishing *coup de théâtre*, the statue moves, and the queen appears to have miraculously come to life. Hermione is then revealed to be still living, and spousal reconciliation and familial reunion ensues. The pairing of Camillo and Paulina theatrically compensates for the loss of Antigonus, and, of course, Leontes has gained a son-in-law. For all that, there remains an irremediable, irreparable loss, that of Leontes' male heir, Mamillius. He is the character who announces the play's title: "A sad tale's best for winter" (2.1.25). His death represents a sense of abiding grief even in the midst of life's triumph of regeneration.

This is an extraordinary story of rebirth and regeneration, from winter to summer, from death to life, and from the delusions of hatred to the healing power of love. Its plot contains all the implausible and impossible features of the romance and, as befits that genre, they are the stuff of art rather than life. The play's often difficult language has been most noted in the well-nigh incomprehensible tirade of the jealous Leontes, in his jumbled itinerary of facial features "noses, ears, lips" that conveys a sense of his paranoid voyeurism as he observes his wife and friend in conversation. However, the language of the play, as Stephen Orgel has noted, is often obscure, not just in those passages intended to convey temporary insanity. This works to intensify the sense that life is a mystery that cannot be grasped by the prosaic factual knowledge required in everyday life but can be approached via the dispensations of art.

How did Shakespeare's own audience respond, then, to *The Winter's Tale*, especially to Antigonus's pursuit by a bear (the jury is still out on whether it was real or an actor in a bear costume) or to Hermione's revivification at the play's end? If Simon Forman was surprised or impressed by the bear or the statue scene, he did not think fit to mention it. It may be that a bear on stage, or alternatively, a representation thereof, was not such a novelty, given the proximity of Globe to the Paris Bear Garden, which featured bearbaiting. Exhibitions of cruelty such as bearbaiting and public executions were enormously popular in early modern England and were thought of as species of entertainment, which means that we cannot assume that our own reactions to *The Winter's Tale* would necessarily have much in common with those of Shakespeare's spectators. From another perspective, namely that of religious ritual, the statue scene might not have been such an astonishing moment to audiences attuned to the miracle of Christ's resurrection as an event staged in medieval drama not just as a sacred reality but also as an historical one. Certainly, the dramatic revivification of Hermione is on a continuum with religious miracles, which were foundational ideas in both sacred and secular culture.

Simon Forman's brief account of the play is in many ways most notable for what it omits, namely the bear and the statue. Yet, Forman does remember the spectacle of cruelty that initiates the play's action, namely Leontes' rage and his accusation of Hermione. He remembers also the oracle of Apollo. This latter we might expect, since he himself was an astrologer-physician who accurately predicted the date of his own death, which occurred while rowing a boat across the Thames only four months after seeing the play, on September 8, 1611. What Forman found most memorable was "the Rogue that came in all tattered," the vividly comic figure of Autolycus who: "cozened the poor man of all his money, and after came to the sheep-shear with a peddler's pack, and there cozened them again of all their money."[2] Importantly, Forman's final pronouncement is that what he has taken away from the play is a moral: "Beware of trusting feigned beggars or fawning fellows."[3] This tendency to draw a moral from literature had persisted since the Middle Ages so that even non-didactic texts, like *The Winter's Tale*, that resist such readings might still be subject to this pervasive habit of interpretation.

But what of the royal spectators who might well have attended keenly to the political danger spelled out by the oracle: "*the king shall live without an heir if that which is lost be not found*" (3.2.132–3). Since Perdita is found, and her marriage with Florizel promises the unification of the kingdoms of Sicily and Bohemia, as well as future progeny, the play seems to have averted political chaos. Similarly, especially in comparison to the childless reigns of the three previous English monarchs, the fecundity of James I and Anne of Denmark augured well for the future of the realm. Shakespeare could not have known at the time of the play's court performance that Princess Elizabeth would one day become queen of Bohemia when, in 1619, her husband, who had no direct hereditary connection to it, would be offered the throne. Nor could he know that in 1612, only months after the play's November performance at court in 1611, Prince Henry, the heir to the English throne, would be dead at the age of eighteen. However, he did know that in 1608 Princess Elizabeth had taken up residence at court, where, Perdita-like, she took part in sumptuous and elaborate court festivals and danced, along with her brother Henry, in the court masque *Tethys* in 1610.

Even though the production of an heir meant that the births and deaths of royal infants were proportionately magnified life events in comparison to survival and mortality among infants and children in the general populace, James I and Anne of Denmark held in common with even the most lowly members of any audience in the public theatre their quotient of joys and griefs in relation to their children. By 1611, James and Anne had already lost four children: Margaret, Robert, Mary, and Sophia. So devastating were these losses that the royal couple refused ever again to attend a funeral.[4] Anne was only fourteen when she married James in 1589, and after a series of miscarriages, she finally gave birth to Prince Henry in 1594. This became a source of discord between the erstwhile happy royal couple when James insisted on having their son fostered, just as he had been. His parents' dispute about Henry's custody began when he was only two days old. He was fostered to John Erskine, the Earl of Mar and sent to live at Stirling Castle, legally separated from his mother, Anne of Denmark. His younger siblings, Elizabeth and Charles, were also sent out to foster homes.

While we cannot know what Queen Anne thought of the play, a number of surprising parallels between her own maternal situation and that of Shakespeare's slandered queen readily present themselves. Hermione describes her separation from Mamillius and her daughter as insupportable griefs: "from his presence / I am barred" and the new-born infant "is from my breast, / The innocent milk in it[s] most innocent mouth, / Haled out to murder" (3.2.97–9). Importantly, this reveals that Perdita was being breastfed even though in the throes of his jealousy in Act 2, Leontes' rage discloses that Hermione did not nurse Mamillius: "I am glad you did not nurse him" (2.1.56). It was not, of course, unusual for scions of the aristocracy to be given to wet nurses, but the practice was being challenged in this period primarily on the grounds that children were thus exposed to the dubious manners and morals of such women. For this reason, in *The Countess of Lincoln's Nurserie* (1622) Elizabeth Clinton urged wealthy women to breastfeed their own infants. Leontes' remark, however, suggests that even before his jealous tirade, he has orchestrated the separation of Hermione from her offspring and that it is her behavior rather than that of any wet-nurse that constitutes a malign influence.

There were no fewer than twenty-three signatures to the February 1594 ordinance that bound young Henry to be kept from his mother: "His Grace's person [is] no wise to be removed or transported forth of the said castle to any other place."[5] Reports reached England of the conflict between James and the increasingly Catholic Anne over their children, the king arguing, "In the surety of my son consists my surety."[6] On October 21, 1598, when Anne was pregnant with the future King Charles I, Sir John Carey, deputy governor of Berwick wrote to Robert Cecil that Anne was being kept under surveillance:

> Our border news is that the Queen of Scots is very narrowly looked unto, and a strait watch kept about her; and it is further said that after she shall be brought to bed, she shall be kept as a prisoner ever after, and the King will no more come where she is.

But Anne's objections were fierce and she gathered about her some of her husband's enemies in an endeavor to lend force to her claim on her son. Since the personal and the political were inextricable in relation to royal offspring, it would be a mistake to separate Anne's claims on her son and her maternal feeling from their inevitable dynastic consequences. Anne's increased inclination towards Catholicism was reason enough for James to want his son kept away from her influence. The *Calendar of State Papers Scotland* records the "suspicion and jealousy" that James felt against his wife and her supporters.[7]

Anne was four months pregnant in 1603 when Elizabeth I died and James moved to London. Anne was ordered to travel there too, and James's plan was to leave all three children behind in Scotland. On May 4, 1603, Anne went instead to Stirling Castle for her son, stopping off to visit her daughter, Elizabeth, on the way. On James's orders, the Earl of Mar refused to release the young Prince Henry. Anne's despair was so intense that she suffered a miscarriage, news of which was reported to the reading public by David Calderwood.[8] In a private communiqué, the Venetian ambassador elaborated that the queen "flew into a violent fury, and four months gone with child as she was, she beat her own belly, so that they say she is in manifest danger of miscarriage and death."[9] Her miscarriage on May 10, 1603 alarmed James sufficiently that he permitted the eight-year-old Prince Henry to accompany his mother on her progress to the English court.

The little boy of Shakespeare's play, Mamillius, like Macduff's son in *Macbeth* and the acutely intelligent Lucius in *Titus Andronicus*, is one of Shakespeare's witty children. Leontes inquires of his son in Act 1, "Mine honest friend, / Will you take eggs for money?" to which he retorts with precocious masculinity: "No my lord, I'll fight" (1.2.160–1). Although still at that point of life when he is in the charge of women, he tells them not to speak to him "as if / I were a baby still" (2.1.5–6). William Haydon, the "Most Senior Groom" of Prince Henry's bedchamber wrote an account of the young prince's life, featuring especially his remarkably acute conversations with his father. When James asked if he preferred the English or the Germans, he answered that he preferred the English, and when asked why this was so given that his mother was German (though she was, in fact, a Danish princess, German was the language of the Danish court), he said, "Sir, you are the cause thereof."[10]

These historical realities bespeak the immense importance attached to royal children, "the heir and the spare" as the current English royal progeny are now popularly known. Women were indispensable to the production of heirs, but apart from that, they had little power. Anne of Denmark, daughter of King Frederick of Denmark, sister of Christian IV of Denmark and Norway and wife of James, was fond of saying that she was the wife, daughter, and sister of a king. Hermione also reminds Leontes at her trial that "The Emperor of Russia was my father" (3.2.117), an assertion of her proper place in the patriarchal order that should command respect and protection.

In the play, the most important female voice is that of Paulina, who has dared to speak truth to power, confronting Leontes even in his most tyrannical rages. It is she who preserves Hermione and who reveals her at the end in the "wink of an eye" in a fashion that echoes St Paul's account of the resurrection of the dead on the Day of Judgment in 1 Corinthians 15.52 or, as the Bishops' Bible of 1568 puts it, "in a moment, in the twinkling of an eye, at the last trumpet. For the trumpet shall blowe, and the dead shall rise incorruptible, and we shall be changed." Yet this notion of instantaneous transformation runs counter to the sense of gradually unfolding events and natural temporal progression (the triumph of time of Shakespeare's source) that might aptly be described in the words of Shakespeare's great tragedy of jealousy, *Othello*: "There are many events in the womb of time which will be delivered" (1.3.370–1). In that play, these words are uttered by the arch-manipulator, Iago, but in *The Winter's Tale*, there is a decidedly feminine temporality controlled by women from the pregnancy which dominates the opening of the play, to the final unfolding and revelation of events is the birthing of truth that has been gestating in the course of the action: "if ever truth were pregnant" (5.2.30–1). We first see Hermione in the last stages of pregnancy, and although she has been held in a kind of temporal stasis for sixteen years, her body, far from being incorruptible like the raised bodies of Paul's Epistle, is pointedly marked with the signs of time. As Leontes rather crudely observes when he looks at what he takes to be a statue: "Hermione was not so much wrinkled" (5.3.28). This sense of "pregnant time," like the common early modern expression, "pregnant wit" conveys a sense of being at once potential and replete. As Haydon wrote of his young charge, Prince Henry, "I come now to the rehearsal of sundry of his pleasant and witty speeches during his young and tender years, wherein the pregnancy of his wit and virtuous disposition do appear."[11] This sense of the rather gentle temporality of gestation, the unfolding of a child's character or of life events, is the antithesis of the way Leontes has tyrannically abbreviated his wife's period of childbed privilege and his infanticidal rages in relation to the infant Perdita: "The bastard brains with these my proper hands / Shall I dash out" (2.3.138–9).[12] Indeed, the play requires a chorus in the figure of Time to allow a definitively feminine truth to unfold:

> I, that please some, try all; both joy and terror
> Of good and bad, that makes and unfolds error,
> Now take upon me, in the name of Time,
> To use my wings. Impute it not a crime
> To me or my swift passage that I slide
> O'er sixteen years . . . (4.1.1–6)

The initial "I" here is not in fact Time; but rather Time is the shape this first person narrator will take upon himself in line 3: he is none other than the dramatist himself. This first-person voice is a remarkable – and in Shakespeare, a highly unusual – revelation.[13] Writing only about six years before his death, Shakespeare here reprises some of the key themes of his earlier work – jealousy, fraternal rivalry (especially that between Claudius and the deceased king of Denmark), the pervasive theme of family reunion; and, most importantly, the false accusation of women (especially Hero in *Much Ado* and Desdemona in *Othello*), and that of the loquacious truth-speaking, "shrewish" woman (Beatrice in *Much Ado*, Emilia in *Othello*, and Kate from *The Taming of the Shrew*). His ideas and his oeuvre were still unfolding.

## The Tempest

One of the most remarkable facts of Shakespeare's biography is that he never left England. In this, he differs from other writers of the period, who, like John Donne, often spent prolonged periods on the Continent. Donne was a member of the Virginia Company, a joint stock company chartered by James I in 1606 for the exploration and colonial settlement of the New World. His Elegy 19, *To His Mistress, Going to Bed*, wittily deploys the analogy between sexual and geographical exploration in the line "O my America, my new-found land." In addition, Donne himself had experienced a terrifying storm at sea when he was part of the English expedition to Cadiz in July 1597, and his poem *The Storm* is in part a record of that experience.[1] Although there is no record of Shakespeare ever having gone to sea or travelled abroad, there is considerable evidence of his knowledge of travel literature, as well as of his links with those of his contemporaries who had ventured to foreign parts.

There is, indeed, a fascinating chain of personal associations that illuminates Shakespeare's compelling and self-consciously artistic allusion in *The Tempest* to real events that had occurred on the other side of the world. That chain begins with Leonard Digges (1588–1635), whose contribution of a commendatory verse to the First Folio suggests that he was one of Shakespeare's friends. Digges hailed from an eminent family of scientists, and indeed his grandfather, another Leonard Digges (c.1515–59), wrote pioneering treatises on the use of surveying implements and other aspects of practical geometry. Sir Dudley Digges, Leonard Digges's elder brother, was a member of the London Council of Virginia Company and contributed a commendatory verse to one of the era's most popular travel narratives, *Coryats Crudities* (1611), written by Thomas Coryat. Leonard and Dudley's mother, Ann (or Agnes) Digges, was a neighbor of the editors of the First Folio, John Heminges and Henry Condell and, indeed, of Shakespeare himself when he lodged on Silver Street. This network of connections between the Diggeses and Shakespeare tightened even more when, after her first husband's death in 1595, Mrs Digges married Thomas Russell, who later received a bequest of five pounds in Shakespeare's will and was appointed one of his executors. Shakespeare had probably known Russell all his life because he lived at Alderminster, not far from Stratford.[2]

Sir Dudley, like his father, was a member of Parliament and a keen supporter of exploration, and he was interested especially in the discovery of the Northwest Passage as a new trade route. Thomas Digges had been one of the country's most eminent mathematicians, and his work included a revision of previous theories of navigation and ship and harbor design. Crucially, however, Thomas Digges was concerned with the practical applications of mathematics, and he tested his navigational computations during fifteen weeks spent at sea. This was direct experience with the ocean, which Shakespeare himself did not possess.

What Shakespeare did possess in great abundance, however, was the capacity to imagine events he had not experienced. In relation to *The Tempest* this is especially important because it is, as we shall see, a refracted version of current events. In this, it is quite unlike most other Shakespeare plays, where typically the plot is adapted from identifiable historical or literary texts. As Peter Hulme and William H. Sherman point out, "No such source has been identified for the story of *The Tempest*."[3] Although *The Tempest* was written very late in his career, Shakespeare was still expanding his powers of invention and addressing these new events, the voyages of discovery, that were currently underway. In a second dedicatory verse, Leonard Digges evidences considerable perspicacity about Shakespeare's creative process:

> Reader his Workes (for to contrive a Play:
> To him twas none) the patterne of all wit,
> Art without Art unparalelld as yet.
> Next Nature only helpt him, for look through
> This whole Booke, thou shalt find he doth not borrow,
> One phrase from Greekes, nor Latines imitate,
> Nor once from vulgar Languages Translate,
> Nor Plagiari-like from others gleane,
> Nor begges he from each witty friend a Scene
> To piece his Acts with; all that he doth write,
> Is pure his owne, plot, language exquisite.[4]

Digges praises Shakespeare's work as being natural and uncontrived, "Art without Art," and as the pure product of his own invention rather than labored imitations of classical or European authors. Thus, Shakespeare's creative imagination is "the patterne of all wit." While painstaking critical attention has been paid over the years to Shakespeare's sources, Digges's early homage to Shakespeare emphasizes instead his originality, his capacity, so to speak, to "make it new." This dimension of Shakespeare's work is especially significant in relation to *The Tempest*, a play about both the old world and the new, in part because all the play's action occurs in the wake of a shipwreck on an unnamed island, a place of the imagination that is deliberately evasive about matters of geographical specificity. The shipwrecked Europeans find themselves somewhere that seems to be between Italy and Tunis, and thus ostensibly in the Mediterranean, although the topography of the isle is also forcefully connected to the far-off, "still-vexed Bermudas" (1.2.229).[5]

Digges's general (albeit not entirely accurate) claim that Shakespeare did not "borrow" or "imitate" in his writing is nonetheless worth affording consideration in relation to *The Tempest*. He draws our attention to the fact that Shakespeare was not looking primarily either to the historical past or to literary precedent in this play but rather working with up-to-the-minute current events. He was especially concerned with the exploits of vessels belonging to the Virginia Company, specifically the *Sea Adventure*, which had been part of a fleet that set sail from Plymouth on June 2, 1609 and had run aground without loss of life in Bermuda during a "cruel tempest" on its perilous voyage toward the

Virginia coastline. The governor of the colony of Virginia, Sir Thomas Gates, had been on board when the fleet was scattered by a ferocious storm on July 24. On May 23, 1610, the company arrived at last in Jamestown with quite a story to tell about their sojourn on the uninhabited but fertile island. While this was the talk of the town in London in 1610, what is remarkable is that Shakespeare had clearly gained access to what was essentially a confidential document, the *True Report of the Wrack and Redemption of Sir Thomas Gates*, prepared for the Virginia Company by the governor's secretary to the Council of Virginia, William Strachey. The manuscript of this report was written in 1610, but it was not published until 1625. Shakespeare may have gained access to the manuscript in any number of ways, and the avenue most often suggested is William Herbert, the Earl of Pembroke, a theory especially favored by those who believe him the dedicatee of the *Sonnets*. Mr W.H. Herbert was also a dedicatee of the First Folio, and he was a member of the Virginia Company. Certainly, Herbert is a potential source, but more likely is Leonard Digges's brother, Sir Dudley, who was engaged in the detailed operations of the company and whose family had such strong ties to Shakespeare.[6]

*The Tempest* is also indebted to the printed reports of the voyage to the New World that Londoners were eagerly reading. Sylvester Jourdain's *Discovery of the Bermudas: Otherwise Called the Ile of Divels* (1610) was a firsthand account, and the Council of Virginia's *A True Declaration of the Estate of the Colony in Virginia, with a confutation of such scandalous reports as have tended to disgrace so worthy an enterprise* (1610) was the official report and defense of the enterprise, which may have been edited by Sir Dudley. The *True Report*, however, which was not available for public consumption, records not only the means by which the shipwrecked men survived but also the breakdown of authority once Gates and his crew arrived on the island. Gates managed to quash all threats of mutiny, to build two new vessels, and finally to reach Jamestown. The incident revealed in the starkest possible terms that the structures of authority that were taken for granted at home could be enforced only with great difficulty and some violence when they were wrenched from their completely naturalized, English context.

*The Tempest* opens in the midst of a raging storm aboard a ship whose passengers are on their return from the wedding of the king of Naples's daughter to the African king of Tunis. King Alonso, with a train of sundry courtiers and servants, is also accompanied by his son Ferdinand and his ally Antonio, the current Duke of Milan, who twelve years earlier had usurped the dukedom from its rightful ruler, his brother, Prospero. The good offices of Gonzalo saved Prospero from death at that time, and the deposed duke was set adrift in a boat together with small daughter, Miranda, and, crucially, his books. These books had been the source of his distraction from government in Milan, but they are also the source of his knowledge and his magic on the island. Prospero manipulates the natural world there and creates the storm that drives his enemies aground on the island and thus delivers them into his power.

When Prospero himself came to the island it was inhabited by only one other human being, Caliban, and by a spirit, Ariel. Prospero has released Ariel from his imprisonment in a cloven pine tree to which Caliban's now deceased mother, the sorceress Sycorax, had confined him; but Prospero does not set Ariel free. Instead, he is now at Prospero's disposal and must do his bidding, a situation about which Ariel voices repeated complaint. While Ariel is a kind of indentured servant, Caliban is kept as a loathed but indispensable slave imprisoned on a rock: "He does make our fire, / Fetch in our wood, and serves in offices / That profit us" (1.2.312–14). The audience learns that it has not always been thus, and that Caliban lived with Prospero until he attempted to rape Miranda. Prospero, however, has other plans for Miranda whom he seeks to match with Ferdinand, son and heir to the king of Naples. Prospero has counted (correctly) on the fact that she will fall in love with the first European male she lays eyes on other than himself. Prospero then enslaves Ferdinand, to test him, but eventually celebrates his betrothal to Miranda in an elaborate though interrupted masque.

The other groups of courtiers are distributed about the island according to Prospero's design, and among them, the power struggles of the old European regime and of the new colonial situation are worked through. In the last act of the play, Prospero renounces his magical robes and his occult books, but he does not burn them. Instead, "deeper than did ever plummet sound / I'll drown my book" (5.1.56–7). He renounces magical and intellectual power only to resume secular authority and again don the garments of his ducal office. He brings in, too, the rebels against his authority from the lower orders, Caliban, Stefano, and Trinculo, and Caliban admits his folly in deifying his co-conspirators. Ariel is promised his freedom once he has provided a wind to allow the Italians to return home.

In *The Tempest* Shakespeare did not write a documentary drama but rather staged a series of complex issues around power and emergent colonial structures. The story of the shipwreck and the New World enterprise in general opened the way for skepticism about the operations of power and the necessity of obedience that European theories of absolutist monarchy could not hitherto readily entertain. The French essayist and philosopher Michel de Montaigne's essay, "Of Cannibals" (1580), translated into English by John Florio in 1603, pondered with some admiration the lives of the indigenous population of Brazil. Montaigne provided Shakespeare with his source for both of Caliban's anagrammatic name and for Gonzalo's speech about the utopia he would establish if he were in charge. This is at once a fantastic idyll and an astonishingly radical, even seditious, demystification of conventional political rationalizations of the power human beings seek to wield over one another:

> for no kind of traffic
> Would I admit; no name of magistrate;
> Letters should not be known; riches, poverty
> And use of service, none; contract, succession,
> Bourn, bound of land, tilth, vineyard – none;
> No use of metal, corn, or wine or oil;
> No occupation; all men idle, all . . . (2.1.149–55)

Shakespeare's audience, royal and common alike, however, manifestly did not live in a world where the fertile earth would yield of itself enough to sustain the entire population without government ("magistrate"), contracts, wealth, servitude, inheritance rights, without labor ("occupation") or agriculture ("tilth," "vineyard"), and thus couched in the context of a utopian fantasy, its potential radicalism would not be understood as the imminent threat of anarchy: "All things in common nature should produce / Without sweat or endeavour" (2.1.160–1). Later in the seventeenth century, however, after the execution of Charles I, groups like the Diggers would seek to institute precisely a social order devoid of hierarchy, and they did so despite the necessity of all manner of arduous labor. The one item that potentially strikes modern readers as anomalous in Gonzalo's list of things he would abolish is literacy: "Letters should not be known" (2.1.51). The sense here is that literacy and knowledge are instrumental forms of power. Writing in particular is the vehicle for the articulation of those documents that establish property rights, that generate commerce, and that articulate authority as law.

   Gonzalo's ideal commonwealth sharply contrasts with the master–slave relationship between Prospero and Caliban. This is the most mysterious relationship of the play. Prospero harbors an obsessive loathing for Caliban's mother, "the foul witch," (1.2.258), the "blue-eyed hag" (1.2.269) Sycorax, which is all the more remarkable because, by his own account, he has never met her. She was dead, or so he says, before he came to the island. Caliban also remembers a time before his relationship with Prospero was embittered, a time when Prospero and Miranda were kind to him and taught him their language, "how / To name the bigger light and how the less" (1.2.335–6). Now, as he reports, "You taught me language, and my profit on 't / Is I know how to curse" (1.2.364–5). Language is the defining characteristic of human identity, and Caliban's is some of the most powerful and eloquent in the play. Yet, Prospero treats him as subhuman, and Trinculo, finding him sheltering under a "gabardine" in the rain, takes him for a monster – a word that is repeatedly applied to him in the course of the play. The word "gabardine" (2.2.37) is also an interesting one. Shakespeare used it to describe Shylock's distinctive ethnic dress in *The Merchant of Venice*. Unlike the inhabitants of Montaigne's Brazil, who were naked, Caliban is clothed in a garment the Europeans see as a marker of his savagery, and which was also the conventional dress of the indigenous Irish. Indeed, the English claimed that in Ireland, England's closest colony, the native population was, like Caliban, both savage and subhuman. John Speed's illustration for the map of Ireland in *The Theatre of the Empire of Great Britaine* (1611), published in the same year that *The Tempest* was written, represents "The Wilde Irish man" with long hair and cloak, known as an Irish mantle, that mark him as an uncivilized racial other. In Shakespeare's time, the indigenous Irish were regarded as being every bit as racially different from the English as they were from, say, indigenous Americans or black Africans. Further, there was a strong conviction that difference in apparel hid more fundamental anatomical differences between the Irish and the English. Thirty years after Shakespeare's play, an entire company of militia swore under oath that when they had stripped the corpses of the slain Irish after the Cashel Massacre in 1647, they found them to have tails nine inches long.[7] This conflation of the bestial and the demonic was a standard feature of colonial encounter since Columbus first voyaged to the New World, and it appears in relation to Caliban's alleged demonic monstrosity, or what Miranda calls, "thy vile race" (1.2.359). This trope bespeaks the projection of European terror onto those whose difference is found to be disturbing, and which, tragically, has been used to justify racial segregation, and especially the sexual segregation of the races. Caliban points out the consequences of sexual intermingling that would unnerve colonists: "I had peopled else / This isle with Calibans" (1.2.351–2).

Prospero's dialog with Caliban is littered with abusive language: "Filth" (1.2.347), "lying slave" (1.2.345), "bastard" (5.1.273), "hag-seed" (1.2.366). Yet at the end of the play, he makes an astonishing if cryptic admission: "This thing of darkness I / Acknowledge mine" (5.1.275–6). Is Prospero acknowledging the responsibility of possession, the master's responsibility for the slave? Or, does the darkness (evil) indeed belong in this instance to Prospero? Or is Caliban merely the projection of some "darkness," some spell – his dark "art" (1.2.1) – for which Prospero now assumes responsibility? The play does not tell us, though Prospero's admission does uncannily hint towards the tortured, sordid, social and seigniorial relations that were to become hallmarks of the slave trade where so many children "of darkness" belonged, unacknowledged, to their white father-masters. In this, as in so many ways, *The Tempest* is imaginatively predictive of the "brave new world" (5.1.183) that had not yet been born.

*The Tempest* was long believed to be Shakespeare's swan song to the theatre; in it, the magus, Prospero, forswears his theatrical magic and prepares to leave the island where he has lived for the past twelve years with his daughter, Miranda. Certainly, *The Tempest* was given prominence in the First Folio (1623), where it was printed as the first play in the volume, which might lend credence to the idea that it was placed there because it was the most recently composed of Shakespeare's works. However, if this was a farewell to theatre, Shakespeare's departure from it was rather more gradual than Prospero's renunciation of magic implies. For Shakespeare went on to coauthor with John Fletcher *Cardenio* (a now lost play), *All Is True* (*Henry VIII*), and *The Two Noble Kinsmen*.

*The Tempest* saw its first court performance in November 1611 and was performed again in the winter of 1612–13 during the marriage celebrations of the Princess Elizabeth to Frederick, Elector Palatine. Full of music, song, and enchanted sleep, *The Tempest* would have been entirely appropriate for such an occasion. Yet the world depicted is, as we have seen, one as much indebted to historical reality, and indeed to current news, as it is to the dreamy lyricism of art. Of course, Shakespeare does incur literary debts, too, especially to Ovid's *Metamorphoses* in 5.1.33–57 and to the great classical text of voyaging, Virgil's *Aeneid*, especially in relation to Aeneas's sojourn in Carthage and his love affair with and abandonment of its queen, Dido. From Ovid's story of Medea, Shakespeare took Prospero's renunciation of his magic. Medea is a far from benign sorceress, and her language is hardly the suitable model for a retirement speech. Even here, however, in one of the play's explicit borrowings, the tension between poetic and historical reality comes into view. What Prospero renounces specifically is the source of his occult power, which, as Caliban has insistently pointed out during the course of the play, lies in his books, and it is possible that he took something of this idea from his acquaintance with the Digges family. Leonard Digges's grandfather (after whom he was named) had died before he had been able to complete the education of his son (the future seafaring Thomas), so he left his mathematical education in the hands of the greatest magus in England, John Dee (1527–1608). Dee for a time enjoyed the favor of Elizabeth I as an alchemist, astrologer, and magician. He thus belonged to the older, pre-scientific order, even though he had serious interests in the new worlds of mathematics, navigation, and geography. Dee bears a further resemblance to Prospero in that he established a monumental library of books and manuscripts at his home in Mortlake in Kent. He had a recurring nightmare about people who "come to my house to burn my books."[8] In the play, it is Caliban most of all, and not the Europeans, who recognizes Prospero's books as the source of his power:

> Remember
> First to possess his books, for without them
> He's but a sot, as I am, nor hath not
> One spirit to command. They all do hate him
> As rootedly as I. Burn but his books. (3.2.91–5)

Prospero gets to dispose of his own books, but John Dee was not so fortunate. His nightmare came true in 1590 because while he was away on the Continent his library was sacked of his books and scientific instruments. As William H. Sherman points out, "Dee was acutely aware of the value of his library and of the extent to which his ability to command information, influence people, and shape events was bound up with his textual possessions – and it is this form of magic rather than a reputation for conjuring that connects Dee with Prospero."[9] Nor was Dee's library vandalized by an ignorant mob. Rather, as Sherman goes on to argue, "virtually every major contemporary collection" was the target of *government* suspicion or suppression.[10] That Shakespeare staged what seems like the very modern idea that knowledge is power as much as brute force bespeaks, then, not only the uncanny prescience of his imagination but also his very careful attention to the world around him.

A final word is in order about the structure of this play. *The Tempest* carefully observes the classical unities of time, place, and action. Only once before, in the much earlier *The Comedy of Errors*, did Shakespeare attempt to observe this particular aesthetic decorum, and in another late play, *The Winter's Tale*, he seems at pains to violate it. All the play's action takes place on a single day, in a single place – on the island. Paradoxically, then, while the action of *The Tempest* stays put in time and space, Shakespeare transported his audience to the far-off wonders of the globe, information about whose contours were, in 1611, still relatively new.

# Notes

### *The Winter's Tale*

1  All quotations from *The Winter's Tale* are from William Shakespeare, *The Winter's Tale*, ed. John Pitcher (London: Methuen, 2010).
2  *The Winter's Tale*, ed. Pitcher, p. 85.
3  *The Winter's Tale*, ed. Pitcher, p. 85.
4  Maureen M. Meikle and Helen Payne, "Anne [Anna, Anne of Denmark] (1574–1619)," *ODNB*.

5  J. Leeds Barroll, *Anna of Denmark, Queen of England: A Cultural Biography* (Philadelphia: University of Pennsylvania Press, 2001), p. 21.
6  Barroll, *Anna of Denmark*, p. 23.
7  *Calendar of State Papers Scotland*, 11: 662–3.
8  David Calderwood, *History of the Kirk of Scotland* (Edinburgh: The Woodrow Society, 1844); Barroll, *Anna of Denmark*, p. 28.

9   Barroll, *Anna of Denmark*, p. 29
10  Excerpted in Mario DiGangi ed., *The Winter's Tale: Texts and Contexts* (Boston: Bedford St Martin's, 2007), p. 230.
11  Excerpted in Mario DiGangi ed., *The Winter's Tale*, p. 229.
12  Frances E. Dolan notes that the play allows for forgiveness by not associating him with female infanticides and the cultural belief in maternal violence. *Dangerous Familiars: Representations of Domestic Crime in England, 1550–1700* (Ithaca: Cornell University Press, 1994), p. 167.
13  See R.S. White, *Let Wonder Seem Familiar: Endings in Shakespeare's Romance Vision* (New Jersey: Humanities Press, 1985), p. 146.

*The Tempest*

1   See Theodore Redpath, ed., "Introduction," in *The Songs and Sonets of John Donne* (New York: St. Martin's, 1983), p. 7.
2   Peter Alexander, *Shakespeare's Life and Art* (London: J. Nisbet, 1946), p. 212.
3   Peter Hulme, and William H. Sherman, eds, *A Norton Critical Edition: The Tempest* (New York: W. W. Norton, 2004), p. vii.

4   *Upon Master William Shakespeare, the Deceased Author, and his Poems*, prefixed to *Shakespeare's Poems* (1640). Reproduced in Brian Vickers, ed., *The Critical Heritage: William Shakespeare Volume 1, 1623–1692* (1974; New York: Routledge, repr. 2000), p. 27.
5   All references to *The Tempest* are from William Shakespeare, *The Tempest: The Arden Shakespeare*, ed. Virginia Mason Vaughan and Alden T. Vaughan (London: Thomas Nelson and Sons, 1999).
6   Hobson Woodward makes the case for the printer William Welby as Shakespeare's source for the manuscript, though we do not, in fact, know that Welby had it in his possession. *A Brave Vessel: The True Tale of the Castaways Who Rescued Jamestown* (New York: Penguin, 2009), p. 155.
7   See Dympna Callaghan, *Shakespeare Without Women: Representing Gender and Race on the Renaissance Stage* (New York: Routledge, 2000), p. 97.
8   William H. Sherman, *John Dee: The Politics of Reading and Writing in the English Renaissance* (Amherst: University of Massachusetts Press, 1995), p. 52.
9   Sherman, *John Dee*, p. 51.
10  Sherman, *John Dee*, p. 52.

# INDEX

Note: page numbers in italics denote illustrations

Who Was William Shakespeare?: An Introduction to the Life and Works, First Edition.
Dympna Callaghan.
© 2013 John Wiley & Sons, Ltd. Published 2013 by John Wiley & Sons, Ltd.